moto · europa

The complete guide to European motor travel

by

Eric Bredesen

SEREN
PUBLISHING

ISBN 0-9641488-3-8   LCCN 95-070769

The thing that I call living is just being satisfied with knowin' I got no one left to blame.
—Gordon Lightfoot, "Carefree Highway"

acknowledgments:

Rob Ankel, Dr. Jeffery Ant, Amy Boardman, Arlo & Judy Bredesen, Chris Bredesen, Doug Bredesen, Janelle Bullus, Todd Byers, Julio Casares & family, Mark & Holly Chidley, Dave Chmelnitsky & family, John Claude, Sylvie Debacq, Eric Engelby, Svend Erik Enger, Chris Festa, Court Fisher, Michael Gannon, John Greenwald, Marc Hoffman, Ernst Karlsen, Melvin Ketchel, Diana Kollacks, Wes Kuhl, Naomi Leonard, Arnaud Loquet, Janet Luth, Denise Malaxas, Joan Marsden, Bobbi Meana, Jeff & Michele Menzel, Mike Metelak, Amy Peters, Doug Rippe, Olivier Saget, Jay Schiltz, Dr. Ron Schope, Liv Julie Sordal, Jean Starr, Damian Sutcliffe, Jerry Svoboda, Fred Tompkin, Lacey Wunder.

disclaimer of responsibility:

This edition of *Moto Europa* was exhaustively researched. The persons, companies, and institutions named in this book are believed to be reputable and engaged in the business or service they purport to. Inclusion or exclusion of mention of a firm or organization is not necessarily a reflection on the suitability of their services or product. Facts have been checked and re-checked. Yet things change, and a small number of mistakes are to be expected. Indeed, expect some of the information presented in this book to differ from what you actually experience. Neither the author nor the publisher can be held responsible for such discrepancies or any inconvenience or other injury they may lead to.

you can help:

We at Seren Publishing want to keep maintaining and improving *Moto Europa's* standing as the most practical guide to European motoring. We encourage you to help in this process. We'll accept suggestions all year at the address below. *Thanks!*

seren publishing
2935 saint anne drive
dubuque, iowa 52001 USA

contents

All prices presented herein, unless otherwise noted, are in terms of US dollars. You should also note my convention regarding telephone numbers: To avoid confusion, none of the foreign telephone numbers I list include the country code; I list country codes in Appendix H. *Also, depending on the country and depending on whether you make an internal call in the country or call the country from another, you may have to add or delete a prefix of "0" to or from the numbers listed.*

a true story . . .

What gives value to travel is fear.
—**Albert Camus,** *Notebooks*

"Are you the American who doesn't know how to drive?"

asked the middle-aged man at the open passenger window of my car, his sharp double-breasted suit and suave but good-natured delivery—with only a slight French accent—intimating that he was a bigwig. *Uh-oh,* I thought, *I'm in trouble.* I leaned slightly toward the passenger window, fired back a *"That's me"*, and held a shrug of an expression on my face as I waited anxiously for a response.

My words shot past the bearded French mechanic who sat in the passenger seat next to me. The mechanic couldn't say *yes* or *no* in English, but for the past fifteen minutes he'd been amiably trying to teach me how to drive a manual transmission car. I kept my eyes on the bigwig. I held my leaning position. I held my facial shrug. The bigwig remained silent at the window, but surprisingly he didn't seem at all upset with me. I relaxed a bit, the shrug leaving my face as I settled back in my seat.

Meanwhile, I noticed, the bigwig had produced a small rectangular case and was holding it open in front of the mechanic. Exotic brown cigarettes lined the case. (I was told later in my trip that they weren't cigarettes but *cigarillos,* miniature cigars.) Ap-

parently my situation was so serious that it called for some sort of contemplative smoke—not, it seemed, a good sign, especially for a jet-lagged non smoker from Iowa who couldn't drive and who sat behind the wheel of a car in downtown Paris one hour before rush hour. The mechanic took the case and snapped up a cigarillo while the bigwig introduced himself to me. "President of the *Renault-USA* division" is all I heard. This was a bigger wig than I'd expected. *They've called in the big guns,* I thought. The mechanic was offering the cigarillos to me. I pinched one. The mechanic took a light; I took a light; the bigwig lit up too. *Voilá,* the cig was smooth. I took another drag. The jet lag, Paris, the bearded French mechanic, the businessman, the crazy-smooth cigarettes . . . Surreal. *Hey,* I thought, *I'm in Paris and smoking with two French guys. This is* <u>cool</u>.

"Why didn't you get an automatic transmission?" asked the bigwig.

"Uh, well, the manual transmissions were quite a bit cheaper," I answered. "I didn't think it would be so difficult to learn."

My anxiety was back and it punctuated the end of my statement with a series of nose-laughs exhausted across my ironical grin. But both these expressions deliquesced quickly, all evidence of my anxiety retreating to the two darting poles that were my eyes. I looked at the businessman, then at the mechanic, then back at the businessman. *Go ahead, laugh at me. Please. I know I'm foolish, but you gotta credit my bravado. Typical American bravado—both our strength and our weakness. Laugh. Laugh. Laugh. Pleeease, I need a good laugh.*

The businessman looked at me, nodded slightly, took a drag and looked away in thought. The mechanic stared at the car floor and began his own subtle nodding. I wasn't gonna get my laugh. These guys were too cool to get mad or laugh *at* me; they just wanted to help. Nevertheless, I wanted to escape. Suddenly I remembered sleep and instantly began to drift off to it; but my ego, considering this phase of the trip more a mission than a vacation, sprung from its depths and slapped me with the stolid injunction it'd been holding all along: *There will be no escaping.* Adhering to the mission meant driving a manual transmission. I knew that an automatic would cost some $500 more; I didn't wanna pay $500 more. *Still,* I thought, *maybe I should give in and get an automatic.* I asked the bigwig if any automatics were available and how much they'd cost.

"I'd have to see what we have available," he responded. "It will take about one-half hour. How long do you want the car for?"

"Ninety days," I said.

He pondered. *Perfect.* I had a half-hour in which to hone enough skills and mix in enough guts to get out and about on the streets. If I couldn't cut it with the manual, I could come back and get an automatic. I put out the cigarillo.

"Why don't you go do that," I suggested. "If I'm not here when you come back, it means I decided to take this car."

The bigwig agreed and went off. The mechanic got out and tended to other business. I methodically put the car in gear and circled where I'd been circling, around the pillars dividing the entry and exit to the parking garage. First gear, second gear, first gear, neutral, reverse, neutral, stall. First gear, second gear . . . I circled several times before pausing, consciously taking a deep breath, re-reconciling my mental map of the city with the stylized one—half map, half advertisement for McDonald's—on the seat next to me, and tentatively rolling out toward the street.

Now under the hard, afternoon, early May sun, I was in full view of everyone. I promptly stalled the engine for the umpteenth time that day. *These people are ignorant of the dangerous novice now on their streets,* I thought. Pedestrians were going about their business—old men shuffling, mothers issuing children across the busy street, fashionable women strolling with purpose—as if the two-ton projectiles zipping past them were targeted by drivers possessed of Mario Andretti's skill. I chuckled in the high pitch of disbelief and set out to make my unique contribution to the chaos.

Less than a hundred meters later—and *before* making my first turn—the high resistance set up by Paris's desultory web of arteries had upped my anxiety enough to melt the mental map which moments before had seemed so crystalline, leaving a shrinking gossamer remnant which, despite all my straining to read street signs and to reinterpret Ronald McDonald's Paris, I couldn't build on or even save. If taken as the summation of my wrong turns, I was effectively dissolved, here there and everywhere, Schrödinger's Cat in the black box of the "City of Light". Paris, it seemed, had swallowed me with all the perfunctory efficiency of a septuagenarian taking a pill. . . . But I wasn't going down smooth: I stalled the car one, two, three, four—I don't know how many times. The French reserve honks for the most awful driving exhibitons; I felt like a hated goose on some mad migration I'd caused to go awry. I refused to make eye contact with anyone for fear of suffering a just humiliaton. I shrunk down like the vowels in the word *fool,* the car's body affording thin consonants of protection against an imaginary paragraph—no, *page*—of aproned old women who from every position logical shared singular delight in deriding my every action. *Maybe I should take this thing back,* I thought. . . . *No, it doesn't matter unless you hit something or someone,* I told myself, remembering the advice of my high school driver's education instructor. "If you miss'm by the width of a hair," he'd said, pausing for effect, holding his thumb and forefinger in front his scrunched up face so that the tiny gap between them measured the same as and aligned with the slits of his eyes—looking through that gap and in through those slits you could see his eyes, eyes like teeth, eyes that he showed to each student before straightening and relaxing in front of the class he'd hypnotized—". . . it doesn't matter—*as long as you don't hit'm!*"

I turned on the radio and a familiar song erupted from the speakers—it was a new hit by Lenny Kravitz, and one of my favorites. The initial buzzing guitar riffs and screaming vocals soon gave way to the title question—"Are you gonna go my way?" I stopped at a red light. Without breathing or taking my eyes off the light, I took the spent cigarillo from the clean ash tray of the spanking-new car and stuck it, Eastwood-style, in the corner of my mouth. The light turned green. I took a deep breath. The tobacco hit my taste buds. Lenny hit a high note. I hit the accelerator. Ninety days and 24,696 kilometers (14,817 miles) later, on schedule, unscathed, and guilty of only a few minor and inconsequential traffic offenses, I would return the car to Paris.

In planning for this my first true "tour" of Europe, I considered all the intra-European transportation options: trains, of course, and cars, motorcycles, bikes and buses, and even hitchhiking. I read what relevant literature I could find, but there wasn't a book that satisfactorily treated the subject of planning and executing a motor tour of Europe. Then I called a friend who'd spent a year studying in and traveling around Europe. I told him about my research and asked his opinion. "I'd do it by car," he said with little hesitation, confirming my feeling that traveling by car would offer the greatest value. Five days later I was driving a brand-new leased *Renault* in Paris (if "driving" is what you'd call it).

It took about a week before I was comfortable with a manual transmission, but the high quality and heuristic nature of the French roads and signage—plus the laissez-faire approach the French take to driving—eased the transition. But I was winging it and I had much to learn.

In this book I impart what I learned before, during and after that tour. And because I wrote the first edition immediately after I'd finished—when I couldn't help but remember the kinds of questions and anxieties that arise naturally in a first-time European motor traveler—this book tends to include answers that you may damn other guides for omitting or forgetting. Indeed, I present so much information herein that even a veteran of the *autobahn* will turn each page in anticipation. What's more, I include only that information which you should consider. You'll choke on no fluff in reading this book: no worthless maps, no verbose descriptions of the terrain. Where a good ol' fashioned map or atlas—or ignorance even—will do you better, I tell ya so. Only on occasion and only with your best interests in mind do I exercise my poetic license. In short, this book means business. I've written a guide that you need, the guide I wish I'd had: a guide that walks you step by step through the decisions you need to make, a guide that presents a reasonable amount and type of information in an easy to follow format, a guide that doesn't waste your time, and—above all else—a guide that **SAVES** and *s t r e t c h e s* your dollar. This is not a typical travel guide, in that I don't detail sights and accommodations: other guidebooks already do an excellent job of that. Instead, I designed this guide to go hand in hand with such accommodations- and sights-oriented guidebooks.

In the *In Preparation* section I direct you in your decision about if and where to travel by motor vehicle; about what type of vehicle—car, van, motorhome or motorcycle—to use; and about whether and how to rent it, lease it, buy it new or used, and/or ship it to and/or from Europe. I also discuss the nature of European camping, the essence of traveling on the hostel circuit, and how to arrange other types of alternative accommodations such as homestays or home-and-vehicle exchanges. And I devote a whole chapter to the particulars of planning for travel in the problematic but preeminently popular British Isles. In spirit I aim to help you leave the beaten path, and it's with this spirit in mind that I purposefully abstain from delineating specific itineraries. For me to attempt a proper description of the myriad possible destinations a motor vehicle can take you to would be laughable. Besides, I'm dubious about the value of such paint-by-the-numbers itineraries. But if it's European motoring itineraries you're after, a host of guides include or consist of them; I list those guides in the *Resources* chapter. Note that the information in those guides hardly overlaps with the information in this book, and thus, like the previously mentioned guidebooks, perfectly complements it. Nevertheless, I do include an entire chapter presenting suggestions that will help you to optimize your personal itinerary and to avoid common pitfalls, overlooks and misconceptions. Finally, in alerting you to other resources which may help you plan and execute your trip and how to get them, any documents you may need and how to get them, what to pack and how to increase your safety, and the often bewildering issues associated with getting refunds on the steep VAT (value-added tax) you'll pay upon purchasing merchandise and services in Europe, I make the *In Preparation* section your one source and shopping catalog for *all* the necessary information you need to thoroughly and efficiently plan a wonderful trip.

Next, in the *On the Road* section I provide the motoring-specific information that will serve you best when you're finally set to roll onto the European roads. In the *Country-by-Country Information* chapter I include information about customs issues, motoring-related concessions for hostellers, toll roads and tunnels and mountain passes, non-toll tunnels and mountain passes, fueling issues, road signs, rules of the road, parking, bank hours, shop hours, national holidays, BBC broadcasting hours and frequencies, safety and security, and what to do in case of breakdown or accident. I cap off the section with the *Ferries and the Chunnel* chapter, a thorough analysis of Europe's ferry routes and of the Channel Tunnel.

Finally, I provide oodles of information in the *Appendices*—including an eight-language motoring-specific phrasebook.

Motoring isn't only my way; it's the most value-adding and—often—the cheapest way. In smoothing that way, this guide will help you save much time, expense and anxiety. Indeed, you'll realize a rich return on your relatively small dollar- and time-investment in this book. *Bon Voyage!*

Eric Bredesen

a true story

part 1

in preparation • • • • • • • • • •

1. why drive?

No one has seen Europe who has not traveled in it by car. The life of the continent from an auto window is a closely felt, personal experience.

—Arthur Frommer

If you were to tour your own country, you'd do it by driving; you know motoring imparts a freedom and a sense of landscape and culture that train and bus travel cannot match. Well, traveling in Europe by car, van, motorhome, or motorcycle is easier, more popular, and more economical than ever before. Indeed, motoring is now likely the *cheapest* way for you to get around in Europe. Besides, nowhere is driving more fun. Yet several myths about European motoring persist and scare untold numbers of travelers from its paramount value. By exploding these myths, we can launch into a rewarding understanding of European motor travel.

Myth #1:

Europeans drive on the left side of the road. For the most part, no. Only the British Isles (England, Wales, Scotland, and Ireland), Cyprus and Gibraltar have adopted the convention of driving on the left.

Myth #2:

It's difficult to get the proper documents. Not so. Usually your driver's license is all you need. However, the Commonwealth of Independent States (the former USSR), Greece, Hungary and Spain require an International Driving Permit (IDP); and Austria, Germany and Italy require you to carry either the IDP or a translation of your license. An IDP repeats the information on your domestic driver's license, with legends in several foreign languages to allow officials in other countries to read it. Your local auto club (AA, AAA, CAA, or NAC) sells IDPs for a scant $10. If you need an IDP, take your license, two passport-sized photos and $10 to the office of your local club. Ten minutes later you'll be able to legally drive on any European road—assuming you're at least 18 years of age. Since several other European countries *recommend* carrying an IDP, you should strongly consider getting one regardless of the country or countries you'll be driving in.

Myth #3:

Fuel costs in Europe make driving there three to four times more expensive than driving in the US. Not necessarily. It is true that *gasoline* prices in Europe are generally three to four times higher than gasoline prices in the US. Yet in continental Europe, *diesel* fuel costs about two-thirds as much as gasoline—and in Norway it's less than *one-half* the price. Moreover, diesel engines are more fuel-efficient than their gasoline-powered counterparts (25 to 35 percent more fuel efficient than gasoline-powered engines of the same horsepower). These two characteristics combine to render the cost of fueling a diesel vehicle in Europe *half* the cost of fueling a similar gasoline-powered vehicle in Europe—and only one to two times the cost of fueling a similar gasoline-powered vehicle in the US. Indeed, if you drive a vehicle in North America that gets about 20 mpg, you're paying the same amount per mile to fuel it as you would in Europe to fuel a typical diesel vehicle; if your vehicle gets 40 mpg at home, you're paying half as much.

Myth #4:

Parking in Europe is a nightmare. Nope. Parking in Europe is surprisingly easy and cheap. Free parking spots abound on the streets, at train stations, at hostels, at hotels and motels, and at sights and special attractions—especially in the out-of-the-way areas that a motor vehicle can take you to. It's true that public and private (as in the case of a hotel) parking ramps in major cities *do* charge $15–25 a day; and parking meters, pay-and-display machines, and zones requiring parking discs (see the *Country-by-Country Information* chapter for more on these) *are* quite common in cities and towns. Yet despite their rather clever pay-for-parking schemes, Europeans are not uptight about parking. In many parts of France, for example, drivers tend to park half on and half off the sidewalk; you won't get a ticket when parked this way if you leave a lane wide enough to allow a person to walk past on the sidewalk. Another example is the chronic double parking which qualifies as a fact of life in Italy. The further north you go, however, the more the ethos compels you to pay for parking.

Not only do free parking spots abound and not only are Europeans relatively relaxed about parking issues, but since government officials in Europe want to promote motoring tours by big-spending tourists and due to the inherent difficulty of effectively billing foreign travelers, European traffic police tend to ignore or only warn foreign violators. And it's likely that during much of your trip you and your vehicle *will* stand out as foreign: the design of each country's plates is unique and any vehicle that crosses a border in Europe must bear an oval sticker designating the country in which the vehicle is registered; moreover, tourists who buy and register a vehicle receive special tourist plates. If pay-and-display machines are in force in an area, I'll pay into them on occasion, but often I'll take my chances. And I found out about parking discs only after I returned from my first tour. Not once have I been fined for parking improperly.

All told during a recent ninety days and nearly 15,000 miles of driving around Europe (which included overnight stays of multiple nights in Paris, Bordeaux, Barcelona, Madrid, Seville, Munich, Salzburg, Florence, Budapest, Vienna, Oslo, Copenhagen, Amsterdam, the Hague, Brugge, Brussels, and Strasbourg, along with dozens of other smaller cities and towns) I ended up paying a total of only $86 for parking—$65 of which I spent for four days and nights of parking at one of Madrid's train stations. And I made no extraordinary effort to keep down my parking costs.

Myth #5:

Europeans are crazy drivers. The European driving style *is* faster and more chaotic than the North American style, but don't jump to the conclusion that it results from a chronic, senseless, and dangerous disregard of rules. On the contrary, this driving style results from a full *appreciation* of the nature of rules. Most of us sing the praises of market economics. We base our faith in market economics on the maxim that a system, whether an economy or a highway, whose order springs largely and naturally from the independent decisions of the individuals composing it blossoms into a more robust and fruitful system—in some sense a *safer* and more effective system—than a system whose order is for the most part imposed from above. Both mathematical and historical evidence seem to prove this maxim largely true. With this in mind, European officials and the general public alike make a conscious effort to give the individual driver more credit and responsibility—more freedom—for making proper decisions on the road. As such, Europeans drive "wildly", but they cannot drive at all until they're 18 years old, and then only after passing rigorous driving

tests. Furthermore, financial circumstances and excellent public transportation combine to keep many Europeans off the roads until their mid to late twenties. If you add to these considerations the fact that most drivers in Europe operate versions of the more demanding and versatile *manual* transmission vehicle instead of the automatic transmission vehicle so predominate in North America, you can begin to understand why, overall, Europeans are better drivers than are North Americans. The statistics concur: although the average mile of European roadway bears 60 percent more vehicles than its counterpart in the United States, four countries—Great Britain, the Netherlands, Germany (with its speedy *autobahns*) and Italy—count fewer traffic deaths per million registered vehicles than do the United States.

Of course you should drive defensively when in Europe, but often the best defense is a good offense: driving aggressively may be your best bet. Italians, for example, are notorious for their aggressive driving, but your life is safer on an Italian road than on its US counterpart. What's more, driving aggressively can be tremendous fun, especially if you're not driving

your own vehicle. Whether you drive aggressively or reservedly, however, the most important thing to do is get into the right frame of mind. The laxity designed into the European motoring system allows newcomers to relax, have fun, and not feel under the constant scrutiny of official and unofficial judges. Moreover, European drivers habitually demonstrate remarkable patience and good will: horn honking is kept to a minimum; slow drivers pull over onto the shoulder or otherwise signal to let faster drivers pass; the faster drivers wave or beep in appreciation; even the fiercest shouting match on a clogged Italian road is more an exercise in civility than in vulgarity.

Myth #6:

European roads are prohibitively vestigial and confusing. Wrong again. A comprehensive network of new expressways (variously called *autoroutes, autobahns, autopistas, autostrada,* etc.) crisscrosses the entirety of Western Europe. In France, Italy, Spain and Switzerland you must pay tolls—expensive tolls, averaging about $0.10 per mile or $0.06 per kilometer—to travel on most of these sleek roads; but in the rest of Europe you can travel the expressways free of charge. In the *Country-by-Country Information* chapter I list all toll roads, bridges, tunnels, and mountain passes so you can avoid them if you want. And avoiding them is easy and advised. Parallel to the expressways run the highways that once served as the main highways. Typically these secondary highways are in excellent condition and offer much more interesting scenery and experiences than the expressways. As such, I recommend that you use these secondary highways to accomplish the majority of your long-distance driving.

In general I find European roads superior to North American roads. I attribute this superiority in large part to Europe's climate. Whereas the climates of Western and Southern Europe draw their character from the ocean, which, acting as a great heat sink, buffers them from severe temperature swings, the climate of North America draws its largely from the land, which can't absord (and subsequntly release) nearly as much energy and thus does little to moderate the temperature. The more dramatically the temperature changes the more roadways expand and contract and the more they deteriorate. Therefore,

the weather causes North America's roads to deteriorate faster than Europe's.

Indeed, the whole of the infrastructure supporting European motoring is of superior qulaity—in terms of both construction and design. Spain provides several good examples of this. All the major roads in Spain, both toll and non-toll, consist of smooth black asphalt marked with rich yellow and white lines: that is, the roads seem brand new (and most of them are). You can use a major credit card to pay some tolls in Spain: just roll down your window, flick out your card, and in five seconds it's back in your hand as you drive away. Automatic sensors placed just ahead of community boundaries detect the speed of incoming vehicles: if a sensor determines that such a vehicle's speed is too high, it activates a red light at that boundary, forcing the violator to slow down. And Barcelona harbors parking garages right out of the 21st century. When you enter these garages, an attendant directs you to drive into a chamber. After properly aligning your vehicle in the chamber, you exit both the vehicle and the chamber. Finally, the attendant closes the chamber, and the vehicle is hydraulically moved to some

secret, subterranean vault. (Be sure, however, to remove your luggage when you remove yourself from such a chamber—recently I didn't and had to recall the car, drive it out and pay before being able to re-park it. My mistake was fortuitous though: I searched for cheaper parking and found a spot on a nearby sidestreet—a spot I occupied free of charge for three days.)

"But isn't it difficult to navigate in Europe?" I get this question often, and my answer is an emphatic *"No."* To control and facilitate traffic, the European governments have employed measures that are either remarkably similar to those employed in North America or else sufficiently heuristic as to be easily followed by foreigners. Across Europe, green lights mean *GO,* red lights mean *STOP,* and amber lights mean *Prepare to Stop (or Go).* Even the good ol' stop sign—complete with the English word *"STOP"*—is used everywhere on the continent. What's more, the signage supplementing European roads is essentially graphic—as opposed to linguistic—and is standardized across the continent. Indeed, the road signs are designed to be foreigner friendly. Those international signs whose meaning may elude you, however, I illustrate and translate in Figure 13.1 of the *Country-by-Country Information* chapter; and in the various sections of that same chapter I illustrate and/or describe signs that are unique to a country. Unlike Australia, Canada, New Zealand and the US, the countries of Europe accommodate large numbers of foreign motorists from dozens of countries—and motoring abroad concerns a German driving in France or a Brit driving in Germany almost as much as it concerns you. Consequently, in going about their own vacations and business, Europeans have smoothed the way for you. And because English is now the universal language, you, as an English speaker, will find the way especially smooth. Indeed, the vast majority of Northern Europeans speak English; Southern and Eastern Europeans, however, have not adopted the language as eagerly.

Regardless, European languages are easy to figure out in many cases. The translations of the question "Can I park here?" which I include in Table 1.1 help illustrate this point. Of course these phrases differ, but the similarities are striking. Because so many similarities are inherent between the European languages, scraps of

Table 1.1

Translations of "Can I park here?"

Danish	*Kan jag parkere her?*
Dutch	*Kan ik hier parkeren*
French	*Puis-je stationner ici?*
German	*Darf ich hier parken?*
Italian	*Posso fermarmi qui?*
Portuguese	*Posso estacionar aqui?*
Spanish	*¿Puedo aparcar aqui?*
Swedish	*Kan jag parkera här?*

one language reinforce scraps of the others. Thus, in a sort of chain reaction, a practical understanding of the language systems tends to blossom quite spontaneously. To further abate the language barrier, I include an eight-language, motoring-specific phrasebook in the *Appendices*.

Since most of the languages you'll come across are cognate with English, road signs are inherently easy to navigate by. But history makes navigation simple in at least one other way: each city and town grew from an old town center, and these town centers are what most travelers wanna

see; everything tends to fall into place if you follow the ubiquitous signs to the town center or simply head toward the tallest church spire. Most of the signs denoting town centers bear variations of the word *center,* such as *"Centro", "Centrum", "Centre Ville", "Centro Cittá",* or *"Zentrum".* On the way to the town center, you can stop to read the many well-placed tourist info boards or go directly to the tourist office by following the ubiquitous signs pointing to it. Usually these signs read *"i"* for information; in France they read *"Office du Tourisme"* or *"Syndicate d'Initiative";* in the Netherlands they read *"VVV";* sometimes they bear a lone *"?".* Of course the streets in the old city centers tend to be confusing and narrow, but you're not gonna be doing much driving in the city: most of the town centers are do-able on foot, and usually those that aren't offer excellent public transport. Still, a good city map is a big help. In the *Resources* chapter I recommend country and city atlases you should consider buying.

Ironically, another way to get your bearings when entering a town is to follow the signs that point to the train station. Both the signs and the stations they point to are ubiquitous in Europe. Look for signs reading *"Gare", "Estacion"*, or some variation of the word *station*. Many guidebooks use the train station as the origin for their directions to sights and accommodations. Furthermore, the famous and (here we go again) *ubiquitous* Hostelling International sign (see the *Alternative Accommodations* chapter) tends to be nearby, pointing the way to the nearest hostel. Most hostel proprietors have placed these signs in a series and with a frequency designed to lead all but the most clueless along the best route to the hostel door. In addition, a tourist office usually operates out of the local train station. At the very least you'll find city maps dispensed inside or a single city map displayed on a large public board just outside. Perhaps what's more important, many of your fellow travelers at the station will be more than happy to give you the scoop on the best places to stay, the best sights, and the best places to hangout. Moreover, the parking lot at the station will be at your disposal—often free of charge; you can just leave your vehicle in the lot and continue on foot or by metro, bus, or taxi. And since governments tend to build train stations near places of interest, and business

people who cater to travelers tend to locate their establishments around either train stations or places of interest, you probably won't feel compelled to stray too far from the station.

Even the infamous roundabouts that increase in frequency with your proximity to a city or town make navigation easy. These little circles quickly become practical roller rinks of sorts—complete with the same giddifying G-forces tugging at the child in you. A roundabout allows you to circle and circle and circle while you figure out which turn to make. I fully describe roundabouts in the *Country-by-Country Information* chapter.

Myth #7:

Crossing borders is a time-consuming and hair-raising process.—Au contraire. Border crossing is a quick and hassle-free process. Indeed, in 1994 nine members of the European Union dropped their centuries-old customs checks. Although potentially you are subject to passport checks and searches of your person and vehicle upon crossing a border, often you can zip across the borders of Northern European countries without even slowing down. Sometimes you'll be required to slow down

and stop before the guards simply wave you through. Most likely you'll just queue-up your vehicle, wait a minute or two, hand each passenger's passport to the guard when you reach the station, flash a smile, wait a moment until the guard returns the passports, and proceed forward a couple hundred meters to the border station of the next country (where you'll repeat the process).

Myth #8:

You'll be on your own in the event of a breakdown, accident or other emergency. Probably not. All vehicle rentals or leases to which you agree should guarantee 24-hour roadside assistance and timely replacement of stolen or wrecked vehicles. And if you're a member of a motoring club such as the AA, AAA, CAA, or NAC, the club will give you a booklet that proves your membership in their internationally affiliated club and thus obliges dozens of likewise-affiliated European clubs to reciprocate a variety benefits, including breakdown assistance (free of charge or at a special rate) and technical and legal advice. Moreover, the booklet will contain letters of credit which help cover such costs as vehicle repair and medical and legal fees. If you feel you need even better coverage, you can buy breakdown insurance from several sources in Britain. (See the *Documents* chapter.) Regardless, European motoring clubs will come to your aid—some for no charge and many at any time of the day. In the *Country-by-Country Information* chapter, I include for each country the addresses and/or phone numbers of the various breakdown, police, fire, and ambulance services. In *Appendix F,* I list step-by-step instructions describing what to do in case of an accident. And in *Appendix G,* I include phrases specific to breakdown and accident situations.

So there you have the myths. In relating the nature of these myths, I've told you the fuel costs, the toll costs, and the parking costs associated with a motoring tour of Europe. In this and the following chapters, I go on to present qualitative and quantitative descriptions of the costs inherent in renting, leasing, buying and shipping the vehicle you use in Europe. Additionally, in the *Ferries and the Chunnel* chapter I include detailed cost analyses of representative routes that bridge the most significant gaps in the European motoring circuit. All this cost information *is* necessary, but you must couple a knowledge of costs with an understanding of what you *get* for those costs. As such, I'll guide you through a *value* analysis instead of a simple *cost* analysis.

So-called budget travelers need to exercise special care in determining value, and thus they provide perhaps the best example to illustrate the nature of its proper determination. The ultimate issue for all budget travelers is *"How much* should my budget be?" Many of these travelers, however, misunderstand the *meaning* of the word *budget,* treating it as a simple financial figure instead of a *process* punctuated by such figures. Simply put, such travelers treat the word *budget* as a noun, forgetting it's also a verb. Yet even after fully appreciating and properly exercising the word *budget,* value tends to elude predetermination. For example, most budget travelers, to quote budget-travel guru Rick Steves, discover that they ". . . don't have a good time *in spite* of traveling on a budget but *because* of it." Explains Steves, "Budget traveling forces you to travel close to the ground, meeting and communicating with the people, not relying on service with a purchased smile." So we must temper our measurement of costs with a reckoning of value. But perhaps the most important lesson to be learned from budget travelers is that we must also temper our reckoning of value with an acknowledgment of the essential unpredictability of value. In other words, *we must strategically surrender to the unexpected.* I'll expound on this surrender later.

Many people hold that the value realizable in European travel is inversely proportional to the number of people traveling Europe at any one time. This is partly true. Europe *does* accommodate millions of tourists, and the crowds *do* become overwhelming at times, spoiling the integrity of the experience. Yet Europe is a big place. In most cases travelers who claim that the whole continent is saturated assume this based on a sampling of anomalous concentrations of people. Apart from the sights that tend to concentrate visitors, the modes of transport which most visitors opt for—trains and bus tours—play a primary role in contributing to these anomalous concentrations. Trains and bus tours tend to lock you onto the beaten path, where you'll visit the same places and meet the same—often, understandably, jaded—locals that other travelers meet. This phenomenon results in something like 90 percent of the travelers frequenting 10 percent of the places. To this I say, "Great! These mobs are leaving the rest of the place to my friends and me."

A motor vehicle allows you to wave good bye to the sweaty throngs and the sometimes nasty, phony and fraudulent establishments that dine on them. Once you're away from the tourist hordes, finding accommodation becomes easier. And all the prices tend to be cheaper off the beaten path. Regardless, traveling by motor vehicle forces both budget traveler and royalty alike to travel—to live—more like a local. Indeed, I've found that the more *business* I do in Europe—including the obtaining and driving of a motor vehicle— the less I act and feel like a tourist and the more I feel charged with integrity. A motor vehicle is your ticket to the museum of the present, your ticket to authenticity. When given the chance, time travelers from the future will trip over each other, offering millions upon millions of dollars for the same ticket, a ticket you'll get for just a few hundred to a few thousand dollars.

What makes the ticket so valuable is its flexibility. With a motor vehicle you can go where you want when you want. You won't be subject to train or bus schedules and the strikes that all too often wipe them out. You have door-to-door capability. You can toss in virtually as much luggage as you like and transport it straight to a place where you can undue all the zippers. You don't have to pay for all the short bus trips to outlying accommodations and sights. Essentially, you have no down-time. Some people might argue that motor vehicles are slower than trains and that the time spent driving should be considered down-time. *Bad attitude*. I just mentioned the advantage of of doing otherwise mundane business in Europe. As the operator of your own vehicle—of your own tour—you're doing business of sorts. Even if you never get out of your vehicle, driving forces you to look at a physical map and to work at creating a *mental* map, an understanding of the continuum that *is* Europe. You'll read the landscape while navigating it, and it's just as good a read as any book. Remember, necessity is the mother of invention; when riding trains or tour buses—which allow you to exercise your vision but don't require you to exercise a map—your understanding of the continuum, your mental map, is rarely constructed. It's only natural: the more you let other people think for you during your trip the less you'll know about the place when you leave. This phenomenon reminds me of an old Burma Shave sign that I'm told once graced US 30 in Iowa, the "Lincoln Highway", as it ran from New York to California. "DON'T LOSE YOUR HEAD TO GAIN A MINUTE," the sign warned. "YOU NEED YOUR HEAD; YOUR BRAINS ARE IN IT." This message evokes images of violent accidents, but there are many more ways to compromise the value of your head than by banging it into a dashboard or telephone pole. Jumping on an overnight train or bus in Seville, for example, and waking the next morning in Paris has its advantages, but the increased value of your head that results from experiencing how Seville connects to Paris is not among them.

And even during the day, trains constrain your vision. Trains, of course, run on tracks. Train tracks are much cheaper to build and trains more efficient to operate if the tracks run across flat ground. Thus train routes tend to follow the flattest land available—and the flattest land available tends not to be very exciting. Even when trains venture into the mountains, they spend much of the time in pitch-black tunnels. And even if the train window isn't dirty and you have a great view, it's gonna to be the same view that everybody else sees. What's more, you won't be able to smell the pine or feel the breeze or hear the birds or taste the local wine. While train travel *passively* constrains your vision of the outside world, it *strives* to completely shield all your other senses.

Indeed, you'll exercise the most important aspect of a motor vehicle's flexibility when you stop and open its doors. If when passing a mountain stream on a hot day you see people swimming in a cool natural pool below, you can pull over and join them. You can drop into this or that intriguing winery, taste a few samples of red, and buy a bottle for dinner. You can stop and talk with that farmer or that group of old men or children on the corner. You can pull up and watch that local soccer or rugby or cricket match. In a train all you can do is zip by such joys, wondering. Compared to a day of motoring, a day of traveling by train greatly diminishes the chances that you and your stories will serve

as the objects of fascination later on. You're going to Europe to further your understanding of the world. Well, Europe and the world are infinitely more than hundreds of disjointed cities. Between those cities are thousands upon thousands of wonders, many of them untold or undiscovered, the perfect ingredients for adventure—get mixed up in 'em.

Among the wonders you can explore are thousands of campgrounds and ideal spots for free-camping that only a motor vehicle will allow you to frequent. See the *Alternative Accommodations* chapter for more on this subject. It's worth noting that without a partner or two, camping is a bit too lonesome for me. As such, I do most of my camping when traveling with friends.

Indeed, for many people, organizing a motoring trip to Europe is not so much a question of money or desire as a question of getting someone to go along. You might desperately wanna travel in Europe, but finding someone who has the time to go with you—much less someone who wants to see the same things and move at the same pace as you and someone you can *get along with* in close quarters for several weeks or months—is difficult. In the *Resources* chap-

ter I describe how you can find travel partners before you leave. Most people are terribly anxious about traveling alone, maybe so anxious that they don't even consider it. The prospects for meeting travel partners abroad may justify this anxiety if you *don't* plan to stay in hostels, but the prospects in hostels are so great that you'll hardly end up traveling alone if you frequent such establishments. See the *Alternative Accommodations* chapter for more on the nature of hostels and the hostelling circuit.

Still, I need to include one caveat. Anyone who travels alone should expect to experience an occasional yet clawing loneliness—especially in the first week of a trip and especially if driving. This feeling is only natural. Every traveler gets it. It'll pass. And when it passes you'll feel foolish for being anxious amidst all your freedom.

Regardless, you may worry that by driving you'll miss out on the social situations that inevitably pop up on train rides. You *will* miss out on these, but if you stay in hostels, you'll meet enough people and have enough fun with them to last a lifetime. And driving will make it even easier. Driving is a great subject for conversation,

why drive?

10

giving you an added mystique when you exchange stories with fellow travelers. As a result many of these travelers will wanna travel with you; and you'll be able to *choose* whom you wanna share the traveling and costs with. (Although you'll have a tough time getting tag-alongs to pay for more than their share of the fuel costs.) Furthermore, you'll rediscover the special intimacy that develops during a road trip: something about driving with good company spawns the best conversations. In fact, driving may lead to more—and more meaningful—social interactions than does train travel.

Another putative advantage of rail travel is the overnight train ride, which allows travelers to save a night's lodging expense and to maximize their sightseeing time. Yet apart from missing all the sights along the way, these passengers often arrive at their destination tired. Indeed, you can expect to get only about five or six hours of sleep on a typical overnight train ride. I don't know about you, but that's not enough sleep for me to feel good the next day. And I wanna to feel good while I'm in Europe. As a motor traveler, I average about eight hours of sleep each night.

Moreover, not marching to someone else's schedule, I wake without an alarm—a vacation in itself. To get more than five or six hours of sleep on a train, you'll have to fork-over $15 for a *couchette*. A *couchette* is a bed in a compartment—sometimes lockable, sometimes not—with two triple coed bunks (blanket, pillow, clean linen, and up to five compartment mates included). An attendant monitors the *couchette* compartment and deals with conductors and customs officials for you. You could also opt to pay $40–80 for a still-crowded two- or three-bed sleeper with a tiny sink. Either way, getting a *good* night's sleep on a train will cost more than staying in a typical hostel.

Whether you travel by train or not, you should expect to make several mistakes and face several surprises along the way. By giving you the ability to turn around in an instant, to act immediately on what intrigues you, to seize the moment, a motor vehicle empowers you to manage and exploit these inevitable wildcards. Note what William Least Heat-Moon writes in *Blue Highways,* his critically acclaimed account of traveling around the US in a camper van: "A traveler who leaves the journey open to the road finds unforeseen things come to shape it. 'The fecundity of the unexpected,' Proudhon called it." This *fecundity of the unexpected* assumes a much more powerful dimension in motoring tours than in train or bus tours. It's this factor that, as I alluded to earlier, renders value impossible for us to completely predetermine. It's this factor that the wise traveler ultimately and strategically surrenders to in both the planning and execution of a trip.

It is prudent, however, to focus for a moment on the *unpleasant* unexpected happenings that may occur. Crime is a prime example. When traveling, of course, you're subject to a higher likelihood of petty crime than are the locals. Still, in many ways Europe is the safest continent in the world, and virtually no place in Europe is prohibitively dangerous for travelers. Nevertheless, in the *Itinerary Suggestions* chapter and again in the *Country-by-Country Information* chapter I discuss specific places and vehicle security procedures you should be aware of. And in the *Packing* chapter I discuss how to secure yourself and your personal possessions while on the street and in your place of lodging. In choosing to travel by motor vehicle you're choosing to travel closer to the ground, to open yourself more to the local population—including the subgroup of criminals. But the criminals probably won't be there to take advantage of you: their prospects are much better on trains, around train stations, and amongst the mobs I mentioned earlier. In other words, criminals go where the crowds go.

Perhaps no other phenomenon takes the potential for both pleasant and unpleasant experiences to the extreme as does hitchhiking—or "autostop", as Europeans call it. Many sources advise that picking up hitchhikers in Europe is a mistake. I'm not gonna to go that far. Unlike North Americans, Europeans accept hitching as an integral mode of transport. Thus, a much wider sample of European society sticks out its collective thumb along the highways, improving the chances that your experiences with hitchhikers there will be pleasant if not wonderful. There's even an association—called Eurostop—that matches riders with drivers throughout Europe. In the *Resources* chapter I describe Eurostop and list some offices. Use *your* best judgment when it comes to hitchhiking. You're under no obligation to pick up anybody. And

note that if you don't share a common language with the person you pick up, the communication barrier will lessen your chances of enjoying the experience.

Many people consider touring Europe by bicycle. Of course bicycling leads to intimate experiences with the landscape and the people. But you'll pay for that intimacy: bicycle touring is *hard* work, and there's no way you can get around much of Europe by bicycle unless you have a ton of time and tremendous stamina. I know because I've met several bicyclists during my travels, and I recently attempted—with limited success—to bike around the British Isles in a month and a half. A good bicyclist on a long tour typically covers about 66 miles (100 kilometers) a day, an effort which each day requires about six or seven hours on the road and which results in mild exhaustion in the evenings. You *will* sleep well, but unless you're an experienced bicyclist you may get in over your head and end up dreading the next day. The great effort inherent with such bicycling means that you can't justify many deviations from your planned route; and to avoid superfluous physical expenditure, you must plan that route with extreme

care. The overwhelming tendency, then, is to limit yourself, to keep on the move, to pass up the fecundity of the unexpected. In short, you'd better love bicycling for the sake of bicycling. Moreover, you should seriously consider covering only 30 to 40 miles per day.

However, even if you travel by motor vehicle you can still do substantial bicycling. In fact, a motor vehicle facilitates enjoyable bicycle travel. With a bike carrier and/or industrial strength rubber bands, you can secure your bike or bikes on the back or top of your vehicle (most vehicle-rental agencies rent bike carriers as well) and drive across boring or hilly country before mounting the two-wheelers; and you can travel comfortably on those days that bring inclement weather. See the *Packing* chapter for more information about how to bring a bike to Europe and what accessories to bring with it. Of course you can also rent or buy a bike in Europe, but bicycles there are roughly twice as expensive as those in the US.

An all-out and unguided bicycle tour is, of course, the cheapest way to go; but it's a toss up between rail and motor travel as to which is cheaper. If you choose wisely,

why drive?

however, the value inherent in motoring will nearly always justify the costs. Recently I chose to lease a car in Europe. I spent $1842 to lease a new *Renault Clio RN 1.9* diesel for ninety days. I ended up spending $719 on diesel fuel ($979, minus money that riders chipped in), $90 on maintenance, $85 on tolls, $80 for parking ($86, minus money that riders chipped in), and $123 for ferries ($241, minus money that riders chipped in): a total of $2939 out of my pocket, and $3323 in all. To travel for the same number of days by train would've cost me $1260 for a 3-month consecutive-day Eurailpass ($1206 if I'd been under age 26 upon validation of the ticket, and approximately $2200 if I'd bought individual second class tickets). Of course, the cost of supplementary transportation would've upped the effective cost of traveling by train. Thus I paid roughly 2.25 times more for motor travel than I would've paid for train travel. I think I got *at least* twice the value. And if I'd had just *one* person to split all the costs with, motoring would've cost me only 1.28 times as much as train travel — an unmistakable value.

I'm only one example. Listen to what the people at *Consumer Reports Travel Letter* had to say in their January 1994 issue.

> We listed rental of a four-passenger car in Europe as one of the year's best buys . . . that sort of rental is also an ideal way for a family to tour Europe. . . .The most economical way for four people to travel comfortably in Europe is to share a mid-sized automobile. When we checked last year the cost per person of touring that way was about 1/3 to 1/2 the cost of four of the cheapest Eurailpasses or second-class rail tickets . . . Even for just 2 people, sharing a car is often cheaper than Eurailpasses.

Note that the *Travel Letter's* analysis doesn't consider the use of cost-reducing diesel vehicles; nor does it fully consider the unbeatable *value* inherent in motoring tours.

Earlier, when discussing budget travel, I quoted Rick Steves. Rick's guidebook-and free newsletter-producing, Eurailpass-and travel product-selling, tour-operating and almost legendary organization Europe Through the Back Door (see the *Resources* chapter) is comprised of another group of experts who recognize the increasing value afforded by European motoring. In one of the recent editions of their newsletter, ETBD made the following observation.

Every year, as train prices go up, car rental becomes a better option for budget travelers in Europe. It's surprisingly easy. While the lion's share of travelers are planning on train travel, you should at least consider the driving option.

Indeed, most budget travelers leap to the assumption that trains offer the only economical way to get around in Europe. But what's worse, most never gain an understanding of the myriad different train passes available. For remarkably detailed analyses of the offerings of European train systems, go to your library and look through issues of *Consumer Reports Travel Letter* and write or call Europe Through the Backdoor and ask for their outstanding— and *free—Guide to European Railpasses*. (See the *Resources* chapter.)

But as alluded to, Eurailpasses aren't the deal they used to be. Recently, their prices have been raised roughly 10 percent per annum. In concert with this inflation, cheaper but more limiting rail passes called "Europasses" have been introduced which cover only three to five of the following countries: France, Germany, Switzerland, Italy and Spain. And because their domains are smaller, Europasses do not offer three of the major benefits of the

Eurailpasses: free or greatly discounted ferry travel between the central continent and Greece, Ireland, and Scandinavia.

Now let's assume that, given all we've discussed so far, you've decided that motoring is the way for you to go. Your next step, then, is to determine what type of vehicle to use. Let's first consider vans and motorhomes. (Motorhomes are called "caravans" or "motorised caravans" in Europe, and often I refer to them in this book as "caravans".) The most obvious benefit of these vehicles is that they're commodious: you can pack in many people and things, and you can sleep and even cook inside, thus saving bigtime on hotel and restaurant costs and on the hassle of constantly packing and unpacking—this is all especially nice if you're traveling with children. Another benefit is the better view you get from the high seat. This view is uniquely helpful if you plan to drive a British vehicle on the continent or a continental vehicle in the British Isles. The main problem with doing so is that it's difficult to see *around* a vehicle you wanna pass: the high seat of a van or caravan allows you to see *over* many types of vehicles.

Of course the relatively large size of these vehicles leads to higher procurement

and fuel costs. A *VW California* rents for $450–550 per week from October through April, $510–610 per week in May and September, and $570–670 per week from June through August; tack on $40 for an automatic. Larger motorhomes which sleep 4–6 go for about $570 per week in the low season, $700 per week during the shoulders, and $850 per week in the high. Good *VW* campers sold at dealerships start at about $5000; a *VW Westpahlia* will set you back some $10,000. Buy-back arrangements usually promise 50–70 percent of the purchase price if you return the vehicle within the year and in good condition. If you plan to buy and then sell a vehicle in Europe, note that despite the generally larger resale market for cars the often more obliging and salient market consisting of fellow travelers is larger for vans and caravans.

Though these vehicles are large relative to other European vehicles, they're small compared to their North American counterparts. The most common motorhomes, for example, are 5.5–6 meters (18–20 feet) long, sport a bunk over the cab, and pack a 2–2.5 liter four-cylindar diesel engine unleashing 75–100 hp through a 5-speed manual transmission. Altogether,

though, a surprisingly zippy package. Most trailers, meanwhile, owing to the smaller engine of the average European car, are rated at less than 2000 kg (4000 lb.) fully loaded. Given the higher fuel prices and the more challenging streets and terrain, such modest numbers allow for reasonable fuel economy and maneuverability. A good used campervan gets about 24 mpg (10 kpl).

Of course even at these economical sizes such vehicles are relatively difficult to park. Moreover, they'll cost you higher tolls, ferry fares and campground fees. Campground fees, however, run only a dollar or two higher per night, averaging $10–12 for two people in a van or motorhome without electrical hookups, $15–30 if hookups are utilized; add $3–4 if you're using a trailer instead of a motorized caravan. See the *Alternative Accommodations* chapter for more detail on camping with vans and motorhomes. Note also that a caravan weighing more than 3.5 tons requires its operator to possess a special driver's license.

On the other end of the size spectrum, motorcycles offer great fuel economy and a more intimate relationship to the environment than do larger motor vehicles.

Their small size makes motorcycles easy to park, cheap to transport on ferries, and inexpensive to admit to campgrounds. Yet the motorcyclist pays in several ways for the small size of his or her vehicle: motorcycles provide less security and are more dangerous to operate than other motor vehicles; motorcyclists are much more subject to the whims of the weather; motorcycle riding is harder work, and thus it doesn't suit plans to cover long average distances; and, finally, motorcycles limit the operator's ability to share thoughts, costs, and the driving with passengers. However, you can do the following to counteract some of these shortcomings:

- Get a helmet that has a full face cover; all European countries require a rider to wear a helmet.

- Bring a good motorcycle lock.

- Bring a jacket that is warmer than you think you'll need.

- Buy the best brightly colored rain gear you can find; it can double as a windbreaker.

- Bring heavy boots and waterproof gloves.

- Get crash bars: they may save your legs if you wipeout.

- Buy a luggage rack, hooked rubber straps, and a plastic bag to secure and cover your luggage; or else buy a lockable luggage carrier.

- Pay extra for an electric starter: it'll save much effort and anxiety.

- Replace a side kickstand with another type: side kickstands sink into many surfaces.

- Forego buying a tank lock: such locks rattle and are a pain to get open.

- Carry spare light bulbs and spark plugs: the plugs consistently foul.

- If you plan to cross borders, display a distinctive nationality plate near the rear number plate: this is a legal requirement in all countries. The plate must have black letters on a white background and conform to a certain regulatory size.

- Replace with a better one the cheap rearview mirror that's standard on most motorcycles: otherwise it'll constantly vibrate and quickly come loose.

Cars, of course, don't offer the comfort or passenger-carrying capacity of vans and caravans; and they aren't quite as fuel efficient, intimate with the road, easy to park, or downright cool as motorcycles; still cars are likely to be a happy medium for you. Be careful, however, when picking the particular type of car for your journey. The smallest class of car that I recommend is the subcompact class. This class consists of such cars as the two- or three-door *Citroën AX, Fiat Uno, Ford Fiesta, Nissan Micra, Opel Corsa, Peugeot 205, Renault Clio, Toyota Starlet, Vauxhall Nova,* and *VW Polo.* The five-door *Renault Clio RN 1.9* diesel comfortably transports three people and is an economical compromise for four. Many companies push four-door versions of cars such as the *Citroën ZX, Fiat Tipo, Ford Escort, Opel Astra, Peugeot 309, Renault Clio/19,* and *VW Golf,* claiming these can comfortably yet economically carry four adults; these cars *are* comfortable for two to three adults, but parties of four will probably find the comfort afforded by the next size up well worth the extra cash. The group on the next step up includes the *Audi 100, Citroën BX, Fiat Tempra, Ford Sierra, Nissan Primera, Opel Vectra/Omega, Peugeot 405/505, Renault 21/25, Vauxhall Cavalier,* and *VW Jetta/Passat.* For more information ask your travel agent to show you a copy of Hertz's

European Car Guide. Or use a modem to call 818 786 2032 and access Key Travel's wonderful new color-picture database (currently IBM-compatible only, but Mac-compatible soon) free of charge; if you don't have a modem, call 213 872 2226 to order a free diskette bearing the same info.

Of course motorcyclists aren't the only motorists who need to worry about equipping their vehicle:

- If traveling with children, you may need to obtain a child-safety seat or two or three or . . . See the relevant country description(s) in the *Country-by-Country Information* chapter.

- You must carry a warning triangle in Austria, Belgium, Bulgaria, the CIS, the Czech Republic, Denmark, France, Germany, Greece, Hungary, Italy, Luxembourg, the Netherlands, Poland, Portugal, Romania, and the Slovak Republic. Two triangles are necessary if traveling through Cyprus, Spain (if the vehicle has nine or more seats or weighs over 3500 kg) or Turkey.

- If traveling in the CIS, Greece or Turkey, you must carry a fire extinguisher.

- If traveling in Austria, Bulgaria, the CIS, the Czech Republic, Greece, or the Slovak Republic, you must carry a first aid kit.

- Carry spare bulbs of the correct wattage for your lights: bulbs may be difficult to obtain abroad. In Spain and certain other countries it's compulsory to carry a spare set of bulbs.

- In Spain vehicles are required to have at least two rear view mirrors. Drivers there must have a clear rear view of at least 50 meters; thus caravans should be equipped with extension mirrors.

- If you plan to cross borders, display a distinctive nationality plate near the rear number plate: this is a legal requirement in all countries. The plate must have black letters on a white background and conform to a certain regulatory size.

- If you plan to drive on the continent with a vehicle that's designed for driving on the left side of the road, or in the British Isles with one designed for the right side, the headlight beams should be adjusted before you make the switch. Of course you can buy a headlight conversion kit in Europe. The kits contain specially shaped adhesive black plastic which sticks to the glass and alters the direction of the beam.

Earlier I mentioned two benefits of diesel-powered vehicles: diesel fuel is about 33 percent cheaper than gas, and diesel engines are about 25 percent more fuel efficient. What's more, diesels require less maintenance than gasoline-powered engines. Diesel combustion occurs by the heat of air compression, not because of an electric spark. As such, diesel engines do not need spark plugs, points, coils, or a carburetor. To cold start a diesel you must turn the key over one notch and wait until the glow plug indicator light switches off; then the vehicle is ready to start. If the vehicle has just shut off (as in the case of a stall), you don't have to wait to restart it: the glow plug will already be hot. Don't worry about finding diesel fuel: every station that has a gasoline pump has a diesel-fuel pump. To help you make sure that you put gasoline in a gasoline engine and diesel fuel in a diesel engine, I include fueling instructions and special translations in the *Country-by-Country Information* chapter and in *Appendix G*.

Diesel fuel is cheap because it requires less refining than higher-grade fuels such as gasoline. Yet the nature of diesel fuel results in several negatives. Although modern diesel engines meet US standards for hydrocarbon and carbon monoxide emissions—often creating less than their gasoline-powered counterparts—they produce more nitrogen oxides (NO_x), sulfur dioxide (SO_2) and aldehydes, plus 30 to 100 times more particulate matter by mass than a catalytic converter-fitted gasoline-powered engine of the equivalent volume and weight. The particulate matter is what most people associate with diesel engines. A modern diesel car won't rumble and fume like a truck or bus, but it will run a bit rougher and noisier than a gasoline-powered car, and it won't be quite as powerful as a gasoline-powered engine of the same volume and weight. Nevertheless, engineers continue to significantly advance the environmental friendliness and mechanical capability of diesel engines. Indeed, the ten or so people who at one point or another drove my leased diesel car found it surprisingly and adequately powerful.

Yet because of the above-mentioned negatives—and since a diesel costs more than its equivalent-horsepower, gasoline-powered counterpart—gasoline-powered vehicles far outnumber diesels. As a result, it's easier to find parts for a gasoline engine. This is not an issue if you're renting or leasing a vehicle and thus are supported by the company-guaranteed timely service; but if you're driving a vehicle that you outright own and it breaks down in,

say, Southern Spain, you may experience a substantial delay in your trip.

As an alternative to a diesel vehicle, consider a vehicle that runs on Liquefied Petroleum Gas (LPG, sometimes called "Gepel"). LPG, too, can double your fuel economy, and it's also more environmentally friendly than gasoline or diesel fuel. In Northern Europe and Italy, LPG is available at nearly every fuel station; but in Spain, Portugal, and the East, LPG is scarce. Several European companies retail LPG in Europe. These companies can provide a list of all the stations they service.

As for whether to go with an automatic or a manual transmission vehicle, many people, uncomfortable or completely inexperienced with driving a manual (like I was on that fateful Paris day described in the opening), leap to embrace the automatics without giving the decision enough thought. Besides having significantly higher rental and lease rates and, of course, higher sticker prices, automatics generally require more fuel than do manuals—and often no diesel automatics are available. Indeed, since virtually all Europeans drive manuals, the variety of manuals available to renters and leasers and, for that matter, to

outright buyers, is much greater than that of automatics. Are you sure you don't wanna give a manual a shot? Manuals can be great fun to drive; and because they give their drivers more precise control over the vehicle, they can be driven more safely. And, hey, if the experience inspires you to buy a manual someday instead of an automatic, you'll realize a lower sticker price on that purchase and lower fuel and maintenance costs down the road.

In a similarly questionable leap of faith, many folks, because of the extra security they presume a trunk provides, prefer a vehicle with a full trunk instead of a hatchback. But because the back seat of almost every car folds down for trunk access, any thief worth his or her latest grab will be able to get into the trunk as easy as a hatch. And since the hatchbacks come with a panel that closes when you close the hatch—obscuring the contents—they provide the same degree of protection as a fully enclosed trunk. In fact, hatchbacks provide *more* protection. In the first place, you don't wanna leave anything of value in a vehicle. But beyond this, you don't wanna tempt thieves with the mystery of what *might* be in your vehicle. By removing the aforementioned panel on a hatchback, you can prove to passing thieves that you're not a fool.

By now you should understand the costs and benefits associated with European motoring. The following chapters should answer any other questions you might have. Even if the costs associated with your motoring preference are sub-stantially higher than the costs associated with other transportation options, remember that skimping, by definition, is stupid. A dollar spent wisely and presently in the life of a person has much more of an effect on that life than does the same dollar spent wisely later on. You could make this trip the time of your life—don't skimp on it. Furthermore, whether you choose to rent, lease, buy or ship a vehicle for use in Europe, the work you put into preparing for the trip will pale in comparison to the great feeling you'll experience when you're finally over there on the open road. Think how jealous your friends will be; think how justified they'll be in their jealousy.

why drive?

2. renting

Many of the same companies that rent vehicles in Australia, Canada, New Zealand, and the United States rent vehicles in Europe as well. Although the European rental fleet differs substantially from those of the above countries, the process of renting a motor vehicle for use in Europe is virtually the same. I say "for use in " because probably you should secure and pay for the deal before you go abroad: given the current comparative value of the dollar a rental from a major company tends to cost much less if you negotiate and pay for it at home rather than in Europe.

Perhaps *negotiate* is too strong a word, but the ways that prices, policies, services, and products vary within and between rental companies serving any one country—and perhaps what's more important, the ways these factors typically vary from one European country to another—require you to exercise the acumen of a corporate executive if you want to choose the best deal. This chapter will help you develop that acumen and guide you, step by step, through the often confusing process of renting a vehicle.

You'll find one of the best tools to help you step through the confusion is the check-list of questions I include as *Appendix A*. Paralleling the treatment of topics in this chapter, the checklist chronologically walks you through the questions you should ask concerning all aspects of motor-vehicle rental. The first portion of the checklist is for use when you discuss auto-rental insurance issues with representatives of your current auto-insurance or credit or charge card company, or with representatives of other sources that automatically provide or else sell auto insurance covering vehicles rented abroad. The next portion of the checklist consists of the appropriate questions to ask when on the phone with a representative of a rental company. Two more portions outline the issues you should address and the questions you should ask at the rental counter and when actually being introduced to the vehicle. A final portion lists the issues associated with returning a vehicle. Besides organizing the questions on the checklist in careful sequence, I designed the layout so you can jot right on the page the answers from several sources; as such, you can easily compare and retrieve them at any point during the planning and execution of your trip.

Insurance

To insure or not to insure a vehicle rental — that is *not* the question. Rather, the question — and it's the most confusing and thus most common question regarding the rental process — is *how* to do so. Rarely does the *basic* insurance included by rental companies cover collision damage, fire damage, damage from natural disasters, damage from vandalism or attempted theft, or theft of the entire vehicle — damages and losses against which you *need* to be somehow insured. To let you conveniently erase or decrease your responsibility for such occurances, rental companies sell supplemental insurance (or, technically, insurance *waivers* stating that the rental company waives the right to charge you for certain damages or losses, provided the vehicle is used in accordance with the terms and conditions of the rental agreement). However, at about $12–15 per day these waivers are expensive; and collectively the rental companies make over $1 billion a year by selling them. Furthermore, the names given to these waivers — and the effective coverage the waivers represent — vary somewhat from country to country and from company to company. As for the aforementioned basic insurance that *is* included in most European rental agreements, it almost always excludes certain European countries from the domain of its coverage; and since it usually amounts to only the legal minimum of liability coverage, it may not, depending on your assests, adequately protect you in the countries where it *is* effective. But don't despair: there are several ways to secure proper and inexpensive coverage.

First of all, the auto insurance you now own may cover vehicles you rent abroad; though this is rarely so. Secondly, several domestic companies sell relatively cheap foreign auto insurance. For example, Travel Guard International, 1100 Center Point Drive, Stevens Point, WI 54481, tel. 800 782 5151, offers a package that includes eight days of primary CDW (later I'll discuss the meaning of primary insurance and the CDW) for $19, with additional days charged at $3. See the *Documents* chapter for a listing of other travel-insurance providers. Thirdly, members of certain national organizations qualify for additional auto insurance free of charge. For instance, several rental companies entitle members of the American Association of Retired Persons (AARP) to discounts and additional liability coverage if the member provides the company-specific AARP identification number for listing on the rental agreement. To get this number AARP members should contact the organization. Members of the National Council of Senior Citizens qualify for similar benefits.

Perhaps the easiest, most inexpensive, and thus most popular way to secure supplemental insurance, however, is to use a certain credit or charge card to pay for the rental. American Express, Visa Gold, MasterCard Gold, and Diners Club provide what's known as *primary* auto insurance to cover rentals in most countries. Primary insurance lets you file directly with the underwriter of your credit-card insurance. *Secondary* coverage, on the other hand, requires you first to obtain a letter from your personal auto-insurance provider stating what they do and do not cover regarding your overseas incident. You must then forward this letter along with all the other relevant documents to the underwriter of your credit card insurance.

The secondary coverage will pick up the charges that are not covered by your personal insurance. For $5, Bankcard Holders of America, tel. 800 553 8025, will send you a list of no-annual-fee gold cards that offer secondary coverage. Always beware, however, that the policies of credit and charge card companies can change overnight; immediately before you embark on your trip, confirm that your card still entitles you to the coverage you think it does. Of course to activate a credit or charge card's auto-insurance benefits, you must use the card to pay for the rental: simply *having* the card is not enough.

Since the supplemental coverage offered by the rental companies costs so much and since the stakes associated with improper coverage are so high, it's well worth your time to thoroughly investigate the insurance offered by the above-mentioned sources. You should speak with representatives of these sources first. Start the dialogue by asking for the representative's name: your knowledge and use of a representative's name serves to personalize the interaction and gives you credibility and further recourse should things turn sour somewhere down the road. Be cheerful and pleasant. In other words,

start off on the right foot; the person on the other end of the line will be remarkably more cooperative if you do—and that cooperation can mean a great deal.

If the representative you speak with confirms that their organization does offer some sort of auto insurance that covers European rentals, get ready to note several points concerning the insurance. Note which countries it covers you in. Note if it covers other drivers besides yourself. Note the deductible. Note whether the insurance covers damage resulting from collision, fire, natural disasters (such as hail), vandalism or attempted theft. Note if it covers theft of the vehicle, at-fault drivers, only certain types of vehicles, traffic violations, and baggage. Note also the number of consecutive days it covers you for. Most supplemental providers impose a limit on the duration of their coverage, usually ranging from fifteen to thirty-one days. If you're covered for, say, fourteen consecutive days, you may mistakenly void the insurance by agreeing to a fifteen-day rental. You can get around such a policy by returning the vehicle before the fourteen days are up and arranging another rental for the remainder of your trip. Continue by asking if the insurance covers "loss of use" charges—

the amount of money the rental companies claim they lose when a rental vehicle is out of the fleet for repairs. If you plan to drive in Greece, ask if the insurance covers damage that the bumpy roads there may cause to the underside of your vehicle; many policies don't cover such damage.

When investigating credit or charge card insurance, ask if the insurance is primary or secondary. Regardless, determine if the card company will let the rental company bill your account directly for any damages that occur. If so, confirm that the status of such a billing will not require you to pay the charge and will not eat into your available credit unless ultimately the underwriter of the card's policy denies your claim. The dollar amount that a rental company equates with certain damages could approximate the value of the entire vehicle. As such, using your credit card to effectively pay up front for damages could cost you substantially if as a result you exceed your credit limit or must pay a finance charge—or both.

If you cannot identify or arrange proper supplementary coverage from other sources, you'll need to consider buying the collision damage waiver (CDW) and/or loss damage waiver (LDW) and/or theft protection (TP) waiver from the rental company you go with. All these *and/ors* are necessary because no universal definition of *CDW, LDW* or *TP* is in use. Often, a waiver termed *CDW* provides coverage against damages or losses due to collision, vandalism, natural disaster, theft or fire— in other words, essentially the full range of coverage. In some countries, rental companies use the term *LDW* instead of *CDW* to designate the same wide spectrum of coverage, and in others the term *collision damage reduction (CDR)* is used instead to indicate that an unwaivable deductible is associated with the waiver. When the CDW or LDW or CDR does not cover vandalism, attempted theft or theft, a TP waiver is offered. On top of all these waivers, the counter agent may offer personal accident insurance (PAI) when you take delivery; such insurance provides the renter and passengers with coverage for accidental death, disability or medical expenses; it's probably not worth its price.

Sometimes you'll run across a confusing jumble of definitions. For example, one company offers a CDW while integrating TP with an LDW in a package they call "TP/LDW", which according to their brochure consists of "personal accident insurance and loss damage waiver." I called this company to inquire about this strange combination of packages. The representative told me that the CDW covers any damage to the vehicle, the LDW covers theft of the vehicle, and the TP covers personal accident. *Whatever*.

No matter how confusing the process may be, you need to ensure that you and every potential driver of your rented vehicle are covered against damage to the vehicle that results from collision, fire, natural disaster, vandalism or attempted theft, and for theft of the vehicle. Your effort to confirm such coverage might require you to assume a fastidious air that may annoy you as well as the representatives you contact. So be it.

Later in the chapter, when I outline the discussion that you should engage the rental company representatives in, I'll address the issue of liability insurance.

Other Issues

Before you begin contacting rental companies, you should consider several issues apart from insurance. First, note that your age may limit your ability to rent a vehicle. All rental companies require their customers to be of some minimum age—usually either 21, 23, or 25 years. Also, many companies deal only with persons who have held a driver's license for at least a year or two. As for the other end of the age-spectrum, most companies enforce a maximum age limit of 65 or 70 years. Some companies, however, override such restrictions if the customer in question can demonstrate his or her driving proficiency to an agent at the delivery site. If because of your age or the age of your license you don't make the cut, don't take it personally. Instead, consider *leasing* a vehicle: anyone eighteen years of age and up can lease a vehicle in Europe for as few as sixteen days.

If you do make the cut, several options allow you to combine relatively cheap motor travel with other modes of transportation. Fly/drive packages are one such option. Recently you could fly Iberia to Spain, TAP to Portugal, Sabena to Belgium, or Lufthansa to Germany or Austria and consequently get a free rental car for a week. Meanwhile, Air France offered a fly/drive package with a rental rate of $69 per week—including tax and CDW. One rental company offered 20 percent discounts to customers who flew Alitalia from the US to Rome or Milan; while they

renting

offered similar deals in concert with Air France, British Airways, SAS, and Swissair. Nevertheless you should exercise caution when considering such programs. After an initial week of free vehicle rental, the charge for each additional day may be exorbitant. Moreover, the flight portion of the package may cost significantly more than other flights, thus wiping out any savings you realize from the cheap vehicle rental. Also, such a package may not let you take advantage of any auto insurance your credit or charge cards otherwise provide. And some packages prohibit one-way rentals or offer only a few vehicle-return options. Note that most of these packages require advance payment, and most have a cancellation charge associated with them.

Self-drive packages—including accommodation and vehicle but not airfare—are available from tour operators like CIE Tours, tel. 800 243 8687, offering programs to Great Britain and Ireland only, and DER Tours, tel. 800 782 2424. Here are some points to address when considering such tour packages:

- Is an advance deposit required? If so, how much and when?

- Can you cancel without penalty? If you can, how far in advance must you give notice? If not, what's the penalty?

- Are airport taxes included in the total price? If not, how much are they?

- Is the transportation to and from the airport included?

- Are meals included in the tour price? If so, which meals?

- Are tips included?

The efficiency of the European rail network coupled with the high cost of short-term European car rental once deterred the majority of travelers from blending the two modes of transportation; this is no longer the case now that "rail 'n drive" passes have arrived on the scene. These passes combine x number of days of train travel with y number of days of motor-vehicle rental at a good daily rental rate—a rate that approximates per-day rates you'd otherwise realize only if renting on a weekly basis. As such, these passes are ideal if you plan to use train travel to form a backbone or ring of long-distance travel on which you'll string motoring day trips. Such passes also suit someone who wants to explore a particular region with a motor vehicle for

three or four days. The passes allow for unlimited miles (or kilometers) and free return at other agencies within the country issuing a certain pass (and sometimes in neighboring countries as well). The prices include all taxes and legal *minimum* insurance. Often the programs allow you to buy additional rail- and/or motor-vehicle days, but you must do this at the time of purchase. Either Avis or Hertz will provide the vehicle. When you order your pass you must declare the date you want the pass to become valid. Be sure to reserve your first day of vehicle rental at least a week before leaving home, otherwise the vehicles are subject to availability; call Avis or Hertz to do this. Order passes through Europe Through the Back Door. (See the *Resources* chapter.) Before you can use your rail 'n drive pass for train or motor travel you must take it to a participating European train station and have it validated. This step is necessary even if you plan to begin your trip by using the pass to rent a vehicle.

As I mentioned previously, reserving and paying for your European rental before you go abroad will probably allow you to secure much lower rates than if you'd conduct the business overseas. Some rental companies offer 21-day advance-purchase discounts which currently result in 30 to 40 percent savings. Although to secure such a discount you'll probably have to prepay—agreeing to pay a charge if you cancel or otherwise alter your reservation. And note that a falling dollar could easily push prepaid rates higher. If prepaid rates are indeed significantly lower at the time of your trip but you find yourself having to arrange a rental after you're abroad, you may be able to reserve from a US-based company a vehicle at the discounted, pre-paid rates by stopping into an office of a US airline and arranging a rental through the airline's reservation system. Alternatively, you could place a transatlantic call to a US rental company's reservation office or to your travel agent.

Many companies offer special low rates if you reserve and pay before, say, April 1. Vans, motorhomes, and motorcycles oftentimes sell out well in advance of the summer season: if you're after one of these, consider making your reservations, say, six months in advance.

Note that most travelers who rent vehicles for use in Europe rent them on a weekly basis: vehicles tend to be quite expensive to rent by the day (though some companies offer decent weekend deals).

Here's something that may strike you as ridiculous: some rental companies consider a "week" to be five days long, not seven; up front get this definition straight.

One-way rentals are quite common. You can usually rent a car in one city and return it in another of the same country — sometimes of neighboring countries as well—without suffering an extra charge. And some agencies offer one-way rates between major European cities, rates which you'll likely find cheaper than adding a dropoff charge to the cost of a regular rental.

Before comparing prices between companies, educate yourself so you don't compare apples to oranges. Most rental companies place their vehicles into a lettered or numbered class. Unfortunately, these classifications are not consistent across companies—and they may vary within the companies themselves. Near the end of the *Why Drive?* chapter I discussed several cars and mentioned how you can find out more about these and other vehicles. Even with the limited information I gave you there you can perform a reasonably extensive analysis. Essentially, the progression of vehicle classes is as follows: economy (eg., *Ford Fiesta*), compact (*Ford Escort*), mid-

size (*Ford Sierra*), full-size, and luxury. Non air-conditioned, manual-transmission models are the norm in Europe. Air-conditioned and automatic-transmission models are usually available, but only in the form of larger, higher-priced vehicles. As a result, opting for these relative luxuries costs usually 1.5 to 2 times more than biting the bullet and settling for an economy or compact class vehicle.

Remember from the preceding chapter that employing a diesel vehicle will cut your fuel costs in half. To get a diesel, however, you may have to jump up a vehicle-class; this may wipe out any savings you'll realize from the reduced fuel costs. As such, try to estimate the number of miles or kilometers you'll be driving. Next, using the expected fuel efficiency of the vehicles you're considering, figure the amount you'll pay to fuel each vehicle. Finally, add these figures to the rates charged for the various vehicles.

Many experienced renters make it a practice to reserve the popular and cheap economy class vehicles. This because rental outlets often run out of such vehicles, and subsequently anyone who has reserved one of the missing economy class vehicles gets a free upgrade. Rental companies should not charge you more if they're forced to give you a more expensive vehicle than the one you reserved. If you have no intention of driving the economy class vehicle you've reserved and if the fleet of such vehicles is *not* depleted, you'll probably be able to upgrade—for a charge of course.

Rental rates vary widely from company to company. But rates fluctuate dramatically from *country to country* as well. Consequently, you may want to rent a vehicle in a country that neighbors the country you plan to travel in. In Table 2.1, I list the average weekly rental rates—including any applicable taxes—for cars in several countries. The table's entries are ordered by the average of the first three cost-columns. For an incredibly detailed analysis of rental rates—company by company for each country and vehicle-type—see the May issue of *Consumer Reports Travel Letter*. Each year that issue contains the results of a *Consumer Reports* phone poll conducted the previous September. Your local library probably subscribes to this extremely helpful publication. Note that the *Travel Letter* is separate from the famous magazine but under the auspices of the same organization, Consumers Union.

Table 2.1

Average Weekly Rental Rates in Various Countries.

Country	Cheapest	Compact	Midsize	Cheapest Automatic
Germany	$127	134	233	275
Switzerland	139	145	223	229
Great Britain	153	166	283	280
Belgium	171	177	259	305
Netherlands	162	179	267	290
Luxembourg	162	181	284	354
Spain	203	214	402	424
Austria	222	239	372	446
Portugal*	188	202	484	493
France	248	260	499	486
Sweden	306	317	431	723
Greece*	240	274	562	510
Ireland*	311	315	472	579
Hungary	297	310	514	460
Denmark	290	339	510	598
Italy	273	319	557	538
Romania	374	374	468	—
Czech Republic	362	362	499	681
Bulgaria	360	396	512	892
Norway	363	398	542	681
Turkey	376	405	611	—
Poland	420	457	546	527
Slovak Republic	406	406	611	—
Finland	500	500	794	1540

*Rates in Greece, Ireland and Portugal are especially subject to seasonal changes.

Call 800 234 1970 or 919 378 2000 to order; each issue costs $5.

Switzerland amounts to an interesting case. Switzerland's average rental costs are some of the cheapest in Europe. And as I show in Table 13.1, fuel is relatively cheap in Switzerland. Moreover, vehicles rented in Switzerland come bearing a sticker or *vignette* which signifies someone has paid the necessary annual tax for the privilege of driving that vehicle on Switzerland's expressways. If your vehicle doesn't have a *vignette* but you want to use the Swiss expressways, you must buy the sticker at a Swiss border station or from a Swiss National Tourist Office for 30 SwF, about $22. (Of course, many rental vehicles in cities *nearby* Switzerland, such as Milan and Munich, come with this sticker as well since their former renters tend to have ventured into Switzerland and opted to travel the expressways there.) In short, consider renting a vehicle in Switzerland if you want to include Switzerland in your itinerary—especially if you'd otherwise rent in France or Italy.

Perhaps to compete with neighbors such as Switzerland, Austria makes an enticing offer. Austria lets you refund a portion of the 21.2 percent VAT (value-added tax) paid on an Austrian motor-vehicle rental; the portion is directly proportional to the amount of driving you do with the vehicle *outside* Austria. So if you plan to rent a vehicle in Austria and to then exit the country in that vehicle, get a tax exemption form from the counter agent when you take delivery. Then each time you exit and enter Austria with the vehicle, jot down the date and time and odometer reading in the appropriate spaces on the form and have an Austrian customs official validate it. Finally, submit the form to the rental company when you return the vehicle; they'll prorate the VAT so that you're taxed only for the fraction of time and mileage *you* spent taxing the Austrian transportation infrastructure. One caveat: Austria charges a 33.3 percent VAT on vehicles rented for any period longer than twenty-one days.

Also noteworthy are the high rates in Scandinavia. I highly recommend touring these countries, but you should consider beginning in Germany, where some of the cheapest rental rates are found. As I relate in the *Ferries and the Chunnel* chapter, for just $40 you—along with a vehicle and up to two other people—can make the five-hour crossing from Rostock, Germany, to Trelleborg, Sweden, on the TR-Line. Besides, you'll enjoy the cruise.

Indeed, the ferries which ply the international waters between the central European continent and its marginal constituents—specifically the British Isles, Scandinavia, and the Eastern Mediterranean—now approximate full-blown cruise ships. Perhaps because of this blossoming, more packages are arising which combine vehicle rental with ferry travel. Hertz, in cooperation with Stena Sealink Line, offers one such program. This program combines car rental in Britain with return ferry travel to Ireland. (See *The Special Case of the British Isles* chapter for more.) Such deals may represent substantial savings if the land mass in which the rental originates—Britain in the above case—is home to substantially lower rental rates than the other land mass. Note, however, that many rental companies don't allow customers to transport vehicles on international ferries.

Another offer from Hertz is *le Swap,* which for one price lets you rent a car on either side of the English Channel, drive it, return it to the agency at the Chunnel port, ride the train through the Chunnel, and pick up another car on the opposite side.

If you plan to take delivery of or return a vehicle at an airport, some of the favorable disparities made evident above may be eaten up by airport surcharges. Certain countries or airports charge rental companies a fee to operate on-site. The rental companies tend to pass this charge on to the consumer. While individual rental companies vary in how they assess airport surcharges, the following surcharges are typical: Austria—7 percent of the rental price; Brussels, Belgium—9 percent; Bulgaria—$3; Czech Republic—8 percent; Copenhagen, Denmark—$18; Helsinki, Finland—$16; France—$11; Germany—DM 10 (about $7); Hungary—7 percent; Italy—10 percent; Luxembourg—6 percent; Schipol in Amsterdam, Netherlands—$22; Norway—$8; Poland—$11–28; Portugal—$10; Slovakia—$11; Spain—$8; Sweden—$10; and Switzerland—9 percent. Another reason to opt against airport delivery is that you may not be alert upon arrival if you've just flown in from overseas.

Airport delivery in Europe does have its benefits though. For one thing, it's often easier than in North America because European agencies keep the vehicles at the terminals instead of at far-removed parking lots. Furthermore, rental vehicles kept at airports are likely to be newer and more reliable than those kept at non-airport sites.

Rental Companies

Below I list the leading car rental companies and their phone numbers. The bigger ones toward the top *may* offer more reliability, flexibility and services, but the consolidators (outfits that subcontract through local independent suppliers) making up the bottom half of the list *may* be cheaper—especially (and surprisingly) in the *summer* months when business travel is down. Note that I stress *may*.

Alamo, tel. 800 522 9696, 800 327 9633 in Canada.

Avis, tel. 800 331 1084, 800 TRY AVIS in Canada.

Budget, tel. 800 472 3325, 800 268 8900 in Canada.

Campanje, (for vans and motorhomes), tel./FAX 209 245 3129.

EuroDollar (Dollar), tel. 800 800 6000.

Europcar (National), tel. 800 227 3876, 800 227 7368 in Canada.

Global Motorhome Travel, tel. 800 468 3876.

Hertz, tel. 800 654 3001, 800 263 0600 in Canada.

Holiday Autos, tel. 800 422 7737.

International Travel Services (ITS), tel. 800 521 0643.

Payless, tel. 800 237 2804.

Thrifty, tel. 800 331 9111.

Woods Car Rental—UK/British Network, tel. 800 274 8583, 800 526 2915 in the UK.

World Wide Car Hire, tel. 01273 203366 or 01273 205025 in the UK.

Auto Europe*, tel. 800 223 5555, 800 458 9503 in Canada.

DER Tours, tel. 800 782 2424.

European Car Vacations, tel. 800 223 6764.

Europe by Car, tel. 213 272 0424 or 212 581 3040 or 800 223 1516, or 800 252 9401 in California.

European Car Reservations, tel. 800 535 3303.

Eurorent, tel. 800 521 2235.

Foremost Euro-Car (also goes by Bon Voyage by Car), tel. 213 872 2226 or 800 272 3299, or 800 253 3876 in Canada.

Kemwel, tel. 800 678 0678.

Kenning, tel. 800 227 8990.

Claim they'll beat any offer, and they charge no penalties for changes or cancellations.

Although local independent rental companies in Europe sometimes offer cheaper deals than do the international companies, they may not offer the same high degree of integrity in their vehicles, insurance and service. *Be careful.*

On the Phone with Rental Companies

The rest of this chapter models—in sequential order—the discussion you should engage a rental company representative in. Again, I mirror yet simplify this discussion in *Appendix A*. And remember, you can use *Appendix A* as a guide and note pad when making these calls.

Of course you should begin by asking the name of the representative with whom you speak. If you're of marginal age, determine immediately whether you qualify to rent from the company. Young drivers should determine if they've held a driver's license long enough. If you don't have a credit or charge card, you should mention this fact right away: it may be tricky to make a reservation without one. Relate

where you want to take delivery. Ask if you must have an International Driving Permit. Ask if the company is a consolidator; if they are, ask which local European supplier will provide your vehicle—and confirm that the supplier's policies will match those of the consolidator. Tell the representative that you want this confirmation specified in writing along with the rest of the information you're soliciting. Next, explain to the representative the type of vehicle you're researching; make sure the prices quoted to you reflect such a vehicle. Establish the period the representative will base the rates on: three days, one week, two weeks, three weeks, or more. Ask that the rates be quoted in dollars and that they include tax. You want the prices in dollars because it makes the figures more simple and intuitive for you.

If you've determined that you can obtain supplementary insurance from other sources, ask that the cost of the CDW or LDW or TP not be included in the quoted rates. The rental company representative may claim, however, that you must either buy theft protection insurance or place a large deposit on the vehicle. By law at least one country—Italy—requires renters to fulfill one of these demands. What's more,

Italian rental agencies have recently banded together to refuse to honor credit card coverage altogether.

Often, rental companies take deposits by putting a "hold" on or by "blocking" one of your credit cards. A *hold* means that you cannot use the card until the rental company removes the hold. A *block* means that a certain amount of your available credit has been temporarily taken from you. In the case of a vehicle rental, this amount tends to be quite large (between $5000 and $14,000). If you won't be driving in Italy, you should stipulate up front that your final agreement will state that you don't have to buy the theft insurance nor place a deposit. If you must buy TP or place a deposit, ask how much the TP costs and the amount and means of the deposit.

Once the representative quotes both the rate and the cost of any necessary insurance waivers, you should confirm that unlimited mileage is included. Furthermore, ask if there's a surcharge for additional drivers. And since you'll probably be pre-paying for the rental, determine what alteration or cancellation charges may apply.

With this information in hand, it's time to get the details about the basic insurance that the rate *includes*. Some companies may "include" CDW or LDW or TP, but this is probably just a ploy to get you to buy them. The truly *basic* included insurance is almost always liability-only. Begin by asking which countries the basic insurance and the registration allow you to drive in. Make sure the insurance is or amounts to Green Card insurance; in other words, the insurance should provide minimum legal liability coverage in most European countries. If you plan to transport the vehicle on an international ferry or via the Chunnel, make sure this is allowed.

If you determine that the domain of the basic insurance satisfactorily accommodates your itinerary, ascertain the integrity of the coverage. Ask about the limits of the liability insurance. Depending on these limits you may not be adequately protected from a law suit. Because insurance standards vary from country to country, most domestically sold personal policies, if they provide liability coverage of rentals at all, don't cover foreign rentals. As a general rule, you should have enough liability insurance to cover all your assets—but no more.

Ask if the basic insurance will cover other drivers besides yourself. Ask if it covers at-fault drivers. If you'll be driving in Spain or Greece, ask if the insurance includes bail bonds: if you're at all at fault in a traffic accident in these countries and you don't have a bail bond, the police will detain you and impound your vehicle until you can prove you have funds to pay for any damages. As I pointed out earlier, if you plan to drive in Greece, determine if the insurance covers damage that the bumpy roads there may inflict to the underside of your vehicle.

If the basic insurance proves to be more comprehensive than liability-only, you should ask the standard questions. Is damage from collision, fire, natural disasters, vandalism or attempted theft covered? Is theft covered? What is the deductible? Often the deductible is very high and may approximate the vehicle's value.

If you decide you need to buy the CDW or LDW, ask about these. How much do they cost? Do they cover damage from collision, fire, natural disaster, vandalism and attempted theft? Is theft protection inherent in the CDW or LDW? If not, how much does TP cost? Do the waivers cover at-fault drivers? Is there a deductible? Remember that in some countries the waiver is offered as collision damage reduction (CDR) instead of a CDW, implying a deductible which cannot be waived.

Also, determine if the rental company offers baggage insurance, and note the cost and terms of such coverage. (Although you should carefully consider buying baggage insurance, don't plan to leave valuable property unattended in a vehicle.) Ask, too, if personal accident insurance is offered, what it covers, and how much it costs.

Overlapping somewhat with the topic of insurance is the issue of service. Ask what services the rental company provides in the event of accident, damage, breakdown and theft. Ask if the company guarantees *timely* service. Ask how long it would take to obtain a replacement vehicle. Furthermore, ask if any special services (such as translation services) or materials (such as maps) are available.

After clearing all these hurdles you're ready to determine the specifics concerning your taking delivery of and returning the vehicle. Ask about any surcharges associated with relevant airport locations. If your itinerary may require you to return the vehicle at another location, ask about the associated charges. Note the cost of extra days—and how far ahead of time you must give notice if you want to add days without incurring a penalty. Also find out if you would be eligible for a refund should you decide to return the vehicle early. Conversely, some companies will charge you the daily rate instead of the weekly rate if you return the vehicle early—resulting, of course, in a greater expense to you; determine if this is the case. Also note the business hours during which you can take delivery of and return the vehicle.

As I detailed in the *Why Drive?* chapter, most countries require motor vehicles to carry certain safety-promoting items. Vehicles rented in a particular country should come with the equipment required by that country. If you'll be driving in several countries, however, you may have to buy equipment to satisfy the requirements of all these countries. If it seems that the countries included in your itinerary will oblige you to obtain further safety equipment, try to get the rental company to include the equipment as part of your agreement. It's probable that government officials will check for these items only if you're in an accident or if your vehicle breaks down, but it's better to be on the safe side. Luggage racks, bicycle racks,

tire chains for driving in snow, and other such items are not always immediately available; you should book them in advance and determine if they cost extra. Also ask if a parking disc or "blue card" is included: as I detail in the *Country-by-Country Information* chapter, many European cities require such a disk or card to be displayed on your vehicle's dashboard while it's parked in certain zones called *"Blue Zones"*.

If renting a van or motorhome it's especially important to determine what's included in the rental cost. Oftentimes you'll be charged extra for bedding, kitchen utensils, cleaning and the like.

The company's policy concerning the initial fueling of the vehicle is also important. It's best if the company fills the tank initially and agrees not to charge you for fuel unless you return the vehicle with less than a full tank; this way you avoid both the annoying task of trying to return the vehicle with some specific but less-than-full amount of fuel and the roughly doubled fuel prices that rental companies charge. If the representative claims that the company won't accommodate this wish, at least feign you've lost interest as a result.

Certain services and organizations— and myriad companies, firms and corporations—have forged agreements that entitle customers, members or employees to special offers or discounts on rentals. (One such organization is Hostelling International.) For one reason or another the rental company representative may refuse to give rates for these programs in the same conversation in which they relate rates that don't reflect any special offers or discounts. If this is the case and you think your affiliation with one or more groups may entitle you to one or more such discounts, just call back and ask for the special rates. Note, however, that a special rate or discount from some organization is no guarantee you'll get a better deal. Often these discounts apply to only the more luxurious classes of vehicles, and they may not apply to rentals that are not returned to the delivery site. Furthermore, many corporate accounts don't result in better prices but rather in perks of another nature (such as allowances for young drivers).

Before you close a deal, ask for a written guarantee of the price—in the foreign currency. Also get any further agreements in writing—including a statement

renting

that any foreign representative of the company (or, if you're dealing with a consolidator, the company that will be subcontracted by the company) will honor these agreements. As described above, these agreements may concern insurance, equipment, or fueling. Have a calculator and a reliable exchange rate handy to convert the final financial figures into dollar figures and to ensure that the representative calculates the final price using a fair exchange rate. By securing the final price in terms of the foreign currency, you'll avoid dealing with unexpected price fluctuations and the confusion associated with currency exchange rates. Of course if you feel you know the future of the exchange rate, you can play this game either way to come out ahead. In other words, if you feel that the dollar will get stronger compared to the relevant foreign currency, go ahead and get the price guaranteed in the foreign currency; but if you feel the opposite is true, get the price guaranteed in dollars. *The Wall Street Journal* includes predictions of future exchange-rate activity.

The last thing to do is to ask for and confirm a reservation confirmation number. Ask that this number be placed on the written agreement. Rental companies give every reservation an identification number. Counter agents who "can't seem to find your reservation" will have remarkable success if they punch in your confirmation number.

Before You Leave

If you pre-paid, you probably paid for the vehicle *and* the tax. The rental company will send you a voucher for this transaction. Make a photocopy of this voucher and bring it along. Counter agents—especially those working at a location other than where you took delivery of your vehicle—may not be well informed about the transactions that transpired when you reserved and/or took delivery of the vehicle. For example, some agents may inveterately add on VAT when you return a vehicle; if you already paid the VAT but cannot prove this fact, you may have a hassle on your hands.

Taking Delivery

When you arrive to take delivery of your vehicle, the counter agent may claim that you have to either buy theft protection or place a large deposit. Even if you present the agent with the company's written confirmation that you do not have to submit to either of these precautions, the agent may balk. Foreign outlets will go to great lengths to ensure quick reimbursement for any loss they suffer. I suppose it's only natural for the policies of a North America-based company to carry less weight in its foreign outposts than in, say, Chicago. If you face such a demand from an agent, there isn't much you can do at the time but comply with it. If an agent compels you to buy insurance or place a deposit contrary to your contract, at least you'll have recourse to eventually get a refund from the company. If you place a deposit using your credit or charge card, be careful that the amount doesn't exceed your credit limit. Consider putting the deposit on an American Express Card, Diners Club or Carte Blanche—none of which impose a credit limit. You may be asked to sign a *blank* charge slip as a deposit—don't do it: always make sure your signature is associated with a specific amount. Finally, if you pay for a rental with a credit or charge card because of the extra coverage the card gives you, make sure you put the deposit on the same card: this minor precaution will simplify and expedite the processing of any claim you might have to file.

Regardless, ask the agent if you can upgrade to a more luxurious class of vehicle free of charge. You'd be surprised how often this works. Agents may be in touch with potential customers who are only willing to rent the class of vehicle you've reserved—and yours may be the last one. The solution to the agent's problem is to let you have a free upgrade. Of course, as mentioned earlier, there's always a good chance that you'll get a free upgrade anyway. On the other hand, if offered a smaller vehicle than the one you reserved, demand a discount.

Always refuse to pay more for a vehicle that's more expensive that the one you reserved. If the agent presses you to upgrade for a price—under the pretense that the vehicle you've reserved cannot comfortably accommodate your party or, say, negotiate the local terrain—you're probably being subjected to the old *bait and switch*. The agent may know that the smaller vehicles are all out, and if you, not being privy to the same information, agree to pay for an upgrade, you've been had.

Before you leave the counter, write the names of any additional drivers on the contract. If you don't add these names, you may be traveling without proper insurance when the other person or persons are at the wheel. You'll probably be offered some sort of personal accident insurance (PAI) at this time; it's probably not worth its price. Regardless, determine if you have the following: Green Card insurance papers; bail bonds; a nationality sticker on the vehicle to ease border crossings; contact addresses and phone numbers in case of an accident, breakdown or theft; and a list of return sites and corresponding charges. And note again the business hours during which you can return the vehicle.

Of course you must inspect the vehicle. Note if all the accouterments specified in your agreement are indeed present. Be sure you know where the jack is and how it works. How about the lug wrench? Understand where the spare tire is and how to get it out. Check out the quality of the tires and the vehicle. Make sure that the head lights, tail lights, windshield wipers, seat adjustments, and seat belts work. A recent study of rental cars in Greece and Spain revealed that 33 percent were either "dangerous" or "very dangerous". (Quality levels are much higher in the more northern parts of Europe, however.) The major problems discovered by the study included cut or bulging or bald tires, bad brakes, inoperative brake lights, and dysfunctional windshield wipers. Remember,

if you sign a rental contract, you may be agreeing that the vehicle is in fine condition. Note, along with the rental company employee assisting you, any mechanical or cosmetic problems the vehicle exhibits. If such flaws exist, make sure the staff either fixes those of a mechanical nature or provides you with another vehicle. Make sure any flaws that are not fixed at this point are noted on the contract. (Try to take some pleasure in being a pest.) Note how much fuel is in the tank so that you can return the vehicle with about the same amount. Determine if a European Accident Statement form is in the glove compartment or the compartment on the driver's-side door. This form provides a standard format on which to record the details of an accident. Finally, if the vehicle is a diesel and you've never driven a diesel get a quick lessen from a competent employee—there are a few tricks.

Returning the Vehicle

Upon returning the vehicle, confirm with the rental agent that no damage occurred to it. Get this fact written on the contract. If you placed a deposit using your credit or charge card (in other words, if the rental company put a hold or block on the card), be sure that the counter agent removes this deposit. On the other hand, if an accident did cause damage to the vehicle, note this damage accurately and precisely on the contract. Consider taking photographs of the vehicle which show the vehicle from every major direction and which substanti-

ate that the pictures were taken in the presence of rental company personnel after you returned the vehicle. Note on the contract the amount of fuel in the tank. Keep a copy of this contract; keep copies of all the documents associated with the rental. In Germany it's considered bad manners to

leave the keys in the ignition. If returning a motorhome, the toilet's holding tank should be empty. If you have a hotel concierge return a vehicle for you, make sure you explain the need for him to return the vehicle punctually and to send you copies of the final rental documents.

3. leasing

To a non European, leasing a vehicle in Europe means buying a brand new vehicle direct from the manufacturer with the agreement that the manufacturer will buy it back at a certain date (the period of the lease being as short as sixteen days or as long as six months) and price (the leaser making just one, up-front payment equal to the difference between the buying and selling prices). Such agreements are known as a *short-term* leases. In many respects, these leases are easier to arrange than are rentals. What's more, they tend to be cheaper.

Several factors contribute to the relative ease of leasing. To begin with, only a few manufacturers grant short-term leases; thus prudent shoppers need not spend much time and effort looking for the best deal. Moreover, for *one* price you get a factory-fresh vehicle with full factory warranty, 24-hour roadside assistance, unlimited mileage, and—here's a biggy—comprehensive insurance that imposes no deductible and allows insured driving in several more countries than does typical rental insurance. (But ask whether Spanish and Greek bail bonds are included.) In addition, you need only be eighteen years old and possess a minimum one-year-old driver's license to lease a vehicle in Europe—and there is no *maximum* age limit. Finally, the process of ordering, taking delivery of and returning a leased vehicle is analogous to doing the same with a rental. After a few phone calls and mailings done several weeks before you depart, you just show up at a European airport or city office, sign a few papers, and take off in your brand-new vehicle; returning the vehicle is even easier. I recently leased a *Renault;* by paying a $35 rush fee I was able to take delivery of the car in Paris just five days after ordering it in the US.

The potential monetary savings, however, are the most intrigueing aspect of a lease. Indeed, short-term leases can be so much cheaper than renting that you may feel guilty for paying so little. But don't feel bad. Manufacturers can offer such good deals because the governments of Belgium and France do not apply a value-added tax (VAT) to short-term leases. (Since these governments can't afford to extend the same break to their own citizens, short-term leases are available to non Europeans only.) The main reason manufacturers *want* to offer short-term leases is that they can re-sell slightly used vehicles at significantly lower tax rates; in other

Table 3.1

**Recent Rental Rates vs.
Recent Leasing Rates.**

	Renault 19 **five-door**			
	1 week	*2 weeks*	*3 weeks*	*extra days*
Rental w/CDW	$53/day	53	50	53
Rental w/o CDW	42	41	37	41
	23 days	*extra days up to 33rd*	*33 days*	*extra days*
Lease	$43/day	20	35	20

words, they can sell the same vehicle twice, each time for an enticing price but in the end for a profit greater than if they'd sold the vehicle just once. Of course the longer you plan to travel the more likely a lease will be a better deal. Leasing also tends to be the best way to find an affordable vehicle that has air conditioning.

Still, several factors—some of which aren't obvious—contribute to the cost of a lease. Indeed, sometimes these factors combine to render a lease more expensive than a rental. Chief among them may be your choice of delivery and return sites. Not only are there far fewer delivery/return sites for leases but most outside France entail a rather steep charge, usually between $50 and $200.

If you plan to travel between the continent and the British Isles, this choice is especially important. Indeed, you should consider five delivery/return options.

Lease one vehicle . . .

(1) delivery on continent + ferry + ferry + return on continent.

(2) delivery on continent + ferry + return in London.

(3) delivery in London + ferry + ferry + return in London.

(4) delivery in London + ferry + return on continent.

or rent or lease two vehicles . . .

(5) delivery & return on continent + ferry + delivery & return in Britain.

Note that you can probably take delivery of and/or return a leased car in Calais, France—a primary crossing point to Britain—free of charge. Furthermore, note that any leased vehicle that's delivered in London will nevertheless be designed to drive on the right side of the road (steering wheel on the left, gear shift on your right) instead of the left (steering wheel on the right, gear shift on your left).

Renault recently made an offer that may influence your choice of a return site. If you return your leased vehicle to *Renault's* downtown Paris headquarters, you qualify for a $50 refund. When you return the vehicle you'll be given a receipt that proves where you returned it. If you then mail this receipt to *Renault* when you get home, they'll send your refund. I know what you're thinking: "It's not worth it to drive in downtown Paris." Don't worry; it'll be easy. *Renault* has conveniently located their headquarters next to an exit off the *périphérique,* the four-lane highway that rings Paris. Zip into town on an expressway *(autoroute),* join the *périphérique* and stay on it until you get to the *Porte de Pantin* exit, exit and turn onto *Avenue Jean Jaures,* and you're almost there: address 186 is just a hundred meters down on your left; circle behind the building to find the garage. This location may be easier to get to (and away from) than any other in Europe. Besides, *Renault's* offer is a good excuse to spend some time in Paris before you go home. You'll enjoy the city much more at the end of your trip: by that time you're sure to be an experienced and suave European traveler—and a traveler without jet lag.

In addition to delivery and return charges, a lease may lead to another set of costs in the form of safety equipment and other accouterments for the vehicle. Rented vehicles should include the safety equipment necessary for the country in which you take delivery (see the *Why Drive?* chapter), but this is not necessarily so with a lease. Furthermore, accouterments such as child seats and bicycle racks, which may be free (or at least available) with a rental, may be extras (or unavailable) with a lease. What's more, the kind of perks which some rental companies provide free of charge—such as guidebooks, information hotlines, message centers or personalized itineraries—probably won't come with a lease. It's also worth noting that vehicles rented in Switzerland come with the $22 *vignette* which allows you to legally drive on the Swiss expressways; leased vehicles delivered in Switzerland do not come with this *vignette*.

One final factor may contribute to the cost of a lease. A typical lease agreement requires you to bring in the vehicle for its scheduled first maintenance by a certain kilometer threshold (usually either 3000, 7500 or 10,000 kilometers; that is, roughly 1800, 4500 or 6000 miles). This maintenance consists of the standard checks and replacements of fluids and filters. Depending on the vehicle, you either will or will not have to pay for the labor. Regardless, you must pay for the materials (oil, oil filter, air filter, etc.). Beyond this standard service and the associated materials, you won't have to pay for any parts or labor associated with mechanical problems the vehicle may develop or incur. In other words, the vehicle will be under full factory warranty.

The availability of mechanical service is a primary concern for anyone endeavoring to drive abroad. Indeed, although the *Renault* vehicle I leased impressed me with its comfort and performance and although *Renault* offers a much wider range of delivery and return sites—and offers them at better prices—than the other main lease providers, I recommend *Renault* over other European manufacturers for one reason: *Renault's* trademark yellow and black sign

bedecks service stations that cover the European continent like follicles cover your skin—one every ten or twenty miles from Portugal to Italy to Hungary to Norway to Britain, and, of course, to France. The presence of other European automobile manufacturers is nowhere near as obvious. Thanks to these ubiquitous service stations, a 24-hour hotline, and guaranteed 24-hour service, you'll experience minimal trouble in promptly getting a *Renault* vehicle to a qualified service station if you must. "*Renault* Assistance TT" is the name of *Renault's* assistance program. *Renault* agents will arrange for towing and repair of your car and will help you with car replacement, car rental, and hotel reservations as necessary. This service can be reached 24 hours a day in France by phoning 05 05 15 15 (toll free) and outside France by phoning 1 47 11 13 13. Simply put, leasing a *Renault* is the closest thing on Earth to *guaranteeing* a hassle-free motor tour.

The story of Naomi and Denise—two young Australians I met in Brugge, Belgium—will serve to illustrate *Renault's* assistance service in action. At the time of our meeting, Naomi and Denise were, or so they were told, the only people *ever* to have backed out on their lease contract with *Renault*. Each of the ladies had paid about $1200 for a four-month lease. After just two days of driving, however, Naomi and Denise piloted their car smack into another car in Lille, France. Thankfully, nobody was hurt. *Renault* offered to provide the ladies with a new car in Brugge or Lille or Paris. Meanwhile, *Renault* put them up for two nights in what Naomi called a "clean, comfortable, and well-located" hotel in Lille. During their time in Lille the ladies decided to return to Paris and pick up the new car there. *Renault* paid for their first class rail transport back to Paris, put them up for three more nights in a nice, downtown hotel, and covered all their taxi rides. All along, *Renault* directly paid the servicers involved, so the ladies didn't need to handle any of the transactions. Finally, however, intimidated by the accident and the novelty of driving on the right side of the road (Australians of course drive on the left at home), Naomi and Denise decided they didn't want to drive after all. As a result, *Renault* gave an $808 refund to both Naomi and Denise; thus in effect, the ladies had to pay only for their post-accident hotel accommodation and transportation. If the ladies hadn't can-

celed, *Renault* never would have charged them a dime extra.

What about insurance against theft of your vehicle's contents? Well, such baggage insurance won't be automatically provided, but you can buy it from the leasing company. The cheapest and best way to hedge against such theft, however, may be to buy travel insurance before you go abroad.

Another thing to consider up front is the price you should expect to pay for the vehicle's first scheduled maintenance. This cost may vary sharply from country to country. For example, having a *Renault* serviced in France will cost markedly less than having it serviced in Spain. Thus if you can't avoid paying for the first service of a leased car, you can at least avoid paying too much for it: the *Renault* lease agreement demands only that you have the vehicle serviced before you reach the kilometer threshold. Always ask for a price quote before you have any work done.

Upon taking delivery, determine if the vehicle has a nationality sticker and a European Accident Statement form. The sticker is required for border crossing. The EAS, which is usually in the glove compartment or the compartment on the

driver's-side door, provides a standard format on which to record the details of an accident. Finally, ask where the nearest service station is: your vehicle will be delivered filled with very little fuel.

Once out on the road, you can, if you like, arrange extensions to your contract. For example, you can extend a *Renault* contract by calling the Paris office at 1 40 40 33 68 no less than ten days before the contract's expiration; *Renault* will advise you of the payment due and will ask for an address in Europe where they can send the extended registration and insurance contract. (An American Express Office will do nicely for this if you have the card or the traveler's checks; a hostel or hotel address is another possibility.) If you make such a change and you plan to return your vehicle to an airport location, you should call the appropriate office to notify them of your new schedule. Notify the head office if you decide to return your vehicle at a location other than that specified on your lease contract. Early return refunds are available from *Renault,* but only after thirty-three days and only in blocks of seven days— remaining days being truncated. For example, a return after thirty-three days on a forty-five day contract would qualify for a seven-day refund.

The following are the lease brokers in the US.

Auto France, Inc., tel. 800 572 9655.

DER Tours, tel. 800 782 2424.

Foremost Euro-Car, tel. 213 872 2226 or 800 272 3299, or 800 253 3876 in Canada.

Europe By Car, tel. 213 272 0424 or 800 223 1516, or 800 252 9401 in California.

Kemwel, tel. 800 678 0678.

Some brokers offer sixteen-day leases; otherwise leases begin at a minimum of twenty-three days. Likewise, some brokers accept Visa and MasterCard; while others may demand you pay with a certified check.

Of course you can lease directly through a manufacturer's office outside Europe, but it'll cost you about $50 more than leasing through a broker. Here are some *Renault* offices outside France.

Renault Eurodrive, 650 First Avenue, New York, NY 10016-3214, tel. 800 221 1052, or 800 477 7116 from Western states, FAX 212 725 5379.

Australia: tel. 02 299 3344 or 008 221 156, FAX 02 290 3963.

Canada: tel. 514 461 1149, FAX 514 461 0207.

Ireland: tel. 01 260 222, FAX 01 260 241.

New Zealand: tel. 09 570 4056, FAX 09 527 7964.

South Africa: tel. 011 803 3068, FAX 011 803 2815.

UK: tel. 081 992 5544, FAX 081 993 2734.

You can also lease directly through a European office (*Renault,* tel. 1 40 40 32 03, FAX 1 42 41 83 47); it takes just one or two days to get the vehicle (one week in the summer), but it'll be 25 to 35 percent more expensive than if you'd gone through a broker or an office outside France.

leasing

4. buying

There are several ways to go about buying a vehicle in Europe, each way promising a different degree of savings. This chapter describes essentially all these ways—all these *roads,* if you will—and the savings inherent with them. Yet any vehicle owner on any road must address at least two issues: insurance and registration. As such, I open the chapter by presenting the common aspects of these two issues. With that foundation established, I go on to describe the nature of buying a vehicle that conforms to your country's emissions and safety and bumper standards, of buying a vehicle that doesn't comply with these standards, of importing either of these vehicle-types, of buying from a private party or a dealer, and of the significant disparities within the European automotive market. Other factors have coupled with these disparities to make London, Amsterdam and Germany by far the most popular places in Europe for non Europeans to conduct the business of buying and selling a vehicle. So I culminate the chapter, after briefly outlining the issues unique to the process of selling a vehicle in Europe, by focusing on the particulars of buying, insuring and registering a vehicle in these three specific locales. But I cap things off by explaining how you can obtain further information to suit your specific needs.

Insurance

Let's begin by discussing basic liability insurance, what Europeans call "third-party" insurance. Drivers in Europe must *at least* insure themselves with third-party insurance; you cannot register a vehicle in Europe without first presenting proof of such insurance. Note that liability or third-party insurance does not cover damages to your car, or injury to the occupants of your car—including you. Rather, it covers damage or injury you and your vehicle may cause to other vehicles, properties, and persons. In considering any third-party insurance, note if it covers additional drivers and at-fault drivers. Note also the monetary limits of the coverage. And note if you can settle a claim from your home: some companies may require that you stay in Europe to settle a claim.

If you wanna cross borders, your insurance should be International Motor Insurance—what's commonly called "Green Card" insurance. Green Card insurance covers your minimum legal liability in a varying array of countries. The Green Card is actually a folder filled with green documents, one of which is small enough to be displayed in a clear plastic pocket adhered to a vehicle's windshield. This small card assures customs and border guards that you've got some sort of liability insurance; still, it doesn't prove that you're properly covered in their country. Listed at the foot of the papers in a Green Card folder are the countries in which the insurance is valid.

Be sure to check this list before buying such insurance. If you plan to travel in Turkey, make sure your Green Card is valid for both the European and Asian sectors. And if you're headed to Scandinavia, note that reciprocal insurance agreements between Finland, Norway and Sweden require your insurance to cover all or none of these countries: a policy that on paper excludes one is a policy that effectively excludes all three. International third-party insurance in Europe should include at least one other element: bail bonds. If you have an accident in Spain or Greece and you don't have a bail bond, the police will detain you and impound your vehicle until you can prove you have the funds to pay for any damages or fines. Another document—the European Accident Statement—can simplify things in case of an accident; get this form from your European insurer.

In considering insurance that's more comprehensive, note if it covers damage from collisions, damage from fire, damage from natural disasters (such as hail), damage from vandalism or attempted theft, theft of personal items stored in the vehicle, theft of the vehicle itself, and personal injury. Of course you should also note the deductibles and limits associated with these protections. Regardless of what insurance package you arrange, a statement of accident-free driving from your home insurance company, or a copy of your driving record, may qualify you for lower rates. Preferably, these documents should account for at least a three- to five-year period terminating within the last three years. You can get up to 65 percent off the gross premium if you can prove you haven't filed an accident claim in the past five years.

Independent European insurance companies offer the most *inexpensive* European auto insurance—and most have English-speaking staff. Although some companies may be reluctant—or will flat out refuse—to deal with foreign tourists, you should, in the end, have little trouble finding a European insurer who'll sell you good and relatively inexpensive insurance. Sometimes, however, you, as a foreigner, will have to pay a slightly higher rate than the locals; try showing the agent this book to demonstrate that you aren't such a risk.

However, if you don't want the hassle of dealing with a foreign insurance company either before or during your trip (it's really not much of a hassle), you can arrange European auto insurance from a domestic provider before you leave. Although it's quite unlikely that your current auto insurer offers such insurance, at least one North American insurance company does: American International Underwriters, 505 Carr Road, Wilmington, DE 10809, tel. 800 343 5761 or 302 761 3107, FAX 302 761 3302.

If you buy a new car as part of a manufacturer's tourist delivery program or from one of Europe's new car brokers, you may be offered auto insurance as part of the deal. Unless this insurance is given free of charge as part of an incentive, it will probably be much more expensive than the insurance available through the other channels discussed. More on this later.

Most Green Card insurance excludes certain European countries from the domain of its coverage. And if you buy your own insurance to cover a vehicle you ship to or buy in Europe, you'll have to buy it in minimum one-month increments. However, certain non-Green Card auto-insurance policies—designed specifically for foreign motorists, sponsored by one European country or another, and effective in

that country only—allow you to augment Green Card insurance so that you can drive in more countries and/or be insured over periods that are not multiples of one month. Most countries make such insurance available through their embassies or consulates or through offices located at their border entry points. Italy, for example, sells auto insurance—good in Italy only—that covers fifteen, thirty or forty-five day periods; but if you want to buy this insurance, you must do so before you arrive in Italy.

Many people have trouble finding auto insurance to cover them in the Baltic States and the CIS. You can arrange such insurance for vehicles (except motorcycles) registered in the UK by contacting Black Sea & Baltic General Insurance Co., Ltd., 65 Fenchurch Street, London EC3, England, tel. 071 709 9202 or 017 709 9292. Auto insurance covering only the CIS is available through the agency *Ingosstrakh* (offices in several European countries) or at the border posts at Brest (on the Polish border) and Uzhgorod (on the Czech border). Contact embassies, consulates or tourist information offices for more information. (See the *Resources* chapter.)

What about breakdown coverage? As discussed in the *Why Drive?* chapter, you

may be adequately covered if you're a member of your national automobile club. If not, you can buy European-wide breakdown coverage from either of Britain's automobile clubs—the Automobile Association (AA), tel. 0256 21023, or the Royal Automobile Club (RAC), tel. 0800 678000—but you must first buy a membership, which is an expensive proposition; a cheaper and adequate alternative is the coverage offered by the London-based outfit National Breakdown, tel. 071 499 0039.

Registration

Registering a vehicle is another common point of concern. As a tourist, you'll qualify for "tourist plates". You may have to pay a nominal registration fee or "road tax" if you buy such plates, but you should eventually be able to get part of this fee refunded, a part proportional to the amount of time you spent outside the country during the registration period—so get your passport stamped at the border when you exit from and return to the country. You can also get a small refund for returning the plates themselves.

If you plan to export a vehicle from Europe, you must register it for export.

Vehicles—whether new or used—are subject to value-added tax (VAT) and Customs duty unless you register them for export. However, a vehicle you register for export but keep in one country for more than six months may become subject to heavy taxation and be dutied unless you take certain steps. In Britain, for example, you must extend the tax-free status of your registration by the end of six months or else pay a special tax and VAT that sums to 40 percent of the vehicle's value. Meanwhile, Germany charges a tax of several hundred dollars if the duration of your German export registration exceeds three months; but this tax is refundable if you prove that you drove across the German border within six months after registering the vehicle. In most cases, the terms of export registration will require you to export the vehicle from Europe within one year. If you buy a factory-fresh vehicle through one of the sales programs that I discuss later, you *must* export the vehicle from Europe within one year or else pay extremely high taxes and possibly surrender the vehicle to European authorities.

I need to make one thing clear at this point. You may have noticed that the above discussion implies that you can buy a vehicle, avoid the VAT tax by registering it for export, and all the while plan to sell it before leaving Europe. It's not that easy. Such a vehicle cannot be re-registered under non-export registration unless the new owner pays the back VAT tax. If it were possible for Europeans to register such vehicles without paying tax, they could pay foreigners to buy vehicles for them and thus avoid their country's VAT. Technically, the buyer will be responsible for paying the tax; but in effect, you'll absorb the cost of the tax because you'll have to lower the asking price to appeal to the tax-paying European public. Still, there is one way to avoid this tax altogether if you must sell an export-registered vehicle before you leave Europe. Any non-European citizen traveling in Europe can, with written permission of the owner, drive a properly insured vehicle. Therefore if you sell the vehicle to another non-European traveler who intends to export it under its current registration, you can avoid the tax. (If you sell such a vehicle to a traveler who doesn't plan to export it, he or she won't be able to register it as a vehicle not for export without first paying the back VAT tax; essentially, then, you'll pass the buck—not cool.) If you find such a buyer (and that's a tall order), you can figure the remaining insurance cost into the price of the vehicle, give the buyer the registration and Green Card plus a signed note stating that the person can use the car as they wish and a signed note stating that you sold it to this person. Leave the date on the bill of sale open; the buyer can eventually complete the bill when he or she gets back home. Of course the buyer must pay you at this point.

Conforming Vehicles

Most vehicles manufactured abroad that conform to your country's emissions, safety and bumper standards spend no time on the European market; instead their manufacturers immediately export them to your country. One exception to this rule is the case of dealers who service US and Canadian military bases; they may stock US-version vehicles. Of course you'll find such dealers in the immediate vicinity of a military base. See *Appendix B* for the names, locations, phone numbers, and addresses of US military bases that remain in Europe. Be skeptical of claims made by any other European dealer or private individual that a vehicle either complies with or needs

buying

only minor adjustments to comply with these standards. A vehicle that does comply should bear a label that clearly states this fact. Manufacturers affix such labels in readily visible positions in the engine compartment and/or on the vehicle body inside the driver's side door. If such a label is not present but the vehicle is nonetheless in compliance with your country's standards, you should obtain a letter of conformity from the manufacturer's representative in your country—not from a dealership—before buying the vehicle with the intent to import it.

You can order factory-fresh, conforming vehicles through domestic- or European-based brokers, through your local dealer, or through a manufacturer's office in your country. Although you should place such an order at least three or four months before you plan to take delivery of the vehicle, some orders can be filled in just four weeks or less—and some brokers can fill certain orders in as few as three days. The pros handle all the shipping and importation paperwork for you. And not only do some manufacturers pay for your European motoring insurance but some may sweeten the deal with free or cut-rate airfare and hotel accommodation. Ask about rebates and warranties. You should qualify for factory rebates, but European warranties are usually void in the US. If you're told that you'll receive a valid warranty, ask if it's valid in your country as well as in Europe. If the warranty *is* void in your country, ask if you're still entitled to certain free parts and service. There should be few hidden costs: one price will include at least the sticker price, tourist registration fee, transfer fee, catalytic converter, marine insurance, and ocean freight. This total will probably be about 10 percent less than the price you'd pay otherwise—although brokers may offer deals that are better still, often up to twice as good. Of course, *you* must arrange the financing. Be sure to arrange this financing before you place your order: banks may hesitate to extend a loan for a vehicle delivered abroad. Usually you must place a 5 percent downpayment with your order, with full payment due some forty-five days later.

Lead-free fuel is now almost universally available in Europe. Therefore you should experience no problems driving a vehicle with a catalytic converter. Still, if your itinerary is unusual, ask if you should wait until you return home to have the catalytic converter fitted; the manufacturer will pay for such delayed installations. Waive the installation of expensive and removable options like CD players: theft of such accessories is common across Europe and notorious at sea ports. Although most marine insurance covers the theft of these items, settling claims can be a pain.

If the manufacturer doesn't arrange and pay for your European auto insurance, they (or the broker you may go through) will at least suggest, and at most insist, that you buy their insurance. Beware. Such insurance is almost twice as expensive as the typical auto insurance sold in Europe and significantly more expensive than the European auto insurance sold outside Europe (such as AIG's personal policies). If you must buy insurance through a motor-vehicle manufacturer or broker, buy it to cover the shortest period possible. Meanwhile, secure insurance from another source to cover the remainder of your trip.

A caveat is necessary at this point. If outside Germany you take delivery from a German manufacturer, you still have to fill out paper work that registers the vehicle in Germany. No big deal. But here comes the tricky part. German law requires a vehicle's registration and insurance to cover the same duration. Therefore on the day you take delivery you cannot register your vehicle for the duration of your trip, buy the expensive factory-offered insurance to cover a period shorter than the registration period, and drive off. Rather, you must either (1) buy the expensive insurance for the duration of your trip, (2) leave the vehicle at the site while you spend a day or two shopping for insurance, or (3) insure and register the vehicle for the same short period with the intention of driving to Germany during that period, buying more insurance, and extending the registration. If you hadn't planned on traveling to Germany during the initial stages of your trip, each option entails an expense in terms of money or inconvenience—or both.

Most manufacturers offer tours if you take delivery at the factory. And delivery charges apply to sites other than the factory. Moreover, vehicles designated for factory delivery require less lead time. The charges and site selection for non-factory pickup vary from company to company—and change frequently; be sure you're working with up-to-date information concerning these charges. Some brokers customarily deliver vehicles at or very near a major international airport. Regardless, you can be ready to hit the roads in (or on) your new vehicle just two hours or so after landing in Europe.

Before you close any deal concerning delivery of a new vehicle in Europe get the delivery date in writing—and confirm it with the factory. If the responsible party does not deliver your vehicle on time, you'll have recourse to ask them to pay for your lodging while you wait. At the very least you'll be in a better position to speed the process along.

You need to address several more points before you hit the road with your brand-new vehicle. Upon taking delivery, tell the clerk that you have a first-aid kit and warning triangle: these are expensive to buy at the factory. Also, get a list of service stations. Next, be sure everything on and in the vehicle (including the jack) works and that *you* know how to work them. Check the lug wrench. Check the spare tire. Check the fluids. Fuel at the factory is expensive; get the minimum amount necessary.

After you finish driving the vehicle in Europe, you'll just drop it off at the designated site. (Before doing this, however, you need to educate yourself about shipping issues; I discuss these in the next chapter.) You won't see your vehicle again until you pick it up several weeks later at a port or dealership in your home country.

Note that for one year or more after you buy a European vehicle factory-direct the manufacturer may prohibit you from selling it outside Europe: such a policy deters profiteering.

Brokers tend to offer cheaper deals than the manufacturer's representatives—dealers or otherwise—in your country. As for your local dealer, he'll initially discourage you from taking delivery abroad, but once he realizes that you're serious, he should happily assist: the dealership probably won't make money on an overseas delivery, but, inevitably, they'll profit by performing the maintenance on the vehicle and by gaining a customer who is more likely to buy from them in the future.

Below is a list of brokers. It's worth checking out what each has to offer.

Europe By Car, Inc., 1 Rockefeller Plaza, New York, NY 10020, tel. 212 581 3040 or 800 223 1516.

Europe By Car, Inc., 9000 W. Sunset Blvd., Los Angeles, CA 90069, tel. 213 272 0424 or 800 252 9401.

buying

Foremost Euro-Car, 5658 Sepulveda Blvd., Suite 201, VanNuys, CA 91411, tel. 213 872 2226 or 800 423 3111, 800 272 3299 in California.

Shipside Tax Free Cars & Trading Corp., 600 B Lake St. Suite A, Ramsey, NJ 07446, tel. 201 818 0400, FAX 201 818 1525.

Europe Auto Brokers, Box 214, 3430 AE, Nieuwegein, Netherlands, tel. 3402 644 94, FAX 3402 60994; as of October '95 tel. 30 606 44 94, FAX 30 606 09 94.

European Automotive Compliance, Gevers Deynootweg 1130a, 2586 BX, the Hague, Netherlands, tel. 70 355 9245, FAX 70 3500624.

Here's a list of what are likely the most convenient offices of European manufacturers.

Alfa Romeo, 8259 Exchange Dr., Orlando, FL 32809, tel. 407 856 5000.

BMW, 1 BMW Plaza, Montvale, NJ 07645, tel. 201 573 2100.

Ferrari, 777 Terrace Ave., Hasbrouck Heigh, NJ 07604, tel. 201 393 4080.

Jaguar Cars, 555 MacArthur Boulevard, Mahwah, NJ 07430-2327, tel. 201 818 8500.

Lotus, tel. 800 24LOTUS or 404 822 4566, FAX 404 995 7698.

Maserati, 1501 Caton Ave., Baltimore, MD 21227, tel. 410 646 6400.

Mercedes, 1 Mercedes Drive, Montvale, NJ 07645, tel. 201 573 0600.

Peugeot, 1 Peugeot Plaza, Box 607, Lyndhurst, NJ 07071, tel. 201 935 8400.

Porsche, 100 W. Liberty St., Reno, NV 89501, tel. 702 348 3000.

Rolls Royce and *Bentley*, P.O. Box 476, 120 Chubb Ave., Lyndhurst, NJ 07071, tel. 201 460 9600, FAX 201 460 9392.

Rover, International House, Bickenhill Lane, Bickenhill, Birmingham, B37 7HQ, United Kingdom, tel. 021 782 8000, FAX 021 781 7000.

SAAB Scania, P.O. Box 9000, Norcross, GA 30091, tel. 800 955 9007.

VW & Audi, 3800 Hamlin Road, Auburn Hills, MI 48326, tel. 810 340 5000.

Volvo, Building B, 1 Rockleigh, NJ 07647, tel. 201 768 7300.

Non-Conforming Vehicles

If you bring home a vehicle that *doesn't* satisfy your country's emissions, safety and bumper standards, you'll fight a maze of paperwork and pay for expensive shipping, Customs and conversion fees. Despite all these costs, you can still realize bargain savings. Bargains endure because European-version models run the gamut from plain and moderately powerful to luxurious and faster than hell; while the models marketed outside Europe tend to be on the luxurious and racey end of the spectrum. Of course with lower-end models come lower sticker prices. And most new European-version models come with a kill switch installed, making the vehicle very difficult to steal. But be careful not to buy a vehicle whose body style is not safety-approved by your country. *BMW's Z-1* roadster, for example, is illegal in the US no matter what emissions and bumper modifications are done to it. Lower sticker prices are not the only savings you can realize: over time, lower-end models tend to require smaller and less frequent expenditures on maintenance and fuel.

Still, shipping and importing a vehicle is very tricky business. As such, I devote the next chapter to the subject.

Big Savings at Import Time

Whether the vehicle you import does or does not satisfy your country's emissions, safety and bumper standards, you may be able to realize further savings.

To illustrate one component of these potential savings let's take the example of a hypothetical US citizen who bought a *SAAB 9000CSE* Turbo in Europe for $31,550 instead of the $37,460 he would have paid to his hometown dealer. Citizens of the US must pay a 10 percent luxury tax on the amount of a vehicle's cost that's over $32,000. Therefore, our US citizen would've saved $5910 on the purchase price and another $546 or so in tax—over $6456 in all. As with customs duty and sales tax, the US government calculates luxury tax based on the price paid for the vehicle *minus* the depreciation it incurs abroad. Therefore, even if your vehicle is slightly above the $32,000 mark, you can bring it under the threshold by driving it a sufficient distance in Europe.

As for depreciation, it's *your* responsibility to claim a certain amount and to back up your claim with a reasonable argument: the government won't volunteer to downgrade the value of your vehicle. You can calculate the depreciation of your vehicle using whichever generally accepted accounting method suits you. However, the best method for a car that's less than a year old is the 200 percent declining balance (or double declining balance) method, which lets you depreciate a car's value by a full *20 percent* regardless of whether it's been driven for only a day or for up to 355. To prove the value of your vehicle you need to provide documentation of the price you paid for it, the date of the purchase, and the corresponding odometer reading. Although the methods for calculating depreciation are defined in terms of time only (based on the assumption that the average vehicle is driven 14,000 miles per year), Customs officials will take distance and damage into consideration.

The mention of damage brings up a noteworthy point. If during your trip the vehicle you buy and plan to import becomes damaged but remains driveable, wait to have the repairs done until after you return home (assuming you don't have to stay in Europe to settle the claim). The damage will make the vehicle's dutiable and taxable value just that much less. In such a case, of course, you'll need to provide a police report to prove that the damage occured after you purchased the vehicle.

In addition to the subtraction for depreciation, US Customs allows citizens to subtract their and their accompanying family members' standard $400 Customs exemptions from the dutiable value of the vehicle. With the value of the vehicle finally determined, US Customs applies a flat duty rate of 10 percent toward the first $1000 before applying one of the following rates to the remaining amount: 2.5 percent for autos, 3.7 percent for motorcycles up to 700 cc, and 25 percent for trucks valued at $1000 or more.

US citizens employed abroad or government employees returning on TDY or voluntary leave may import a foreign-made vehicle free of duty provided they enter the US for a short visit, claim non-resident status, and export the vehicle when they leave. Military and civilian employees of the US government returning at the end of an assignment to extended duty outside the Customs territory of the US may include a conforming vehicle among their duty-free personal and household effects. The vehicle must have been purchased abroad and been in its owner's possession prior to departure. Generally, extended duty is considered to be duty lasting 140 days or more.

Some states and territories may consider vehicles to be *used* if they were kept abroad for a certain amount of time before importation (the usual threshold is ninety days). Because some of these states and territories don't place a sales tax on used vehicles, you may be able to avoid such a tax by keeping your vehicle in Europe for a few extra days. Contact your local department of motor vehicles to determine the exact taxing policies concerning used vehicles.

Apart from the luxury tax, the US government imposes no federal tax on post-1985 automobiles that have a combined fuel-economy rating of at least 22.5 miles per gallon; other vehicles, however, may be subject to a federal gas-guzzler tax.

Private Party or Dealer?

Unless you buy a vehicle direct from a manufacturer or broker, you'll have to decide whether to buy from a private individual or from a dealer. As I mentioned earlier, the vehicle you buy in Europe will be subject to VAT unless you register it for export. Technically, this means that used vehicles bought from individuals are also subject to VAT. In other words, the seller should calculate the VAT, include it in the selling price, and eventually pay the tax portion of the selling price to the government. As you might expect, however, in many cases private sellers neither include the VAT in the selling price nor report the sale to the government. Thus one advantage of buying from a private seller is that you may be able to avoid much if not all of the VAT. Moreover, vehicles available from individuals are usually cheaper than those available from dealers, regardless of tax considerations.

You can find such vehicles for sale on the streets (especially around universities), through ads in the classifieds, through bulletins posted on community or university boards, at auto flea markets, at police and post office sales, and at US military bases.

Although private parties may offer lower prices on vehicles, dealers may offer warranties and services which more than compensate for their higher prices. Some dealers, for example, can authorize repairs at facilities throughout Europe; and they may even offer to reimburse you for such repairs. Furthermore, some dealers offer to buy-back—under certain terms—the vehicles they sell; these dealers are most likely to offer a warranty and good service. Finally, most dealers will also help you insure and register any vehicle you buy from them.

You're likely to be asked to pay in cash if you buy from a private individual. But if you don't wanna walk around with tons of cash on you, there are other options. You may be able to make a wire transfer of funds from your account back home into the account of the seller; before you go abroad, ask your bank what's involved. Many sellers will accept traveler's checks since these give you the same credibility as a certified check. And some dealerships may even let you use a charge card such as the American Express card

See *Appendix C* and *Appendix D,* respectively, for discussions about how to evaluate a vehicle and how to perform preventive maintenance on the vehicle you buy.

But which is the best European country or city in which to buy and/or sell a vehicle? The answer, of course, largely depends on you and your itinerary. Still, the *grand*-scale state of Europe's automotive market is worth analyzing here.

Despite the ongoing homogenization of the general European market, striking disparities persist within Europe's *automotive* market. European Community law stipulates that EC citizens are free to buy and sell vehicles in any EC country and at the local prices. But by making it difficult to permanently import a foreign vehicle and by keeping the public in the dark about the price disparities, cabals consisting of national governments and their pet domestic manufacturers have successfully discouraged cross-border shopping. What's more, European automotive manufacturers wield maximum leverage in the market because auto dealers in Europe tend to sell the products of just one or another manufacturer: as such, the dealers don't play the mediating role that they otherwise would.

The widely varying taxes imposed by the various countries add another twist to the price disparities: in high-tax countries such as Denmark, manufacturers typically reduce the wholesale price to dealers so the overall retail cost will remain affordable.

Since non Europeans do not have to pay taxes on the purchase of a vehicle if they register it for export, and since you may be able to avoid the VAT by buying from an individual, you can take advantage of not only the after-tax price disparities but also the before-tax disparities. With this information in mind, take a look at Graphs 4.1 and 4.2. I base these graphs on a 1992 study by the BEUC, an organization of European consumer groups.

According to this data, Germany and Luxembourg present the best economic environment in which to buy a vehicle if you buy it from a dealer and do not register it for export; in other words, they're the best countries—price-wise—in which to buy a vehicle if you must pay tax on the purchase. Denmark, on the other hand, although the priciest country in terms of after-tax cost, appears to offer the best economic milieu in which to buy a vehicle if you register it for export or if you buy it used from an individual; in other words,

it's the best country—again, *price*-wise—in which to buy a vehicle if you do not have to pay tax on the purchase. Conversely, Britain appears to present the best economic environment in which to *sell* a vehicle—though it'll be hard to sell a left-hand-drive vehicle there.

However, in some countires—Austria and Denmark, for example—non residents cannot buy auto insurance. This makes it impossible for a you to register a vehicle in these countries unless you first secure insurance from a company at home or in, say, Germany. But you don't necessarily have to register the vehicle right away: you can ask the owner to give you written permission to drive the vehicle for a specific time under his or her insurance and registration, giving you the leeway you need to insure and register the vehicle in another country.

Italy is another special case: it's illegal for non residents to buy a vehicle in Italy unless it's registered for export.

Along with sales price, factors such as geographic location, the English skills of the population, the quality of the vehicle population, the ease of insuring and registering a vehicle, the cost of airfare, and the typical traveler's itinerary have conspired

buying

Graph 4.1

Relative Average Car Prices, *Including* Tax.

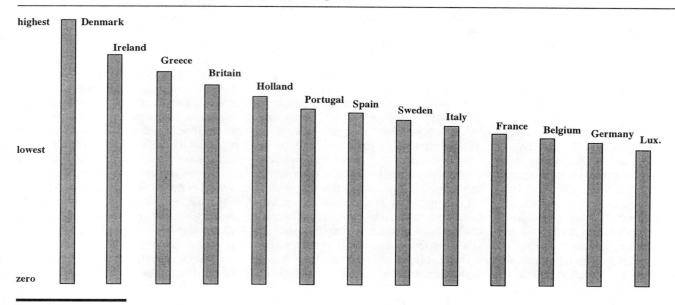

highest — Denmark, Ireland, Greece, Britain, Holland, Portugal, Spain, Sweden, Italy, France, Belgium, Germany, Lux. — lowest — zero

Graph 4.2

Relative Average Car Prices, *Excluding* Tax.

highest*

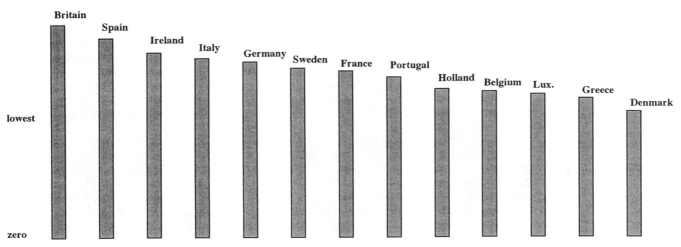

lowest

zero

*in this case I don't include the most expensive country.

to make Britain, the Netherlands and Germany by far the most popular places for non Europeans to conduct the business of buying and selling a vehicle in Europe. Among the first two countries, the cities of London and Amsterdam stand out as the best suited and most popular venues. Therefore I'll culminate this chapter by describing in detail how to buy a vehicle in London, Amsterdam and Germany.

Selling

But before I focus on these three specific places, I'll discuss the topic of selling a vehicle in Europe. Since the selling process virtually mirrors the buying process, I need to make only a few specific points about selling.

For one thing, the spring season amounts to a seller's market; while the fall season amounts to a buyer's market. For another, it *is* legal to sell a vehicle outside the country you bought it in; though because the buyer in another country—if a citizen of that country—*may* have to deal with substantial hassles and expenses associated with importing a vehicle, it *may* be easier and more lucrative to sell the vehicle in the country where it's registered. Of course, if you plan to sell your

vehicle to a traveler who'll register it like you did—as a tourist's vehicle—importation won't be an issue.

The case of Germany, however, demands special attention. The German government will force a citizen who buys a German-registered, tourist's vehicle to pay the registration fees that the government originally waived for the tourist. And regardless of where the vehicle is registered the German citizen must immediately submit a tourist-registered vehicle to a meticulous inspection of its mechanical and structural integrity (a *"TUV"* inspection). The citizen must pay to fix any significant flaws discovered by this inspection—including rusty body parts. On the other hand, the German government waives the registration fees and *TUV* inspection for non Germans who buy a vehicle from a tourist. Thus, Germans will tend to offer much less for your vehicle than will non Germans. It's also worth noting that German-made vehicles are in high demand outside Germany.

Turning to London, consider running a free add in the *Loot,* London's most popular classified ad paper (tel. 01891 888888; deadline at 2:00 P.M. each day); or

in *Exchange and Mart* (tel. 01202 671 171, FAX 202 678 156) or *Auto Trader* (tel. 0181 543 8000), two other weeklies. Three other effective mediums may be *Southern Cross* magazine (tel. 0171 376 0211, FAX 0171 938 4943; deadline for Wednesday publication is noon on Monday), *TNT Magazine* (tel. 0171 937 3985; deadline for Monday publication is noon on Thursday), and *New Zealand News UK* (tel. 0171 930 6451, FAX 0171 930 8780; deadline for Wednesday publication is noon on Monday): all three are weeklies that cater specifically to Aussie and Kiwi travelers. (Don't dial the leading *0* if calling from outside Britain.)

If you wanna sell your vehicle in Amsterdam, run an ad in the newspaper *De Telegraaf* (tel. 585 91 11). If you wanna sell in Paris, run an ad in the *International Herald Tribune* (tel. 1 46 37 93 00).

If you place such an ad, do so several weeks in advance, explaining when you'll be in town and asking interested parties to mail their name, address and phone number to you at the American Express office (if you have an American Express Card or traveler's checks) or some other address where you can receive mail.

Of course you can always sell your vehicle to a dealer, but you probably won't get a good price.

London

If you wanna buy a vehicle in Europe and drive it around the continent and/or the British Isles before selling it, several factors combine to make London an excellent starting and/or ending point for your trip: (1) English is the native language, so all transactions will be that much easier for you; (2) the "tube" (or subway) renders London's motor-vehicle market easily accessible; (3) London is home to a truly phenomenal, concentrated and thriving market where campervans (or "combis") and motorhomes change hands between spirited travelers, mostly Aussies and Kiwis (or "combi trippers"), who are beginning or finishing their grand tours; (4) several automotive repair and insurance services in London cater specifically to combi trippers; and (5) as I detail near the end of the *Itinerary Suggestions* chapter, London is the best place to start and end a grand tour regardless of your mode of transportation.

On the downside, right-hand-drive vehicles (steering wheel on the right, gear shift on your left) make up the bulk of London's vehicle population. Driving a right-hand-drive vehicle on the continent makes it extremely difficult to pass other vehicles unless you have a passenger in the left front seat who is acting as your eyes or unless you're driving a vehicle that has a seat high enough to let you see *over* the majority of vehicles. Furthermore, you must adjust the headlights of a right-hand-drive vehicle before taking it to the continent. Although a headlight conversion kit, containing specially shaped adhesive black plastic that sticks to the glass and alters the direction of the beam, will make this procedure easy; such kits are widely available in Europe. It may be legal to drive your right-hand-drive vehicle on the continent, but transporting it over or under the English Channel will cost you more than simple passenger fare; check out the fares in the *Ferries and the Chunnel* chapter. Finally, note that the vehicle population in England is of poorer quality than the vehicle populations of the Netherlands and Germany.

If you wanna know how to get from here to there in London, get a *Mini London AZ Street Atlas and Index;* it's used religiously—even by the residents. The *Atlas* illustrates and indexes every street, alleyway, tube line and tube stop in London. You can pick up an *Atlas* in one of the countless shops and bookstores in London or from a bookstore in your country.

Before you search London for the perfect vehicle, you need to understand what an MOT certificate is. To keep dangerous vehicles off the road the British Ministry of Transport (MOT) subjects every vehicle to an annual inspection. If a vehicle passes inspection, the MOT issues a certificate to the owner. Make sure the vehicle you're considering has such certification. If you plan to either keep the vehicle in Britain or return to Britain to sell it, it's important that the MOT certificate will be valid for the duration of your trip. If the certification runs out, you'll have to pay for a new inspection and any required repairs. Moreover, the longer the certification is valid the easier it will be for you to sell the vehicle in Britain.

If it's a used van or caravan you're after, one London spot demands your attention: a stretch of Market Road two blocks west of where it intersects Caledonia Road just south of the Caledonia Road tube stop. As you stroll up the slight grade of Market Road and the tops of the vans and caravans that line it begin to appear—mirage-like at first and then snapping, like a 60s flashback, into salient superreality— you'll feel the buzz of being in a truly holy place. The place is called The Van Market—the capital letters reflecting, apart from the aforementioned sacredness, a certain state of organization, but an organization which arises soley from the individuals who go there to buy and sell. Although London's city officials have forced the Market to move from place to place over the years, countless groups of intrepid travelers continue to sniff it out, making it, ephemeral as it is, an apotheosis of the European budget travel scene. Most of the vans are *VWs* in the $1500 to $3800 (£1000 to £2500) range. Such vans—if they're in excellent condition—get about 24 mpg (10 kpl). The sellers sleep right there in their vans and caravans, showering at the adjacent tennis club for £1.5. Of course this concentration assumes a social dimension; indeed, it's not a bad place in which to wile away a few days before you sell your vehicle.

Many of the buyers begin their tour in late June, crossing to Calais and heading down the coast to Pamplona and the famous San Fermin Festival (a.k.a., The Running of the Bulls), where they intend to meet some of their new Market Road buddies. Well, those buddies bring some buddies who meet up with their buddies who . . . And out of the seven-day frenzy of drunken bovine virility that is San Fermin come sundry convoys of van trippers, their ultimate goal to converge on and help fertilize Munich and the Oktoberfest two-and-a-half months down the road. A recent summer saw one such convoy grow to twenty-three vans.

The Market crowd does tend to be young, but when I happened to check it out one October day I met a friendly—and very normal—middled-aged Australian couple who were selling their van after a tour of Europe.

Of course there are also *dealers* in and around London. Here's a partial list.

Bilbo's Trading Company, South Godstones, E. Surrey, tel. 01342 89 24 99. All vehicles are *VW* campers, both right- and left-hand-drive; no buy-back offered.

Bromley Motor Caravans, 55–65 Abbey Road, Belvedere DA17 5DG, tel. 0181 311 3500. Big rigs, all right-hand-drive; buy-back negotiable.

Campervan Company, Unit 1, 22 Stable Way, London W10, tel. 0181 960 5747. All left-hand-drive, *VW* vehicles; primarily rentals; no buy-back offered.

Campervans and Motorhomes Bought and Sold, 42a Summerhill Road, Tottenham, London N15, tel. 0181 360 0818 or 01836 329940. Nearest tube: Seven Sisters. All makes available; 4–6 berths; insurance arranged.

Eurocamper, Manner Farm Road (beside New Bridge), Alperton Tube, Wembley, tel. 01831 396878. All *VWs* from £1000. Pre-purchase checks for £20.

The Garage Car and Van Rental, tel. 0181 681 2885 or 01860 541 658. From £66 per week. You can rent before you buy. They sell camping gear as well.

Global Motorhome Travel. Office in London. In the US, tel. 800 468 3876.

Heathrow Campers, Bell Weir Garage, Wraysbury, Berkshire TW18 4TW, tel. 01784 81 34 38. All *VW* vehicles, both right- and left-hand-drive; buy-back of 60–80 percent is offered; they'll sell your vehicle for a commission.

Sunseeker Rental Ltd., Stable Way W10, N. Kensington, tel. 0181 960 5747. Mechanical repairs, body work, servicing, MOTs; buy-back offered.

VW Campercentre, M25 J 13 (near Staines), day tel. 01784 483438, evening tel. 0831 190433. *VWs* sold *and* bought. Buy-back of 70 percent is available for one year from date of purchase. They'll sell your *VW* camper for a commission. Discount *VW* spare parts and tires also available, tel. 01784 483303.

The following company rents Honda motorcycles and sells them with a buy-back option that promises repurchase of the vehicle at 80 percent of the selling price.

H.G.B. Motorcycles, 69–71 Park Way, Ruislip Manor, Middlesex HA4 8NS, England. Contact Sue Hale, tel. 01895 676451, FAX 01895 676822. Minimum age: 17 years for the *Honda H100* model, 21 years for others. Any license designated for motorcycle use will be accepted. Open Monday through Saturday, 9:00 A.M. to 6:00 P.M.

If you're looking for a *car*, Market Road *may* be worth checking out, but you'll probably have better luck shopping elsewhere. Try stopping in the New Zealand News UK office, address 25 in the alley of shops just west of and running parallel to Haymarket, off Piccadilly Square. On the board just inside the front door, travelers

and others post messages concerning, among other things, the following: vehicles for sale, vehicle insurance and repair, travel partners, tour packages, and jobs. It's a good place to check out regardless of your transportation plans. While in the office, you might as well pick up free copies of *New Zealand News UK* and *Overseas* magazine. Travel articles aimed at the Kiwi expatriate crowd fill both and make interesting reading for any traveler. Another free weekly publication you should grab in London is *TNT Magazine,* which caters to Australian expatriates and contains travel articles as well as classified ads listing vehicles for sale. *Southern Cross* is a similar magazine; it seems to contain more classified ads listing vans for sale than do the others. You can also check the various papers. The best for classified ads is the *Loot,* updated and available every day from newsstands. Also try *Exchange and Mart* and the *Auto Trader,* both published weekly. (Note that British classified ads give odometer readings in terms of miles.) London's tube is so comprehensive that you should have little trouble getting to private residences to check out cars.

The following establishments will perform a thorough inspection and testing of a

vehicle before you buy it. These guys are good; unless you're a mechanical whiz, you'd be wise to enlist their services.

Archie's Garage (*VW* specialists), 208 Kensal Road, W10, London, tel. 0181 969 2692. Open Saturday.

DUUO Motors, Unit 5, No. 2, Upper Tollington Park, NW4, London (just off Stroud Green Road, Finsbury Park), tel. 0171 281 9898. Open six days a week. Camper van experts and Kiwis, Garth and Richard charge $50 (£30) for pre-purchase checks; but they're skilled and experienced mechanics *and* travelers. As such, they'll offer especially relevant advice. DUUO stocks a full range of second hand parts, reconditioned and guaranteed motors, and more. DUUO fully services vehicles for around $105–160 (£70–100)—including parts.

Peter Norris, tel. 0171 733 6520. Free pre-purchase checks. *VW/Audi* specialists; boxer engines are another specialty. Peter is an Aussie who's been serving London's *VW* owners for fourteen years.

As I mentioned already, you cannot register a vehicle anywhere in Europe until you present proof of its insurance. I recommend the following insurance agency; they act as a broker to arrange insurance from

buying

any one of a multitude of British companies.

Down Under Insurance Services, 24A Bristol Gardens, Maida Vale, W9 2JQ London, tel. 0171 286 2425, FAX 0171 289 6562, specializes in arranging motor insurance for travelers. They offer the best long- and short-term rates available. Prices include a Green Card and Spanish bail bonds. If your vehicle is over twenty years old, you can buy only third-party insurance for it. Note that for some cars, insurance is good only for drivers 25 years of age or older. One policy covers up to six drivers. You can buy policies for drivers younger than 21 years, but they cost much more. Some tips from Down Under: (1) avoid buying a vehicle that's over twenty years old; (2) a campervan over 2500 cc or a saloon car over 1600 cc is expensive to insure; (3) if you're entitled to a no-claims discount, bring documentation of this fact with you. Down Under also offers European and UK breakdown coverage, personal possessions coverage, and travel medical and health coverage. A Down Under representative told me "you can walk into our office this morning and go to Europe this afternoon if you want." Comprehensive cover costs £750–1650, depending on the vehicle. The following price quotes pertain to vans, low cc-rated cars, or cars costing under $2250 (£1500)—for which the lowest premiums are charged.

six months for drivers 23 years of age or older: $390 (£254) for third party, theft and fire; $330 (£215) for third party only.

six months for drivers 21 years of age or older: $515 (£336) for third party, theft and fire; $430 (£283) for third party only.

two months for drivers 23 years of age or older: $197 (£128) for third party, theft and fire; $170 (£110) for third party only.

two months for drivers 21 years of age or older: $250 (£162) for third party, theft and fire; $220 (£142) for third party only.

Also try contacting the British Automobile Association Insurance Services, Ltd., Fanum House, Basingstoke, Hampshire RG21 2EA, England, tel. 01256 20123; or the RAC Insurance Services, Spectrum House, P.O. Box 700, Bond St., Bristol BS99 1RB, England, tel. 01800 678000.

Apart from proof of insurance, you need to secure two other documents before you can register a vehicle in Britain. The first document is the bill of sale. Usually the bill is simply a hand-written note from the seller. The note should describe the vehicle, the vehicle identification and license numbers, and the price you paid; both parties should sign and date it. Second, you need the Vehicle Registration Document; also get this from the seller. If the registration document is in the process of being replaced at the time of sale, you can apply for a free Certificate of Registration (form *V379)* at the local Vehicle Registration Office. European governments recognize this certificate in place of the registration document; you should keep it in the vehicle always. Unless your insurer tells you otherwise, take the bill of sale and the Vehicle Registration Document to the Department of Transport, Vehicle Registration Office, 1 Zoar Street, London SE1 OSY, near the London Bridge tube station. This office will present you with a Certificate of Registration—proof that you own your vehicle. You'll have to register the vehicle for a minimum of six months and pay a minimum registration fee (or "road tax" as the Brits call it) of £72.50 ($110). This fee is refundable in proportion to the amount of time you spend outside Britain during the registration period.

Amsterdam

The following characteristics make Amsterdam a popular place for non Europeans to buy or sell a vehicle: (1) most people in the Netherlands speak fluent English; (2) Amsterdam harbors a wide selection of used vehicles; (3) these vehicles tend to be in better condition than those in England; (4) of course these vehicles tend to be designed for driving on the right side of the road; (5) Amsterdam is compact and boasts good public transportation; (6) the easy-going Dutch keep the red tape to a minimum; and (7) Amsterdam is centrally positioned on the continent.

The Dutch government, too, requires regular motor vehicle inspections. Like the British MOT certification, the Dutch inspection—termed an *"APK"* inspection—determines if a vehicle presents a prohibitive risk to public safety. As such, any Dutch-registered vehicle you consider buying should have a valid *APK* sticker on the windshield. Be sure to check the expiration date printed on this sticker, and ask for the accompanying papers—some people use counterfeits. Try to buy a vehicle whose next *APK* inspection date is well after the date you plan to sell the vehicle. If you plan to sell the vehicle in the Netherlands, a youthful *APK* sticker will bring a higher price. And if you must get a new *APK* sticker, you'll have to pay about $30 (55 guilders) for it, submit your vehicle for inspection, and pay to repair any defects that don't pass. You cannot register a vehicle that isn't *APK* certified. If you drive a Dutch-registered vehicle in the Netherlands without the proper certification, the Dutch authorities can fine you about $70 (125 guilders)—and they may confiscate the vehicle.

You can look up dealers' addresses in *De Gouden Gids (The Yellow Pages)* under "caravans" or "autos". The following dealers sell vans and/or caravans.

ACC Osdorp, Akersluisweg 4, 1069 MB Amsterdam, tel. 020 610 1819.

Braitman & Woudenberg, Droogbak 3-4, 1013 GE Amsterdam, tel. 020 622 1168, FAX 020 620 3855, or tel. 800 468 3876 in the US.

Alias Smith and Willard, Krugerstraat 6, 3531 AP Utrecht, tel. 030 93 71 63.

Campanje, P.O. Box 9332, 3506 GH Utrecht, tel. 030 447070, FAX 030 420981; in the US, tel./FAX 209 245 3129.

Corn. Dirkszstaat 1771, P.O. Box 9332, 3506 GH Utrecht, tel. 030 447070, FAX 030 420981.

The Dutch auto brokers listed earlier may be able to locate used vehicles—including demos—as well as new ones.

If you know Dutch or if you can corner a Dutch interpreter, check out the classifieds in *De Telegraaf*. (Of course Dutch classified ads list odometer readings in terms of kilometers; remember that 1.67 kilometers equal one mile.) Regardless, note the phone number used to place classified ads; if you decide to sell your vehicle in Amsterdam, you can place an ad in the paper before you return.

Several areas tend to harbor vehicles that bear *"Te Koop"* ("For Sale") signs: the streets around the Centraal Station (train station); the Dam Rak, off Dam Square in front of the American Express office; and across town near the Olympisch Stadion. Check for used vans and caravans for sale at the main campgrounds: Camping Vliegenbus and Amsterdamsche Ijsclub (behind the Olympisch Stadion). The *VVV* (tourist office) in front of the Centraal Station provides lists of upcoming auto flea markets, as well as lists of dealers who specialize in vans and caravans.

You can arrange insurance from one of the agencies listed in the yellow pages

buying

under *"Verzekering"*. Otherwise, dealers can arrange insurance for you. Registering the vehicle is easy: Take the insurance documents and the vehicle's title and registration to the local post office; a clerk there will transfer the vehicle to your name before you can say *"Dank u well."*

Germany

For the following reasons, Germany is an attractive country in which to buy a vehicle: (1) most people in Germany speak fluent English; (2) Germans tend to take *excellent* care of their vehicles; (3) each vehicle is subject to an extremely thorough inspection every two years; (4) the many US military installations in Germany amount to good places in or around which to buy and sell vehicles; (5) virtually all vehicles in Germany are designed for driving on the right side of the road; and (6) Germany is centrally located on the continent.

Like the governments of Britain and the Netherlands, the German government requires vehicle owners to submit their vehicles for inspection every two years. However, unlike the analogous inspections conducted by Britain and the Netherlands, Germany's inspection evaluates a vehicle not only on the basis of the threat it poses to public safety but also on the threat it poses to the reputation of German engineering and manufacturing and to the classic German sensibility. In fact, a vehicle showing rust will fail. The Germans call their inspection a *"Technischer Uberwachungs Verein"* or *"TUV"*. The government stamps the due date of the next inspection on the rear license plate of each vehicle. In classified ads, *"TUV 5/95"* means that the buyer must submit the vehicle for inspection in May 1995. In Germany—again, unlike in Britain and the Netherlands—a vehicle registered to a tourist will not become subject to government inspection unless someone buys it and registers it as a permanent German vehicle instead of a tourist's vehicle. This policy is so because Germany assumes that any tourist registering a vehicle will export the vehicle from Germany. Thus you have one reason to buy a vehicle whose *TUV* inspection is imminent: the German citizen selling the vehicle will be trying to avoid the cost of a new inspection and therefore will tend to offer a good selling price. Of course, buying such a vehicle can also work against you. Such a vehicle represents a greater risk because almost two years will have gone by since it last passed a *TUV*. And unless you plan to ship the vehicle home or sell it to another traveler—or to someone else who won't register it in Germany—the same phenomenon that you originally took advantage of will erase any savings you realized in the purchase price; in other words, you'll have to lower the price commensurate with the impending inspection. Because, as I explained earlier, you should avoid selling the vehicle to someone who must re-register it in Germany, this second point doesn't carry as much weight as you might think it would. Apart from the *TUV* document, there's another document that can clue you in on the mechanical integrity of a vehicle. That document is the ownership book, or *Kraftfahrzeugbrief,* that the manufacturer issues with each new vehicle. The ownership book lists all the past owners *and* any major repairs done to the vehicle.

But where to find the vehicles? Frankfurt, being a hub for Lufthansa, is a popular point of entry into Germany. As such, you may wish to contact the following dealers in Frankfurt.

Moserim Kunze-Hans GmbH, Berner Straße 99, Gewerbegebiet Nieder-Eschbach

60437 Frankfurt am Main 50, tel. 69 5072005 or 69 5083250, FAX 69 5072021.

Ralf Moses, Kurt-Schumacher-Straße 1, 6392 Neu Anspach, tel. 49 60818046, FAX 6081 7855, or tel. 800 468 3876 in the US.

Reise-mobil Rutenkolkb, Friedberger Landstraße 434, D-W6000 Frankfurt am Main, tel. 69 474545, FAX 69 474207.

University towns amount to good places in which to buy a cheap vehicle. All students know English; and if you throw in a promise to mail them a Green Bay Packers or Toronto Blue Jays or Wallabies or All Blacks T-shirt, they're likely to help you get the vehicle insured and registered. Note that the university school year in Germany runs from mid October to mid July. Go to the student union, the *Mensa,* and look for a bulletin board with vehicle ads posted on it. Also check the streets around the university. The German equivalent of "For Sale" is *"Zu Verkaufen".* You'll find a flock of *VW* cars for sale in front of the Art Institute on the Hardenbergstraße in Berlin. Because of its historic interest, large university, and nearby US military bases, Heidelberg is a good place in which to base your search. Note, however, military bases amount to

better places for selling a vehicle than for buying one; the soldiers tend to ask more and pay more for vehicles than do the German citizens. Munich is another university town replete with historic and cultural attractions. Vehicles up for sale line Munich's Leopoldstraße just past the Siegestor Arch in the Schwabing section of town. And used vans and caravans are usually up for sale at Munich's wonderful Thalkirchen campground. Moreover, Munich's Bodensee Straße (*street*) harbors one of the largest concentrations of camper dealers in Europe. The following towns and cities are home to large universities as well: Bonn, Bremen, Cologne, Dusseldorf, Frankfurt, Freiburg, Goettingen, Hamburg, Hanover, Karlsruhe, Mannheim, Marburg, Meersburg, Nureburg, Stuttgart, Tuebingen, Ujm, and Wurzburg.

Auto flea markets take place each weekend in many cities. Because the transactions that occur at these markets do, in fact, occur between individuals, you may be able to avoid the VAT by buying at such a market. Usually these markets take place on the grounds of outdoor movie theaters near the edges of cities or towns. If this is the case the market is an *Autokino Markt,*

kino being the German word for a movie theater. Otherwise, the market is a *Private Automarkte* or *AUTOPRIVAT.* You'll be charged a small fee to enter these markets. Ask at local tourist offices or service stations about the times and locations of upcoming markets. German police and postal services hold auctions several times a year. Vehicles sold at these auctions can go at unbelievably low prices. Call or stop by the local German police or post office and ask about such auctions.

To read the classifieds, you must know some German. Table 4.1 is an alphabetically ordered list of terms that are typical in car ads. (Of course, German classified ads present odometer readings in terms of kilometers. Remember that 1.67 kilometers equal one mile.) If you see the letters *"gew"* in an ad, it means a dealer placed the ad; the word *"privat"* means an individual placed it. In *VW* ads the word "export" does not mean the vehicle is up to export standards; rather, it designates a luxury model. By the way, it may help you to know that *ß* in the German alphabet is pronounced "ss", not "b".

Regardless of how you go about buying your vehicle, note the phone number used to place classified ads. If you decide

buying

Table 4.1

Typical Words Used in German Car Ads.

1 Hd.	one owner
3 Leigen	camper has 3 beds
50 PS	50 horsepower
68tkm	68,000 kilometers
ATM	new motor
Bestzustand	very good condition
Bj. 84	Built in 1984
Cabrio	convertible
Dachst.	pop-up roof
einwandfreier Zust.	mint condition
Gasheizg.	gas heater
guter techn. und opt. Zust.	excellent condition
Hubdach	pop-up roof
in gut. Zust	in good shape
mit zusatzlicher Campingeinrichtung	additional camping equipment included
Neu bereiftnew	tires
Neu bremse	new brakes
Neu kuppelung	new clutch
TUV 95	Next inspection due in 1995
TUV neu	just inspected
TUV uberpruft	TUV inspected
VB	asking price
VB 20% unter neupreiss	asking 20 percent under the new price
VW Automat	VW Automatic
VW Kafer	VW bug
viele extr.	many extras
wie neu	as new
Wohnbus	camper

to sell your vehicle in Germany, you can place an ad in the paper before you return.

Of course you'll need to insure a vehicle before you can register it. The word that designates *insurance* in German is *Versicherungs*. Of the myriad insurance companies in Germany, most can deal in English. Some insurance companies, in fact, cater largely to US military personnel. German auto-insurance providers, however, do not base premiums on vehicle or driver age but, rather, on vehicle horsepower and the length of time a driver has held his or her license. What's more, some companies charge higher premiums for tourists.

Your German auto-insurance agent can tell you exactly how to register the vehicle, but I'll give you the basics. First, you need to obtain three documents: the *Kaufvertag,* the *Kraftfahrzeugbrief,* and the *Kraftfahrzeugschein.* Buyer and seller must sign the *Kaufvertag*—the contract of sale. Stationary shops sell this simple form, but usually the seller supplies it. Each party should keep a copy. The *Kraftfahrzeugbrief* proves ownership of the vehicle and lists each owner, but the seller doesn't sign it. The *Kraftfahrzeugschein* is another ownership document; keep it in your vehicle.

Take these three documents, the Green Card you get from the insurance company, your passport, your International Driving Permit, your domestic license, and the vehicle itself to the *Kraftfahrzeug-**zulassungsstelle*** (The Department of Motor Vehicles). Somebody at the Department will be able to speak English. As a tourist, you should request *Zollnummer* or tourist plates; registering a vehicle under such plates allows you to avoid German registration fees. The clerk will ask you to fill out a few forms; the department officials will conduct a cursory inspection of your vehicle (not a *TUV* inspection); you'll pay a nominal fee; and you'll receive the proper papers—including your vehicle's tourist-specific registration, the *Internationaler Zulassungsschein.* The clerk will have cut off the lower right corner of the *Kraftfahrzeug**brief,*** invalidating it based on the assumption that you will export the vehicle. Keep this document if you plan to sell the vehicle in Germany. Finally, go to the local Customs office (the clerk will tell you where it is) and pick up your tourist plates. German Customs will charge a nominal fee for the plates, but the fee is refundable if you return the plates in good condition.

Conclusion

Although I present in this chapter a substantial if not sufficient amount of information about how to buy, insure, register and sell a vehicle in Europe, you may be wise to search out more information from more sources before you embark on such an enterprise. Certainly before you leave for Europe you should confirm with the appropriate government department, embassy or consulate all crucial points that are uniquely subject to change at the hands of government—importing/exporting policies being a primary example. To hunt down contacts not listed herein, try calling your local libraries and asking if they stock a phone book and/or newspaper from the city or country you plan to buy a vehicle in. Because university libraries cater to foreign students, they're likely to have such resources. Using the relevant yellow pages, you can look up the addresses and phone numbers of auto-insurance companies and auto dealers; using the relevant newspaper or newspapers, you can study the classified ads to determine the deals being offered by dealers and individuals. To find a particular phone number, it'll be easier if you call the relevant tourist office, embassy, or national chamber of commerce: they usually stock directories. The US Armed Force's newspaper *Stars and Stripes* (tel. 703 697 6695 in the US; tel. 06155 601 349/447 civilian, tel. 348 8349/8447 military, FAX 0429 29332 in Germany) is an excellent source for classified ads in English. Unfortunately, the paper is not distributed in the US. But if you call the US number listed above, the staff may send you some recent classified-ads sections free of charge. You can also check the classifieds in the *Army Times,* tel. 800 424 9335 or 703 750 8900. If it's a van or motorhome you're after, contact the European camping magazines I list in the *Resources* chapter: they can send back issues advertising vehicles for sale. You might wanna compare the prices charged for vehicles in Europe to the prices charged for the same vehicles near your home. In the US the *N.A.D.A. Official Used Car Guide* and the "Blue Book"—both available at libraries and banks—will help in this comparison. Note, however, that European models may differ in composition if not in name from the models marketed in North America; if you have questions concerning such a discrepancy, call the manufacturer.

5. shipping
& importing

For purposes of economy, much of the discussion in this chapter assumes that you're a US citizen. Still, the majority of the principles and a significant number of the details here presented in terms of the US apply to citizens of other countries as well. I begin the chapter by discussing the pros and cons of shipping a vehicle *to* Europe. Then, I describe how a US citizen can import a vehicle that does *not* meet US standards. In the last section of the chapter, I explain how to arrange shipping. Any person planning to ship a vehicle should read that last section.

Shipping Your Vehicle to Europe

Shipping your own car, van or motorhome to Europe and then bringing it back is probably not a good idea. Apart from the depreciation that your vehicle will incur while you drive it in Europe, shipping by freighter will cost at least $3000 return.

One interesting alternative to freighters, however, is Cunard Line's *Queen Elizabeth 2*. This grand passenger ship accepts vehicles as accompanied baggage. The cheapest fares (including port and handling charges of $155 each way) are about $2650 return and $1550 one way; although you can save 15 percent by booking and placing a deposit 120 days before your cruise. The fare covers all your meals and entertainment while onboard. If you purchase a one-way ticket, you can bring your vehicle free of charge, notwithstanding an extra $75 port and handling charge. This offer of free vehicle passage substitutes for

the complimentary one-way British Airways airline ticket that customarily accompanies a one-way ticket on the *QE2*. The customary free airline ticket covers travel between London and any one of seventy-nine cities in North America, with the option to fly the supersonic Concorde one way between New York or Washington and London or Paris free of charge or at a reduced fare. If you travel one way and accept the customary airline ticket but still bring your vehicle, Cunard charges about $2225 extra for any vehicle up to 5500 pounds. If you travel return and take your vehicle both ways, Cunard charges about $3650 for a vehicle up to 5500 pounds. Rates vary for vehicles that weigh between 5501 and 8000 pounds. Cunard accepts no vehicle weighing over 8000 pounds or exceeding any of the following dimensions: 6 feet high, 20 feet long, or 6 feet wide. The *QE2* makes the five-day crossing from New York to Southampton, England, twice a month from April to October and much less frequently during the remainder of the year. Space on the *QE2* is limited however, so make reservations well before your sailing date. You can contact Cunard Line at 555 Fifth Avenue, New York, NY 10017-2453, tel. 800 221 4770 or 212 880 7545 or 212 880 7500, FAX 212 949 0915.

Taking a vehicle to Europe and selling it there is an option you may want to consider. Europeans are nuts about anything that smacks of Americana. Many Europeans would consider a *Harley* or a big 'ol model from Detroit the find of a lifetime; in other words, you may get a very good price for it. However, don't casually approach such an endeavor; you must *thoroughly* investigate your responsibilities, as well as the costs Europeans would face in buying and importing your vehicle. Contact the Customs officer at the nearest embassy or consulate of the country you want to ship to. (See the end of the *Resources* chapter for the addresses of embassies and consulates.)

Shipping a motorcycle over or back, or both, is more practical than shipping other motor vehicles. Shipping a motorcycle to Europe costs as low as $350 one way and is generally less than half as expensive as shipping a car. And since a motorcycle relates more intimately to both the road and your body than does a car, your comfort and safety depend more on the particular bike you ride than the particular car, van or motorhome you drive: you may not get a good "fit" buying or renting a motorcycle. In addition, motorcycle rentals in Europe are more expensive than car rentals, averaging about $100 per day plus mileage; and they're not easily available in every country.

Similarly, motorhomers who've converted their vehicle into their castle may not wanna pay $170 a day to visit real castles in a modest European surrogate. Remember, however, that a larger North American model will be significantly more expensive to fuel and difficult to maneuver than a typical European model. And though American manufacturers such as Airstream, Holiday Rambler, and Winnebago maintain representatives in Europe, their networks are not impressive, and spare parts are difficult to come by. What's more, your vehicle's electrical system won't jive with European standards. As such, you'll need to install a transformer before you go. If you forget to do this, a soldier at an American military base in Europe might be nice enough to procure one for you. One of very few European companies that sell them is Trueblood RV, Justinianstraße 22, 60322 Frankfurt, Germany, tel. 69 34 53 54. In addition, since most European motorhomes sport chemical toilets feeding into small removable holding tanks, few European campgrounds offer facilities for emptying the large built-in tanks gracing most North American models. Instead of removing the tank and gayly skipping to the campground's receptacle, you — assuming you're conscientious — will find yourself in frequent intimate relations with something less than an attraction, a modern-day wonder nonetheless, the municipal sewage treatment plant; but, hey, you *will* be off the beaten path! See the "Camping" section of the *Alternative Accommodations* chapter for more on the availability of dumping stations.

Before you make a decision, read the beginning of the *Buying* chapter to come up to speed on insurance issues. Compare the insurance offerings I relate in that chapter to the insurance sold by International Insurance Underwriters, tel. 800 248 4998, a GEICO affiliate.

If you do decide to ship your own vehicle, you need to gather the necessary paperwork to satisfy US and foreign Customs. US Customs needs to determine that a vehicle shipped abroad is not a stolen vehicle. As such, you need to present Customs with two copies of a notarized title. You'll also need a *Shipper Export Declaration* form and a *Declaration of Dangerous Goods* form. Stationary stores sell these forms, but only in $15 pads of one hundred. You'll have to deliver your vehicle and the proper documents at least three days before the vehicle's scheduled departure. For details, citizens of the US should contact the US Customs Service Trade Operations, 1301 Constitution Ave., NW, Washington, DC 20229, tel. 202 927 0300. While inquiring about such issues, ask how you can get an oval nationality sticker for your vehicle: "AUS" signifies it's registered in Australia; "CDN", Canada; "NZ", New Zealand; and, you guessed it, "USA", the United States.

But what about foreign Customs? Customs documents, issued in accordance with the terms of the UN Customs Conventions, are still required by a number of *non-*European countries in order to avoid the payment of the often substantial deposits demanded for the temporary importation of a vehicle (whether via a land-locked point of entry or a sea port). If you're a member of your national motoring club, the international organization it belongs to—either the *AIT* or the *FIA*—will extend to you such a document, the *"Carnet de Passages en Douane"*, that, in lieu of deposits, guarantees foreign governments that the organization will pay any Customs duties and taxes required if you don't re-export your vehicle. But before providing this document, your club will require you to place a deposit with *them;* the idea being that it's better to leave your deposit with someone you trust rather than in the hands of some capricious if not corrupt foreign government. But to repeat, European countries do *not* require such deposits or guarantees. Nevertheless, contact the nearest embassy or consulate of the country you're shipping to and ask for copies of any mandatory forms and instructions for getting cargo through their Customs. While you're at it, ask how *long* it takes to clear their Customs and what steps you must take to export *from* their country. (Again, see the end of the *Resources* chapter for the addresses of embassies and consulates.)

One option that's much easier and less expensive than shipping your vehicle to Europe—and more popular and practical each year—is a home and vehicle exchange. From 1988 to 1992 the number of Europeans visiting America grew steadily from about 5.5 million to nearly 8 million; while the number of Americans traveling to Europe wavered between a high of 8 million (in 1990) to a low of 6.35 million (in 1991). I'm sure many of these Europeans would've loved to swap homes and vehicles with you. The biggest hurdle for such an arrangement is trust: the easier it is for both parties to establish the more practical this option becomes. Several organizations arrange such swaps and provide the kind of professional third-party assistance that is the catalyst of this trust. I list these organizations in the *Alternative Accommodations* chapter. If you have a motorhome, a couple of services can help you arrange to swap it with motorhome owners in Europe: Vacation Home Exchange Club, P.O. Box 650, Key West, FL 33041 USA, tel. 800 638 3841; and Camper Exchange, Inc., P.O. Box 947, North Bend, WA 98045 USA, which for a fee of $60 will send you a list of potential caravan swappers in Europe. And the European camping magazines I list in the *Resources* chapter offer an effective forum for advertising your interest in a swap.

Table 5.1

US EPA-authorized Independent Commercial Importers.

Champagne Imports Inc., 200 West 5th Street, Lansdale, PA 19446. Representative: Mr. Joe Marino. Tel. 800 535 9728 or 215 361 1304.

G & K Automotive Conversion, 3231 S. Standard Ave., Santa Ana, CA 92705. Representative: Mr. George Gemayel. Tel. 714 545 9503.

ICI International, 7303 Monetary Dr., Orlando, FL 32809. Representative: Mr. Ed Sequel. Tel. 407 851 5699, FAX 407 851 5055.

Import Trade Services USA, Inc., 177 Red Hill Road, P.O. Box 677, New City, NY 10956-0677. Representative: Mr. Ken Shaffer. Tel. 800 872 3727 or 914 638 9039, FAX 914 638 9016.

J.K. Motorcars, Inc., 3500 Sweet Air Street, Baltimore, MD 21211. Representative: Mr. Jonathan Weisheit. Tel. 410 366 6332.

Liphardt Associates, Inc., 15 Trade Zone Drive, Ronkonkoma, NY 11779. Representative: Mr. Peter Dibernardi. Tel. 800 322 3702 or 516 588 8288.

Wallace Environmantal Testing Laboratories, 2140 Wirtcrest, Houston, TX 77055. Representative: Mr. Les Weaver. Tel. 713 956 7705.

With a little work, however, *you* may be able to make all arrangements for a home and/or vehicle swap. If you're an academic, work for an international company or firm, or belong to some other reputable international organization (such as a church or a medical society), contact some of your European colleagues. If you can tap into the so-called electronic super-highway, send out messages asking for information about potential international swaps; and keep an ear or an eye tuned for individuals or new services that offer European homes and vehicles for temporary swapping. See the *Resources* chapter for more info about electronically based resources.

If you succeed in securing someone else's vehicle in Europe, you should obtain written permission from that someone and carry it in the vehicle always, along, of course, with proof that the owner has properly insured and registered the vehicle. You need to carry a special form of authority, an *Autorizacao* certificate, if you plan to drive someone else's vehicle in Portugal; get the form at a registration office in Europe, or contact your local motoring club or a Portuguese tourist office or embassy. If you lose any of the registration or permissive documents, contact the police.

Importing a Non-Conforming Vehicle

If you plan to import a European vehicle that does not conform to your country's vehicle standards, you need to do some substantial homework. If you know exactly what vehicle you'll be buying abroad, you should be able to determine all the costs associated with importing it. On the other hand, the slightest misunderstanding by any party involved in such an enterprise can result in unexpected and overwhelming costs to you and you alone.

US citizens must deal either directly or indirectly with three separate government agencies, each with its own agenda: Customs, which I addressed largely in the previous chapter, will concern itself with establishing the value of your vehicle and placing a proper duty and federal tax on it; the Environmental Protection Agency (EPA) will concern itself with establishing that your vehicle does not pose an unacceptable threat to the environment; and the Department of Transportation (DOT) will concern itself with establishing that your vehicle does not pose an unacceptable threat to the immediate safety of the population. In the end, a US citizen importing a vehicle must be able to prove to Customs that he or she has satisfied the requirements of the other two entities; otherwise the citizen will face long delays and high port-storage fees while he or she arranges the necessary paperwork and modifications to the vehicle.

The US EPA does not restrict the importation of vehicles manufactured before EPA requirements took effect. Such vehicles include gasoline-powered passenger vehicles manufactured before 1968 and motorcycles manufactured before 1978. Any person may import such ve-hicles without bond, under the applicable declaration category on *EPA Form 3520-1*.

The US government does not permit *individual* US citizens to import non-US version vehicles other than those described in the previous paragraph. Instead, an individual must enlist an Independent Commercial Importer (ICI) to handle the importing. The ICI must possess a currently valid qualifying certificate of conformity for the particular vehicle the individual wants the ICI to import. The ICI will be responsible for performing all necessary modifications, testing, and labeling, as well as providing an emissions warranty. In Table 5.1, I list the seven ICIs authorized by the US EPA.

Any US citizen planning to import a non-US version vehicle should use these ICIs as a primary source of information. *Never buy a non-US version vehicle without first speaking with an ICI who assures you they can bring the vehicle into compliance for a certain price.* The ICIs are remarkably helpful; after all, they stand to make lots of money if you contract their services. An ICI will even suggest certain vehicles that are good deals and tell you how to locate such a vehicle in Europe.

One ICI contracted by the US military is Import Trade Services, Inc. As such, ITS maintains an office with seventy employees near the Frankfurt airport (Kelsterbach) in Germany. Contact Kay Lester at Langer Kornweg 16, 65451 Kelsterbach, Germany, tel. 06107 8051, if you determine which vehicle model you want only *after* you arrive overseas—a likely scenario.

It's worth noting that Ken Shaffer, owner of ITS, tells me his company must either flatly turn down or at least discourage roughly nine out of ten people who solicit its services. The rejection rate is so high because, as with all ICIs, ITS lacks a license to modify certain models and because the cost of modifying some models is so high that ITS would not be serving its customers' best interests if it agreed to modify such vehicles. Not all ICIs may exercise the same integrity concerning the second point, however.

US citizens can call the EPA Imports Hotline at 202 233 9660 for information regarding ICIs that may have obtained approval since the issuance of the list that I reproduced as Table 5.2. For further information US citizens should contact the US EPA Manufacturers Operations Division (EN-340F), Investigation/Imports Section,

Table 5.2

US DOT-authorized Registered Importers.

Eastern United States

Auto Enterprises, 850 N. Rochester Road, Clawson, MI 48017, tel. 313 589 3600.

Automotive Research & Design (trades as CXA), 190 Egel Avenue, Middlesex, NJ 08846, tel. 908 271 9440.

Champagne Imports*, 200 West 5th Street, Lansdale, PA 19446. Representative: Mr. Joe Marino. Tel. 800 535 9728 or 215 361 1304.

J.M. Motors, 941 Ridge Road East, Webster, NY 14580, tel. 716 924 0308.

Pierre Enterprises, 4413 South US 1, Fort Pierce, FL 34982, tel. 800 322 3702.

Superior Auto Sales, 5201 Camp Road, Hamburg, NY 14075, tel. 716 649 6695.

Western United States

Double Decker Bus, 1212 South Broadway, Denver, CO 80210, tel. 303 744 7049.

Europa International, 1570 A Pacheo Street, Santa Fe, NM 87501, tel. 505 984 8888.

Mesa Auto Wholesalers, 63 East McKellips Road, Mesa, AZ 85201, tel. 602 390 9939.

Northern Califonia Emissions Laboratory, 2748 Jefferson Street, Napa, CA 94558, tel. 707 258 1753.

affiliated with Import Trade Services USA, Inc., one of the ICIs.

Washington, DC 20460, tel. 202 260 2504, FAX 202 260 6089; or the EPA Investigation/Imports Section (6405-J), Washington, DC 20460, tel. 202 233 9660, FAX 202 233 9596. Canadians should contact the Road Safety and Motor Vehicle Regulation Directorate, Transport Canada, Ottawa, ON K1A 0N5, tel. 613 998 2174, FAX 613 998 4831, and ask for the brochure *Private Importation of a Motor Vehicle into Canada.* Also, Canadians should contact Revenue Canada, Customs & Excise Travelers Division, Connaught Building, 5th Floor, Ottawa, ON K1A 0L5, tel. 613 954 6370, FAX 613 954 1765, and ask for the brochure *Importing a Motor Vehicle into Canada.*

Regardless of your citizenship, the emission requirements of your state or province or territory may be more strict than those of your national government. So before importing a vehicle, you should confirm with the appropriate state or province or territory authorities that the vehicle and your plans to modify it are satisfactory.

Now it's the US DOT's turn to enter the picture. In planning to import a vehicle, you must determine that your government considers the vehicle model and model year eligible for importation. An owner attempting to import a vehicle ineligible for importation must pay to return the vehicle to its point of origin or surrender the vehicle to Customs for imminent destruction. US Federal regulations *49 CFR,* parts *593* and *594,* specify the petitioning process and fees required for a US citizen to obtain such a determination of eligibility. For additional information or details on these requirements, contact the US Department of Transportation, National Highway Traffic Safety Compliance (NEF-32), 400

shipping & importing

Seventh Street SW, Washington, DC 20590, tel. 202 366 5313, FAX 202 366 1024; or contact some of the RIs I list in Table 5.2. (All the previously listed ICIs are authorized RIs also.)

In the US the importer (*you* if the vehicle being imported is a US version, an *ICI* otherwise) must file form *DOT HS-7* at the time of entry, indicating whether the vehicle conforms with applicable safety and bumper standards. You can obtain this form from Customs brokers (see the last section of this chapter) or at ports of entry. The importer must enter non-US version vehicles under a DOT bond equal to 150 percent of the vehicle's dutiable value. The government requires this bond in order to ensure that the vehicle is brought into conformance within 120 days after importation. The bond is in addition to the regular Customs entry bond. Bonds may be difficult to obtain and can be expensive; the issuer may require security deposits equaling 50 percent or more of the bond's value.

Unless specifically excepted, the importer must sign a contract with a DOT-Registered Importer (RI) who will modify the vehicle so it conforms with all applicable safety and bumper standards and who can certify the modifications, just as

an ICI can do for the EPA-required modifications. The importer must attach a copy of the RI's contract to the *DOT HS-7* form and furnish these documents—along with the DOT bond—to the Customs Service at the port of entry.

Other documents that you need to present upon importation include the shipper's or carrier's original bill of lading, the bill of sale, foreign registration, and any other documents concerning the vehicle. Note the following words of caution from the US Customs Office.

> The EPA certification of ICIs does not guarantee the actions or work of the ICIs, nor does it regulate contractual agreements and working relationships with vehicle owners.

> The EPA strongly recommends that before shipping a non-US version vehicle for importation the importer either make final arrangements with an ICI for modifications and testing, or obtain EPA approval in writing for importation. Storage fees at the ports are costly, and the vehicle may not be eligible for importation.

> The US government has eliminated the policy which permitted importers a one-time exemption for vehicles at least five years old.

The EPA considers a US-version vehicle that has had modifications to its drive train or emission control system to be a non-US version vehicle, even though it may be labeled a US-version vehicle.

For US-version vehicles driven in Europe, a bond will *not* be required upon return to the US if the vehicle participates in one of the EPA-approved catalyst control programs operating in Europe.

Arranging Shipping

Of course there are two ways to send freight: by air and by sea. Shipping by air, with the exception of a few carriers such as Lufthansa, is expensive. Furthermore, shipping a car, van or motorhome by air is impractical. Shipping by sea is less expensive, but it takes much longer. Shipping to or from the East Coast of North America takes about two weeks by sea; while shipping to or from the West Coast takes about three to four weeks. Shipping to or from Australia or New Zealand takes about eight to twelve weeks by sea. Always allow for delay: your items could be delayed clearing customs; a dock workers strike could be on; and an item like a vehicle may be seriously damaged or else stolen in transit.

Before I further discuss the mundane subject of shipping, I must reiterate one delightful option: Cunard Line's *Queen Elizabeth 2,* which accepts vehicles as accompanied baggage. See the first paragraph of the first section of this chapter for a detailed description of the *QE2's* service.

At the end of this chapter I list several shipping companies. If you make your own arrangements to ship your vehicle, contact some of these companies. Begin the correspondence by asking whether the company is a broker (or freight forwarding company) and not just a carrier. Brokers maintain rate contracts with airlines and cargo ships, contracts that make their prices less than those of carriers. Besides, shipping lines often refuse to carry cargo that's not booked through a broker. What's more, brokers know the *ins* and *outs* of Customs issues. As such, brokers have rapport and leverage with Customs officials at home and abroad; if your shipment has trouble clearing Customs, a broker can usually clear up the problem over the phone. If you're unfamiliar with Customs rules and shipping, I *highly* recommend using a broker. Lufthansa Airlines, however, is one carrier that offers competitive rates and service.

Regardless, the carrier that either you or a broker eventually enlist should offer a payment protection scheme against their going out of business. If a carrier tells you that they do offer such a scheme, get a copy of the protection policy in writing, and read it thoroughly before you make any arrangements. The best schemes are the Customer Payment Guarantee or CPG (operated by the Association of International Removers) and the IMMI (operated by the overseas division of the British Association of Removers). Any member of these associations has a proven track record in the industry. US citizens can call the Interstate Commerce Commission (tel. 215 596 4040 in the East, 213 894 4008 in the West) to help determine the integrity of a broker or a carrier.

When investigating the cost of shipping a particular vehicle, you'll need to tell the shipping company the exact weight and dimensions of the vehicle, where you're departing from, where you want to go, and what your schedule is. Ask about the costs of air freight (for motorcycles) and/or sea freight (for motorcycles and other vehicles), shipping insurance, preparation for shipment (fuel drainage, oil and transmission fluid drainage, battery disconnection, crat-

ing, steam cleaning and waxing), other port and handling fees, special delivery and return, documents, and the time it will take to ship the vehicle. Also ask about reduced rates from certain ports (Amsterdam, Antwerp, Rotterdam and Hamburg are among the cheapest). Finally, ask if the freighter takes passengers; many do. I'm told that the companionship, food and lodging on a freighter are wonderful. With the crew and, usually, about twelve other intrepid travelers, you dine on delicious food; and you stay in your own spacious and well appointed outside cabin with a huge window (instead of a tiny porthole). In the *Resources* chapter I list several publications devoted to relating the specifics of freighter travel.

Be sure you understand the terms and conditions of the marine insurance available. Watch out for the following in a marine insurance policy: exclusions for bruising, scratching and denting; exclusion of accessories such as stereos; high deductibles; and anything less than complete coverage from the moment you hand over the vehicle until you touch it again back home. Always ensure that a company with offices or settling agents in your home country underwrites your marine insurance: it's essential that the policy allows you to settle claims in your home country. The best way to confirm this allowance is to get the name and address of the settling agent in your home country before you book your shipping. Remember to ensure your vehicle and any accompanying items for their full *replacement* value in your home country.

You may have to put your vehicle in a crate and arrange to get it to a terminal. You can crate the vehicle yourself or have a dealer, packaging company or freight company crate it for you. One good solution is to have a trucking company package and send it, but ask to watch the packing. Brokers will arrange to get the crated vehicle to the terminal; this will cost extra, but it's the simplest way.

If you have a motorcycle that you want to crate, you can get a crate from a dealer for about $50. Make sure there's no mud or grass on the machine. Customs officials worry about contaminates that may come in on dirty items. The June 1986 issue of *BMW Owner's News* contains instructions for building a *reusable* crate. You do this by bolting the top, sides and bottom of the crate together instead of nailing them together. Here's a real killer:

every motorcycle has identification numbers—one on the engine and the other on the frame—which Customs officers must be able to see to match them with your title. If they can't see these numbers, you'll have to uncrate the bike. To avoid this inconvenience, cut a hole in the crate so the serial number can be seen.

When shipping from Europe, consider surrendering the vehicle at the dock or shipping agent's warehouse. If instead you have the vehicle picked up, you may open yourself to trouble. Marine insurance doesn't take effect until the vehicle has arrived at the warehouse, and the insurance covering the vehicle in the meantime may require you to stay in Europe to settle a claim if an accident occurs during that short transport.

Before surrendering a vehicle, there are several things you should do. For one, try to gage the vehicle's fueling so that you leave little fuel in the tank: the shipping company will drain the fuel before loading the vehicle. To safeguard against the importation of dangerous pests, the US Department of Agriculture requires that the undercarriage of imported vehicles be free from foreign soil. As such, your vehicle must be steam sprayed or otherwise cleaned

thoroughly before shipment. And have your shipper or carrier notify you of the freighter's arrival date, and be sure to inform Customs of this date: this info will allow Customs to quickly clear your vehicle.

Note that if you leave the vehicle in port storage for more than three days you'll pay a steep daily storage charge. Customs clears shipments at the first port of entry unless you arrange for a freight forwarder in your country to have the vehicle sent in bond to a Customs port more convenient for you. Customs ports exist in virtually every US state.

Theft is a major problem at ports and during transit. As such, remove loose or detachable parts of your shipment; and do not use your vehicle as a container for personal belongings. Indeed, many shippers and carriers will not accept your vehicle if it contains personal belongings. Regardless, you must declare the entire contents of your vehicle to Customs upon importation. Failure to make such a declaration can result in you being fined and your vehicle and its contents seized. And you may incur a personal penalty and your vehicle may be seized if *anyone* conveys illegal narcotics in your vehicle.

If you do go ahead and put possessions in your vehicle or in the crate that the vehicle is in, make sure you have proper insurance. Marine insurance falls into three main categories: if you insure your *entire* consignment against loss and theft, you can only make a claim if *everything* disappears; coverage against loss and theft of the entire consignment or any one package allows you to make an acceptable claim if all or any *complete package* (suitcase, etc.) doesn't arrive; coverage against loss or theft of either of the above plus any individual item or piece of goods out of a package allows you to make a claim for *anything* missing. You can also elect to have your loss and theft policy cover breakage of professionally packed items and/or owner packed items.

Besides arranging the proper insurance to cover your possessions, you must take care in packing these items. Note that suitcases and trunks often get marked or scratched on the outside. It's acceptable to lock such luggage and keep the keys, but the keys must be available at the destination when the luggage arrives. Weight does not affect the shipping cost, but movers are more likely to drop heavy containers. If you have many books or heavy items, split the load so each container (or "tea chest") is half full of heavy items and half full of light items. Most important, always pack boxes tight and to the top, filling in gaps and holes so that nothing can move. Ultimately, freighters carry all cargo in sealed steel containers, some of which travel above deck. The temperature changes during a voyage can be extreme, causing condensation. Clothing, books, etc., wrapped in plastic can arrive covered in mildew. Wrap items in paper or clothes instead. Marine insurance policies exclude damage caused by atmospheric temperature extremes.

Some North American Shipping Companies

Aid Forwarding Co., Inc. (yes, that is "Aid," not "Air"), 19914 Via Baron, Rancho Dominguez, CA 90220–6104. Contact Lucille Clark, tel. 310 638 6600, FAX 310 638 1200.

Allied Transportation Services, tel. 800 229 9781 or 408 727 9781.

American Export Lines, 1756 S. Robertson B1, Los Angeles, CA 90035, tel. 800 777 2888.

Homebound International Shipping, Inc., tel. 800 750 1313.

Schumacher & Associates, Inc., 411 N. Central Ave., Glendale, CA 91203, tel. 213 245 1811.

Sea-Land Service, Inc., 669 Panorama Dr., Long Beach, CA 90802, tel. 213 775 6761.

Sunny International Shipping, tel. 800 690 4500.

Warren Motorcycle Transport, 7106 NW 108th Avenue, Tamarac, FL 33321. Contact Mr. Warren Goodman, tel. 800 443 7519, FAX 305 726 0494. Warren uses Lufthansa airlines from a variety of North American airports.

Air and Ocean Export Packing, 1604 W. 34th, Houston, TX 77018, tel. 713 680 9400 or 800 231 0350.

Trailblazers International, 8203 Willow Place South #430-C, Houston, TX 77070, tel. 800 945 6102.

American Export Lines, tel. 718 917 7702 or 800 439 9999.

Penbroke Marine Services, Inc., tel. 800 227 8096 or 718 816 8778.

Auto Overseas Ltd., 630 Palisades Ave., Englewood, NJ 07631, tel. 212 594 3939.

Gdynia American Lines, Plainfiled, NJ, tel. 908 412 6000.

Motorcycle Transport Inc. 1232 Hooper Ave., Toms River, NJ 08753. Contact Ralph Freitas, tel. 908 244 0200.

Overseas Brokers, 111 Great Neck Road, Great Neck, NY 11021. Contact Doron Weissman, tel. 516 773 6100, FAX 516 773 6103.

Ozark Fast Freight, Ltd., PSC #2, Box 1457, Apo, NY 09405, tel. Germany at 03943 6101.

Overseas Car Shipping, tel. 800 334 6228. Ship through Charleston, South Carolina.

Motorcycle Transport Inc. 1232 Hooper Ave., Toms River, NJ 08753. Contact Ralph Freitas, tel. 908 244 0200. Office in San Diego too.

Accord Export Lines, 640 Army St., San Francisco, CA 94124, tel. 415 821 0800.

American Export Lines, tel. 800 477 5377.

American Freight Line (they speak German), tel. 800 974 5055.

Jaguar Intermodal Transport, tel. 415 826 4141 or 800 899 4548.

World Wide Shipping, tel. 415 495 6794.

Air Tiger Express Inc., 15215 52nd S., Seattle, WA 98188, tel. 206 248 8073.

Some British Shipping Companies

Austpac International, 3rd Floor, 207 Regent Street, London W1R 7DD, tel. 081 452 6460.

Britannic Shipping and Air Freight, Unit 4, The Wyvern Estate, Beverly Way, New Malden, Surrey KT3 4PH, tel. 081 942 0955, FAX 081 949 0040.

Cargo Forwarding, A2 Broomsleigh Business Park, Worsley Bridge Road, London SE26 5BN, tel. 081 698 8815.

Double E Overseas Removals, Ltd. Movements House, Ajax Works, Hertford Road, Barking, Essex IG11 8BW, tel. 081 591 6929, FAX 081 594 5935.

Karman Shipping Services, Ltd., tel. 081 858 8268.

Personal Shipping Services, 8 Redcross Way, London SE1 9HR, tel. 071 407 6606.

SANZ International Shipping. 159 Earls Court Road, Earls Court SW5 9QX, tel. 071 244 7866

SBS Freight, Unit 2, Staples Corner Business Park, 100 North Circular Road, London NW2 6LU, tel. 081 208 1677, FAX 081 208 3200.

Seaworld Cargo International Movers, Freepost, V.I.C. Industrial Park, West Street, Erith, Kent, DA8 1BR, tel. 0322 439439.

Some Continental Shipping Companies

Brauns & Co., 2857 Langen bei Bremerhaven, Landstraße 94, tel. 0 47 43 50 67. Other offices include Frankfurt: 0611 590311; Munich: 089 6906419; Stuttgart: 0711 841014 or 0711 841015 or 0711 841016.

E.H. Harms Gmbh & Co., Postfach 15040, 2800 Bremen 1, tel. 0421 3689 104.

European Automotive Compliance, Gevers Deynootweg 1130a, 2586 BX, the Hague, Netherlands, tel. 70 3559245, FAX 70 3500624.

G. Albrecht Co., Steunstraße 7b, Postfach 120426, 2850 Bremerhaven 12, tel. 0471 40174.

Karl Gross Co., Hafenhaus Columbusbhf, Postfach 120244, 2850 Bremerhaven, tel. 0471 4838 20.

mhs Motorradtouren GmbH, Donnersbergerstraße 32, D-8000 Munich 19.

Contact Herbert Schellhorn, tel. 89 168 4888, FAX 89 166 5549. Air shipment of motorcycles to and from Frankfurt.

Transcar Gmbh, Langer Kornweg 16, 6092 Kelsterbach-Frankfurt, tel. 06107 8051.

Other Organizations

Panama Canal Commission, 2000 L St. NW, Suite 550, Washington, DC 20036, tel. 202 634 6441.

US Department of Defense, Department of the Army, Deputy Chief of Staff, Logistics, Washington, DC 20310. Rep.: Mr. Gary Bull.

US Department of State, 2201 C St. NW, Washington, DC 20520, tel. 202 647 6441. Rep.: Mr. John Miller.

6. the special case of the british isles

Nowhere else in Europe are the benefits of motor travel so immediate and so markedly without parallel as in the British Isles. Mostly it's the English language that makes the difference, by facilitating interactions between English-speaking travelers and natives; but it's the infrastructure and anatomy of the Isles as well. Yet nowhere else in Europe do so many idiosyncrasies—several of which tend to lessen the appeal of motoring—challenge the traveler's savvy. The principal idiosyncrasies are as follows: (1) you must drive on the left side of the road; (2) most of the vehicles are right-hand-drive vehicles (steering wheel on the right, gear shift on the left); (3) rental rates in Britain are some of Europe's cheapest, but (4) rates in Ireland are much more expensive; (5) the Isles being isles, special costs (for ferry, Chunnel, or airline fares) are associated with travel between them and to/from the continent; (6) diesel fuel in the British Isles costs virtually the same as gasoline; (7) BritRail's tickets are the most expensive in Europe, and (8) BritRail does not honor Eurailpasses; but (9) their round-trip tickets cost just 10 percent more than their one-way tickets; (10) a handful of unique bus and van services whose benefits approximate those associated with motoring have popped up in England and Scotland; (11) hitchhiking is relatively safe in the Isles; and, finally, (12) the Isles' gentle landscapes and the propinquity of the discrete villages and such that dot them constitute a seemingly ideal matrix for bicycling.

First things first. The term *British Isles* refers to *Great Britain* and the whole of *Ireland*—Great Britain encompassing England, Scotland and Wales, and tacking on Northern Ireland to become the so-called *United Kingdom;* and Ireland consisting of Northern Ireland and the much larger Republic of Ireland. Despite this impressive congeries, the British Isles all told—with their human population of 60 million, some 57 million of which reside in the UK—reduce the surface of the sea by an amount slightly less than does the US state of Oregon.

The main trouble that most North Americans face when driving in the British Isles is this business about driving on the left side of the road. Not only is the traffic flip-flopped, but the steering wheel is on the other side of the vehicle—and the gear shift is at your left hand instead of your right. (Although the shifting pattern is the same; and the accelerator is still at the right foot, with the brake pedal off to its left.) It's virtually impossible for a North American to practice driving this way before arriving in a country where left-side driving is the norm; the best we North Americans can do is use mental imagery to shed the right-side-of-the-road mindset. Yet the adaptability of the human brain is remarkable. In a matter of days a North American driving in the British Isles (or, for that matter, an Aussie or Kiwi driving on the continent) can supplant the mindset he or she assumed over a whole lifetime. It reminds me of an experiment in which scientists asked a man to wear a contraption that inverted his vision. He agreed. At first, the upside down world confused the man so that he stumbled around and could hardly feed himself. Within a week, however, he was functioning normally. When the scientists finally took the contraption off the man's head, the rightside-up world seemed upside down to him. Again he stumbled around and could hardly feed himself. This went on for years—no, just kidding; in a couple of days the man readjusted to the conventional world. If the human mind can adapt so quickly to the inversion of the whole world, surely you'll adapt to sitting on the right side of a vehicle, shifting with your left hand, and driving on the left side of the road.

Not only will you quickly adapt, but the benefits of driving will counteract the anxiety you'll experience in the transition period. In the meantime, the right attitude can minimize both this anxiety and the real danger that fuels it. Be cool. Take your time. Most Brits and Irish, experienced in motoring on the continent, empathize with and are thus tolerant of disoriented foreign drivers. When someone does honk at you, open your smile like a jackknife and wave at the irritated bloak like a bloody fool. Who cares? Remember, all will be OK as long as you don't hit anything. Soon you'll be zipping around like Jackie Stewart. The whole experience will make for good stories when you get home, and the you'll feel a genuine and justified pride in your accomplishment.

I must reiterate that it *is* legal to drive left-hand-drive vehicles (steering wheel on the left, gear shift on your right) in the British Isles and right-hand-drive vehicles on the continent, but it makes it virtually impossible to safely pass other vehicles unless you have an astute and trusted navigator in the passenger seat or unless the driver's seat is high enough to let you see *over* the majority of vehicles. But as I alluded to in the *Renting* chapter, some rental agreements forbid transport of a vehicle between Britain and the continent, and some may prohibit transport between Britain and Ireland as well. Check for such stipulations if you plan to drive on two or all three of these land masses.

Note from the tables in the *Renting* chapter that Great Britain is one of the cheapest and Ireland one of the most expensive countries in which to rent a vehicle. This disparity—coupled with the cost of crossing the Irish Sea—makes it difficult to determine the most cost-effective way to tour the two islands by rental car. This being so, Hertz, in cooperation with Stena Sealink Line, offers a program called "Seadrive" that may interest those who desire a vehicle for a week or more both in England and in Ireland. The program allows you to rent a car in England, Wales or Scotland and transport it and up to five passengers on a return ferry trip to Ireland all for one charge. Call Hertz in Dublin at 01 2808844 or in London at 0181 759 2499 to get more information or to make reservations. Hertz representatives in North America seem to be uninformed about this program.

If you wanna drive a rental vehicle into Northern Ireland, confirm first that the rental company allows this.

Probably the cheapest way to cross — without bringing your vehicle along—between Britain and Ireland or between Britain and the continent is by the bus-ferry-bus or train-ferry-train services. One ticket covers the land *and* sea legs. Contact any National Express or Slattery bus office in Britain, any Bus Éireann office in Ireland, any Eurolines office on the continent, or an appropriate train station.

Note that the Young Person's Railcard and the Senior Card are available only in Britain and cost £16 ($25). Persons 16–23 years of age or persons over 60 years of age, respectively, qualify for one of these cards, cards which in turn qualify the owner to a 30 percent discount on train trips and boat rides between Britain and Ireland or between the the Isles and the continent. If you don't plan to use a bus-ferry-bus or train-ferry-train service, be sure to compare this discount to the separate discounts that some ferries already offer to students and seniors: discounts are not cumulative. Note also that Eurailpasses allow for free ferry travel between the continent and Ireland but *not* between the continent and Britain or between Britain and Ireland.

See the *Itinerary Suggestions* chapter for a discussion of the motorail service—a motor vehicle-carrying train service you can use in conjunction with the ferries to make quick time to destinations all over Southern and central Europe.

And see the *Ferries and the Chunnel* chapter for a discussion of the car-and-people-carrying *Le Shuttle* and the high-speed, people-only-carrying Eurostar trains that run through the new Channel Tunnel. The Eurostar trains compete most closely with cross-channel airline services. Early on, the lowest air fares from London to Amsterdam or Paris cost about $80 one-way (or "single"), $120 return, roughly the price of the Eurostar fares. (Flights that originate on the continent, however, are more expensive.) Meanwhile, the quick shuttle flight from London to Dublin costs about $125.

As for travel *within* the British Isles, note that the price of diesel fuel in Britain and Ireland roughly equals that of gasoline—about £0.52 per liter or $3.13 per US gallon. This fact in combination with the relatively short driving distances inherent in the Isles means that you won't save as much by using a diesel vehicle there as you would on the continent.

Great Britain's rail system, BritRail, is unusual, too. Not only does BritRail

Table 6.1

Typical Second Class ("Standard Class"), One-way British Train Fares.

London—Dover	£16 ($25)
London—Bath	23
London—Fishguard	42
London—Holyhead	58
London—York	42
York—Edinburgh	33
Edinburgh—Stranraer	23
Edinburgh—Aberdeen	26
Edinburgh—Loch Ness	23
Loch Ness—Skye	13

refuse to honor Eurail passes, but their point-to-point tickets are the most expensive in Europe. For example, the number of kilometers you can travel per dollar in various countries or sections of Europe are as follows: Turkey—40 km; Eastern Europe—17 km; Spain—13 km; Italy—12 km; France—10 km; Germany—8 km; Scandinavia—7 km; and, finally, England—6 km. What's more, BritRail's couchettes cost a steep $37 per night. In Table 6.1, I list some typical second class British train fares. For the most part, these high point-to-point fares translate into high prices for the various BritRail passes.

There are, however, some ways to avoid these high fares. For one thing, as I noted earlier, BritRail's return tickets cost just 10 percent more than their one-way or "single" tickets. Moreover, the Family Card, available in Britain only, costs just £20 ($31) and entitles parents traveling with children to a 25 percent discount—while it lets kids under 16 years of age travel for only £1.

Bus (or "coach") fares are about 40 to 60 percent cheaper than rail fares, but bus travel takes about twice as long. Still, British bus service is timely and the system extensive. And for £12 ($18) you can buy a BritExpress card that entitles you to 30 percent off on all bus fares for the thirty days after its purchase. Or for £7 ($11), seniors over 59 years of age and youths under 26 years of age can buy a card that entitles them to discounts of up to 30 percent on all National Express coach fares. Both of these discount cards can be bought in Britain. Just bring a passport-sized photograph to any National Express coach station; the staff there will prepare your card while you wait. The London Coach Station (serving National Express, Eurolines, and Slattery's) is on the corner of Buckingham Palace Road and Elizabeth Street, near Victoria train and metro station. Britain's Tourist Trail bus pass entitles holders to unlimited travel on Britain's extensive network of National Express and Caledonian Express buses. If you buy this pass in Britain rather than domestically, you'll save about 20 percent.

The Student Travel Center—just north of Victoria Station, at the corner of BPR and Grosvenor Gardens—sells a wide variety of bus and train passes and plane tickets.

Many other British bus and rail passes are sold only *outside* Britain. To buy them in the US or Canada, contact Europe Through the Backdoor and be sure to ask for their free *Guide to European Railpasses*. (See the *Resources* chapter.)

When you add up all the idiosyncracies discussed so far, it's not surprising that special bus and van services—whose fares undercut the fares charged by the train and bus services just described—have arisen in Britain. These services offer many of the benefits of automobile travel, but without the anxiety. Moreover, by using them to form a ring or backbone of long-distance travel, you can take advantage of the relatively cheap return-fare train tickets by stringing short return train trips onto the bus or van circuit.

The first such service I wanna describe is the Slow Coach. The Slow Coach is a minibus that leaves London three times a week, picking up and dropping off passengers along the way at Windsor, Bath, Stratford-upon-Avon, the Lake District, Edinburgh, York and Cambridge, before returning to London to start over. The service is personable and, usually, door-to-door. The ride offers a great opportunity to cruise the English countryside while meeting other passengers from around the globe. While you ride along, the driver expounds on local history and offers tips about places to stay and eat and drink. The bus even makes stops when the sights or the riders demand it. The Slow Coach's clientele ranges from high school-age backpackers to retired adults but tends to consist largely of persons in their 20s or 30s. The common denominator of the clientele is a desire to meet a variety of people while visiting exciting new places. Tickets for the Slow Coach cost £69 and are valid for two months. You can purchase tickets by phoning/FAXing 01249 891959 (24 hours) in England or by stopping in at one of the youth hostels along the route. Reservations should be made a couple of days in advance. Bicycles *are* taken with a reservation.

A new service, tangential and analogous to the Slow Coach, has emerged to haul you around Scotland—the land of bagpipes, kilts, lochs and haggis. Haggis Backpackers, Ltd., which began operating in the summer of 1993, derives its name from the famous Scottish delicacy made from the innards of the sheep which dot Scotland's craggy hills. Siblings Donald and Alastair got the idea for their company from a similar service they happened upon in New Zealand. Now the brothers get to hangout together only once a week: they spend the rest of their time hauling travelers in separate vans on staggered legs around the Scottish circuit. In most cases the service is door to door, and stops are made along the way for food, castle tours, and photo ops of the myriad vistas and historical sights. This is the most personable transportation service you can expect to find. Once enroute, you'll have to listen closely at first to discern the historical tidbits, wisecracks and inevitable bullshit clothed in Donald and Alastair's thick Scottish accent; but soon you'll be in the front seat, eating candy bars, drinking coffee (provided gratis, donations accepted) and giving Donald or Alastair some of his own. As with the Slow Coach, Haggis is a *wonderful* way to get close to the land, meet a variety of people—again, most in their 20s or 30s—and get the scoop on the local establishments, sights and activities. The route and schedule are as follows.

Edinburgh, Pitlochry, Aviemore, Inverness, Loch Ness, Skye.

Fort William, Glencoe, Oban, Loch Lomond, Glasgow, Edinburgh.

Leaves Edinburgh: M, T, W, F, S, S to Skye.

Leaves Skye: M, T, W, T, S, S to Edinburgh.

A ticket costs £55 and is good for three months. Haggis *will* take bikes. Call Haggis in Edinburgh at 0131 557 4060, FAX 0131 558 1177. Phone from 10:00 A.M. to 1:00 P.M. or from 3:00 P.M. to 7:00 P.M. Or write to Haggis Backpackers, Ltd., c/o The Backpackers Centre, 7-9 Blackfriars Street, Edinburgh. Reservations should be placed a couple of days in advance.

Note that if their vehicle is not full, the operators of the Slow Coach and Haggis Backpackers services will allow you to pay for a certain leg on their circuit. To do this, find out where and when the services pick up passengers. When the Slow Coach or Haggis van arrives, ask the driver if the vehicle is full and if you can pay for a ride to one of the next stops.

A comparable service, the Go Blue Banana van, tel. 0131 220 6868, will, for £39, take you on a three-day, 450-mile jaunt from Edinburgh into the Highlands.

An intimate, cheap and versatile way to get around the *back* roads of Scotland is by riding along on postal vehicles. Post offices in Scotland offer the *Scottish Postbus Guide* free of charge. You don't need an envelope or a stamp: just a couple of £s allow you to go wherever the mail goes.

Back in London, the Budget Tours UK minibus leaves the metropolis each weeweek, taking travelers on a four-day tour of Southwest England. Experienced travelers operate Budget Tours with the stated objective of offering a fun and interesting mixture of popular tourist attractions along with some less-exploited sights

that lie off the beaten track, sights which travelers cannot access directly using public transport. The tour—complete with shared accommodation, English breakfasts, and entrance fees to Stonehenge and Tintagel Castle—costs just £125. Day one finds you departing early in the morning and cruising to Stonehenge, Avebury, Silbury Hill, various pagan hill carvings, and finally to the spot considered by most to be the site of Camelot. On the second day you're off to Dartmoor National Park and it's picturesque villages, wild countryside and prehistoric stoneworks. Day three takes you to the Cornish coastline, Tintagel Castle, and Merlin's Cave. Finally, on your way back to London you stop on day four to explore the mystical heart of England— Glastonbury or "Avalon", the legendary resting place of the Holy Grail. All told, you'll travel over 1000 kilometers. Weekly tours depart every Monday at 8:30 A.M., returning Thursday. The tours depart from London's Prince of Teck Pub at Earls Court Road and Kenway Road, London. For information and bookings contact Budget Tours UK, 12b Kingswood Road, Penge, London, SE20 7BN England, tel. 0181 778 1614.

Finally, there are a variety clubs and outfits leading day- and weekend-trips out of London. The clubs include the Drifters Club, 10 Norfolk Place, Paddinton W2, tel. 0171 262 1292; and SANZ Travellers Club, 200 Earls Court Road, SW5 90X, tel. 0171 244 7866. Tracks Day Trips, meanwhile, operating out of 12 Abingdon Road, W8 6AF, tel. 0171 937 3028, captains weekend trips to sample English wines and ciders, to the beach resort of Margate, to tour breweries that make real Sussex Ale, or to Bath for £9 each. Deckers Day Trips, 131-135 Earls Court Road, SW5 9RH, tel. 0171 370 4555, runs weekend trips to Bath and the Cotswolds, Brighton and Arundel Castle, Hever Castle and Penshurst Vineyards, or Oxford and Blenheim Palace for £10 each. See London's *TNT* and *New Zealand News UK* magazines, descibed in the *Resources* chapter, for more.

Let's turn now to Ireland. Ireland's rail service and most of Ireland's long-distance "expressway" buses honor Eurailpasses. The rail system, however, fanning out from Dublin, neglects much of the countryside. The bus system is more comprehensive and, given the short distances, nearly as fast. Beware that many of the train and bus routes *between* (not necessarily *to*) smaller towns like Galway and Killarney stop running or reduce their frequency starting in late September. Note further that train fares and comfort vary during the week. For example, the Dublin-Killarney route costs only IR£48 return on Tuesday, Wednesday, Thursday and Saturday; but on Monday, Friday and Sunday it costs IR£80 return and is quite crowded. Bus tickets cost about 60 percent less. In Table 6.2, I list some typical Irish train fares. A Travelsave stamp entitles any student with an ISIC to 50 percent discounts on rail and bus travel. To get the stamp, students should take their ISIC and at least IR£10 to any USIT student travel office in Ireland.

Rather than buying point-to-point tickets, you may be better off buying one or more of the passes I list in Table 6.3. These passes can be bought from CIE Tours in Dublin or Limerick, Bus Éireann in Dublin (tel. 01 366111), Ulster Bus in Belfast, and CIE Tours/Irish Rail in the USA (108 Ridgedale Ave., Box 2355, Morristown, NJ 07962, tel. 800 243 7687); but they're significantly more expensive when bought *outside* Ireland. Europe Through the

Table 6.2

Typical Second Class ("Standard Class") One-way Irish Train Fares.

Dublin—Galway	IR£25 ($40)
Galway—Killarney*	14
Killarney—Cork	11
Cork—Rosslare	16
Rosslare—Dublin	19
Dublin—Cork	32
Dublin—Killarney	32
Dublin—Sligo	27
Sligo—Galway*	5
Dublin—Belfast	14
Belfast—Derry	8
Derry—Sligo*	8

*these routes stop service approximately September 25 each year.

Backdoor sells a railpass called the BritIreland pass that covers the whole of the British Isles and includes return ferry passage between Britain and Ireland. (See the *Resources* chapter.)

Hitchhiking is another option. Europe's best hitching is found in Ireland, but it's not as easy as you might expect—especially for males. Altough female hitchhikers usually get picked up quickly, it's often to the chagrin of a guy or two who got to the spot first and stood in the rain for an hour. I met a dozen or so hitchers during my bicycle tour of Ireland; all seemed to be doing quite well. One couple from Pamplona told me an amazing story. . . . They'd been hitching. A car had pulled over. The couple had run up and told the driver where they wanted to go: about eighty miles that-a-way. They'd asked the driver, a guy from England, if he was going that-a-way. "No," he'd told them. "But I'll take you there anyway. I don't have anything better to do." . . . Still, hitching is probably the most dangerous way to travel, even in jolly Ireland.

Many people fancy a bicycle tour of the Isles. Indeed, nearly everything about the Isles—except the weather—makes for good bicycling. Yet as I mentioned in the *Why Drive?* chapter, long-distance bicycling is a serious endeavor that should not be taken lightly. Distances in the Isles *are* relatively short, but short relative to the size of the *continent;* it's still about 650 miles (1080 kilometers) along the fastest motoring route from London to the top of

Table 6.3

Recent Irish Bus and Train Passes.

Rambler Pass (Bus)

	Adult	Group (over 5)	Child (under 16)
3 days in 8	IR£26	24	13
8 days in 15	60	57	30
15 days in 30	90	80	45

Iarnród Éireann (Train)/Bus Éireann Railroad Rambler Ticket

	Adult	Group	Child
8 days in 15	IR£78	73	39
15 days in 30	115	100	58

Irish Explorer Flexipass: 8 days of bus or rail travel in 15 days (in the Republic of Ireland only) for about IR£85; or a rail-only version with 5 out of 15 days for about IR£60.

Irish Rover Flexipass: 5 train-days in 15 days for about IR£70.

Emerald Card—valid on Iarnród Éireann, Bus Éireann, Bus Atha Cliath, N. Ireland Railways, Ulsterbus & CityBus (Belfast):

	Adult	Group	Child
8 days in 15 IR	£IR105	100	53
15 days in 30	180	105	90

Scotland. To ride in a circuit around either island is a huge physical effort. Bicycle tourists usually budget no more than 60 miles (100 kilometers), or about seven hours, on the road per day. In Britain or Ireland you can expect to use a combination of narrow country lanes, busy highways and everything inbetween. Few of these roads will have much of a shoulder; you'll be sharing the road with trucks and buses. *Wear a helmet.* On the brighter side, you'll also be sharing the road with pheasant and grouse, cattle and horses, and friendly locals who'll give you direction or bicycle along with you for a while—and may even invite you home for tea or coffee. You'll feel every bump of the land, smell every field of flowers, whiff each pile of manure, hear every bird's song, every bell's ring, every call—English or Gaelic—from the fields. You'll sleep very well at night.

In fact, if you're planning to travel by car, van or motorhome, you should consider bringing a bicycle along. As I describe in the *Packing* chapter, you can bring a bicycle on a plane free of charge if you claim it as one of your two checked bags. On the other hand, you can buy a bike in Europe. Expect to pay about $400 in Britain for a bicycle that costs $300 in the

the special case of the british isles

US; this is about half the cost of bicycles on the continent. Of course you can also rent bicycles there. Try some of the following.

London

The *Loot* classified ads paper. The paper comes out each day. Free ads can be placed by phoning the Express line at 01891 888888. The deadline is 2:00 P.M. Bikes should sell in two or three days.

Go By Cycle, 15 Templeton Place, Earls Court, London SW5, tel. 0171 373 3657. All alloy wheels, VAT refund, 18/21 speed, Shimano geared, fully guaranteed new and ex-demo/rental models, one year free service. Sell locks, racks, tools, bungee cords, etc. Visa and MasterCard accepted. They may buy the bike back in the early summer.

Sunday Cycle Mart, Cygnet Street, E1, adjacent to Brick Cave. Nearest tube stop: Liverpool St. Every Sunday morning. Biggest and cheapest selection in London. Second-hand trade-in cycles from £25, new mountain bikes from £100, new racers from £85.

New Zealand House, at end of Haymarket Street off of Piccadilly Square. Walk through to shops behind. Find the New Zealand News UK, address 25. People sometimes post bike-for-sale bulletins on the board just inside the door.

The camping store on Charing Cross Road on the left side of the road just south of the Tottenham Court Road Tube stop (near intersection of Charing Cross and Oxford Street) sells cheap sea sacks, bungy cords and rain gear.

Dublin

Check the message board at Isaac's Hostel in Dublin. Otherwise, there is a bike shop next door where a new British Eagle Town and Trail model goes for IR£325, a used one goes for IR£125, and bikes are rented for IR£5 per day.

Buy and Sell classified ads paper. The paper comes out countrywide every Thursday. Free ads can be placed by phoning 01 2807191 24 hours a day, 7 days a week. The deadline is 1:00 P.M. on the Monday before publication. Ads run in two issues.

Cork

Cork bicycle hire. Kilgrew's, 6 Kyle St., off South Main, tel. 021 276255. Open 6 days. 5 and 12 speed gents, 6 speed ladies, all Raleigh. IR£7 per day or IR£30 per week.

Cork, Killarney, Galway, etc.

RailBike is the Irish national bicycle hire service for travelers. Based on the Irish Rail network, this service is offered at mainline rail stations in Cork, Killarney and Galway. RailBike bicycles can also be booked for collection or return through any rail station. New model mountain bikes IR£32 per week, IR£6 per day. Group discounts. Credit cards accepted. Tel. 01 971911, FAX 01 970756.

If you use a bicycle that you own, write down the make, model, serial number, and the address of the lock insurer. To register the bike in London, take it and the address of a hostel, hotel, American Express office, or friend in London to a police station; the police will stamp the bike with the address code so you can be contacted if they recover the bike after its theft. If you rent, be sure to note if you'll be responsible for the cost of the bike if it's stolen.

On occasion, even the heartiest bicyclist may want to put themselves and their bike on a bus or train. I already mentioned that the Slow Coach and the Haggis Backpackers take bicycles; several other services as well take bikes. Most ferries, for example, take bicycles free of charge. Although some intra-Britain buses *do* accept bikes, intra-Britain National Express buses don't. The bus-ferry-bus arrangements, on the other hand, will take a bike for an extra £10 fee — if there's room. (Call ahead and ask whether they require that you box the bike.) Irish buses generally take bikes for IR£4.50 per day, but the design of some Irish buses precludes them from taking bicycles; call ahead and ask.

BritRail's trains accept bicycles for £3 a day; while Irish trains take bikes for IR£6 per day. Note that a ticket for the bike's passage is good for as many trains as you can ride in a day. At tiny train stations, you can't buy tickets: you'll buy your tickets from the conductor after you board. While short trains don't have a special car for bikes or other baggage, bigger trains either have a middle car with a small area for bikes and baggage or are so big that they have a special baggage car — which is where your bike will go. The latter are called "Intercity" trains. It's difficult to predict which end of the Intercity trains will accommodate the baggage car, so ask a conductor — if you can find one. Watch the train carefully as it comes in, looking for the baggage car at the front. A cage-like structure and a lack of people on the inside characterize the baggage car. If the baggage car is not in the front, it will be in the rear. The only rule is that Intercity trains terminating in London locate the baggage car in the front. If you get confused and end up at the end of the train opposite the baggage car, be prepared to run your bike to the other end.

See the *Packing* chapter for a list of items that prudent bicyclists bring on a tour. The tourist offices provide useful brochures — including maps and itineraries — about bicycling in Britain and Ireland. You can also contact the Cyclist's Touring Club (CTC), Cottrelll House 69 Meadrow Godalming, Surrey GU7 3HS, England, tel. 01483 417217; ask if they can provide you with an updated list of British buses which accept bicycles.

7. itinerary suggestions

Traveling by motor vehicle offers unparalleled access to the land and to the people and creatures that inhabit it. This is the most redeemable property of motor travel, and you should evoke it to imbue your itinerary with a vital integrity, like a garment designer who exploits the most enchanting property of a fiber to invest a piece with character. If you weave your itinerary with a spirit of adventure, with a desire to learn about places and people*and*

about yourself, with a willingness to shed the familiar, a willingness to change, you'll find it quickened by the unexpected; you'll feel it assuming wonderful dimensions; you'll put it on and go go go, and it'll fit like a glove. Yet you must also reckon many mundane if not tiresome issues when designing your itinerary; so after I expound a bit more on the proper fiber to use, I'll discuss some patterns that these other somewhat tedious issues suggest you weave it into.

Of course you can vitalize your itinerary just by *leaving the beaten path*. But if you *religiously* follow this strategy, you'll end up a bit frustrated and minus some

great experiences. Europe is the most civilized continent in the world: humanity has run rough-shod over the expanse for untold thousands of years. As a result, there are lots of beaten paths. Many of these paths are hard to avoid; many are glorious and should be sought.

What's most remarkable, then, about the state of the continent is its ubiquitous and seemingly irrepressible natural beauty. From the verdant Pyrénées to the savannah-like wilds of Hoge Veluwe National Park in the Netherlands, from the dusty plains of Southern Spain to the misty and precipitous fjords of Norway, from the stretching lochs of Scotland to the angel-hair falls on the sculpted cheeks of Swiss valleys, wonderful nature waits both on and off the beaten path.

As for Europe's civilization, it hasn't yielded fully to the virus of pyramid-bedecked strip malls, coast-to-coast culture-clones, and all the homogenizing effects of

20th-century machinery. In the villages of France, people yet ride rickety black bicycles with a baguette strapped across the rear rack; and groups of old men sit-out the afternoon on corners along the main roads, recounting and making and becoming stories. In Scotland and Wales and Ireland, farmers still call to their children the ancient Gaelic language. Alongside tidal rivers in Portugal, knotty-knuckled fishermen stand, leather-skinned and wincing, in the heavy afternoon, their fingers moving furiously to untangle nets, everything else—from their thick-soled black shoes to their greasy blue-gray pants to their bent backs to the hang of their necks to the slow sideways turns of their heads in the dense shadows of their hats to the oil blue sky—seeming sapped of time and swollen with the ocean's inertia; jazz drifts from the restaurants there and drops in the street. Levity is the rule not far away in Spain, where past low white-washed houses on dusty dirt streets, black-clad men beneath thin black hats ride high in the saddle and hugged from behind by women whose long dresses caparison the horses too. Even in tourist-choked Venice you can stroll as the lone anachronism in alleyways under windows open to the ever coming and

peaceful night, the meal-time cling-clangs and banter of ghostly Venetians the repast of your haunt. *This must be exactly the way it was,* you'll think.

Indeed, from our perspective ghosts still pass for neighbors in Europe: they live on and compose the physical and cultural fabric of the continent. But as such, these ghosts are dynamic and cannot be captured by canned descriptions or preconceived notions—although they will play along. Consider the words of esteemed historian Daniel J. Boorstin.

> Modern tourist guides [circa 1961] have helped raise tourist expectations. And they have provided the natives—from Kaiser Wilhelm down to the villagers of the Chichacestenango—with a detailed and itemized list of what is expected of them and when. These are the up-to-date scripts for actors on the tourists' stage.

Yet if you let the natives tender their story instead of encouraging them to reinforce yours, you may even make friends with a few. In fact *they*—rather than some book—should function as your primary guides.

Nevertheless, you should use a good guidebook or two. Indeed, I specifically designed this book to go hand in hand with one by leaving out detailed descriptions of

sights, accommodations, etc. Guidebooks should function as the islands of information from which you launch journeys of true discovery. In other words, sometimes it's best to put your trust in a guidebook and sometimes it's best to put the guide away.

Besides, you don't wanna work too hard at having a good time: such work can be a pain and it tends to be *mis*guided. Remember the fecundity of the unexpected I spoke of in the *Why Drive?* chapter? How the wise traveler—indeed the *true* traveler—must ultimately surrender to it? Here's what intrepid traveler and novelist Lawrence Durrell had to say about that.

> Journeys, like artists, are born not made. A thousand different circumstances contribute to them, few of them willed or determined by the will—whatever we may think.

An example of this fecundity is a visit I made to the little town of Dômme, in France's Dordogne River valley. I happened to meet an American woman at one of the valley's many caves that house prehistoric paintings. She told me I *must* go to Dômme. She didn't offer much more advice, just that I should go. I'd planned to go to Bordeaux that day; I went to Dômme instead. Well, the view of the valley from the bluff Dômme sits on overwhelmed me as much as a stretch of peaceful space can. Later in my journeys I met a guy who became a good friend, and I told him about the view at Dômme; I was proud to possess this relatively esoteric piece of travel knowledge, and I enjoyed relating the experience, wrestling with it to draw some meaning, verbally painting its picture, making it mine. When I returned home, that friend sent me a letter with this quote by one of my favorite writers, Henry Miller.

> Just to glimpse the black, mysterious river at Dômme from the beautiful bluff at the edge of town is something to be grateful for all of one's life. I believe that this great peaceful region of France will always be a sacred spot for man and that when the cities have killed off the poets this will be the cradle of poets to come . . . it gives me hope for the future of the race, for the future of the earth itself. . . . The Dordogne will live on just as dreams live on and nourish the souls of men.

It was as if back there at Dômme I'd looked at a great painting for the first time — with no preconceptions — and felt exactly what the painter had felt when he created it. Indeed, many artists and art historians abhor the trite explanations which plaques or tapes afford the museum-goer. Such connoisseurs prefer to open themselves to the art rather than to some canned description of it; they trust primarily their own reactions; they know this approach is their only hope of maximally experiencing the art. It's like when you nudge a child and say, "Go take a look": you may wanna describe a wonder to the child, but you know it's in their best interests to let them discover it for themselves. Once a writer describes a place and once you've read that description before arriving there, the place, in at least one way, is lost to you forever: your impression of that place will always be distilled through the eyes and words of another. Not an altogether bad thing, but not the type of thing that makes for discoveries. My original ignorance of that natural work of art that is the view from Dômme, my original ignorance of Henry Miller's or any other writer's or traveler's description it, lets me claim my experience of the place as my own; it let me experience a discovery. And long after I left Dômme, that ignorance let me truly connect with the very thoughts — seemingly still wet in the brain — of one of my favorite writers. Sometimes it's better to learn about a place after you've traveled to it.

Still, most of us already have a collection of knickknack notions about Europe, ideas that we tend to employ as the linchpins of our itineraries. Of course these ideas work just fine to support a bric-a-brac set of experiences, but they give way under an itinerary laden with reality. And that's what we're after isn't it, *reality*. But how to come up with an itinerary that will sop it up?

Well, since the ideal teachers are waiting all over Europe, and since I'm just as likely as you to bias the itineraries I come up with, and, what's more, since it'd be hypocritical to define a path when it's my stated goal to help you leave the beaten path, I'm not gonna delineate specific itineraries. Besides, there are already a handful of guides — which I describe in the *Resources* chapter — that do this. But not only are such itineraries suspect spiritually, they're suspect practically as well: it's virtually impossible to properly treat the continuum that a motor vehicle opens to you. Famed Czech author Milan Kundera captured the essence of these basic faults when he wrote,

> A route differs from a road . . . because it is merely a line that connects one point with

another. A route has no meaning in itself; its meaning derives entirely from the two points that it connects. A road is a tribute to space. Every stretch of road has meaning in itself and invites us to stop. A route is the triumphant devaluation of space, which thanks to it has been reduced to a mere obstacle to human movement and a waste of time.

In attempting to strike the right balance between interacting with the locals (or, for that matter, with your fellow travelers), using a guidebook or two, using your own head, and surrendering to the fecundity of the unexpected, you'll naturally imbue your travels with the kind of spirit that makes for invaluable experiences.

Nonetheless, a systematic analysis of more mundane issues is necessary to manage that effort and let it work its magic amid the unavoidable constraints of time and space and resources, constraints that suggest certain patterns for the grand scale design of your itinerary. In the *On the Road* section, I provide the kind of nuts-and-bolts information that should prove helpful if not essential in this grand-scale planning. You'll notice that I include no topographical and very little road-condition

information in that section's *Country-by-Country Information* chapter. I omit the first kind of info because I don't wanna waste your time with verbal descriptions of landscapes when maps can pictorially give you much more precise, thorough and immediate information. A picture is worth a thousand words, right? Even non-topographic maps are filled with clues about the nature of the landscape: you can bet that the more winding the roads the more problematic and interesting the landscape.

It's worth noting here that mountainous countries such as Austria, Norway and Switzerland boast mountain tunnels — oftentimes marked on maps by dotted lines — which allow roads or trains to carry motor vehicles through. Many of these tunnels are disconcertingly long and many run below natural passes and in an essentially parallel relation to a much older road which painstakingly but beautifully negotiates the vertical as well as the horizontal. I detail all these on a country-by-country basis in the *Country-by-Country Information* chapter.

In Switzerland especially it's often impossible to "make good time" unless you use the expressways and tunnels. Check your Switzerland road map carefully when

planning your schedule. But besides realizing the limits that the hyper-meandering roads impose, you should realize the potential they offer — increasingly breathtaking views on every turn. Plan to drive for driving's sake, and try to minimally constrain yourself with time-related issues. Ask yourself this question: Why do I wanna drive quickly and horizontally through Switzerland?

Switzerland's postal coaches are famous for challenging the third dimension and thus providing unrivaled service to the extents of the country. Experienced chauffeurs with special training captain these coaches (which have three independent brake systems) on half- and full-day excursions along the backroads — both high and low. You can even take hand luggage of up to 50 kg (110 lbs.) free of charge.

As for road conditions, virtually none of the roads in 1990s Europe constitute a prohibitive threat to your safety or your plans; their condition should play little to no role in the planning of your itinerary. Apart from most of the former Yugoslavia, go where you wanna go.

The relative length of a country's description in the *Country-by-Country Information* chapter is an intrinsic clue to the

itinerary suggestions

amount of planning the country's terrain and infrastructure require before you can confidently navigate them. To form the bulk of each country's description in that chapter, I combine information regarding customs requirements, concessions for hostellers, toll roads, mountain passes, fuel considerations, unique road signs, rules of the road, driving tips, parking tips, bank hours, shop hours, national holidays, BBC broadcasting hours and corresponding radio frequencies, and how to handle breakdown or accident or other emergency situations. Countries with toll roads demand more attention if you wanna avoid paying tolls. Mountainous terrain of course, as alluded to earlier, demands especially careful planning because of the up-and-down and winding nature of the roadways—and the unusually slow and difficult-to-predict pace of travel that results.

Still, the information I include in the *Country-by-Country Information* chapter functions in large part as insurance. Your instincts will quickly process most of the driving situations you'll encounter; and what's too complex for them will probably be easy pickings for your analytical side. Hey, besides this or any other guide, you've got untold millions of years of evolution going for you. Indeed, you'll do your best driving by relaxing and letting these instincts and quick decisions take you where they may. This is a primary reason I made a separate *On the Road* section: to emphasize that it's both more realistic and more cost-effective to address many of these issues when you're out on the road rather than when you're at home. Why overwhelm yourself with info you're likely to forget before you need it?

What's more, saving some studying and decisions until later tends to jive with the spirit of adventure and the fecundity of the unexpected that I discussed earlier. Indeed, it's arguable that you should minimize the planning you do each travel-day. There's so much to do and see in Europe that you'll never be at a loss for wonderful new experiences: everything will tend to fall into place. This tendency is especially strong in a motoring tour. Despite all the flexibility that a motor vehicle gives you, it also constrains you. The reasonable per-day distance associated with motor travel is much less than that associated with rail travel. Immediate options are limited: the next day's destination should lie within roughly a two hundred-mile radius. The route that tends to emerge and often makes sense is some sort of circuit or circular route. As such, the next destination usually emerges as obvious.

For those of you without much time in which to travel, adhering to a practical circular route may keep you from experiencing the kind of variety that you wanna experience. Well, by putting your vehicle on a train or by dropping off a rented or leased vehicle somewhere other than where you picked it up, you can effect linear itineraries. Driving an essentially straight route allows you to experience great variety at a leisurely pace and in a relatively short time.

The French rail system, *SNCF,* offers a service called *"Trains-autos-couchettes"* that can take you and your car and passengers overnight to destinations in Austria, France, Germany, Italy, Portugal, Spain, and Switzerland. Finland's trains also provide such a service. In fact, the train systems of most countries offer some sort of auto-train service (called "Motorail" in English, *"Autoreisezuge"* in German, *"Treni per Auto Accompagnate"* in Italian, and *"Trenes de Autos"* in Spanish). Look for signs reading "auto/train" and depicting car-carrying flat beds or box cars. See *Appendix I* for detailed descriptions and fares of the French, Italian and Spanish services.

Apart from offering the merits of a linear route, the advantages of traveling by Motorail include savings on gas and tolls (you'll take toll roads if you wanna make the best possible time; figure about $0.10 per mile, $0.06 per kilometer) and the avoidance of wear and tear on your vehicle and yourself. And of course traveling overnight by train frees the daylight hours for other pursuits. Some sort of sleeping accommodation is compulsory on overnight *SNCF* Motorail services. These accommodations range from first class single-bed sleepers costing $160 to second class couchettes holding six berths costing $16 per.

But the savings don't necessarily stop with the above. The European-wide hotel chains Ibis, Mercure, Novotel, and Minotel grant reduced rates to *SNCF* (not just Motorail) travelers, as does Avis. Several ferry services do the same—but for Motorailers only. These include the following which cross between the British Isles and the continent: Brittany Ferries, Hoverspeed, *Le Shuttle* (through the Chunnel), P&O European Ferries, and Stena Sealink. See *Appendix I* for detailed

schedules of these reduced fares. Motorailers will also get discounts when plying the sea between France, Corsica or Sardinia on *SNCM Ferryterranée,* and between Spain and the Balearic Islands on *Transmediterranea*.

Stena Sealink also offers tickets combining Motorail service with their Landbridge ferry service that connects Ireland to the continent by way of Britain. The offerings include one-way ferry passage plus one-way Motorail travel, return ferry plus one-way Motorail, and return ferry plus return Motorail. Let's take one example: return ferry to Britain plus one-way Motorail between Rome, Italy, and Calais, France. The corresponding fare for two adults who initiate travel during the period early July to early September is approximately $840; each additional adult pays about $192; each child 4–11 years of age, about $103. The return ferry service *alone* for a car, van or caravan plus driver and up to four extra adults costs something like $339 during roughly the same period.

Whether a linear route will save you money depends on several factors. Let's say, for example, you got a good deal on a return flight to London and you wanna taste a little of England before getting a car

and driving at a leisurely pace to Rome. Let's also say that you have three weeks to get to Rome and back to London. Finally, let's say you lease a *Renault* for free delivery in Calais. One option would be to pay the $190 return charge to leave the car in Rome, before returning to Calais by train at a cost of about $190 *per* adult (not including the roughly $75 charge for a sleeper), not to mention children, or by plane to London at a cost of $250–350 *per* passenger (if you buy the plane ticket on the London market, where tickets are exceptionally cheap). Another option would be to make flight arrangements into London and out of Rome—arrangements, however, which may cost much more than a simple return flight to and from London. Motorail allows you to take delivery of the car in Calais, drive it to Rome, and put it on an overnight train back to Calais at a cost of about $450 for the car and the driver, $135 for each extra adult, $68 for each extra child 4–11 years of age, and, say, $75 per person for a two-berth sleeper.

Regardless of whether you plan to travel a circuitous or linear route, you'll have to start from a city. But you do *not* need a motor vehicle to see a European city. At least you don't wanna begin your

itinerary suggestions

trip by doing lots of driving in a city: not only is it unnecessary, but it's also the most difficult driving you'll encounter in Europe. Plan to see the city in the days before you get the vehicle or in the days after you return it—or both. I recommended you do both. A vibrant city may be just what the doctor ordered to battle the jet lag at the beginning of your trip; while as a more experienced European traveler, you'll be more relaxed at the end of your trip and able enjoy the sophisticated side of a place like Paris much more than you were in the beginning.

Once off the beaten path you should have little trouble finding quality and relatively inexpensive accommodations—even during the high season. Unless you plan to rent a property or properties, consider making few accommodation reservations, some to cover the nights you'll spend in the city or cities you fly in or out of and some, perhaps, for your first day or two on the road, just to encourage a smooth start. Abstain from developing a detailed *schedule*. Also, think twice before driving on a holiday weekend. Not only are the roads more crowded on such weekends but so are hotels and restaurants. The Easter holiday and the two weeks around it play host to the worst crowds and traffic—especially in Southern Europe. On the other hand, many interesting festivals take place around holidays. My advice is that you plan your trip to include a national holiday but that you don't plan to travel much during that holiday.

To estimate distances, mark your map's scale on the edge of a piece of paper and then move the marked edge around your general route, adding the miles or kilometers as you go and using your imagination to add miles or kilometers to winding sections. Most atlases and maps, however, boast tables relating driving distances between major cities.

If you plan to do the classic grand tour, consider circling south early in the year, enjoying the early season warmth and avoiding the high season heat, humidity, crowds and prices.

The further south you go the more prevalent becomes petty crime. Most European countries don't experience a high incidence of vehicle theft. Unless you're driving a very expensive vehicle, thieves probably won't consider taking the vehicle itself. The taxis in Western Europe are evidence of this—they're *Mercedes Benz*. Still, the South is noted for its high incidence of theft *from* vehicles. The cities of Seville, Spain, and Naples, Italy, are infamous hotbeds of such crime. Instead of taking your vehicle into Naples, stay on the Ischia or Sorrento Peninsula and take the catamaran or *aliscafi* to the city. Otherwise, try parking out of view of the streets in such cities, or park on the street but near a place where traffic police are working or in front of banks or embassies where security measures are in place already. Parking on the even the busiest street in broad daylight won't help. Thieves, usually in packs of three or four, cruise the streets looking for foreign-registered vehicles, which they pilfer in a matter of seconds.

No matter where you are in Europe, don't leave any valuables in your vehicle if you can help it. Leave the glove compartment open and emptied. If you have a hatchback, take off the shield that conceals the trunk space. Pull down the back seat that gives access to the trunk. Consider leaving the passenger door unlocked: thieves will get in a locked door easily, but they may break a lock or a window doing it. In short, don't tempt; make the vehicle look as if someone else beat the thief to the prize.

You can even make your vehicle repulsive to certain thieves by leaving a lifelike, rubber tarantula or snake in full view on the front passenger seat or on the open door of the glove compartment. This advice may sound ridiculous, but even the most hardened criminal has his phobias. And besides, you'll get a kick out of knowing that you—who most petty European thieves would take to be a fumbling, naive tourist—might be able to freak out one of these jerks.

On top of these tactics, you should take care to avoid a more much more rare type of thief, the type that's not deterred by the prospect of a confrontation with you. From Madrid comes a story about how such thieves might operate. The rental agencies at Madrid's airport park their vehicles in unprotected and unsupervised areas. This being so, thieves in Madrid have learned to puncture the tires of these vehicles, wait outside the parking area, follow the exiting vehicles, and rob them when the unsuspecting driver pulls over with a flat. Always be wary of roadside help offered by anyone other than a police officer or civil guard. If someone stops to help, ask them to contact the police for you. And conversely, don't *you* stop to help a stranded motorist: in the more marginal parts of Europe, roadside brigands are known to feign car trouble then rob you and/or steal your vehicle when you stop to help.

Undoubtedly you'll hear horror stories about driving in Italy. Try to evaluate the source. For example, on my first tour I met a family from Oregon who'd just finished driving in Italy; they resounded that driving in Rome was ridiculous chaos. Two days later, however, I met a couple from Manhattan who laughed and said driving in Rome was a breeze. As I noted in the *Why Drive?* chapter, fewer deaths occur per million registered vehicles in Italy than per million registered vehicles in the United States. After driving extensively in Italy I'll say this: The cars move fast, but the streets in the cities are surprisingly wide, and the highways are fine. Italy, after all, is the home of the paved road. I'm from Iowa; some people call me "Corn Boy"; I've had fun.

Although I wanna abstain from giving specifics, there are at least two campgrounds in Italy that demand special mention. One of these is in Florence, immediately below and to the right of the Piazzale Michelangelo as you face the city from the Piazzale. The view from the Piazzale at sunset is unforgettable: the River Arno running from the grapey night, hugging the bluff's base, passing the silhoutted mountain that is Brunelleschi's magnificent dome, cutting through the city's plateau of desultory red roofs, suffering bridge after antique bridge, and, in a long French kiss with the dying day, taking on before the folded arms of the horizon's hills the glow of memory and promise . . . a tableau of time. The view from the campground is essentially the same. The other campground worth mentioning is across the lagoon from none other than Venice. Camp on the shore and look across to the glorious city. From the campground entrance take the regular boat service across the lagoon for a ten-minute approach to the city that'll have you pinching yourself, thinking that such things were reserved for movie stars.

If, on the other hand, you choose to park at Venice's huge Tronchetto garage, you may be met on approach by a man— seeming to be an employee—who'll direct you to the right side of the garage, away from the Vaporetto dock. He'll try to help you with your bags and usher you to a water taxi charging rip-off fares of about $100. If you balk he'll claim that the boat line you want is not in service. Just ignore

itinerary suggestions

these low lifes and head to the left side of the garage for fairly priced parking and a cheap boat ride to the city center.

Looking to the east of Italy the question arises: How to do Greece by car? This is a good question. Currently, the best answer *may* be that you shouldn't. The war in the former Yugoslavia makes the most direct overland route to Greece impractical if not insane, and traveling across the Adriatic accompanied by a vehicle means a costly ferry ride. (See the *Ferries and the Chunnel* chapter.) Regardless, the myriad-island nature of Greece doesn't lend itself to driving. And the Greek roads are generally the worst in Europe. Perhaps as a direct result of these poor roads, Greece endures Europe's second highest incidence of motor-vehicle fatalities—and the *worst* accident rate in terms of the number of collisions per vehicle. Furthermore, the ports at Bari and Brindisi, Italy, are infamous for their thieves; think twice before you leave your vehicle at one of these ports.

But when will you have a better chance, right? You'll have a better chance if you fly in or return to London, where a return flight to Greece costs less than $150. Persons using train passes should consider doing Greece separately as well. Train travel in Greece is slow and frustrating; the bus system is much better. Note that by going to Greece later in the year, you can avoid the big crowds and the high prices that go with them. Furthermore, you can avoid the uncomfortably hot days and nights. May is considered the best month in which to visit Greece. By October the rains return—but only *one* day a week on average. And averaging 60° Fahrenheit, nights are cooler and more comfortable in May and October (on average, 12° Fahrenheit cooler than July and August, 6° Fahrenheit cooler than June and September). Ferries serve some Greek islands on a daily basis and some on a weekly basis. If you wanna maintain maximum flexibility in your travel plans, consider traveling only to those islands that the ferries serve daily.

You can travel to Turkey by motor vehicle via the Istanbul route—an expressway bypasses the city—or by ferry. Note that Turkey's train system is quite bad; buses there offer much more timely and extensive service and cost only about $1.50 per hour. Perhaps the bus travel is so good because Turkey's roads are surprisingly good; don't hesitate to drive in Turkey.

I mentioned earlier that theft of vehicles is not a problem in Western Europe, but this is not the case in a place like Poland. Poland suffers (or *benefits,* you might say) from a very high rate of theft of western vehicles, which, once swiped, are taken to Russia and sold. (In Poland the taxis are not *Mercedes Benz!*) The same is true for Prague, in the Czech Republic, and for the Baltic States of Estonia, Latvia and Lithuania. In these places consider parking near a train station in outlying areas or towns that tourists don't frequent. Thieves hang out where the tourists hang out. You can take one of the frequent trains (there's usually one every hour) into the major metro areas, where you don't need a vehicle anyway. The ride will cost just a few dollars. I once left my car for four days near the train station in Plzen, the birthplace of pilsner beer and the home of the world-famous *Pilsner Urquell* brew. From there I took a $3 train ride the remaining one hundred miles into Prague. To read the train schedules, however, you should know that in Slavic languages like Czech and Polish the preposition *Do, do,* or *go,* pronounced "doe", means *to* (literally, *until),* as in "departing to"; while the preposition *om,* pronounced "ott", means *from,* as in "arriving from." There's a good chance, however, that thieves *won't* rip-off your vehicle if you drive into the major metropolitan areas of these countries—especially if it's ugly and you're careful. Of course a detterent such as "The Club" or an installed kill switch (standard now on many new European-version vehicles) will help, as will turning your wheels all the way to the curb and engaging the steering-wheel lock.

If you plan to drive a *BMW* or the like, you may be justified in fearing the criminals of Southern and Eastern Europe. As such, one compromise option to consider in the initial stages of planning your journey is the following: take the trains in Southern and Eastern Europe and drive in northwest Europe. Not only is crime more prevalent in Southern and Eastern Europe, but the train tickets are much cheaper there as well. For example, as I noted in *The Special Case of the British Isles* chapter, the number of kilometers you can travel per dollar in various countries or sections of Europe are as follows: Turkey—40 km; Eastern Europe—17 km; Spain—13 km; Italy—12 km; France—10 km; Germany—8 km; Scandinavia—7 km; England—6 km. To take advantage of these price gradients, you'd have to buy point-to-point train tickets or single-country passes instead of inter-country passes. Besides the issues of crime and rail fares, there's the issue of language. The populations of Southern and Eastern Europe do not speak English with anywhere near the frequency or skill as do the populations of Europe's northwest. In the northwest you can realize the full potential of your motor vehicle by getting out to meet and actually *converse* with the people who don't see tourists very often. I've already mentioned that it's better to *buy* a vehicle in the northwest. Well, if you do buy, staying in that region with the vehicle will keep your fuel costs down, and if any problems arise—and they are less likely to arise in the more temperate, industrialized and Anglicized northwest—you can deal with them much easier. Defining the limits of your itinerary on a more geological basis, however, may be the best approach. Here's an idea: Don't drive south of the great mountain ranges (the Alps and the Pyrénées) or east of the former Iron Curtain. You'll want the motor vehicle in the mountains, however, to propel you up into beautiful scenery and hard-to-get-at hideaways.

The criminal, economic, and cultural issues which prompt consideration of the above compromises are complex and generally not weighty. I don't wanna give the impression that enough circumstances, dangerous or otherwise, exist to justify a broad recommendation of these compromises. On the contrary, I recommend that you resist, in spirit at least, such compromises, for they are based largely on fear and fear alone—and fear is usually overblown and much more likely to sabotage your trip than are criminal elements or monetary or cultural constraints.

There's another grand plan which combines train and motor vehicle travel, a plan which is *not* basically a compromise and which *does* arise from weighty issues. Because a motor vehicle is usually a liability in major cities, you may wanna use the high-speed trains to dart disjointedly to the major cities you wish to see, doing this either before you get a motor vehicle or after you return one. You can use the motor vehicle to explore the smaller towns and the countryside. This way you'll experience all the major facets of the European travel infrastructure and subculture, avoiding the most negative aspects of each while exploiting the most positive. The one drawback to this plan is the unbalanced nature of the itinerary—a continuous series of cities followed by a continuous series of small towns and countrysides. Although I hesitate to call such series monotonous, they may not constitute the proper balance for you. You can be flexible, however, using the train to go to some smaller towns or countryside stops and using the motor vehicle to make an occasional excursion into a larger town or city. You may also wanna combine this plan with the compromise of taking trains in Southern and Eastern Europe and driving in northwest Europe.

Moving north we come to the land of my forebears: Scandinavia Norway's cost of living is the highest in Europe—you'll pay $30 a night for a bed in an Oslo or Bergen *hostel*. Surprisingly, however, I've spent less money per day there than in any of the other countries I've visited. Why the paradox? Norway, Sweden and Finland sanction or tolerate camping on just about any unfenced land—even if private—as long as you're 100 meters (about 100 yards) from any dwellings, stay no more than two nights, and pick up after yourself. The long summer days in Scandinavia make camping there easier still. Bring a good sleeping bag though: it can get cold. I've spent three-fourths of my Norwegian nights free-camping.

Sounds like a lot of camping, I know. But Norway's scenery is truly incredible, especially her fjord country—maybe the world's most salient precinct of the possible. And the civilization is ideally and wonderfully integrated: In Norway you always feel close to nature, but never far from civilization. If you do go to Norway, be sure to visit Oslo's Frogner Park. Over 150 granite and bronze statues sculpted over some thirty years by Gustav Vigeland stand in the park—the most remarkable collection of sculpture in Europe, in my opinion. Admittance to the park is free of charge.

Late spring or early summer is the best time to visit Scandinavia. The longest days occur in late June, when it's light until midnight. There *is* snow in the summer, high atop the fjords. In fact, you can ski in the summer near Stryn, Norway, about six hours by car northwest of Oslo. Check the Norway section of the *Country-by-Country Information* chapter for information about road closings.

Of course you'll have to end your motoring tour in a city or town. Note that Paris makes a good transition point. Not only is Paris one of the best places in the world in which to hangout without a vehicle, but if you plan to continue traveling you may be able to sponge a still-valid Eurailpass off one of the many travelers who fly home from there. With this ticket you can get to Ireland and travel around it for free. This trick is illegal, however. If a conductor or ferry operator asks for your passport and compares it to the name on the pass, you may be in some trouble. I'd say such an investigation is quite unlikely and that by far the biggest threat associated with such chicanery is the threat to your good conscience.

Several factors coincide to make London the best place in which to transition or conclude a grand tour. First, you'll make many Aussie and Kiwi friends while traveling on the continent. Most of these folks base their travels out of Britain—London especially—where they've come to spend a couple of years. Late in the summer they tend to return to Britain to work and pay for their summer fun. As such, you can travel the Isles with these temporary Brits or stay at their place and avoid the high costs of London's accommodations. And it's likely that after showing this book to these notoriously high-spirited travelers, you can persuade them to chip in and help you buy a motor vehicle in which you can then travel the Isles together. The market will be a buyer's in late summer. Second, London is the home of the cheap flight. You can fly from London to Greece for the aforementioned $150 return, or to Moscow for $300 return, or to Bangkok for $300 one way, or to Sydney for $425 one way, or to Auckland for $550 one way, or to New York for $150 one way, or to Chicago for $275 one way, or to Los Angeles for $200 one way. Third, your command of the local language will allow you to make complicated arrangements for extensions to your trip. If you do plan an extension to your trip, stop in Stanford's Travel Bookshop, 12 Long Acre, Covenant Garden, London: they claim to offer the largest selection of travel literature in the world. Fourth, note that in the beginning stages of a trip you'll be psyched to try other languages, but by the end you'll pang for good 'ol English. Finally, a special note for budget travelers on a *serious* budget: unlike those on the continent, most hostels in the British Isles take Visa and MasterCard, so if you're running low on funds, you can finance more of your traveling with a credit card.

Also contributing to the above argument are three factors which make Britain an outstanding bookend to a grand tour—

whether it stands at the beginning or the end. First, Britain does not honor Eurailpasses but it does offer many exciting alternatives. Second, the English Channel and Britain's left-side driving convention tend to make transporting a vehicle between Britain and the continent an unwise venture. Finally there's the weather. Rain falls in the British Isles an average of two to three times a week *all year round*. Don't get too cute and go to the British Isles with sun and warmth figured into your plan; sun and warmth are not why you go there. Although the waters that surround the British Isles buffer them from grand climate changes, this just succeeds in making the weather consistently *blah*. But you can work the British Isles' blahness to your advantage by realizing that most people equate high temperatures with good weather and good times. The *vast* majority of people visit the Isles in July and August when the temperature is highest. But what's this? It *rains* much more in July and August than it does earlier in the year. And in the South of England and in Ireland it also rains less in September and October than it does in July and August. A tour bus operator in Killarney, Ireland, told me that in July and August up to 150 tour buses work

the Kerry Peninsula; while in October there are only five or so a day. He also noted the fortuitous nature of the colder temperatures: the days tend to be clearer after the night frosts. Of course, the lower temperatures and smaller crowds mean lower prices and fewer hassles as well. Strongly consider combining the world-famous Edinburgh Festival—held from mid August to early September—with a September and October tour of the Isles, but make your reservations in the spring for accommodation in Edinburgh during the festival. As for spring around the British Isles, you'll love England and Holland in late April and May if you're into flowers. Note also that June is considered the best month—weather-wise—in which to visit Britain.

September/October seems to be festival time in Ireland.

Yeats International Theater Fest—late August to late September.

Writers Festival—Dublin, late September.

Dublin Theater Festival—early October.

Cork Guiness Jazz Festival—late October.

Here are some other major European festivals and happenings.

Midnight Sun—in the Arctic Circle, Scandinavia, the 4 weeks around June 20.

Running of the Bulls—Pamplona, Spain, second week in July.

Oktoberfest—Munich, Germany, late September.

Montreaux Jazz Festival—Montreaux, Switzerland, 2 1/2 weeks in mid July.

Cannes Film Festival—Cannes, France, May.

Semana Santa & Feria de Abril—Seville, Spain, late March & April.

El Rocio festival—60 kilometers west-south-west of Seville, late May.

8. alternative accommodations

As travelers are becoming more sophisticated, intrepid, and value-conscious, they're looking for accommodations that promise a *real* connection with the European people and landscape *and* with fellow travelers—a connection that the modern-day hotel or motel doesn't foster. Well, between hostels, pensions, camping, rentals, homestays, farmstays, home exchanges, volunteer work, paid work, and study there are increasingly many such accommodation options to choose from.

Hostels

Hostels were initiated in post-war Germany as lodges in which to fatten- and brighten-up German youths who'd suffered the ravages of World War II. Hostels are much more than that now—although they still play host to swarming school groups on occasion. Today, hostels operate Europe-wide in the cities, in the villages, in the countryside, in castles, on islands, along the beaches, on sailing ships, and in the mountains. Many of these are spartan, but many rival hotels—offering single rooms, doubles, triples, and quads, apart from the classic summer camp-style bunkhouse arrangement. Most have an area for socializing. Some even sport bars. One hostel I've stayed at, nestled near the base of small medieval town gracing the lip of a yawning Provençal valley, boasts a crystal clear swimming pool extending into a vineyard and serves up a delicious meal— complete with all the wine you want— each night. And the average hostel charges just $12 for a night's stay. As such, hostels attract interesting and fun people of all ages from all over, who either seek out or find themselves caught up in hostelling's unparalleled and positive social dynamic, people with whom you'll exchange travel advice, jokes, addresses, cooking duties and more, people who'll contribute to and share some of the best days of your life. As travel guru Rick Steves says, "Hostelling is a philosophy. A hosteller trades services and privacy for a chance to live simply and in cooperation with people from around the world."

Most people associate hostels with the college-age crowd. It's true that the clientele slants toward the young; but middle-class families, school groups, the elderly, and professionals—young and old—frequent so-called "youth" hostels. Only Bavaria's hostels still impose an age restriction (26 years and under). I've met a jazz musician, a sculptor, an architect, and a private detective in hostels; I've met actors, engineers, Australian Golden Oldies rugby players, teachers, welders, writers, lawyers, doctors, nurses, computer programmers, a group of fifth graders in former East Germany who bashfully practiced their English on native speakers—a friend and me—for the first time; I've met families; I've met ninety-year old women; and I've met several people who work for the same international business consulting firm I once did. If people are as worthy of exploration as are continents, then each hostel is like a Pangea, a supercontinent or conglomeration of continents, waiting for you to discover it. In this sense hostels transcend the physical continent of Europe and become destinations in themselves. Often you'll hear people describing their travel plans in terms of hostels: "I'm going to [this or that] hostel," they'll say.

A remarkably high percentage of hostellers basically travel by themselves—and it's worth noting of this subset that a fantastically high percentage are young women. I say *"basically* by themselves" because a phenomenal and universal tendency exists for lone travelers to bond and band together. Often such bands end up traveling together for several days or weeks or months even, splitting up with great memories and no hard feelings whenever this or that member decides to go his or her own way. It does take a measure of courage to travel alone, but this fact helps explain why lone travelers tend to be even more interesting than people who travel in groups or with old friends. On many occasions I've sat drinking beers or eating dinner with a group of five or six travelers who were all traveling solo. These groups have always been unanimous in concluding that solo is *the best way to travel.* Indeed, solo travel results in *such* an unusual and marvelous dynamic that you'll wonder if it'll change for the better the social approach you take at home; unfortunately, though, I think it's unique to the travel circuit. In fact I've found that when I travel with even just *one* friend, we tend not to meet as many people: we're usually having a good time

as is and so don't *need* to meet others. It's this common *need,* combined with a desire to interact, that's the catalyst of the wonderful hostelling dynamic. What Arthur Frommer said is remarkably true: hostels are the "most dynamic travel facilities on earth."

And a hostelling "circuit" truly exists. On myriad occasions I've run into people I'd met one or two months previous and a thousand or two thousand miles away. Or I've met someone who'd met someone I'd met. You follow? The circuit amounts to a true and powerful, albeit transitory, community that springs from its fun-loving, gutsy, intelligent, multicultural and multinational elements and is catalyzed and intensified by amazing surroundings and the transience inspired by the plurality of those surroundings. Indeed, the hostelling community is one of the most modern communities on earth, analogous to a manifestation of the burgeoning virtual-community that exists traveling fiber optic cables.

It all reminds me of John Cllellon Holmes' description of Jack Kerouac and company.

Though they rushed back and forth across the country on the slightest pretext, gathering kicks along the way, their real journey was inward; and if they seemed to trespass most boundaries, legal and moral, it was only in the hope of finding a belief on the other side.

But apart from recognizing the inwardly spiritual journeys that many hostellers are on, you sense a collective and unmistakable vibe—still spiritual in its nature, but outwardly so—when you're tossing back a few cold ones with, say, a couple of Germans, some Italians, a South African, two Swiss, an Aussie, an Israeli, a couple of Canadians, a Kiwi, three Belgians and a Swede; it's like in e.e. cummings' *Enormous Room,* but with the players brought together by the power of peace instead of war; it's the answer to and the result of centuries of conflict; it's the superreality of a new world, the salty stuff of living history; and you drink drink drink it down.

Of course, not every hostel will jive with your sensibility or catalyze a profound tickling of your spirit. Rely first on word of mouth and second on the budget-travel guidebooks.

Many hostels belong to the Hostelling International organization. Such hostels denote themselves with the stylized logo—standard worldwide—that I show in Figure 8.1. To stay in such hostels you should get a Hostelling International (HI) membership card. You can still stay in these hostels if you don't have the card, but you'll have to pay a bit more. The card costs $10 for persons under 18 years of age, $25 for adults 18–54 years of age, $15 for persons 55 years of age and up, $35 for families with children under 16 years of age, or $250 for life. See the *Documents* chapter for instructions on how to order the card.

Aside from the lower rates at hostels, a membership in HI entitles you to numerous substantial discounts. As part of a country's description in the *Country-by-Country Information* chapter, I list those HI discounts that relate to driving and to ferry passage. Other HI discounts include reduced prices for museum admission, sporting equipment rental, and more. Even if you don't plan to stay in hostels, you may find that these discounts make membership in HI worthwhile.

Furthermore, hundreds of HI hostels operate in wonderful spots across Australia, Canada, New Zealand and the US. I bet you never even knew they were around. Such domestic hostels offer a great way to cheaply travel your home country while

Figure 8.1

Hostelling International Sign.

you act as unofficial ambassador to visiting foreigners.

Thanks to a new international computer system, you can now make reservations with participating HI hostels in over seventy countries by calling one source; in the US the number to call is 202 783 6161. You can use Visa or MasterCard to pay for the reservations. A $2 reservation fee applies. However, only make reservations if you must: your plans are likely to change. (Remember the fecundity of the unexpected.) For example, *do* make reservations for popular big-city hostels during the high season. And always make reservations in Paris, or else get to the hostel before 9:00 A.M. Some hostels, though, don't take reservations.

Hostels operating separately from the HI organization are known as "independents" and, of course, require no membership card. The services provided by these hostels tend to be better than those of HI hostels, the rules less limiting, and the atmosphere more fun and easy going. But of course this rule doesn't always hold true.

Apart from hostels located in the center of a major city, almost all offer free parking. What's more, nearly every hostel sports a well-equipped kitchen (with pots, pans, silverware, dishes, ovens, refrigerators, etc.) where you can cook your own food. Often I team up with other hostellers to cook—and clean up after—rather impressive meals. Many hostels also offer coin- or token-operated laundry facilities (soap included gratis). Of course the sink or a laundromat is always an option. (Laundromats sell soap.) Hostels provide the pillows and blankets; but many HI hostels require a "sleep sheet", a sewn-up sheet that you sleep in. If you don't have a sleep sheet, the hostel will provide one— usually for a small fee. You *could* claim

you have a sleep sheet and then proceed to use, say, your sleeping bag; but for your comfort, and to avoid these small charges piling up, it's worth making your own sleep sheet and bringing it along. You should bring a pair of ear plugs too; the little foam kind are the best. These beauties will add at least one hour of sleep to each of your nights in a hostel. Even if you're in a room with five other people, ear plugs will make it sound like an empty nest. Buy your ear plugs at a pharmacy at home or in Europe, or get them free of charge when you order something such as a sleep sack or neck pouch from Europe Through the Backdoor. (See the *Resources* chapter.) You might also want an eye mask; North Americans can buy a mask and ear plugs from the marvelous *Magellan's Travel Essentials* catalog. (Again, see the *Resources* chapter.)

Hostels have a reputation as being places of theft, a reputation that's largely undeserved. No budget traveler ever comes home and rattles off a list of all the hostels where nobody stole something from them, but be sure they'll tell you of the hostels where such a theft occurred. In other words, these things tend to get blown out of proportion. Many hostels offer lockers for

your use—some with a coin-operated lock, some without a lock. I bring a chain and padlock that I use on lockers without locks and to lock my pack to something if there's no locker at all. Never have any of my possessions been stolen while in a hostel. Yet I'm careful: I take a clue from nature and sleep with my valuables between my legs, and I don't leave other things in view if I can help it—out of sight is out of mind. The overwhelming number of hostellers wouldn't think of stealing your stuff, but it only takes one to ruin your day.

Many hostels—usually only HI hostels—enforce a daily lockout, from, say, 10:00 A.M. to 5:00 P.M. During this time the staff cleans the place. Usually a lockout means that you can't enter your room, but it may mean you can't enter any part of the hostel. Lockouts are an infamous drawback to hostelling, but at least they force you to get off your butt. Don't worry, the operators of the hostel will let you leave your possessions in the room, or, if you're gonna check out later that day, they'll store your possessions in a safe place. To keep costs down, some hostels ask each guest to perform a small chore each morning; try to do it with pleasure.

Pensions

Pensions constitute a major alternative to hostels—especially in the South. Pensions are cheap hotels, often as cheap or cheaper than hostels; but they cater to travelers rather than the down and out, and as such the room-quality tends to be much better than you might expect. (Be sure, however, to check before you pay.) You either get your own room and key or share a room with other travelers. A chief advantage over hostels is that you can come and go as you please. What's more, pensions tend to be located right in the thick of the action. They don't, though, offer the cooking or laundry facilities that most hostels do.

If you plan to stay in a combination of hostels and pensions, and if you plan to adhere to common budget-travel principles, you should budget at least $30 a day to cover your lodging, food, drink, sightseeing, metropolitan public transport, and miscellaneous expenses.

Camping

Most Europeans view camping as being cheap, socially oriented accommodation rather than the rugged, back-to-nature experience that North Americans tend to picture. As such, organized campgrounds are good places to meet the middle class sector of European society, a somewhat different crowd than you'll find in hostels or hotels. Still, since Europeans are relatively reserved, European campers probably won't come up and introduce themselves to you; you should make the first effort.

As detailed in the *Why Drive?* chapter, European campgrounds usually itemize fees—charging for each person, tent, vehicle and trailer. Campgrounds there are rated on a four-star scale; and apart from the basics, four-star operations are likely to provide several of the following: laundromat, grocery store, restaurant, bar, disco, swimming pool, water slide, sauna, tennis courts, fitness facilities, miniature golf course, horseback riding, a library, and a playground. Many campgrounds also offer mobile homes or bungalows for rent. Unless you plan to rent one of these, don't worry about reservations: European campgrounds are never "full"; the operators will pack you in if need be. But beware that most campgrounds lock the gate for the night at about 10:00 P.M. and for lunch from noon to 2:00 P.M. Also, most don't provide picnic tables, and, sad to say, disallow campfires. Though the toilets can be perplexing, I'd rather let you discover their wonders for yourself than force you to suffer through a description here. As for the showers, expect all varieties; and if using one that's token operated, make sure you know how much time a token gives you.

So many well-marked campgrounds dot the European landscape that finding them is a no-brainer. Look for the international camping sign: either a "C" with a tent superimposed or else a stylized trailer. Greece, however, denotes campgrounds with a sign reading *"EOT"*. And if you find a campground labeled *"FKK"* or *"Frei Körper Kultur"*, you've found a clothing-optional campground. The major cities, too, harbor popular campgrounds. For instance, Thalkirchen campground on the Isar River just twenty minutes outside Munich is a wonderful spot, bordered by the river and within a forest and boasting cafes and bars and an international clientele. Most budget guidebooks describe the best campgrounds in and around the bigger cities or otherwise-popular spots. If you plan to do lots of camping, however, a special guide may be worth its price. See the *Resources* chapter for more on these. Also, many of the tourist offices listed in that chapter will send you detailed information about campgrounds.

Camping, of course, is a huge money saver. And Sweden officially sanctions free-camping, and Norway and Finland tolerate it in principle. The people of these countries consider free-camping a right: everyman's right *(allmansratten)*, they call it. Remember, to properly exercise this right you should camp on unfenced land and at least 100 meters (just over 100 yards) away from dwellings, stay only two nights, and clean up after yourself. *Allmansratten* doesn't apply to motorhomes, however. I've camped on Norway's wooded hills, on precipices high above fjords, on the shores of fjords, and even within the city limits of Oslo. When hygiene becomes an issue, I'll duck in to an organized campground and either bum or pay for a shower. Furthermore, I take advantage of the long summer days in the "Land of the Midnight Sun", often setting up camp in daylight between 11:00 P.M. and midnight. (By the way, Europe in general is on a much higher latitude than the US; as such, the summer sun sets much later there.)

When not in Scandinavia, you can either take your chances and free-camp unannounced in some discreet spot or do the right thing by asking permission from the land owner. If you choose the second option, chances are your host will engage you in a fascinating conversation and, if you're lucky, invite you to dinner. Of course you can sleep in your vehicle if you like. Though explicitly prohibited in certain countries, discreet free-camping is tolerated almost everywhere. See the *Country-by-Country Information* chapter for more.

Of course free-camping is an especially viable option for motorhomers. Many spend in the night in the parking lots of tourist attractions—under the pretense that they're waiting to get in early—or, say, supermarkets or marinas. Even more popular are the rest stops along expressways. In fact, these are designed to facilitate overnight stays. In England you're supposed to pay a £3.50 charge to stay overnight at these stops, but this charge is rarely enforced.

Most European motorhomes have chemical toilets with detachable cassettes designed to be emptied in special receptacles—called "Chem WC" units—installed at most campgrounds, or into a regular toilet. As made clear in the *Shipping and Importing* chapter, because irremovable holding tanks are not common on European motorhomes many campgrounds don't have a North American-type dumping station. Campgrounds or free-camping facilities with such a station are denoted by the trailer pictogram and/or the words *"Entsorgungskanal"* (German), *"scarigare"* (Italian), or *"vidoir"* (French). The German auto club *ADAC* (see the *Country-by-Country Information* chapter) publishes and distributes—free of charge to members of affiliated clubs—a list and map of such dumping stations. For a charge, some campgrounds will allow you to dump without staying overnight. Don't dump these tanks by a highway or in a field—this is highly illegal. If you must, visit a municipal sewage treatment plant to do the job.

Most campgrounds provide central drinking-water taps with a hose connected so motorhomers can fill their tank. Bring a length of hose—having a half-inch fitting—so you can fill up from a distance.

Virtually all European motorhomes are wired with 10 Amp circuits that, given the 220 Volt standard, allow you to use up to 2200 Watts (that's 10 x 220) of power at any one time. Note that an appliance such as a hairdryer can demand almost this much power. And where the voltage is lower, you'll have even less power to play with. Though in the mid eighties Europe went to a standard known as *CEE 17* for campground sockets and plugs, many campgrounds are not in compliance. Still, most will provide free of charge any adapter you might need to interface a *European* model vehicle to the camp's system. (See the *Packing* chapter for a discussion of electrical standards.) Some campgrounds offer a meter at each site, charge you to hook up, and then charge per kilowatt-hour. Others impose an inclusive charge. Since you may have to park quite a distance from a socket, bring a 25 meter connecting cord designed for outdoor use.

See the *Resources* chapter for a listing of several books and magazines on the subject. See the *Documents* chapter for a discussion of the camping carnet document. See the *Packing* chapter for a list of necessary camping equipment. And see the *Country-by-Country Information* chapter for relevant country-specific comments.

Rentals

Rental arrangements usually require more lead time than do hotel arrangements, some-times as much as eight months. And although some rentals are available for one-or two-day stays, most require a stay of a week or more. What's more, you may be asked to pay extra and in advance for maid services and the like that are normally included in the price of a hotel room. And if you must cancel, you might lose the entire prepayment. Once you arrive you'll likely be required to meet with a property manager, local agent or neighbor to obtain the keys, turn on the utilities, and arrange phone service. Still, a rental can be well worth all this.

But how to go about arranging a rental? While domestic agenices offer properties that start at about $500 per week, you can rent a house for as little as $150 if you bypass these agencies. Popular guidebooks sometimes list rental accommodations as well as hotels, and many popular magazines contain classified advertisements listing properties available for rental world-wide. (Though these may be placed by agencies.) The twelve-page quarterly newsletter *Villa Report,* Box 4690, Greenwich, CT 06830-0602, lists private homes, apartments, suites, inns, yachts, river barges and other unique and luxurious accommodations throughout the world. The semiannual *World-Wide Home Rental Guide,* available from 369 Montezuma Ave., Suite 338, Santa Fe, NM 87501, tel. 505 984 7080, costs $18 for a year-long subscription and lists both individual owners and rental agencies. And the new *Guide to Vacation Rentals in Europe* (see the *Resources* chapter) may prove invaluable.

You can also make arrangements through many of the tourist offices in Europe; to get their phone numbers call the domestic tourist offices or embassies I list in the *Resources* chapter. Cork Kerry Tourisme, Tourist House, Grand Parade, Cork, Ireland, tel. 21 273 251, FAX 21 273 504, publishes *Irish Cottage Home Holidays,* comprised of a good variety of listings from IR£100–500 per week and of advertisements for agencies. Many regional German tourist offices publish excellent color-photo guides. Here are three.

Familienferien. Schwarzwald Fremdenverkehrsverband, Postfach 1660, 79016 Freiburg im Bresigau, Germany, tel. 761 31317, FAX 761 36021.

Fröhliche Familienferien. Neckarland-Schwaben Touristikverband Lohtorstraße 21, 74072 Heilbronn, Germany, tel. 7131 629661, FAX 7131 68638.

Urlaub auf Bauren-und Winzerhöfen,
Rheinland-Pfalz Tourist Office,
Schmittpforte 2, 55437 Ober-Holbersheim,
Germany, tel. 6728 1225, FAX 6728 626.

A popular option in France is a country cottage or *gîte* ("zheet"). The *Gîte Guide,* published yearly by FHG Publications, Paisley, Scotland, and available in US bookstores for $17.95, lists over 1200 *gîtes* throughout France, describing each in English and including photographs. The guide also gives detailed instructions about how to reserve directly with the owner or through a French booking agency. Gîtes de France is a French government agency that was created after WWII to help the French rural economy stay afloat. It serves as a sort of rental agency for private property owners who wanna supplement their incomes. The units, usually in small villages or in the countryside, must meet certain government standards. A typical unit, sleeping four to six, rented through this agency goes for between $200 and $500 per week. Call their English-language number in Paris at 1 49 70 75 97. Another helpful source for thousands of inexpensive rural rentals in France is the Maison des Gîtes, 35, rue Godot-de-Mauroy, Paris, France, 75009. Write for an order blank listing ninety regional guidebooks costing about $6 each. If you go this route, expect to pay about $130 a week for a *gîte* that can accommodate up to six people, $180 a week in July and August.

Similar sources in several other countries publish listings of or arrange rentals.

Chez Nous, Bridge Mills, Huddersfield Rd., Holmfirth HD7 2TW, England, tel. 484 684 075, FAX 484 685 852. Publishes a directory of French rentals owned by Brits. Prices are reasonable ($150 plus per week) since there's no commission. Moreover, there's no language gap.

FriFerie Danmark, Liselejevej 60, 3360 Liseleje, Denmark, tel. 42 34 63 34, FAX 42 34 64 53. Publishes a listing—in Danish and German only—of rentals that start at $200 per week in the the off season, $350 in the summer.

R.T. Braker, 2, rue du Dome, 75116 Paris, France, tel. 1 47 27 48 80. Friendly and experienced Franco-American couple who operate a $60-per-night B&B in Paris, five minute's walk from the Arc de Triomphe.

Fjordhytter, Lille Markevei 13, 5005 Bergen, Norway, tel. 5 23 20 80, FAX 5 23 24 04. Publishes a photo catalog containing extremely detailed descriptions—in English. Prices start at $165 in the off season, $350 in the high season.

Allrum, Wallingatan 34, S-111 24, Stockholm, Sweden, tel. 8 10 44 37, FAX 8 21 01 76.

Destination Stockholms Skårgård AB, Lillström, S-18023 Ljustero, Sweden, tel. 8 542 481 00, FAX 8 542 414 00. Rents cottages in the Stockholm archipelago, starting at about $200 in the off season, $350 in mid summer. You should book 7–8 months ahead for the high season.

Hotelltjänst, Vasagatan 15–17, S-111 20, Stockholm, Sweden, tel. 8 10 44 37, FAX 8 21 37 16.

SGS Bostäder, Utlandagatan 24, S-412 80, Goteborg, Sweden, tel. 31 81 33 71, FAX 31 81 48 20.

If you wanna physically inspect a property before you rent it, you can book a hotel room for the first day or so and then shop around for a rental. Apart from inquiring at the local tourist office, you can try stopping by the local train station: most of the main train stations host real estate agencies. You can also go direct to the manager of a large rental complex. Don't expect much, however, if you're operating in the high season.

If you're looking for a flat in Britain, the following translations of ad-speak will prove helpful.

BR: Britsh Rail station

bth: bathroom

ch: central heating

dbl: double

db: double bedroom

DSS ok/welcome: doesn't discriminate against beneficiaries

no DSS: no beneficiaries

excl: exclusive (basic rent exclusive of heating, gas, etc.)

f: female

f/f: fully furnished

gch: gas and central heating

incl: inclusive

m: male

mxd: mixed flatshare with male and female flatmates

nr: near

ns: non smoker

pcm: per calendar month

pkg: parking

pp: per person

pw: per week

rm: room

prf/prof: professional

sb: single bedroom

sgl: single

sp: separate

tbe: tube/underground station

wm: washing machine

If you wanna take the easy way out and pay a lot more money, the following rental agencies will prove helpful.

Anitours, 81 New Road, Ste. 144, Parsippany, NJ 07054, tel. 800 243 8264. Properties in the Czech Republic.

At Home Abroad, 405 E. 56th St., Suite 6H, New York, NY 10022, tel. 212 421 9165, FAX 212 752 1591. Rents apartments, houses and castles.

Barclay International Group, tel 800 845 6636 or 212 832 9777. Their free booklet, *The Savvy Consumer's Guide to Short-Term Apartment Rentals,* includes advice for families with small children, health/fitness-conscious travelers, deluxe travelers, and more; there's even a section on why to use a travel agent.

British Homes, London Flats, Box 21, Port Washington, NY 11050, tel. 516 883 2717, FAX 516 944 5264.

Calboccia, 89 Edgecroft Rd., Kensington, CA 94707, tel. 510 987 9724. Restored farm houses in Umbria, Italy.

Castles, Cottages and Flats, 7 Faneuil Hall Marketplace, Boston, MA 02109, tel. 617 742 6030, FAX 617 367 4521. Rentals in Great Britain, France, Ireland and Italy.

Condolink, 743 N. 120th St., Omaha, NE 68154, tel. 800 733 4445 or 402 492 9500, FAX 402 492 8747. Rents timeshare condos.

Cuednet, tel. 800 726 6702 or 805 987 5278.

Eurobed, 818 Druid Hills, Temple Terrace, FL 33617, FAX 813 664 0051. Rents rooms and apartments in Prague at a reasonable rates.

Europa-Let, 92 N. Main St., Ashland, OR 97520, tel. 800 462 4486 or 503 482 5806, FAX 503 482 0660. Rents apartments,

alternative accommodations

houses, farmhouses, manors, and castles. Booking fee, $25.

Four Seasons Villas, Box 848, Marblehead, MA 01945, tel. 800 338 0474 or 617 639 1055, FAX 617 631 8718. Rents apartments, condos and houses in Great Britain. Surcharge.

The French Experience, 370 Lexington Ave., New York, NY 10017, tel. 212 986 1115, FAX 212 9986 3808. Rents apartments, cottages and houses in France. Booking fee, $20.

Heart of England Cottages, P.O. Box 878, Eufaula, AL 36072. Cottages in England, Scotland and Wales from $100 per person per week. Brochure for $3.75.

Hearthstone Holidays, P.O. Box 68085, #70, Bonnie Doon Mall, Edmonton, AB T6C 4N6, Canada, tel. 403 465 2874, FAX 403 478 5517. Britain, France and Italy.

Hideaways International, 767 Islington St., Box 4433, Portsmouth, NH 03802, tel. 800 843 4433 or 603 430 4433, FAX 603 430 4444. Can arrange resort rentals. Membership, $79 a year; includes two guides, quarterly newsletter, asnd discounts.

Home and Host International, 2445 Park. Ave., Minneapolis, MN 55404, tel. 800

SOVIET-U. B&Bs and homestays in the CIS, Baltics, and Prague.

Home at First/De Tours, tel. 800 5 CELTIC or 610 565 5242. Specializes in England, Scotland and Ireland.

Hometours International, 1170 Broadway, Suite 614, New York, NY 10001, tel. 800 367 4668 or 212 689 0851. Rents apartments and houses in Europe (specializes in Italy). Reservation fee, $50 ($25 applied to rental; $40 refund if no rental is arranged).

Interhome Inc., 124 Little Falls Rd., Fairfield, NJ 07004, tel. 201 882 6864, FAX 201 808 1742. Rents apartments, houses and castles. Booking fee, $20.

Italian Villa Rentals, Box 1145, Bellevue, WA 98009, tel. 206 827 3694, FAX 206 827 5125.

Keith Prowse, 234 W. 44th St., Suite 1000, New York, NY 10036, tel. 800 669 8687 or 212 398 1430, FAX 212 302 4251. Rents apartments in central London.

Lynott Tours, 350 5th Ave., Suite 2619, New York, NY 10118, tel. 800 221 2474 or 212 760 0101, FAX 212 695 8347. Rents houses in Ireland.

Marie Lambert, 2011 Burton Ave., Burley, ID 83318, tel. 208 678 4253. Condos on the French Riviera.

Overseas Connection, 31 North Harbor Dr., Sag Harbor, NY 11963, tel. 516 725 9308.

Prestige Villas, Box 1046, Southport, CT 06490, tel. 800 336 0080 or 203 254 1302, FAX 203 254 7261.

Provence West, Ltd., tel. 303 674 6942.

Rent a Home International, 7200 34th Ave. NW, Seattle, WA 98117, tel. 800 488 7368 or 206 789 9377. Rents apartments, houses and castles.

Rent-a-Vacation Everywhere (RAVE), 383 Park Ave., Rochester, NY 14607, tel. 716 256 0760, FAX 716 256 2676. Rents apartments, condos and houses. Booking fee, $25.

Sterling Tours, 2707 Congress St., Suite 2-G, San Diego, CA 92110, tel. 800 727 4359 or 619 299 3010, FAX 619 299 5728. Rents apartments, condos and houses in England, France, Italy and Spain.

Suzanne Pidduck Rentals in Italy, 1742 Calle Corva, Camarillo, CA 93010, tel. 800 726 6702 or 805 987 5278, FAX 805 525 9684. Rents apartments, houses and castles in Italy.

Swiss Touring USA, 5537 N. Hollywood Ave., Milwaukee, WI 53217, tel. 414 963 2010, FAX 414 769 6591. Rents apartments and houses in Switzerland.

Twelve Islands and Beyond, 5431 MacArthur Blvd., Washington DC 20016, tel. 800 345 8236 or 202 537 3549, FAX 202 537 3548. Rents apartments and houses in Greece and Turkey.

Untours/Idyll, tel. 800 5 CELTIC or 610 565 5242.

Vacanza Bella, 2443 Fillmore St., Suite 228, San Francisco, CA 94115, tel. 415 554 0234. Rents apartments, houses and castles in Italy.

Vacation Home Rentals Worldwide, 235 Kensington Ave., Norwood, NJ 07648, tel. 800 633 3284 or 201 767 9363, FAX 201 767 5510.

Villa Holidays, 1 Berkley Lane, Rye Brook, NY 10573, tel. 800 457 0444 or 800 800 5576 (Boston office) or 914 937 6944, FAX 914 937 7069.

Villa Leisure, Box 30188, Palm Beach, FL 33420, tel. 800 526 4244 or 407 622 9097. Rents apartments, condos and houses in France and Spain.

Villas and Apartments Abroad, 420 Madison Ave., Suite 1105, New York,NY 10017, tel. 800 433 3020 or 212 759 1025, FAX 212 755 8316.

Villas International, 605 Market St., Suite 510, San Francisco, CA 94105, tel. 800 221 2260 or 415 281 0910, FAX 415 281 0919.

Villas of Distinction, tel. 800 289 0900. French Riviera, Provence, the Algarve in Portugal. Also, private yacht charters in France.

Villas of the World, 4501 Forbes Blvd., Suite 100, Lanham, MD 20706, tel. 800 638 0930, tel. 301 459 8020. Directory and newsletter lists about 250 rentals worldwide. Discounts are 15–25 percent off listed rates. Membership, $60 a year.

Worldwide B&B & Exchange Services, 3200 SW Eveningside Dr., #19, Topeka, KS 66614–3717, tel. 800 273 7133. B&B homestays in Albania, Bulgaria, Czech & Slovakian Republics, Hungary, Poland, and Russia.

Your Own World, 796 Crestmoor Dr., San Jose, CA 95129, tel. 800 473 6155. Moscow and St. Petersburg homestays.

Homestays and Farmstays

Rather than renting your own hideaway, you can arrange to stay with Euorepans in their homes—sometimes for a charge, sometimes not. The following organizations help arrange homestays.

American International Homestays, Route 1 Box 6, Iowa City, IA 52240, tel. 800 876 2048.

Borton Overseas, tel. 800 843 0602.

Central Bureau for Educational Visits and Exchanges, Seymour Mews House, Seymour Mews, London W1H 9PE, England, tel. 0171 387 8572. Publishes *Home from Home,* a guide to international homestays, termstays and exchanges. £6.99 + postage.

Friendship Force, Suite 575, South Tower, 1 CNN Center, Atlanta, GA 30303, tel. 404 552 9490.

The Hospitality Exchange, 1422 E. Roosevelt Ave., Salt Lake City, UT 84105, tel. 800 580 8759, ask for Allen Rasmussan. For a $15 annual membership the Exchange provides contacts with 350 members worldwide. Two-day minimum stay; no money changes hands.

alternative accommodations

Global Social Venture Network, 721 Montecello Rd., San Rafael, CA 94903, tel. 415 491 1532, FAX 415 492 1046.

SERVAS, Inc., 11 John St., Room 706, New York, NY 10038, tel. 212 267 0252, is an international cooperative system of hosts and travelers. Families and individuals can join for $45 a year.

Also take note of the *People to People* series of directories by Jim Haynes, and the *International Meet-the-People Directory*. I describe these in the *Resources* chapter.

It's especially common for farmers to host travelers who wanna stay for a week or more—in the farmhouse itself, a guest house, or a barn-like structure. As with a typical homestay, there's almost always a charge for such accommodation. Check out the following for more information.

The Austrian Tourist Office distributes the brochure *Erholung auf dem Bauernhof*.

Vacances à la Ferme/Fetourag A.A.B., rue de la Science 21, Boîte 2, 1040 Brussels, Belgium, tel. 02 230 72 95.

The British Tourist Authority distributes the free booklet *Stay on a Farm*.

You can order the annual books *Farm Holiday Guide England, Wales & Ireland* and *Farm Holiday Guide Scotland* from Hunter Publishing, Inc., 300 Raritan Center Parkway, Edison, NJ 08818, tel. 908 225 1900. $14.95 and $6.95, respectively.

You can order the annual book *Britain: Country Lodgings on a Budget* from British Gifts, P.O. Box 2655, Los Angeles, CA 90026 or from GHF, Inc., P.O. Box 1224, Clifton, NJ 07012, tel. 212 765 0898.

Farm Holidays in Britain is available from The Farm Holiday Bureau, National Agricultural Centre, Stoneleigh, Kenilworth, Warwickshire CV8 2LZ, England, tel. 0203 696969, FAX 0203 696900.

The Danish Tourist Office distributes the brochure *Farm Holidays in Denmark*.

The Finnish Tourist Office distributes the brochure *Farm Holidays in Finland*.

You can order the annual book *French Farm & Village Holiday Guide* from Hunter Publishing, Inc., 300 Raritan Center Parkway, Edison, NJ 08818, tel. 908 225 1900. $16.95.

You can order Paul Walshe's *French Farmhouses and Cottages* from Rizzoli International Publications, Inc., tel. 800 462 2387 or 212 387 3530. 1992. 160 pages. $27.50.

Farmholidays/Suomen 4 H-Iiito, Uudenmaankatu 24, SF 00120 Helsinki, Finland, tel. 90 642233.

For a listing of farm lodgings in Germany ask for the annual book *Urlaub auf dem Bauernhof* by calling Germany at 069 716 83 41 or FAX 069 724 15 54.

For farm lodgings in the Rhineland contact Fremdenverkehrsverband Rheinland-Pflaz e.V., Löhstraße 103–105, Postfach 1420, D-5400 Koblenz, Germany, tel. 0261 31079, FAX 0261 18343, and ask for the free brochure *Ferien auf Bauernund-Winzerhöfen*.

Another free brochure, *Urlaub auf dem Bauernhof*, is available from the organization of the same name, Postfach 5443, D-7800 Freiburg, Germany, tel. 0761 271 3391.

Women's Agricultural Tourist Cooperative of Ambelakia, 41000 Ambelakia, Greece, tel. 0495 31495.

Women's Agricultural Tourist Cooperative of Chio, 82102 Pyrghi-Chios, Greece, tel. 0271 72496.

Agricultural Cooperative of Petra, 18008 Petra-Lesvos, Greece, tel. 0253 41238.

Agrotours, Dob utca 53, H-1074 Budapest, Hungary, tel. 01 121 4021, FAX 01 253 4144.

Agriturist, Corso Vittorio Emmanuele 101, 00186 Roma, Italy, tel. 06 685 2342, FAX 06 685 2424. Send a money order of 35,000 lire for their Italian catalog.

Terranostra, Via Magazzini 2, 50122 Florence, Italy. Send money order of 43,000 lire for their catalog.

Turismo Verde, Viale Ettore Franschini 89, 00155 Rome, Italy. Send money order of 18,000 lire for their catalog.

Central Farmers' Organization, International Secretary, 19 Prinsevinkenpark, 2825 HK Den Hague, the Netherlands, tel. 070 526666.

Gromada, Wczasow pod gruszas, Ulica Podvale 23, 00952 Warsawa, Poland, tel. 022 311211.

Direcção Geral do Turismo, Divisão do Turismo no Espaço Rural, Ave. António Augusto de Aguiar, 86, Apartado 1929, 1004 Lisboa Codex, Portugal, tel. 01 57 50 15, FAX 01 55 69 17.

The Spanish National Tourist Office distributes the brochure *Vacaciones en Casas se Labranza*.

Landresor, Vasagatan 12, S-105 33, Stockholm, Sweden, tel. 8 78 75 555, FAX 8 21 83 81.

LRF Turism, Klaraö, Kyrkogatan 12, S-105 33, Stockholm, Sweden, tel. 8 78 75 000, FAX 8 11 01 98.

Fédération de Tourisme de la Suisse Romande, Office du Tourisme, CH-1530 Payerne, Switzerland.

Verkehrsverein Andermatt, Bahnhofplatz, CH-6940 Andermatt, Switzerland.

Zadruzna Zveza Slovenije, Miklosiceva 4/I, 6100 Ljubljana, Solvenije, tel. 061 211 911.

Home Exchanges

As I described in the *Shipping* chapter, one option that gets easier and more popular each year is a home and vehicle exchange. From 1988 to 1992 the number of Europeans visiting America grew steadily from about 5.5 million to nearly 8 million; while the number of Americans traveling to Europe wavered between a high of 8 million (in 1990) to a low of 6.35 million (in 1991). I'm sure many of these Europeans would've loved to swap homes and vehicles with you. The biggest hurdle is trust; the easier it is for both parties to establish the more practical this option becomes. Several organizations arrange such swaps and provide the kind of professional, third-party assistance that's the catalyst of this trust.

The organizations I list below cannot assume responsibility for the actions of the people listed in their publications. It's ultimately your responsibility to screen potential tenants and to take whatever precautionary measures you deem necessary. Make sure your homeowners insurance covers damage done by temporary tenants and includes liability insurance to protect you in case a guest is injured in your home. If you rent to or exchange with strangers, make sure the contract stipulates that they pay for the *replacement* value of anything they happen to damage. Consider asking for a security deposit as well. There's really nothing stopping you from including motor vehicles in the swap. If you do include vehicles, first OK this with your auto-insurance provider, and confirm that the other party has done the same. Here are several organizations that publish directories of potential home swappers.

Annlin Publications' Vacation Homes Unlimited, 18547 Soledad Canyon Rd., Suite 223, Santa Clarita, CA 91351, tel. 805

251 1238, FAX 805 298 0576. Publishes house-exchange directory three times a year. Directory and listing, $55 ($50 for directory only).

Exchange Book, Vacation Exchange Club, Inc., Box 820, Haleiwa, HI 96712–0820, is a 256-page, worldwide directory of families seeking home-exchange vacations. $16.

Global Exchange & Travel Services, P.O. Box 2015, South Burlington, VT 05407–2015, tel. 802 985 3825.

The Great Exchange Ltd., 438 Cambridge Ave., P.O. Box 60147, Palo Alto, CA 94306, tel. 415 424 8455. Britain only.

Home Base Holidays, 7 Park Ave., London N13 5PG, England, tel. 081 886 8752.

Home Exchange International, Inc., 22458 Ventura Blvd., Suite E, Woodland Hills, CA 91364, tel. 818 992 8990. Paris and Milan only.

Home Exchange Network, Box 951253, Longwood, FL 32791, tel. 407 862 7211, modem 407 869 5965. A computer bulletin board service. Free six-month membership.

The Hospitality Exchange, 4908 E. Culver #2, Phoenix, AZ 85008, tel. 602 267 8000. Publishes house-exchange directory three times a year. Membership and listing, $15.

Member must offer reciprocal host services to other members.

Interchange, The Association for World Travel Exchange, 38 West 88th St., New York, NY 10024–2502, tel. 212 787 7706, or Interchange, 286 Park South, Hamilton, ON L8P 3G4, Canada. Publishes a directory of professionals whose residences and vehicles are available for exchange with other professionals.

Intervac US/International Home Exchange, Box 590504, San Francisco, CA 94159, tel. 800 756 4663 or 415 435 3497, FAX 415 435 0492. Publishes house-exchange directory three times a year: Dec 1, March 1, and May 1. International directory and listing, $75, $68 for seniors, $11 more to include a photo. Membership gets you all three directories, plus your listing in one. Roughly 9400 subscribers.

The Invented City, 41 Sutter St., Suite 1090, San Francisco, CA 94104, tel. 800 788 2489 or 415 673 0347, FAX 415 673 6909. Publishes a house-exchange directory three times a year: Mar, June, and Nov. Directory and listing, $50. No photos. Active membership of 2000.

Loan-a-Home, 2 Park La., Apt. 6E, Mount Vernon, NY 10552, tel. 914 664 7640.

SERVAS, 11 John St., Room 706, New York, NY 10038, tel. 212 267 0252. House exchange. Membership, $55 a year.

Teacher Swap, Box 454, Oakdale, NY 11769, tel. 516 244 2845. Bed and breakfast or house exchange for teachers only. But they employ a loose definition of "teacher", encompassing active and retired, volunteer and paid, Sunday school, and adult education teachers. Directory and listing, $42 ($50 for the directory only). Roughly 700 listings. No pictures.

Trading Homes International, Boz 787, Hermosa beach, CA 90254, tel. 800 877 8723, FAX 310 798 3865. Publishes three directories each year. A $65 membership gets you all three, plus your listing in one.

Uptown Reservations, 50 Christchurch St., Chelsea, London SW3 4AR, England, tel. 0171 351 3445.

Vacation Exchange Club, Box 650, Key West, FL 33041, tel. 800 638 3841, FAX 305 294 1448. Publishes a house exchange directory five times a year. Membership and listing, $65 a year; $80 for a listing with a photograph. A listing for a second home costs $10 more.

Vacation Homes Unlimited, P.O. Box 1562, Santa Clarita, CA, tel. 800 VHU SWAP.

World for Free, Box 137, Prince St. Station, New York, NY 10012, FAX 212 979 8167. For $25 a year members receive an address book; they must then make their own arrangements.

Worldwide Home Exchange Club, 6609 Quincy St., Philadelphia, PA 19119. World Headquarters located at 45 Hans Place, London SW1X OJZ, England, tel. 0171 589 6055.

But again, as I described in the *Shipping* chapter, with a little work *you* may be able to make all the arrangements for a home and/or vehicle swap. If you're an academic, work for an international company or firm, or belong to some other reputable international organization (such as a church or a medical society), contact some of your European colleagues. If you can tap into the so-called electronic superhighway, send out messages asking for information on potential international swaps; and keep an ear or an eye tuned for individuals or new services that offer European homes and vehicles for temporary swapping. One such service is at web address www.homeexchange.com. See the *Resources* chapter for more info about electronically based resources and just surf, baby.

If you succeed in securing an exchange, consider exchanging lists of friends, too. And if you agree to exchange *vehicles,* get the agreement in writing, and carry it in the vehicle always, along, of course, with proof that the owner has properly insured and registered the vehicle. You need to carry a special form of authority, an *Autorizacao* certificate, if you plan to drive someone else's vehicle in Portugal; get the form at a registration office in Europe, or contact your local motoring club or a Portuguese tourist office or embassy. A similar requirement is made by Turkey. If you lose any of the registration or permissive documents, contact the local police.

Two books on the subject of exchanges will give you more information.

Trading Places: The Wonderful World of Home Exchange, by Bill and Mary Barbour. Contains a thorough resource list and many anecdotes, plus a chapter on children and home-swapping. Vacation Home Exchange Services, 16956-4 S. McGregor Blvd., Fort Myers, FL 33908, tel. 800 532 4918. $9.95.

The Vacation Home Exchange and Hospitality Guide, by John Kimbrough. This resource guide to home exchange programs contains additional information on person-to-person hospitality clubs.

Kimco Communications, 4242 W. Dayton, Fresno, CA 93722, tel. 209 275 0893. $14.95 plus $2 postage.

Volunteer Work

Apart from the saved cost of accommodation, the *spiritual* rewards of volunteer work can be enormous. Recently I volunteered for a two-week stint (usually the *minimum* required stay) on an archaeological dig in France. The work was hard but interesting (Neanderthal artifacts); and the project provided a great opportunity to eat, drink, and play with the natives. And we ate and drank and played a *lot.* I made many friends—despite the fact that I was the only one on the dig who didn't speak, or at least have some background in, French. It was also a nice way to take a break from traveling.

The *Archaeological Fieldwork Opportunities Bulletin,* a comprehensive guide to excavations, field schools, and special programs with openings for volunteers, students, and staff throughout the world is published by the Archaeological Institute of America (AIA), 675 Commonwealth Ave., Boston, MA 02215, tel. 617 353 9361, FAX 617 353 6550. To order contact Kendall/Hunt Publishing Co., Order Dept., 2460

Kerper Blvd., Dubuque, IA 52001, tel. 800 338 5578.

A certain issue of the AIA's bimonthly *Archaeology* magazine (usually the March/April issue) may describe and list contacts for digs occuring during the upcoming summer in Europe and the Middle East— digs that advertise for volunteers. Check back issues at your library, or contact the AIA at the above address or at tel. 800 829 5122.

Council on International Educational Exchange (CIEE), 205 E. 42nd St., New York, NY 10017, tel. 212 661 1414. The Council arranges workcamps across Europe and sells the 188-page *Volunteer! the Comprehensive Guide to Voluntary Service in the US and Abroad.* $9.

Civil International/International Voluntary Service-USA, Rte. 2, Box 506, Crozet, VA 22932, tel. 804 823 1826. Arranges placement in workcamps across Europe.

The *International Workcamp Directory* is published by Volunteers for Peace, 43 Tiffany Rd., Belmont, VT 05730, tel. 802 259 2759. $10 ppd. For a registration fee of $125 this group arranges placement in workcamps across Europe.

Paid Work

You may wanna work for pay while in Europe. Technically speaking, European governments require most foreigners to obtain a work permit before working for pay in Europe. Contact Council Travel, Travel CUTS, or STA Travel (see the *Documents* chapter) to obtain European work permits. Here are some sources to check for work.

Travel CUTS Students Work Abroad Program or SWAP. See the *Documents* chapter for their address.

International Jobs: Where they are and how to get them is published by Addison Wesley, tel. 800 446 2226. $12.45.

International Employment Hotline . A monthly newsletter in its 15th year, the hotline lists jobs by country of assingment and includes a job's title, description, requirements and employer contact. P.O. Box 3030, Oakton, VA 22124. $30 per year.

Work, Study, Travel Abroad: The Whole World Handbook is published by the Council on International Educational Exchange (CIEE), 205 E. 42nd St., New York, NY 10017, tel. 212 661 1414. $12.95 + $1.50 postage.

Working Holidays is published by the Institute of International Education (IIE), 809 United Nations Plaza, New York, NY 10017, tel. 212 883 8200. $22.95.

Inter Exchange Program, 365 W. 34th St., 2nd Floor, New York, NY 10001. Publishes a pamphlet describing international and au pair work.

Call or write World Teach, HIID, 1 Eliot St., Cambridge, MA 02138, tel. 617 495 5527, for information on teaching English.

Friends of World Teaching, P.O. Box 1049, San Diego, CA 92112, tel. 619 275 4066, will send you a list of foreign schools with ESL programs. The listings are by country. The minimum order costs $20 and allows you to choose three countries; beyond that, each list costs $4.

Directory of Summer Jobs Abroad, £6.95 ($11); *Work Your Way Around the World,* £7.95; *Working in Ski Resorts in Europe,* £5.95. Published by Vacation Work, 9 Park End St., Oxford OX1 1HJ, England.

Looking for Employment in Foreign Countries is published by World Trade Academy Press, 50 East 42nd St. Suite 509, New York, NY 10017. $16.50.

Study Abroad

The following resources will help you arrange a stint as a student in Europe.

Association of Commonwealth Universities, John Foster House, 36 Gordon Square, London WC1H 0PF, England, tel. 0171 387 8572, publishes several guides about studying in Britain's universities.

Study Holidays is published by the Central Bureau for Educational Visits and Exchanges, Seymour Mews House, Seymour Mews, London W1H 9PE, England, tel. 0171 387 8572. The guide gives information on over six hundred language study programs across Europe. £7.95+ postage.

Basic Facts on Foreign Study (free of charge), *Academic Year Abroad* ($39.95 + $3 postage, describing thousands of study programs), and *Vacation Study Abroad* ($31.95 + $3 postage, describing over one thousand programs) are published by the Institute of International Education (IIE), 809 United Nations Plaza, New York, NY 10017, tel. 212 883 8200.

Financial Resources for International Study is published by Peterson's Guides, P.O. Box 2123, Princeton, NJ 08543, tel. 800 338 3282.

Going Places: The High School Student's Guide to Study, Travel and Adventure Abroad is published by St. Martin's Press, Inc., 175 5th Ave., 17th Floor, New York, NY 10010-7801, FAX 212 529 0694. 300 pages. $14.

Guide to Academic Travel is published by ShawGuides, Inc., 625 Biltmore Way, #1406, Coral Gables, FL 33134–7539. Comprehensive source of information about adult academic learning vacations. $17.

UNESCO's *Study Abroad* is distributed by Unipub Co., 4611-F Assembly Dr., Lanham, MD 20706–4391, tel. 800 274 4888. $24 + $2.50 postage.

Work, Study, Travel Abroad: The Whole World Handbook is published by the Council on International Educational Exchange (CIEE), 205 E. 42nd St., New York, NY 10017, tel. 212 661 1414. $12.95 + $1.50 postage.

Transitions Abroad

If you plan to stay abroad for an extended length of time, you should consider subscribing to *Transitions Abroad*. This no-nonsense, information-packed magazine addresses, among other things, all the subjects discussed in this chapter. Furthermore, TA's annual *Educational Travel Resource Guide* is the most thorough directory available of volunteer-work, paid-work, study-abroad, and living-abroad resources; it costs just $5. TA's mission statement is as follows.

Transitions Abroad provides active travelers of all ages with practical, usable information on economical, purposeful international travel opportunites—travel that involves *learning* by living, studying, working, or vacationing alongside the people of the host country.

To subscribe, write to *Transitions Abroad*, Dept. TRA, Box 3000, Denville, NJ 07834. In the US, $19.95/6 issues, $39/12 issues. Outside the US, $26/6 issues in Canada, $38/6 issues in other countries. Back issues are available for $4.50 per copy ($7 overseas), postpaid. A complete index of all back issues (since 1977) is available for $2. Write: Back Issues, P.O. Box 1300, Amherst, MA 01004.

9. value-added taxes

Most European governments impose a *value-added tax* or VAT—a national sales tax of sorts—on goods and services. It's usually about 20 percent and is buried in the price. Although non Europeans often qualify for a partial refund of this tax, they leave roughly a half-billion dollars in refundable VAT unclaimed each year. Generally, travelers are entitled to refunds of the tax on merchandise only—in other words, on the kind of stuff that can be exported. Business travelers, on the other hand, can receive VAT refunds on their vehicle rentals, their gasoline and diesel fuel, and even on their lodging and meals. Austria, however, offers a similarly wide range of refunds to mere tourists.

Let's begin by noting what a VAT refund is not. A VAT refund is not the same as the "duty-free" or "tax-free" offers available at airports, on planes, or on ships: these involve a part or all of the customs duty or tax being waived on certain luxury and highly taxed items such as jewelry, liquor, and tobacco.

You can secure a true VAT refund in one of four ways. The first and easiest way is to buy from a merchant who has enrolled in the Europe Tax-free Shopping (ETS) plan. Over 60,000 merchants now participate in this plan. These businesses display a blue and red "Tax Free for Tourists" sticker—always in English—in their windows; they'll issue a VAT refund check on the spot. (In the Netherlands the sticker reads "Tax-Free Shopping Holland".) Some businesses that *don't* display the sticker *do* participate; always ask. ETS is actually a corporation; it maintains desks at major exit points where you can cash your refund checks.

The second way to get a VAT refund is by mailing a refund application back to the store after originally paying the VAT. If you produce a foreign passport at the time of purchase from a non-ETS merchant, the merchant will write-up a VAT refund form and present you with a copy. (In a few areas, however, you may have to obtain the forms yourself from customs officials or tourist offices.) When you leave the country you simply show your form to customs officials who then validate it with a stamp. Finally, you mail the form back to the store. Of course it's best to mail the form before you leave the country; most exit points—airports, for example—provide a conspicuously placed mail box for such purposes. If you used a credit card to make your purchase—as you should (more on this in the *Documents* chapter)—you'll receive your refund as a credit to your account. If you paid cash, you'll receive a check in the foreign currency. Expect to wait up to three months for a refund.

The third way to get a refund is by the exit method. Certain countries allow you to submit your refund forms to a customs official upon exiting the country. If this is the case, you'll get cash or a check on the spot. Yet qualifying exit points are few; if you leave through an infrequently used exit point, you may have to use the mailing procedure instead.

The fourth and final method is the direct export method. Some countries allow you to avoid paying VAT if the merchant directly sends the merchandise to your home by mail. This method can be expensive, however: the shipping and insurance will cost you, and the package may be subject to customs duty at home. Use this method for ungainly or heavy items only, items that you don't wanna lug around.

Of course the tax rate varies considerably from country to country. What's more, the procedures and requirements necessary to obtain VAT refunds tend to vary from country to country, store to store, and purchase to purchase. Some countries disallow certain of the above methods. Some countries enforce a time window in which you can leave the country before a refund becomes invalid. And the refund might be subject to additional handling fees, fees which may amount to as much as 3 percent of the purchase price. Most countries, in order to avoid processing paperwork for small purchases, impose a minimum purchase value that you must meet to qualify for a refund; individual stores may impose higher thresholds or apply them to each item individually rather than to your total bill. In fact, some countries let individual stores decide if they'll grant any refund at all. In Table 9.1, I describe some of the different rates and refund policies. For more details, contact the relevant tourist office(s).

As I mentioned above and described fully in the *Renting* chapter, Austria lets you refund a portion of the VAT paid on an Austrian motor vehicle rental. The Irish government, meanwhile, allows merchants to set their own rate of refund and minimum purchase amount. Look in the windows of Irish merchants for "Cashback" signs, or ask in the store if they issue *Cashback Vouchers*. In Italy you may be better off if you forego the refund and the ensuing flood of red tape and instead negotiate a reduction *before* you buy something. In Spain goods must leave the country within three months of their date of purchase to qualify for a refund. And in Belgium goods must leave the *European Community* within the same three months in order to qualify.

Sometimes the procedure to get the actual cash is clumsy. For example, many intra-European trains don't stop at the border long enough for you to take care of business; you may have to disembark, do your thing with customs, and get on another train later. [Just one more reason to drive, eh?] Of course if you use the mail method, you won't get your refund until you get home—and then you may find that cashing small refund checks in a foreign currency is a problem: some banks don't deal with them at all, and if they do, chances are they'll apply an unfair exchange rate. Below I list several organizations that can help. To be sure they haven't moved or gone out of business, always telephone these services before you mail your checks to them.

Table 9.1

VAT Refund Policies for Tourists in Various Countries.

	VAT Percentage	Percentage of Puchase Price* that's Refundable	Minimum Purchase	Refund Method			
				1	2	3	4
Austria	20%	16.7%	$75	•	•	•	•
Belgium	19.5	16.3	154	•	•	•	•
Denmark	20	16.7	98		•	•	
Finland	18	15.3	20	•		•	•
France	18.6	15.7	371	•	•	•	•
Germany	15	13	—	•	•	•	•
Great Britain	17.5	14.9	19	•	•	•	
Ireland	16–21	13.8–17.4	50–100		•	•	•
Italy	19	16	665/item	•	•	•	•
Luxembourg	15	13	92/item	•	•	•	
Netherlands	17.5	14.9	169	•	•	•	
Norway	20	16.7	44	•	•	•	•
Portugal	16–20	13.8–16.7	82	•	•	•	
Spain	15	13	314		•		
Sweden	25	20	15	•		•	•
Switzerland	6.5	?	?		•		

*Assuming that the VAT is buried in the purchase price.

For a fee of $3.50 the foreign currency department of Thomas Cook Services cashes VAT refund checks at good exchange rates. Checks of less than $250 are cashed on the spot; larger amounts must first clear a European bank. Offices worldwide.

Deak International, with offices in the US and Canada, cashes foreign-denominated checks. Call them at 800 421 8391 in the US (800 424 1186 in California), or 800 268 8155 in Canada.

New York Foreign Exchange, Inc., changes any European currency into US or Canadian dollars for a $2 service fee. They send out payment the same day they receive your checks.

26 Broadway Suite 767, New York, NY 10004, tel. 800 346 3924 or 212 248 4700.

591 Summit Ave., Jersey City, NJ 07306.

For $2 per check, Reusch International processes VAT refund checks at good rates. They return a check made out in US dollars after about ten days. Sign and endorse each check, write "Payable to Reusch International" along with your signature on each, and mail them to one of the following addresses.

3 First National Plaza, Suite 2020, Chicago, IL 60606, tel. 312 332 5900, FAX 312 332 5901.

1925 Century Park East, Suite 240, Los Angeles, CA 90067, tel. 213 277 7800, FAX 213 277 0832.

450 Park Ave., Suite 2301, New York, NY 10022, tel. 212 421 7100, FAX 212 421 6487.

1350 Eye St., 10th Floor, NW, Washington, DC 20005, tel. 800 424 2923 or 202 408 1200.

New York City residents might wanna check out Chequepoint USA Currency Exchange Bureau at 551 Madison Ave., New York, NY 10022, tel. 212 980 6443. They only cash British VAT refund checks, they only do it in person, and they charge an 8 percent fee.

Tax rates (not necessarily VAT) in the countries that do *not* currently offer refund programs to tourists are as follows: Bulgaria—19.5 percent; Czech Republic—23 percent; Greece—18 percent; Hungary—25 percent; Poland—7 percent; Romania—18 percent; Slovak Republic—23 percent; Turkey—12 percent. Be sure to ask in these countries if refunds are now available to foreigners. You may not be able to garner a tax refund from these countries, but the US government, under a program called the Generalized System of Prefer-ences (GSP), charges no duty on many types of goods bought in several of these countries. Write for the free GSP brochure; I give the address in the *Resources* chapter.

Now what about those refunds for business travelers? In Table 9.2, I describe the multitude of refunds available. There are, however, lots of criteria. Qualifying for these refunds can be a pain, however. Your company must possess a Federal Tax ID Number and cannot be incorporated or registered to do business or collect VAT in the country from which you, as an employee, claim a business-related VAT refund. Also, your company must file a certificate of status as a business in each country where it will conduct business and claim refunds. Note from Table 9.2 that the required minimum purchase amount depends on whether you incur the expenses during the one trip that you'll make to a particular country in a particular year or during one of two or more such trips. Furthermore, refund claims must be filed in bulk for expenditures made over a reasonable period of time, such as a quarter; and they cannot be filed later than six months after the end of the year. Only original receipts are acceptable with the

Table 9.1

VAT Refund Policies for Business Expenses in Various Countries.

	BEL	DEN	FRA	GER	GB	IRE	ITY	LUX	NET	SPA	SWE
once/year minimum	$31	35	33	38	94	27	25	31	39	27	—
multi-visit/year minimum	$246	244	278	317	203	216	179	246	310	222	—
vehicle purchase	50%			•							
vehicle rental	50%	?	•	•				•	•		50%
gasoline	50%	?									
diesel fuel	50%	•	50%	•	•	•		•	•		•
transportation	?	?		?			40%	34%		72%	
lodging	?		•	•				20%	34%	•	72%
gifts	?		•	•			•	•			•
professional costs	*	?	*	*	*	*	*	40%	*		•
conferences	?		•	•	•		•	•	•	•	•
fairs/exhibitions	?	•	•	•	•		•	•	•		•
entertainment		•					•				72%
meals	?		•	•				20%			72%
alcoholic beverages		•					•				

• = full refund; 50% = 50% refund; ? = depends; * = no VAT is charged for such services.

forms, and the forms must be filled out without error or omission and in the language of the refunding country. You can expect a refund six to twelve months after you file.

France, Italy, Portugal and Spain require companies to enlist registered agents, usually accounting firms, to file for such refunds. Regardless, given the hassle involved, your company may wanna hire one of these agents. The following is a list of firms that provide VAT-reclaim services.

Arthur Andersen & Co., 1345 Ave. of the Americas, New York, NY 10105, tel. 212 708 4324. Offices worldwide.

Deloitte & Touche, 2 Prudential Plaza, 180 N. Stetson Ave., Chicago, IL 60601, tel. 312 946 3000. Offices worldwide.

Euro VAT Refund (associated with Coopers and Lybrand), 9005 Exposition Blvd., Los Angeles 90034, tel. 310 204 0805.

FEXCO, FEXCO House, 15 Galena Road, London W6 0LT, England, tel. 44 81 748 0774.

The Global Group, 7614 Newcastle Dr., Annandale, VA 22003, tel. 703 642 2627.

International Sales Tax Refund (INSATAX), 620 19th St., Suite 160, Niagra Falls, NY 14301, tel. 716 284 6287; also at Dorset Lodge, 8 Dorset Square, London NW1 6QJ, England, tel. 44 71 724 3135.

ITS Fabry, 24 Vendue Range, Suite 201, Charleston, SC 29401, tel. 803 720 8646.

Meridain VAT Reclaim, 575 8th Ave., 6th Floor, New York, NY 10018, tel. 212 695 8424.

VRS, Crawley Grange, North Crawley, Buckinghamshire MK 169HL, England, tel. 44 2 306 5581.

10. resources

Free Info

There's a ton of free and relevant information for the asking, much of it equal or superior to what you'd otherwise pay for. Trouble is, after you order such info it may take a week or two or three or four to arrive. That's why I describe such opportunities first, to give you one less excuse for not getting on the ball.

The best way to get on the ball is by writing or calling all relevant tourist offices. (See the listings at the end of this chapter.) Describe to them your travel interests: driving, camping, bicycling, budget accommodations, homestays, farmstays, etc. If you plan to travel in France, you should ask for a map of *Bis* routes. Exits off France's *autoroutes* may be embellished by an orange panel marked *"Bis"*. These signs indicate alternate routes which avoid areas prone to congestion at peak driving times. Each June the French Government publishes a map of *Bis* routes and distributes it free of charge through its tourist offices. If you plan to buy a vehicle in Europe and/or import or export a vehicle to or from Europe, ask about taxing, insurance, registration, and, if relevant, about importing and exporting issues. If the tourist office can't help you, contact the appropriate consulate or embassy. (Again, see the end of this chapter.)

The maps offered by tourist offices, however, tend to be stylized and not very precise. I can't stress enough that you *need* a good, no-nonsense map or atlas, which you should either bring with you or else purchase immediately when you arrive. Maps of European countries are often cheaper in Europe than elsewhere, and since they're essentially graphic it doesn't matter much that they're in a foreign language. The European motoring clubs—especially those having reciprocal agreements with the AA, AAA, CAA, and NAC—may offer maps free of charge or at reduced prices. In the the *Breakdown, Accident or Emergency* section of each country's description in the *Country-by-Country Information* chapter, I list the names and addresses of the European motoring clubs. I suggest, however, that you at least bring a good map of the country you plan to begin your driving in. The AAA offers good maps to its members— *free* to AAA+ members and for a charge to basic members. If you belong to a different motoring club, check if they offer a similar deal. While you're at the club office, you can buy an International Driving Permit and get a passport photo taken—often free of charge if you join up that day. See the *Documents* chapter for more on the IDP and passports.

The Cyclists Touring Club, Cotterel House, 69 Meadrow, Goldalming, Surrey GU7 3H5 England, tel. 0483 417217, will be happy to send you information on bicycling in Britain. Ask the club if they can provide you with an updated list of British trains and buses that accept bicycles.

The governments of The Down Under and North America fund several "free" publications.

Customs Information for All Travelers is a brochure detailing Australian customs issues; it's available from local offices of the Collector of Customs or from Australian Consulates abroad.

I Declare is a pamphlet describing Canadian customs issues; it's available from the Revenue Canada Customs and Excise Department, Communications Branch, MacKenzie Ave., Ottawa, ON K1A 0L5, tel. 613 957 0275. *Bon Voyage, But ...* is another pamphlet covering these issues; it's available from External Affairs, Ottawa, ON K1A 0G3. These materials are also available at Canadian embassies and consulates abroad.

Three brochures—*New Zealand Customs Guide for Travelers, If You're Not Sure About It,* and *DECLARE IT*—are offered by New Zealand customs offices and by New Zealand embassies and consulates abroad. Contact New Zealand Customs, P.O. Box 29, Auckland, tel. 9 77 35 20.

Know Before You Go—Customs Hints for Returning U.S. Residents; International Mail Imports; and *GSP and the Traveler— Information on Bringing Articles from Developing Countries Under the Generalized System of Preferences* are three brochures available free of charge at US post offices, at US embassies and consulates abroad, and from Customs, P.O. Box 7407, Washington, DC 20044.

The Citizen's Emergency Center (Department of State Publication 9746) is a brochure distributed free of charge by the Superintendent of Documents, US Government Printing Office, Washington, DC 20402. The Citizen's Emergency Center issues *Consular Information Sheets* which address many travel matters. Stop by a passport office, US consulate or embassy, call the interactive hotline at 202 647 5225, or use a modem to tap into the Bureau of Consular Affair's computer bulletin board at 202 647 9225.

Even a few players in good 'ol private enterprise contribute to the pool of free info.

Europe Through the Backdoor's free and deliciously candid quarterly newsletter (maybe the best European travel newsletter, regardless of price) and free *Guide to European Railpasses* describe train costs in great detail, present heaps of other useful information, and offer products and services for sale. This is a top-notch operation captained by the oft-quoted Rick Steves.

You may have seen one of Rick's shows on PBS. Rick's *Europe Through the Backdoor, 2–22 Days in . . .* , and phrasebooks are not free, but they've attained a loyal readership because of their insightful, irreverent and spirited treatment. If you order something (a Eurailpass, guidebook, backpack, money belt, etc.) through ETBD, they'll throw in something else (last time I checked it was a *2–22 Days* guide) free of charge. ETBD also runs several excellent, close-to-the-ground, Backdoor tours of Europe. Write or call Europe Through the Backdoor, Inc., 109 Fourth Avenue N., P.O. Box C-2009, Edmonds, WA 98020–0909, tel. 206 771 8303.

Magellan's Travel Essentials, P.O. Box 5485-N, Santa Barbara, CA 93150, tel. 800 962 4943, will send you their free travel catalog listing water purifiers/filters, travel packs, money belts and security wallets, photo gear, electrical adaptors, first aid kits, translators, maps, phrasebooks, rain gear, hats, toilet kits and components, travel alarms, shortwave sets, etc. A fantastic resource—the number, variety and usefulness of the products offered are astounding.

Foreign Electricity is No Deep Dark Secret is a free brochure published by Franzus, Murtha Industrial Park, Box 142, Beacon

Falls, CT 06403, tel. 203 723 6664. Send a self addressed, stamped envelope. This company sells voltage and frequency transformers and plug adapters. See the *Packing* chapter for more on foreign electricity.

To search for a toll-free telephone number, North Americans can call 800 555 1212 without suffering a charge (though you'll only get AT&T 800 numbers, not those of Sprint or MCI); to search for a non toll-free number, they can call the area code plus 555 1212 and suffer a charge of $0.75. To search for a foreign phone number, call the appropriate tourist office, embassy or national chamber of commerce in your country. Otherwise, stop by a university library or a large public library: they often stock a wide variety of foreign directories.

Distributed by Hertz to travel agents only, *The European Car Guide* contains extremely detailed descriptions of the various vehicles available in Europe. Ask your travel agent to let you peruse it.

Also free of charge are the services provided by your local library. Don't underestimate what your library and librarian can do for you. A librarian can take one stupid question and moments later return with precisely the information you need. In

a world struck with information anxiety, librarians often function as psychiatrists.

Budget plenty of time for library research; a whole day or two may not be enough—that's how much pertinent info is out there. Begin by browsing the travel mags. Here are three of the best.

Consumer Reports Travel Letter. A remarkably informative and to-the-point monthly periodical. For a $37 annual subscription write to Consumer Reports Travel Letter, Subscription Department, P.O. Box 51366, Boulder, CO 80321-1366. Back issues (the May issue is especially helpful for Euro-motorists who plan to rent a vehicle) cost $5 each and can be ordered by calling 800 234 1970 or 919 378 200 or by writing to the Circulating Director, CRTL, 101 Truman Ave., Yonkers, NY 10703-1057.

The *Condé Nast Traveler*. An artful yet highly informative monthly magazine. To order a year-long subscription send $15 to P.O. Box 52469, Boulder, CO 80321-2469. For back issues call 800 777 0700. For free indexes call 800 628 1030.

Travel Holiday. Similar to *Condé Nast*. To subscribe to 10 issues a year, send $11.97 to Box 2036, Marion, OH 43305, or call 212 366 8700, FAX 212 366 8791.

Don't forget the *Readers Guide to Periodical Literature*. The *Guide* lists myriad travel articles that appear in magazines. It may have been a long time since you last used this resource to write a research paper for high school or college, but it's remarkably useful and easy to use. Check the *Automobile Touring* section first.

There are literally hundreds of serials—some of which are incredibly obscure *and* incredibly helpful—that your library won't have. To find one that suits your interests, look through *The Standard Periodical Directory* and *Ulrich's International Periodicals Directory Including Irregular Series and Anuuals*. Both are arranged by subject—eg. "Travel". Note that *Ulrich's* is international and includes book series; it's the one to check for guides that are produced and sold by foreign tourist offices.

Of course you won't forget to look over the library's selection of guidebooks. There's no reason why you can't check out one or two, take them on your trip, and return them just a little worse for wear. Below I list some of the most popular guides, followed by guides that are especially relevant to a driving tour of Europe.

Although I recommend that you get these books (if you get them) from your library or local bookstore, I include phone numbers and/or addresses so that you can order them direct from the publishers or distributers.

Consider one of the following budget guidebooks.

Berkeley, tel. 212 572 8757.

Europe Through the Backdoor, and the *ETBD 2–22 Days* guides. See the ETBD address I listed earlier in the chapter.

Let's Go, tel. 800 221 7945.

Lonely Planet, tel. 800 275 8555 or 510 893 8555, FAX 510 893 8563.

The Rough Guide, tel. 800 223 2348 or 212 373 8500.

Or try one of these more upscale-oriented travel guides.

Baedeker's, tel. 201 767 5937

Birnbaum's, tel. 212 270 7542.

Fielding's, tel. 212 889 3050.

Fodor's, tel. 212 572 8757.

Frommer's, tel. 800 223 2348 or 212 373 8500.

For a broader overview of history and culture, you might also want one of the following.

Eyewitness, tel. 800 225 3362.

Knopf, tel. 800 733 3000 or 410 848 1900.

But more experienced art-lovers may prefer the

Blue Guides, tel. 800 233 4843 or 212 354 5500.

Your interests in the countryside will better served by the following.

Berlitz Travellers, tel. 212 598 2499, FAX 212 353 9706.

Insight Guides, tel. 800 225 3362 or 617 272 1500.

Michelin, tel. 800 423 0485 or 803 458 5261.

And here are some especially relevant resources to check out.

Britain's Royal Automobile Club (RAC) will prepare individually tailored routes for members and non members. The RAC's *European Route and Travel Pack* let's you choose a route that's either the fastest, most scenic, most suitable for towing, or that avoids motorways and toll roads. The *Pack* goes on to provide junction-by-junction route directions, total and intermediate distances in miles and kilometers, through-route town plans for major cities, route planning maps for every country visited, and information booklets for each country. Coverage includes Austria, Belgium, France, Germany, Luxembourg, the Netherlands, Portugal, Spain, and Switzerland; marked mapping is provided to cover other countries. The *Travel Pack* costs £16.50 ($25) for members, £18.50 ($28) for non members. The RAC also offers *Travel Packs* that cover the United Kingdom and Ireland; both cost £5 ($8) for members, £10 ($15) for non members. A cheaper alternative is the collection of *European Route and Town Plans;* it costs £11 ($17) for members, £13 ($20) for non members. To order, call the RAC in England at 01345 333 222; have your credit card details available. Allow fourteen days for route preparation; next-day delivery within England, however, can be guaranteed for a £3 ($5) supplement.

The *Driving Tours* series from Prentice Hall Travel includes one guide for each of the following countries: *Britain, France, Germany, Italy, Scotland,* and *Spain.* Each guide is a compendium of dozens of itineraries—complete with maps, historical descriptions and photographs. Prentice Hall

General Reference and Travel, 15 Columbus Circle, New York, NY 10023, tel. 800 223 2348 or 212 373 8500. $19.00 each.

The *Exploring Rural Europe* series includes *England & Wales, France, Germany, Greece, Ireland, Italy, Scotland,* and *Spain*. Each guide is about 200 pages long, and consists of driving tours of one day to one week that acquaint the traveler with the histor, character and cuisine of the region. Passport Books, 4255 West Touhy Avenue, Lincolnwood, IL 60646-1975, tel. 800 323 4900 or 708 679 5500, FAX 708 679 2494. $12.95 each.

Off the Beaten Track Guides. This series includes *Austria, Britain, Northern France, Southern France, Germany, Greece, Italy, Portugal, Scandinavia, Spain,* and *Switzerland*. Each guide is about 300 pages long, includes maps and color photos. Globe Pequot Press, P.O. Box 833, 6 Business Park Road, Old Saybrook, CT 06475–0833, tel. 800 243 0495 or 203 395 0440 or 800 962 0973 (in Connecticut), FAX 203 395 0312. $14.95 each.

Touring Europe: Flexible Day by Day Itineraries for Independent Travelers. Michael Spring. 1994. Chapters consist of: Ireland—the Southwest; England—Bath, the Cotswolds, and Stratford-upon-Avon;

Germany—Heidelberg, the Romantic Highway, Munich and the Alps; Austria—Salzburg to Vienna; Italy—Pompeii, Capri, and the Amalfi Coast; France—The Riviera; Spain—Sevilla, Córdoba, Granada, and the Costa del Sol. Fodor's. $15.00.

The *Best of Britain's Countryside: A Driving and Walking Itinerary* series includes the *Heart of England and Wales*, *Northern England and Scotland*, and *Southern England*. Bill and Gwen North. 1990–1993. 256–272 pages. Mountaineers Books, 1011 SW Klickitat Way, Suite 107, Seattle, WA 98134-1162, tel. 800 553 4453 or 206 223 6303. $12.95 each.

Walks and Tours in Britain. 1990. 320 pages. The British Automobile Association and Ordnance Survey collaborated on this unique guide to 194 walks and 50 driving routes in the UK's most scenic areas. Accompanied by detailed maps and descriptions of sights, each tour is on a removable loose-leaf sheet; a clear plastic cover protects against the wet. Oversized hardcover binder. W.W. Norton, 500 5th Ave., New York, NY 10110, tel. 800 223 2584 or 212 354 550. $40.

AA Tour Guide: Britain; and the *AA Tour Guide Scotland*. These soft-back guides contain many two- and three-day car tours

detailing the most interesting places to visit en route. Distributed by BritRail Travel International, Inc., 1500 Broadway, 10th Floor, New York, NY 10036-4015, tel. 800 677 8585 or 212 575 2667, FAX 212 575 2542. Also available at BritRail's British Travel Shop, 551 Fifth Ave., 7th Floor, New York, NY 10176. In Britain contact the Automobile Association, Farnum House, Basing View, Basingstoke, Hampshire RG21 2EA, England, tel. 01256 20123, FAX 01256 493389. $16.95 each.

Daytrips in Britain. The popular *Daytrips from London* has been expanded to cover not only the easy and interesting day excursions from the capital but also others using Edinburgh as the starting point. Distributed by BritRail and Britain's AA. (See the listing immediately above.) $12.95.

Scotland for the Motorist. Pastime Publications' guide to all sorts of outdoor activities. Distributed by BritRail and Britain's AA. (See the listing above.) $12.95.

Ireland: The Complete Guide and Road Atlas. 1993. 128 pages. This oversized paperback, complete with a 16-page road atlas, presents 10 suggested routes, along with background info on history and culture, and a 75-page gazetteer of major cities and towns. Globe Pequot. (See previous listing.) $19.95.

AA Walks and Tours in France. 1993. 256 pages. Produced by the British Automobile Association and the IGN-F (the French national mapping society) as a guide to more than 200 scenic walks and drives all over France. Copiously illustrated with high-quality color photos and excellent maps. W.W. Norton, 500 5th Ave., New York, NY 10110, tel. 800 223 2584 or 212 354 5500. $35.

The Backroads of Holland: Scenic Excursions by Bicycle, Car, Train or Boat. Helen Colijn. 1992. 224 pages. Serves up 20 scenic tours that will take you off the beaten track by bike, boat, train, car or even foot. Bicycle Books, P.O. Box 2038, Mill Valley, CA 94942, tel. 800 468 8233 or 415 381 2515. $12.95.

Karen Brown's Country Inns and Itineraries series includes a book for each of the following: England, Wales, and Scotland; France; Germany; Ireland; Italy; Spain; and Switzerland. Each book is about 290 pages long. 1992–1994. Travel Press, P.O. Box 70, San Mateo, CA 94401, tel. 415 842 9117. Distributed by Globe Pequot Press. $14.95 each.

Guide to Vacation Rentals in Europe. Michael and Laura Murphy. 1994. 384 pages. First-hand advice about how to cut out unnecessary middlemen and save big bucks by dealing direct with the most reputable European agents, where the best rentals are (villas, apartments, cottages, chalets, farmhouses and condos) and their rates. Globe Peqout Press. $14.95.

Europe's Wonderful Little Hotels and Inns. One guide for Great Britain and Ireland, and one for the continent. Edited by Hilary Rubinstein. 1994. 352 and 496 pages, respectively. St. Martin's Press, 175 5th Ave., New York, NY 10010, tel. 800 221 7945. $14.95 and $17.95, respectively.

Cottages, B&B's and Country Inns of England and Wales. Elizabeth Gundry. 1994. Fodors Travel. $15.

People to People series. Jim Haynes. Includes the following: *The Baltic Republics; Czechoslovakia, Hungary, Bulgaria; France; Poland; Romania;* and *Russia.* Putting you directly in touch with Europe's people, these invaluable little books increase your chance of experiencing the real Europe. Each guide covers a certain geopolitical area and consists of information about one thousand citizens of all ages who asked to participate in this unique experiment of sorts. These people wanna meet you, show you how they live, introduce you to their favorite places, and help you find accommodation—perhaps in their own homes. The info about each person includes address, phone number, languages spoken, profession, age and a brief self-description. Jim Haynes has lived in Paris for twenty years. The dinners he hosts every Sunday evening for Parisians, expatriates and visitors have become legendary. Jim's address is Atelier A-2, 83 rue de la Tombe Issoire, 75014 Paris, France, tel. 1 43 27 17 67 or 1 43 27 19 09, FAX 1 43 20 41 95. Published by Zephyr Press, 13 Robinson Street, Somerville, MA 02145, tel. 800 775 1400 or 203 467 4257. $10.95 each.

International Meet-the-People Directory. Edited by Marianne Cruz. This 32-page directory lists contacts in over 30 countries. International Visitors Information Service, 1623 Belmont St., NW, Washington, DC 20009-4003, tel. 202 939 5566. $6.

Festivals Europe. Margaret M. Johnson. 1992. 240 pages. Mustang Publishing Co., P.O. Box 3004, Memphis, TN 38173, tel. 800 462 6420 or 301 459 8696. $10.95.

Passport's Let's Drive Europe Phrasebook. 95 pages. An eight-language phrasebook *specifically* designed for motorists, it contains detailed graphics showing automotive parts and assemblies. It also contains phrases pertaining to general travel activities and situations. $7.95. Also available is *Passport's World Travel Translator* (NTC/Sony EB-XA, EB-G and CD-ROMXA, price varies), a computer-based product that includes words and expressions in ten languages—and a special automotive section with digitized graphics. Published by Passport Books. (See address above.)

Manston's Europe '91. Peter Manston. 496 pages. The best guide to the practical: how phone systems work, laundromats, etc. Travel Keys, P.O. Box 160691, Sacramento, CA 95816, tel. 916 452 5200. $11.95.

The Camper's Companion to Northern Europe and/or *The Camper's Companion to Southern Europe*. Dennis and Tina Jaffe. 1986. 300 pages. These guides are full to the brim with concise info. Williamson Publishing Co., Church Hill Road, P.O. Box 185, Charlotte, Vermont 05445, tel. 800 234 8791 or 802 425 2101. $13.95 each.

Europa Camping. Lists hundreds of campgrounds across Europe. Distributed by Recreational Equipment. P.O. Box C-88126, Seattle, WA 98188, tel. 800 426 4840.

Michelin Red Guide Series: Camping France. Michelin Travel Publications, Box 19001, Greenville, SC 29602–9001, tel. 800 423 0485. $15.

Europe by Van and Motorhome. David Shore and Patty Campbell. 1994. 232 pages. Overlaps somewhat with the info in *Moto Europa* but provides enough motorhoming/van-tripping specifics to justify its purchase. Shore/Campbell Publications, 1842 Santa Margarite Drive, Fallbrook, CA 92028, tel. 619 723 6184. $13.95 US, $15.95 Canada.

Exploring Europe by RV. Dennis and Tina Jaffe. 1994. 320 pages. Also overlaps with *Moto Europa,* but includes eleven recommended itineraries, featuring details about favorite campgrounds, that can be followed to the letter or tailored to suit your taste. Globe Pequot Press. $14.95.

Britain's Caravan Club publishes in two volumes the most useful English-language guide to Europe's campgrounds: one guide covers the UK, the other the continent. However, many of the smaller UK sites are restricted to Caravan Club members or to members of affiliated clubs such as the AAA. The Caravan Club, East Grinstead House, East Grinstead, West Sussex RH19 IUA, England, tel. 01342 326944, FAX 01342 41 02 58.

AA Camping and Caravaning in Britain. Less detailed than the above, but provides info on on some 1000 best inspected and graded sites. Distributed by BritRail Travel International, Inc., 1500 Broadway, 10th Floor, New York, NY 10036-4015, tel. 800 677 8585 or 212 575 2667, FAX 212 575 2542. Also available at BritRail's British Travel Shop, 551 Fifth Ave., 7th Floor, New York, NY 10176. In Britain contact the Automobile Association, Farnum House, Basing View, Basingstoke, Hampshire RG21 2EA, England, tel. 01256 20123, FAX 01256 493389. $15.95.

Scotland: Camping and Caravaning Parks. Published by the Scottish Tourist Board, this guide lists the facilities, rates, etc. of some 350 camping sites in Scotland. Distributed by BritRail and Britain's AA. (See the listing immediately above.) $7.95.

The British Forestry Commision operates campgrounds in many scenic locations. Contact them at 231 Corstorphine Rd., Edinburgh EH12 7AT, Scotland, tel. 0131 334 0303.

Readers of German will find the German auto club *ADAC's* two-volume guide very helpful. ADAC, AM Westpark 8, 81373 Munchen 70, Germnay, tel. 89 76 760, FAX 89 76 76 2500.

The Recreational Vehicle Association sells a directory of more than 300 member dealers in the US, Canada and Europe, including types of vehicles offered, weekly prices, and whether or not airport pickup is provided. They also publish "Rental Ventures", a booklet listing state travel offices and campground associations, with info on how to choose an RV. Tel. 800 336 0335. $5 for the directory; $3 for the booklet; $7.50 for both.

Motor Caravan Magazine. Link House, Dingwall Ave., GB-Croydon CR9 2Ta, England, tel. 0181 68 62 599.

Camping Car. 24, avenue de Mousquetaires, F-94420 Le Plessis-Trevise, France, tel. 1 45 93 72 72, FAX 1 45 93 25 93.

Camp Magazin. Gansemarkt 24, Postfach 30 54 24, D-20317 Hamburg, Germany, tel. 40 34 700, FAX 40 34 58 90.

Pro Mobil. Another camping magazine. Anzeigenabteilung, D-70162 Stuttgart 10, Germany, tel 711 18 21 639, FAX 711 18 21 349.

Innocents Abroad: Traveling with Kids in Europe. Valerie Wolf Deutsch and Laura Sutherland. 1991. 480 pages. Penguin USA, tel. 800 526 0275 or 201 387 0600. $15.95, or $4.95 paperback.

Miles of Smiles: 101 Great Car Games. Carole Terwilliger Meyers. 1992. 128 pages. Carousel Press, P.O. Box 6061, Albany, CA 94706–0061, tel. 510 527 5849. $8.95.

Take Your Kids to Europe. Cynthia Harriman. 1991. 222 pages. ETBD calls it their favorite book on traveling with kids in Europe. Cynthia covers planning, food, lodging, travel tips, and country-by-country sights and activities that really turn kids on. Sold by Europe Through the Back Door. $13.

Travel With Children. Maureen Wheeler. 160 pages. Lonely Planet Publications, Embarcadero West, 112 Linden St., Oakland, CA 94607, tel. 800 275 8555 or 510 893 8555; also P.O. Box 617, Hawthorn, Victoria 3122, Australia. Within the USA, send $10.95 + $1.50 postage.

Motorcycle Journies Through the Alps. John Hermann. 1993. 250 pages. Whitehorse Press, 154 West Brookline St., Boston, MA 02118, tel. 800 842 7077 or 617 241 5241. $19.95.

Motorcycle Touring: An International Directory is also published by Whitehorse Press. The directory gives bios of tour operators, describes organized tours worldwide, lists motorcycle rental compa-

nies worldwide, and describes shipping issues and companies. 460 pages. $24.90.

Get Up and Go: A Guide for the Mature Traveler. Gene and Adele Malott. 1989. 325 pages. Gateway Books, 13 Bedford Cove, San Rafael, CA 94901, tel. 415 454 5215. $10.95 + $1.90 postage.

The International Health Guide for Senior Citizens (1990, 70 pages) and *The Senior Citizen's Guide to Budget Travel in Europe* (1992, 63 pages). Pilot Books, 103 Cooper St., Babylon, NY 11702, tel. 516 422 2225. $5.95 each.

On the Move: A Motorist's Guide for the Disabled Traveler. 1991. 128 pages. $6.95.

Directory of Accessible Van Rentals. For campers and RV travelers worldwide. Twin Peaks Press, Box 129, Vancouver, WA 98666, tel. 800 637 2256 or 206 694 2462. $9.95.

Trueblood RV, Justinianstraße 22, 60322 Frankfurt, Germany, tel. 69 34 53 54, will send info about how to rent or buy a European motorhome designed for wheelchair users.

More info regarding wheelchair-accessible facilities is distributed by The Society for the Advancement of Travel for the Handicapped, 26 Court St., Penthouse,

Brooklyn, NY 11242, tel. 718 858 5483; and by Moss Rehabilitation Hospital Travel Information Service, 1200 West Tabor Road, Philadelphia, PA 19141-3009, tel. 216 456 9600.

Buying a Bargain Car at Auction. Robert Stock, (a Brit). Robert Hale Publishing. £6.99.

How to Keep Your Volkswagon Alive: A Manual of Step by Step Procedures for the Complete Idiot. 15th edition. 464 pages. John Muir Publications, P.O. Box 613, Sante Fe, NM 87504-0613, tel. 800 888 7504 or 505 982 4078.

Volkswagon Stationwagon & Bus Official Service Manual Type 2: 1968–1979. 4th rev. edition. 468 pages. Robert Bentley Publishing, 1000 Massachusetts Ave., Cambridge, MA 02138, tel. 800 423 4595, tel. 617 547 4170. $34.95. This book actually complements the one immediately above; consider buying both if you're doing a van trip.

As already stated, your choice of maps is important. Although the library will have a European atlas, you won't be able to take it with you. Consider the following.

Michelin Guide, No. 703: Europe, Main Cities. 1993. Tel. 800 423 0485 or 803 599 0850. $24.95.

Michelin Road Atlas: Europe. Scenic routes marked in green. $19.95.

Michelin also sells individual country maps.

Passport's European Atlas for Travelers. 1988. 252 pages. Tel. 800 323 4900 or 708 679 5500, FAX 708 679 2494. $24.95.

Passport's European Road Atlas: Europe. 1991. $16.95.

Passport's Road Atlas: Great Britain. $16.95.

Passport's Map of Switzerland, Austria & the Alps. 1989. $9.95.

Passport's Map of Scandinavia. $9.95.

Passport's Map of Holland, Belgium, and Luxembourg. $9.95.

Rand McNally sells comparable maps and atlases, tel. 800 333 0136.

BritRail distributes a fantastic array of maps from several sources (such as Michelin and Britain's AA) and of many different scales and of all parts of the British Isles. BritRail Travel International, Inc., 1500 Broadway, 10th Floor, New York, NY 10036-4015, tel. 800 677 8585 or 212 575 2667, FAX 212 575 2542. Also available at BritRail's British Travel Shop, 551 Fifth Ave., 7th Floor, New York, NY 10176.

Destination Europe, an add-on to the electronic *Automap Road Atlas* ($59.95), allows you to plan driving trips through more than 8400 cities and over 250,000 miles of roadways, with info on the quickest routes, alternative routes, distances, driving times, weather, and ski resorts, along with phone numbers and addresses of hotels in major cities. Disks for DOS, Mac, and Windows. Automap, Box 690, Buffalo, NY 14207, tel. 800 564 6277, FAX 716 873 0906. $39.95

Map Link, 25 E. Mason St., Depot A, Santa Barabara, CA 93101, tel. 805 965 4402, offers a unique assortment of "hard-to-find" and rare maps purchased on location by world travelers and shipped or hand-carried back. Ask for their free catalog of over 4500 map titles.

World Image, 6348 W. 95th St., 104-I, Oak Lawn, IL 60453, tel. 708 233 0208, sells maps of anyplace in the world: road, city, regional, and topographic. Ask for their free catalog.

The Moscow City Map and Guide. 2nd ed. Contains over 500 significant revisions relecting changes in Moscow over the last two years. RIS, 89 Main St., Suite 2, Montpelier, VT 05602, tel 800 639 4301, FAX 802 223 6105. $6.95.

A couple of books tell you about other books.

Traveler's Reading Guide: Ready-Made Reading Lists for the Armchair Traveler. Edited by Maggy Simony. 1992. 960 pages. Lists both travel literature and guidebooks. Facts on File, 460 Park Ave. South, New York, NY 10016, tel. 800 322 8755. $19.95.

Good Books for the Curious Traveler—Europe. Theodora Nelson and Andrea Cross. Johnson Books, 1880 S. 57th Ct., Boulder, CA 80301, tel. 800 258 5830.

If you can't find just the right book, you should look through the collection of *Books In Print* reference guides at your library. These guides list myriad English-language books; and they do so by *Title*, *Author* and *Subject*. The *Subject* volume will probably prove most useful. Note the publishers of the books that interest you, and glean the publisher's telephone number from the *Publishers* volume. You can take this info to your local bookstore and have them order the book or books for you. Although the bookstore clerk could look up the same info (they'll have a *Books In Print* collection, plus similar directories), it's no fun to wait at the front of a line with four impatient souls breathing down your neck and tapping their feet.

It's said that the quickest way to learn what maps, books, and tapes covering a particular destination are available is to ask for a free computer printout from Travel Books and Language Center, Inc., 4931 Cordell Ave., Bethesda, MD 20814, tel. 301 951 8533, FAX 301 951 8546.

Info on the Electronic Superhighway

Super-up-to-date travel info—including dispatches from travelers abroad—is compiled in *GNN Travelers' Resource Center,* an online magazine-style publication featured in the Global Network Navigator for the internet, www address nearet.gnn.com. The web is burgeoning with other travel sites as well. Many libraries now offer internet access free of charge.

The folks at Foremost Euro-car have developed a cutting-edge electronic travel-information service called *Key Travel.* By using an IBM-compatible computer and modem to dial 818 786 2032, you can access *Key Travel's* bulletin and message boards as well as their full-color, high-resolution graphics of the various vehicles available for rent, lease or purchase in

Europe. A Mac-compatible version may be up and running by the time you read this. If you don't have a modem, you can call Foremost and ask them to send you—again, free of charge—a disk bearing the same info.

One brand-new bulletin board deserves special mention. The Travel Info Exchange (modem 508 287 0660, 24 hours, limit one hour per day) is operated by Tom Brosnahan, the author of Lonely Planet's *Turkey: A Travel Survival Kit.* The Exchange includes a conference hosted by Europe Through the Backdoor's Rick Steves.

The most complete overview of travel information sources available on computer networks is *The Electronic Traveler,* a spiral-bound directory written and published by M.L. Endicott. The book covers the Internet, popular proprietary systems such as America Online (with its Travel Cafe) and CompuServe (with its Travel Forum), computer reservations systems such as Eaasy Sabre, and over 200 independent bulletin board systems (BBS's). The author is moderator of the green.travel mailing list, cohost of the Travel Conference on the WELL, and operator of the Gaia Passage Travel Information Service

BBS (modem 912 265 0784, 7:00 P.M. to 7:00 A.M. EST). The book costs $50 post-paid. To order, send a check or money order payable to M.L. Endicott, P.O. Box 20837, Saint Simons Islands, GA 31522 USA.

A less expensive directory is Savitha Varadan's *A Pocket Tour of Travel on the Internet*. Sybex, 2021 Challenger Dr., Alameda, CA, tel 800 227 2346 or 510 523 8233. $12.99.

Travel Partners

If you have access to the Internet or to a computer bulletin board, consider placing or looking for a message asking for travel partners. You can also place a classified ad in a major newspaper or magazine or in one of the newsletters listed in the *Standard Periodicals* or *Ulrich's* directories. Try the *International Travel News*, 2120 28th St., Sacramento, CA 95818, tel. 800 366 9192; $0.55 per word; deadline: 20th of the month two months prior to issue date.

One of the following publications may help.

Partners In Travel is a sixteen-page newsletter amounting to a contact service for the single traveler. Partners in Travel, 11660 Chenault St. #119, Los Angeles, CA 90049-4527, tel. 213 476 4869. $45 a year.

Travel Companions is a thirty-three page newsletter for singles of all ages. It contains hundreds of listings from singles seeking travel companions and partners. Travel Companions Exchange, Inc., Box 833, Amityville, NY 11701-0833, tel. 516 454 0880, FAX 516 954 0170. $4 per issue.

You may want to enlist one of the following services.

June's International and Sophistacted Women Travelers, 603 Bath Ave., Brooklyn, NY, tel. 718 266 2045.

Singles in Motion, 545 W. 236th St., Riverdale, NY 10463, tel. 718 884 4464.

Singleworld, 401 Theodore Fremd Ave., Rye, NY 10580, tel. 800 223 6490 or 914 967 3334.

Travel Companions, Atrium Financial Center, 1515 N. Federal Highway, Suite 300, Boca Raton, FL 33432, tel. 800 383 7211 or 407 393 6448.

Travel in Two's, 239 N. Broadway, Suite 3, N. Tarrytown, NY 10591, tel. 800 692 5252 or 904 631 8301.

Umbrella Singles, P.O. Box 157, Woodbine, NY 12788, tel. 800 537 2797 or 914 434 6871.

Solo Flights, 63 High Noon Rd., Weston, CT 06883, tel. 203 226 9993.

Golden Companions. Exclusively for those over 45 years of age. P.O. Box 754, Pullman, WA 99613, tel. 208 858 2183.

Tempo Travelers. Caters to single, widowed or divorced travelers who are at least 50 years of age. 938 N. 70th #125, Lincoln, NE 68505.

Alternative Ways to Get There

Of course you can go by either air or sea. Either way it doesn't have to be a ho-hum process. Indeed, why not begin your trip by pushing the envelope? It'll be a little adventure in itself—a rewarding adventure.

I'll start with the most sedate option that can still be called "alternative": You can buy airline tickets from consolidators who buy blocks of unsold tickets from the airlines and then sell them at discounted rates. If you choose this option, call the appropriate Better Business Burea to confirm that no substantial complaints have been filed against the companies you're considering. What's more, get all information in writing, buy confirmed round-trip tickets only, and pay by credit card so you have recourse if something goes foul. Try the following.

Airhitch, tel. 800 326 2009.

1-800-FLY-CHEAP.

Cheap Tix Inc., 8320 Lincoln, Room 101, Los Angeles, CA 90045, tel. 800 234 4522.

Council Charter, tel. 800 800 8222.

Council Travel (see previously listed addresses), STA Travel or Travel CUTS (see the *Documents* chapter).

Euram, tel. 800 848 6789.

International Adventures, tel. 212 599 0577.

JetSet, tel. 800 638 3273

NOW Voyager, 74 Varick St. #307, New York, NY 10013, tel. 212 431 1616.

Travac 989 6th Avenue, New York, NY 10018, tel. 800 872 8800 or 212 563 3303.

Unitravel, 1177 N. Warson Road, P.O. Box 12485, Saint Louis, MO 63132, tel. 800 325 2222.

Consolidators may place classified ads under the headings "Travel", "Tickets", or "Transportation". Check newspapers—especially the Sunday *New York Times'*
Travel section—and alternative publications such as the *Utne Reader* and the *Village Voice.* Your local library probably subscribes to major city newspapers and to certain alternative publications. The June '94 *Consumer Reports Travel Letter* includes an excellent geographically ordered list of North American consolidators.

Barter is a common means of exchange between travel suppliers. Try contacting Travel World Leisure Club, tel. 800 444 TWLC or 212 239 4855.

There's yet another air-travel option: You can exchange your checked-baggage allowance for a cheap airline ticket. Such an arrangement is known as *air courier travel,* and there are several companies that specialize in it. Although you won't be able to check any bags when traveling as a courier, you *can* bring carry-on luggage aboard. (And, hey, if you're trying to "travel light", carry-ons are all you should bring anyway.) You never touch whatever it is the courier company is transporting; someone else takes care of getting that on and off the plane and the premises. All you do is meet an agent at the airport, sign some papers, and show Customs some documents when you arrive abroad. There are at least four books about air courier travel.

Air Courier Bargains. Kelly Monaghan. Intrepid Traveler, tel. 800 356 9315. $14.95 in bookstores, $17.45 from Intrepid.

The Insider's Guide to Air Courier Bargains and *The Courier Air Travel Handbook*. Thunderbird Press, 5930–10 W. Greenway Rd., Suite 112, Glendale, AZ 85306, tel. 800 345 0096. $14.95 and $10.95, respectively.

Air Couriers Guide Book. Owen Publications, Box 32172-A, Charleston, SC 33733. $6.95 ppd.

You can arrange such travel by contacting an air courier broker; find them listed in the Yellow Pages under the following headings: "Air Courier Service", "Courier Service", "Delivery Service", or "Freight Service". Like the aforementioned consolidators, air courier brokers sometimes place classified ads under the headings of "Travel", "Tickets", or "Transportation". Here are a few such brokers.

Discount Travel International, tel. 212 362 3636.

Excalibur International Courier (c/o Way to Go Travel), tel. 213 466 1126.

F.B. On Board Courier Services, tel. 514 633 0740.

Halibut Express, tel. 718 656 8279.

International Adventures, tel. 212 599 0577.

Midnight Express, tel. 310 672 1100.

NOW Voyager, tel. 212 431 1616.

The Shoestring Traveler, a newsletter for and about air couriers, has established a bulletin board for its members that includes daily courier updates and a flight-search program that searches for the lowest courier and non-courier airfare to foreign destinations, including charter flights, consolidator fares, and other bargains that don't show up on most travel agents' computers. A subscription costs $42 per year; for more info call 407 582 8320.

And the International Association of Air Travel Couriers publishes a bi-monthly newsletter detailing trips and fares available from dozens of courier-booking agencies in the US and overseas. IAATC, South J St., Box 1349, Lake Worth, FL 33460, tel. 407 582 8320. $45/year.

If you have to leave from an airport far from your home to get a good deal, try doing a "drive away" to that city. In other words, call one of the following outfits and arrange to deliver a vehicle for them. (You pay for the fuel only.)

AAA Driveaway, tel. 800 466 7775.

Across America Driveaway, tel. 219 852 0134.

All America Auto Transport, tel. 800 942 0001. DC and LA.

Auto DriveAway, tel. 800 346 2277 or 212 967 2344. Nationwide with 85 offices.

Dependable Car Travel tel. 800 826 1083. NY, LA, and Miami.

If the sea beckons, there are several options for you—the most luxurious of which is an old-fashioned oceanliner crossing. Try contacting the following.

Cunard Line's *Queen Elizabeth 2*. From April to October the *QE2* sails twice monthly between New York and Southampton, England, with less frequent sailings the rest of the year. Cunard Line, 555 Fifth Avenue, New York, NY 10017-2453, tel. 800 221 4770 or 212 880 7545 or 212 880 7500, FAX 212 949 0915. See the *Shipping and Importing* chapter for details about bringing your vehicle on the ship.

Royal Viking Line, 750 Battery St., San Francisco, CA 94111, tel. 800 634 8000, ships out to Europe several times a year.

And then there's the intrigueing option of freighter travel. The accommodations on freighters are wonderful—you have your own spacious outside cabin with a big window instead of a port hole; you dine on good food with the captain and the rest of the crew; and you get to hang out with about a dozen other intrepid travelers like yourself. But it costs a lot: each day will run about $100, and the trip will probably take one or two or three weeks. The following resources will help.

Cruise and Freighter Travel Letter, Klevens Publications, Inc., 7600 Avenue V, Little Rock, CA 93543–9436, tel. 805 944 4111. 12 pages.

Ford's Freighter Travel Guide, Ford's Travel Guides, 19448 Londelius St., Northridge, CA 91324–3511, tel. 818 701 7414, FAX 818 701 7415. Gives information on passenger-carrying freighters and other casual forms of ship travel. 144 pages. $15 per copy.

Freighter Space Advisory, Freighter World Cruises, Inc., 180 South Lake #355I, Pasadena, CA 91101, tel. 818 449 3106. $33 per year, twenty-four issues.

Freighter Travel News. First-hand accounts of recent freighter trips along with late-breaking news in the field. Freighter Travel News, 3524 Harts Lake Rd., Roy, WA

98580–9125, tel. 206 458 4178. 8 pages. $2 per copy. $18 per year, $20 in Canada.

Mediterranean Shipping Co. (c/o Sea the Difference, 420 5th Ave., 8th Fl., New York, NY, tel. 800 666 9333 or 212 354 4409.)

Pearl's Travel Tips, 548 East Shore Road, Great Neck, NY 11024, tel. 516 487 8351. Offers a free newsletter about freighter travel.

Traveltips, Traveltips Cruise & Freighter Travel Association, 163–07 Depot Road, Flushing, NY 11358, tel. 212 939 2400. Gives first-hand accounts of cruises taken by members of the association. Offers a free eight-page pamphlet.

Ocean-going yachts are always looking for cooks, cleanup persons and sailors. Experience is key. Can you hoist the sails? Are you a doctor or nurse? Can you cook? Do you have a video camera so you can document the trip? Are you a photographer? A writer? Can you dive? Regardless, you should bone up on the jargon of sailing. Bring a résumé, and secure letters of recommendation from previous employers: the more professional you seem the better your chances. Many yachting magazines include help-wanted advertisements.

If these don't produce a definite contact, you can check the marinas in Miami, Newport, etc. Look for laundry and self-steering gear hanging out to dry. Signs asking for long-haul sailors and live-aboards may be posted. Hangout at the yacht clubs and yuk it up with the regulars. Many owners are happy to exchange free passage for help; this allows them to avoid the hassles of hiring and accounting for a paid employee. But note that "sharing expenses" usually means you're expected to chip in for food at least. Common destinations include Britain and the Mediterranean ports of France, Gibraltar, Italy, Malta, and Spain. But since you won't be traveling with an onward airplane ticket you *may* need to have money available for posting a bond of roughly $1000 when you dock in a country; such bonds are of course refundable upon your exit. If you're serious about this option, you should get a copy of Greg Becker's wonderful new book, *The Seagoing Hitchhiker's Handbook: Roaming the World on Other People's Yachts,* Upper Access Books, tel. 800 356 9315, $11.95. Greg covers the skills that would make you most desirable, pretrip planning, money matters, where to look and when, what to

consider before signing on, captain and crew relations, and lists the best-traveled cruising routes.

Consumer Protection

US Citizens who have problems with transportation services that serve the US can get help from the Better Business Bureau and from the USDOT Consumer Affairs Division, 400 7th St., SW, Room 10405, Washington, DC 20590, tel. 202 366 2220. To order the publication *Flyrights* (Publication #050-000-00513-5) free of charge, contact the US Government Printing Office, P.O. Box 371954, Pitsburgh, PA 15250-7954, tel. 202 783 3238.

Once Abroad

You may wanna meet some natives who are in your career field. To do this, look for "institutes" for foreign visitors. These organizations schedule such meetings. The Swedish institute, tel. 8 789 2000, is the best. Some local German tourist offices match travelers and natives through the "In Dialogue" program. Friends Overseas, 68-04 Dartmouth St., Forest Hills, NY 11375, sets up meetings with individuals, families or couples; write and include your name, address, telephone number, age, occupation or occupational goals, when and where you'll visit, and an SASE. Of course you can do your own footwork. Scan major bulletin boards, like those at the University of London (in Senate House on Malet St., and at Birbeck College). These boards list lectures, speeches, workshops, and gatherings that are open to the public—great opportunities to meet interesting people in an atmosphere where you don't stand out as a gawking tourist.

If you wanna know how to get from here to there in London, get a *Mini London AZ Street Atlas and Index;* it's used religiously—even by the residents. The *Atlas* illustrates and indexes every street, alleyway, tube line and tube stop in London. You can pick one up in one of the countless shops or bookstores in London; though they are available domestically.

In London try stopping in the New Zealand News UK office, address 25 in the alley of shops just west of and running parallel to Haymarket, off Piccadilly Square. On the board just inside the front door, travelers and others post messages concerning, among other things, the following: vehicles for sale, vehicle insurance and repair, travel partners, travel packages, and jobs. While in the office you might as well pick up a free copy of their *Overseas* magazine. Travel articles aimed at the Kiwi expatriate crowd fill the magazine and make interesting reading for any traveler. Two other free weekly publications that you should grab in London are *TNT Magazine* and *Southern Cross* newspaper. Both of these publications are similar to *Overseas* but cater to Australian expatriates.

To get road condition information call Britain's Automobile Association at the following numbers. (Calls are charged at 36p per minute cheap rate, 48p per minute at all other times.)

Hourly U.K traffic reports: 01336 401 110.

French *autoroute* toll information: 01336 401 884.

European fuel prices & availability: 01336 401 883.

Laws, paperwork, and driving conditions:

Austria:	01336 401 866.
Belgium:	01336 401 867.
Denmark:	01336 401 868.

France:	01336 401 869.
Germany:	01336 401 870.
Gibraltar:	01336 401 871.
Greece:	01336 401 872.
Ireland:	01336 401 873.
Italy:	01336 401 874.
Luxembourg:	01336 401 875.
Netherlands:	01336 401 876.
Norway:	01336 401 877.
Portugal:	01336 401 878.
Spain:	01336 401 879.
Sweden:	01336 401 880.
Switzerland:	01336 401 881.

An association called Eurostop matches drivers with riders across Europe. Drivers give the date, departure city, destination, and the number of passengers that can be taken. The driver pays a small reservation fee, and the passenger pays a small mileage fee. Here are some Eurostop locations to contact.

Allostop Provoya, Passage Brady 84, 75010 Paris, France, tel. 1 42 40 00 66 or 1 42 46 00 66 or from abroad 1 47 70 02 01.

A Dedo, Calle Estudiod 9, 2nd Floor, 2801 Madrid, Spain, tel. 265 65 65.

I.L.C. International Life Center, N.Z. Voorburgwal 256, 1012 RS Amsterdam, Holland.

Alonsanfan, Via Guelfa 66 Rosso, Florence, Italy, tel. 28 33 95.

Impuls Mitfahrzentrale, Fierzgaße 16, 8031 Zurich, Switzerland, tel. 271 23 00.

Contact the Paris office to learn of other offices.

Tourist Offices in Australia

Austrian National Tourist Office, 36 Carrington St., 1st Floor, Sydney NSW 2000, tel. 02 299 36 21.

British Tourist Authority, Midland House, 171 Clarence Street, 4th Floor, Sydney NSW 2000, tel. 02 298 627.

French Tourist Bureau, Kindersley House, 33 Bligh Street, Sydney NSW 2000, tel. 02 233 32 77, FAX 02 233 45 76.

German National Tourist Office, Lufthansa House, 12th Floor, 143 Macquarie Street, Sydney NSW 2000, tel. 02 367 38 90, FAX 02 367 38 95.

Greek National Tourist Organization, 51–57 Pitt Street, P.O. Box R203, Royal Exchange, Sydney NSW 2000, tel. 02 241 1663, FAX 02 241 1664.

Irish Tourist Board, 5th Level, 36 Carrington Street, Sydney NSW 2000, tel. 02 299 61 77, FAX 02 299 63 23.

Latvian Embassy, P.O. Box 23, Kew, Victoria 3101, tel. 3 499 69 20.

Netherlands Board of Tourism (NBT), 5 Elizabeth Street, 6th Floor, Sydney, NSW 2000, tel. 02 247 69 21, FAX 02 223 66 65.

Spanish Tourist Office, 203 Castelreagh Street, Suite 21A, PO Box A685, Sydney NSW 2000, tel. 02 264 79 66, FAX 02 235 28 20.

Tourist Offices in Canada

Montréal

Austrian National Tourist Office, 1010 Sherbrooke St. W, Suite 1410, Montréal, PQ H3A 2R7, tel. 514 849 3709.

French National Tourist Office/Maison de la France, 1981 Avenue McGill College, Suite 490, Montréal, PQ H3A 2W9, tel. 514 288 4264, FAX 514 845 4868.

Greek National Tourist Organization, 1233 Rue de la Montagne, Montréal, PQ H3G 1Z2, tel. 514 871 1535, FAX 514 871 1498.

Intourist Travel Information office (Russia), 1801 McGill College Ave. #630, Montréal, PQ H3A 2N4, tel. 514 849 6394.

Italian State Tourist Office, 1 Place Ville Marie, Montréal, PQ H3B 3M9, tel. 514 866 7667, FAX 514 392 1429.

Toronto

Austrian National Tourist Office, 2 Bloor St. E, Suite 3330, Toronto, ON M4W 1A8, tel. 416 967 3381.

British Tourist Authority, 94 Cumberland St., Suite 600, Toronto, ON M5R 3N3, tel. 416 925 6326.

Danish Tourist Board, Box 115, Station N, Toronto, ON M8V 3S4, tel. 416 823 9620.

Estonian Consulate General, 958 Broadview Ave., Toronto, ON M4K 2R6, tel. 416 461 0764.

Finnish Tourist Board, 1200 Bay St., Suite 604, Toronto, ON M5R 2A5, tel. 416 964 9159.

French National Tourist Office/Maison de la France, 1 Dundas Street West, Suite

2405, Box 8, Toronto, ON M5G 1Z3, tel. 416 593 4717.

German National Tourist Office, 175 Bloor Street East, North Tower, Suite 604, Toronto, ON M4W 3R8, tel. 416 968 1570, FAX 416 968 1986.

Greek National Tourist Organization, 1300 Bay Street, Toronto, ON M5R 3K8, tel. 416 968 2220, FAX 416 968 6533.

Irish Tourist Board, Suite 934, 160 Bloor Street East, Toronto, ON M4W 1B9, tel. 416 929 2777, FAX 416 929 6783.

Latvian Embassy, 700 Bay St. 19th Floor, Toronto, ON M5G 1Z6, tel. 416 408 2540

Netherlands Board of Tourism (NBT), 25 Adelaide Street East, Suite 710, Toronto, ON M5C 1Y2, tel. 416 363 1577, FAX 416 363 1470.

Portuguese National Tourist Office, 2180 Yonge St., Toronto, ON M4S 2B9, tel. 416 250 7575.

Spanish Tourist Office, 102 Bloor Street West, Suite 1400, Toronto, ON M5S 1M8, tel. 416 961 3131, FAX 416 961 1992.

Swiss National Tourist Office, 154 University Avenue, Suite 610, Toronto, ON M5H 3Y9, tel. 416 971 9734, FAX 416 971 6425.

Vancouver

Austrian National Tourist Office, 200 Granville St., Suite 1380, Vancouver, BC V6C 1S4, tel. 604 683 5808.

Tourist Offices in New Zealand

British Tourist Authority, Suite 305, 3rd Floor, Dilworth Building, corner Customs & Queen Streets, Auckland 1, tel. 09 3031 446, FAX 09 3776 965.

Tourist Offices in the United States

Atlanta

British Tourist Authority, 2580 Cumberland Parkway, Suite 470, Atlanta, GA 30339, tel. 404 438 7019, FAX 404 432 9641.

Chicago

British Tourist Authority, 625 North Michigan Avenue, Suite 1510, Chicago, IL 60611, tel.800 462 2748.

French Government Tourist Office/Maison de la France, 645 North Michigan Avenue, Suite 630, Chicago, IL 60611. Tel: 312 337 6301 or 312 751 7800. FAX: 312 337 6339.

Greek National Tourist Organization, 168 North Michigan Avenue, Suite 600, Chicago, IL 60601, tel. 312 782 1084, FAX 312 782 1091.

Italian Government Travel Office, 500 North Michigan Avenue, Suite 1046, Chicago, IL 60611, tel. 312 644 0990, FAX 312 644 3019.

Netherlands Board of Tourism (NBT), 225 North Michigan Avenue, Suite 326, Chicago, IL 60601, tel. 312 819 0300 or 312 819 1636 for rotary phones, FAX 312 819 1740.

Polish National Tourist Office, 333 N. Michigan Ave., Chicago, IL 60661, tel. 312 236 9013.

Spanish National Tourist Office, 845 North Michigan Avenue, Chicago, IL 60611, tel. 312 642 1992.

Swiss National Tourist Office, Suite 2930, 150 North Michigan Avenue, Chicago, IL 60601, tel. 312 630 5840, FAX 312 630 5848.

Los Angeles

British Tourist Authority, World Trade Center, 350 South Figueroa Street, Suite 450, Los Angeles, CA 90071, tel. 213 628 3525, FAX 213 687 6621.

French Government Tourist Office/Maison de la France, 9454 Wilshire Boulevard, Beverly Hills, CA 90212–2967, tel. 213 272 2662 or 213 271 6665, FAX 213 276 2835.

German National Tourist Office, 11766 Wilshire Blvd.., Ste. 750, Los Angeles, CA 90025, tel. 310 575 9799.

Greek National Tourist Organization, 611 West 6th Street, Suite 2198, Los Angeles, CA 90071, tel. 213 626 6696, FAX 213 489 9744.

Spanish National Tourist Office, San Vincente Plaza Bldg., 8383 Wilshire Blvd., Suite 960, Beverly Hills, CA 90211, tel. 213 658 7188.

Swiss National Tourist Office, 222 Sepulveda Boulevard, Suite 1570, El Segundo, CA 90245, tel. 310 335-5980, FAX 310 335 5982.

New York

Austrian National Tourist Office, 500 Fifth Ave., 20th Floor, New York, NY 10110, tel. 212 944 6880.

Belgian Tourist Office, 780 3rd Ave., #1501, New York, NY 10017-2024, tel. 212 758 8130, FAX 212 355 7675.

Bulgarian National Tourist Office. Balkan Holidays (authorized agent), 41 East 42nd

St., Ste. 508, New York, NY 10017, tel. 212 573 5530.

British Tourist Authority, 551 5th Ave. & 45th St., 7th Floor, , New York, NY 10176-0799, tel. 800 462 2748 or 212 986 2266.

Cyprus Tourist Office, 13 E. 40th St., New York, NY 10016, tel. 212 213 9100.

Czech and Slovak Travel Bureau and Tourist Office (Cedok), 10 E. 40th St., New York, New York, NY 10016, tel. 212 689 9720.

Danish Tourist Board, 655 Third Ave., New York, NY 10017, tel. 212 949 2333.

Estonian Consulate General, 630 Fifth Ave., Suite 2415, New York, NY 10111, tel. 212 247 7634.

Finnish Tourist Board, 655 Third Ave., New York, NY 10017, tel. 212 949 2333.

French Government Tourist Office/Maison de la France, 610 Fifth Avenue, Suite 222, New York, NY 10020–2452, tel. 212 757 1125 or 212 315 0888, FAX 212 247 6468.

German National Tourist Office, Chanin Building, 122 East 42nd Street, 52nd Floor, New York, NY 10168, tel. 212 661 7200, FAX 212 688 1322.

Greek National Tourist Organization, Olympic Tower, 645 Fifth Avenue, New York, NY 10022, tel. 212 421 5777, FAX 212 826 6940.

Hungarian Travel Bureau (IBUSZ), 1 Parker Plaza, Suite 1104, Fort Lee, NJ 07204, tel. 201 592 8585.

Intourist Travel Information Office (Russia), 821 United Nations Plaza, New York, NY 10017, tel. 212 687 2194.

Irish Tourist Board, 757 Third Avenue, New York, NY 10017, tel. 212 418 0800, FAX 212 371 9052.

Italian Government Travel Office, 630 Fifth Avenue, Suite 1565, New York, NY 10111, tel. 212 245 4822, FAX 212 586 9249.

Lithuanian Consulate General, 41 West 82nd St., New York, NY 10024, tel. 212 87 4552.

Luxembourg Tourist Information Office, Beekman Place, New York, NY 10023-4003, tel. 212 370 9850.

Malta National Tourist Office, Maltese Consulate, 249 E. 35th St., New York, NY, tel. 212 725 2345

Monaco Government Tourist Convention Bureau, 845 Third Ave., New York, NY 10022, tel. 212 759 5227.

Norwegian Tourist Board, 655 Third
Avenue, New York, NY 10017, tel. 212 949
2333, FAX 212 983 5260.

Polish National Tourist Office (Orbis), 342
Madison Ave., Ste. 1512, New York, NY
10173, tel. 212 867 5011.

Portuguese National Tourist Office, 590
Fifth Avenue, 4th Floor, New York, NY
10036–4704, tel. 212 354 4403, FAX 212
764 6137.

Romanian National Tourist Office, 573
Third Ave., New York, NY 10016, tel. 212
697 6971.

Spanish Tourist Board, 665 Fifth Avenue,
New York, NY 10022, tel. 212 759 8822,
FAX 212 980 1053.

Swedish Travel & Tourism Council, 655
Third Avenue, 18 Floor, New York, NY
10017, tel. 212 949 2333, FAX 212 697
0835.

Swiss National Tourist Office, Swiss
Center, 608 Fifth Avenue, New York, NY
10020, tel. 212 757 5944, FAX 212 262
6116.

Turkish Tourist Office, 821 UN Plaza, New
York, NY 10017, tel. 212 687 2194.

San Francisco

Swiss National Tourist Office, 260 Stockton
St., San Francisco, CA 94108, tel. 415 362
2260.

Washington, DC

Latvian Embassy, 4325 17th St. NW,
Washington, DC 20011, tel. 202 726 8213.

Embassy of Ukraine, 1828 L St., Ste. 711,
NW, Washington, DC 20036, tel. 202 296
6960, FAX 202 296 2450.

Embassies or Consulates in Australia

Austria: POB 3375, Manuka, ACT 2603,
tel. 06 295 1533, FAX 06 239 6751.

Belgium: 10 Arkana St., Yarralumla, ACT
2600, tel. 06 273 2501, FAX 06 273 3392.

Cyprus: 37 Endeavour St., Red Hill, ACT
2603, tel. 06 295 2120, FAX 06 295 2892.

Czech Republic: 47 Culgoa Circuit,
O'MAlley, ACT 2606, tel. 06 290 1516,
FAX 06 290 1755.

Denmark: 15 Hunter St., Yarralmula, ACT
2600, tel. 06 273 2195, FAX 06 273 3864.

Finland: 10 Darwin Ave., Yarralumla, ACT
2600, tel. 06 273 3800, FAX 06 273 3603.

France 6 Perth Ave., Yarralumla, ACT
2600, tel. 06 270 5111, FAX 06 273 3193.

Germany: 119 Empire Circuit, Yarralumla,
ACT 2600, tel. 06 270 1911, FAX 06 270
1951.

Greece: 9 Turrana St., Yarralumla, ACT
2600, tel. 06 273 3011, FAX 06 273 2620.

Hungary: 17 Beale Crescent, Deakin, ACT
2600, tel. 06 282 3226, FAX 06 285 3012.

Ireland: 20 Arkana St., Yarralumla, ACT
2600, tel. 06 273 3022, FAX 06 273 3741.

Italy: POB 360, Canberra City, ACT 2601,
tel. 06 273 3333, FAX 06 273 4223.

Malta: 261 La Perouse St., Red Hill, ACT
2603, tel. 06 295 1586, FAX 06 239 6084.

Netherlands: 120 Empire Circuit,
Yarralumla, ACT 2600, tel. 06 273
3111,FAX 06 273 3206.

Norway: 17 Hunter St., Yarralumla, ACT
2600, tel. 06 273 4444, FAX 06 273 3669.

Poland: 7 Turrana St., Yarralumla, ACT
2600, tel. 06 273 1208, FAX 06 273 3184.

Portugal: 23 Culgoa Circuit, O'Malley,
ACT 2606, tel. 06 290 1733, FAX 06 290
1957.

Russia: 78 Canberra Ave., Griffith, ACT 2603, tel. 06 295 9032, FAX 06 295 1847.

Slovakia: 47 Culgoa Circuit, O'Malley, ACT 2606, tel. 06 290 1516, FAX 06 290 1755.

Spain: POB 76, Deakin, ACT 2600, tel. 06 273 3555, FAX 06 273 3918.

Sweden: 5 Turrana St., Yarralumla, ACT 2600, tel. 06 273 3033, FAX 06 273 3298.

Switzerland: 7 Melbourne Ave., Forrest, ACT, tel. 06 273 3977, FAX 06 273 3428.

Turkey: 60 Mugga Way, Red Hill, ACT 2603, tel. 06 295 0227, FAX 06 239 6592.

United Kingdom: Commonwealth Ave., Canberra, ACT 2600, tel. 06 279 6666, FAX 06 273 3236.

Embassies or Consulates in Canada

Austria: 445 Wilbrod St., Ottawa, ON K1N 6M7, tel. 613 563 1444, FAX 613 563 0038.

Belgium: 80 Elgin St., 4th Floor, Ottawa, ON K1P 5P2, tel. 613 236 7268, FAX 613 236 7882.

Bulgaria: 325 Stewart St., Ottawa, ON K1N 6K5, tel. 613 232 3215, FAX 613 232 9547.

Czech Republic: 50 Rideau Terrace, Ottawa, ON K1M 2A1, tel. 613 749 4442, FAX 613 749 4989.

Denmark: 85 Range Rd., Suite 702, Ottawa, ON K1M 8J6, tel. 613 234 0704, FAX 613 234 7368.

Finland: 55 Metcalfe St., Suite 850, Ottawa, ON K1P 6L5, tel. 613 236 2389, FAX 613 238 1474.

France: 42 Sussex Drive, Ottawa, ON K1 2C9, tel. 613 232 1795, FAX 613 232 4302.

Germany: 275 Slater St., 14th Floor, Ottawa, ON K1P 5H9, tel. 613 232 1101, FAX 613 594 9330.

Greece: 76–80 MacLaren St., Ottawa, ON K2P 0K6, tel. 613 238 6271, FAX 613 238 5676.

Hungary: 7 Delaware Ave., Ottawa, ON K2P 0Z2, tel. 613 232 1711, FAX 613 232 5620.

Ireland: 170 Metcalfe St., Ottawa, ON K2P 1P3, tel. 613 233 6281, FAX 613 233 5835.

Italy: 275 Slater St., 21st Floor, Ottawa, ON K1P 5H9, tel. 613 232 2401, FAX 613 233 1484.

Netherlands: 275 Slater St., 3rd Floor, Ottawa, ON K1P 5H9, tel. 613 237 5030, FAX 613 237 6471.

Norway: 90 Sparks St., Suite 532, Ottawa, ON K1P 5B4, tel. 613 238 6571, FAX 613 238 2765.

Poland: 443 Daly Ave., Ottawa, ON K1N 6H3, tel. 613 236 0468, FAX 613 232 3463.

Portugal: 645 Island Park Drive, Ottawa, ON K1Y 0B8, tel. 613 729 0883, FAX 613 729 4236.

Romania: 655 Rideau St., Ottawa, ON K1N 8L5, tel. 613 235 5345, FAX 613 567 4365.

Russia: 285 Charlotte St., Ottawa, ON K1N 8L5, tel. 613 235 4341, FAX 613 236 6342.

Slovakia: 50 Rideau Terrace, Ottawa, ON K1M 2A1, tel. 613 749 4442, FAX 613 749 4989.

Spain: 350 Sparks St., Suite 802, Ottawa, ON K1R 7S8, tel. 613 237 2193, FAX 613 236 1502.

Sweden: Mercury Court, 377 Dalhousie St., Ottawa, ON K1N 9N8, tel. 613 236 8553, FAX 613 236 5720.

Switzerland: 5 Marlborough Ave., Ottawa, ON K1N 8E6, tel. 613 235 1837, FAX 613 563 1394.

Turkey: 197 Wurtemburg St., Ottawa, ON K1N 8L9, tel. 613 232 1577, FAX 613 232 5004.

United Kingdom: 80 Elgin St., Ottawa, ON K1P 5K7, tel. 613 237 1530, FAX 613 237 7980.

Embassies or Consulates in New Zealand

Belgium: Willis Corroon House, 1–3 Willeston St., POB 3841, Wellington, tel. 04 472 9558, FAX 04 471 2764.

France: Willis Corroon House, 14th Floor, 1–3 Willeston St., POB 1695 Wellington, tel 04 472 0200, FAX 04 472 5887.

Germany: 90–92 Hobson St., POB 1687, Wellington, tel. 04 473 6063, FAX 04 473 6069.

Italy: 34–38 Grant Rd., Thorndon, POB 463, Wellington 1, tel. 04 473 5339, FAX 04 472 7255.

Netherlands: Investment Centre, 10th Floor, Cnr. Featherston and Ballance Sts., POB 840, Wellington, tel. 04 473 8652, FAX 04 471 2923.

Poland: 17 Upland Rd., Kelburn, Wellington, tel. 04 471 2456, FAX 04 471 2455.

Russia: 57 Messines Rd., Karori, Wellington, tel. 04 476 6113, FAX 04 476 3843.

Sweden: Greenock House, 8th Floor, 39 The Terrace, POB 5350, Wellington, tel. 04 472 0909, FAX 04 471 2097.

Switzerland: Panama House, 22 Panama St., Wellington, tel. 04 472 1593, FAX 04 499 6302.

Turkey: 15–17 Murphy St., POB 12-248, Wellington, tel. 04 472 1292, FAX 04 472 1277.

United Kingdom: 44 Hill St., POB 1812, Wellington, tel. 04 472 6049, FAX 04 471 1974.

Embassies or Consulates in the United States

Albania: 1150 18th St. NW, Washington, DC 20036, tel. 202 223 4942, FAX 202 223 4950.

Austria: 3524 International Court, NW, Washington, DC 20008–3035, tel. 202 483 4474, FAX 202 483 2743.

Belarus: 1511 K St., NW, Suite 619, Washington, DC 20005, tel. 202 638 2954, FAX 202 638 3058.

Belgium: 3330 Garfield St., NW, Washington, DC 20008, tel. 202 333 6900, FAX 202 333 3079.

Bulgaria: 1621 22nd St., NW, Washington, DC 20008, tel. 202 387 7969, FAX 202 234 7973.

Croatia: 236 Massachusetts Ave., NE, Washington, DC 20002, tel. 202 543 5580.

Cyprus: 2211 R St., NW, Washington, DC 20008, tel. 202 462 5772, FAX 202 483 6710.

Czech Republic: 3900 Linnean Ave., NW, Washington, DC 20008, tel. 202 363 6315, FAX 202 966 8540.

Denmark: 3200 Whitehaven St., NW, Washington, DC 20008–3683, tel. 202 234 4300, FAX 202 328 1470.

Estonia: 630 Fifth Ave., Suite 2415, New York, NY 10111, tel. 212 247 1450, FAX 212 262 0893.

Finland: 3216 New Mexico Ave., NW, Washington, DC 20016, tel. 202 363 2430, FAX 202 363 8233.

France: 4101 Resevoir Rd., NW, Washington, DC 20007, tel. 202 944 6000, FAX 202 944 6072.

Germany: 4645 Resevoir Rd., NW, Washington, DC 20007–1998, tel. 202 298 4000, FAX 202 298 4249.

Greece: 2221 Massachusetts Ave., NW Washington, DC 20008, tel. 202 939 5800, FAX 202 939 5824.

Hungary: 3910 Shoemaker St., NW, Washington, DC 20008, tel. 202 362 6730, FAX 202 966 8135.

Ireland: 2234 Massachusetts Ave., NW, Washington, DC 20008, tel. 202 462 3939, FAX 202 232 5993.

Italy: 1601 Fuller St., NW, Washington, DC 20009, tel. 202 328 5500, FAX 202 462 3605.

Latvia: 4325 17 St., NW, Washington, DC 20011, tel. 202 726 8213, FAX 202 726 6785.

Lithuania: 2622 16th St., NW, Washington, DC 20009, tel. 202 234 5860, FAX 202 328 0466.

Luxembourg: 2200 Massachusetts Ave., NW, Washington, DC 20008, tel. 202 265 4171, FAX 202 328 8270.

Malta: 2017 Connecticut Ave., NW, Washington, DC 20008, tel. 202 462 3611, FAX 202 387 5470.

Netherlands: 4200 Linnean Ave., NW, Washington, DC 20008, tel. 202 244 5300, FAX 202 362 3430.

Norway: 2720 34th St., NW, Washington, DC 20008, tel. 202 333 6000, FAX 202 337 0870.

Poland: 2640 16th St., NW, Washington, DC 20009, tel. 202 234 3800, FAX 202 328 6271.

Portugal: 2125 Kalorama Rd., NW, Washington, DC 20008, tel. 202 328 8610, FAX 202 462 3726.

Romania: 1607 23rd St., NW, Washington, DC 20008, tel. 202 332 4848, FAX 202 232 4748.

Russia: 1125 16th St., NW, Washington, DC 20036, tel. 202 628 7551.

Slovakia: 3900 Spring of Freedom St., NW, Washington, DC 20008, tel. 202 363 6315, FAX 202 224 4139.

Slovenia: 1300 19th St., NW, Suite 410, Washington, DC 20036, tel. 201 828 1650, FAX 202 828 1654.

Spain: 2700 15th St., NW, Washington, DC 20009, tel. 202 265 0190, FAX 202 332 5451.

Sweden: 600 New Hampshire Ave.,NW, Washington, DC 20037, tel. 202 944 5600, FAX 202 342 1319.

Switzerland: 2900 Cathedral Ave., NW, Washington, DC 20008, tel. 202 745 7900, FAX 202 387 2564.

Turkey: 1714 Massachusetts Ave., NW, Washington, DC 20036, tel. 202 659 8200.

Ukraine: 1828 L St., Suite 711, NW, Washington, DC 20036, tel. 202 296 6960, FAX 202 296 2450.

United Kingdom: 3100 Massachusetts Ave., NW, Washington, DC 20008, tel. 202 462 1340, FAX 202 898 4255.

11. documents

Passport

You need a valid passport to enter any European country and to re-enter your own.

Australian citizens need to make an appointment to apply for a passport at a local post office, or they can get one at an overseas passport office or Australian diplomatic mission. Parents can file for applicants who are under 18 years of age and unmarried. Proof of citizenship and current name along with other forms of identification and two identical, passport-sized (45 mm by 35 mm) photographs are required. Call 02 13 12 32 for more information. Australians over 11 years of age must pay a departure tax.

Canadian citizens can apply by mail to the Passport Office, Department of External Affairs, Ottawa 1, ON K1A 0G3, or at one of the regional offices. Information is available by calling 800 567 6844 from eastern Canada or 800 567 6868 from western Canada. Allow for at least a five day wait if you apply in person, three weeks if you apply by mail. The fee is CA$35.

New Zealand citizens must contact their local Link Centre, travel agent, or New Zealand Representative for an application. Mail it to the New Zealand Passport Office, Documents of National Identity Division, P.O. Box 10-526, Wellington, New Zealand, tel. 04 474 81 00. The fee is NZ$56.25 for adults, NZ$25.30 for children under 16 years of age. Double these figures for applications lodged overseas. Allow at least twenty-one days for processing. Rush service is available. New Zealanders who are overseas can send their application to the nearest New Zealand Embassy, Consulate, or High Commission.

US citizens may apply for a passport at any US Passport Agency office or at select federal and state courthouses and post offices. If you're over 18 years of age and have a passport that was issued after your 18th birthday and that has expired but is not more than 12 years old, you can renew it by mail for $55. Otherwise, you must renew your passport in person and pay $65, $40 if you're under 18 years of age. Note that you'll need two passport-sized photographs, a birth certificate, social security card, and photo identification. You may not be able to pay by personal check. Parents must apply in person for children under 13 years of age, and they must provide permission for children 13–17 years of age. Allow at least three weeks for processing if you apply at a Passport Agency, longer if you apply at a courthouse or post office. You can pay for rush service if you prove need (for example, if you present a plane ticket). You'll be penalized $100 for returning home with an expired passport. Call 202 647 0518 for recorded information including a listing of cities with Passport Agencies; or call 202 634 3600 and ask for the Passport Duty Officer; or write to the Passport Office,

1425 K St., NW, Washington, DC 20522. Note that the term "passport-sized" photos implies the following: full face forward with your head's image measuring between 1 inch and 1 3/8 inches in diameter, taken against a white background, and measuring 2 inches by 2 inches overall. When getting passport photos, make at least eight extra prints, and keep the negative with you. You can use these extra prints for visas, the international driving permit, hostel cards, youth passes, etc. The negative will come in handy if you need any more prints made. If you join the AAA, they'll snap and develop your passport photos free of charge; otherwise, they'll charge $10 for this service.

Regardless of your citizenship, carry —in a safe place separate from your other valuables—photocopies of the important pages of your passport (or carry an expired passport) and a copy of your birth certificate. If your passport is lost or stolen, report to the local police immediately; the police will give you a receipt that you must carry as a temporary ID. Then, go to your embassy or consulate, where you must somehow prove your identity. The embassy or consulate will replace your passport within a couple of days, but you must pay a rather steep fee to effect this.

Visa

A visa is a stamp placed on your passport by a foreign government. The stamp allows you to visit that country for a specific purpose (tourism, for example) and for a specific duration. Call your local travel agent to determine which countries require a visa for your particular citizenship. Citizens of the US can send a check for $0.50 to the Consumer Information Center, Department 459X, Pueblo, CO 81009, tel. 719 948 3334, to receive the *Foreign Visa Requirements* pamphlet. Of course visa requirements are always subject to change.

A majority of European countries don't require you to have a visa. As a US citizen I didn't need a visa for any of the eighteen countries I visited. Still, the French government presently requires Australians to obtain a visa before they can enter France; likewise, the Czech Republic requires Canadians to obtain a visa. The CIS—comprised of Armenia, Azerbaijan, Beloruss, Kazakhstan, Kirkghizia, Moldova, Russia, Tajikistan, Turkmenia, the Ukraine and Uzbekistan—presently requires visas of all foreigners. Although such requirements seem arbitrary, they usually function as political payback for a disagreement between countries.

Most visas cost $10–30 and allow you to spend about a month in the country. Apply to embassies or consulates of the countries which require a visa. Allow several weeks for processing. Most countries will issue a visa on the spot or within a few days if you visit the consulate (either in your country or in Europe) in person, and most countries sell visas at certain points of entry (such as airports and border stations). Agencies exist which—for a charge—will get your visas for you. Such a service may be necessary if you need a visa quickly. In the US try the Visa Center, Inc., 507 Fifth Ave., #904, New York, NY 10017, tel. 212 986 0924; or World Visa and Document Services, 1413 K St. NW Suite 800, Washington, DC 20005, tel. 202 289 6251. In Britain check the advertisements in *Overseas* magazine, *The New Zealand News UK* newspaper, *TNT Magazine,* and *Southern Cross* newspaper.

Travelers planning to drive in the CIS need to obtain a special *Autotourist* visa and an itinerary card. All visas for the CIS must be obtained in advance; Ukraine-only visas, however, can be purchased at the border for about $45.

Some visas are incompatible. Greece, for example, won't let you in if you have a visa or passport stamp from Northern Cyprus. Morocco and most Arab countries turn away people whose passport bears a stamp from Israel. Ask that such troublesome stamps be placed on a removable page in your passport.

This brings up an important point: Don't tear out or mark up a page in your passport that isn't specified as being removable. The passport pages are numbered; if the sequence is broken or if pages are missing or fouled, the border guards will assume that you're hiding the fact that you committed some offense in another country, an offense that resulted in a stamp of disapproval being placed on your passport.

With the lax borders that now exist within Europe, border guards rarely stamp passports. If you wanna collect stamps on your passport as momentos, you should ask for them. If you're conducting a grand tour, this practice is a good idea anyway: it proves to the country you first arrived in (and from which you'll most likely depart) that you haven't stayed too long within their borders.

Money

Of course you're wondering about cash. Probably the best way to get cash is to use an ATM. Besides convenience, you get a good exchange rate when you use an ATM. My Cirrus ATM debit card works all over France, Spain, Portugal, Italy, the Czech Republic, Denmark, Sweden, Norway, Belgium, Britain and Ireland. It even worked recently in El Rocio, Spain, where all the streets are dirt and half the town gets around on horses. It doesn't work, however, in Switzerland, Austria or Germany. My bank used to charge no transaction fee or commission on my overseas ATM transactions, but this is not true anymore. Typical fees for transactions made abroad run $3 to $5. Check with your bank. Some waive all fees for the elderly or for depositors with a substantial minimum balance. Although such fees are usually levied only by the bank that issued the card, the ATM in which you use your card might apply a separate fee. If you have a Cirrus card, ask your bank to send you a copy of Cirrus's free *ATM Location Directory;* if you have Plus card, ask for the *Visa International ATM Locator Guide;* both list the locations of all participating ATMs worldwide. Cirrus operates a worldwide ATM locator service at tel. 800 424 7787; Plus has an automated service at tel. 800 843 7587. Over seven thousand Cirrus machines now grace Europe; while Plus operates over five thousand ATMs in Britain, and over three thousand in Spain. Of course, more are on the way. It's truly amazing to slide in your card, punch in your PIN (Personal Identification Number), and receive the local currency. Beware though: Most European ATMs only accept numeric, four-digit PINs. If your PIN is four characters long but includes letters, use the letter-number correspondences shown on US phones to translate it into numbers; if your PIN is longer, ask your bank for a new PIN.

Letter-Number Correspondences on Phones
ABC—2; DEF—3; GHI—4; JKL—5;
MNO—6; QPRS—7; TUV—8; WXYZ—9

Also note that ATMs in Europe may not function twenty-four hours. This is especially true in Denmark, where most ATMs work during business hours only. And realize that transfers are usually not possible, and that receipts might not be issued.

A less desireable option is to use a credit or charge card to get a cash advance, either in person at a bank or through an ATM. Such transactions are less desireable because they'll result in a cash advance fee showing up on your statement. Over 44,000 Visa and over 15,000 MasterCard ATM locations now operate in Europe. MasterCard's 28-page leaflet "Shopping with Your ATM Card" is available free of charge; call 800 999 5136. Diners Club has its own club cash program under which any withdrawal is simply added to your monthly bill. American Express, meanwhile, requires you to enroll in their American Express Cash Program to withdraw cash at its European ATMs. One benefit of this plan is that you can link your American Express card directly to your checking account, so your checking account is automatically debited with each purchase or withdrawal you make using your card.

Perhaps American Express's greatest advantage, however, is that any card holder can take a personal check written out to American Express into an overseas American Express Office and receive cash—up to a certain limit, usually either $1000 or $2000—at an excellent exchange rate. Before you leave home be sure to write out as such all the checks you'll need; that way if they're stolen they'll be hard to use. In most cases, American Express charges no commission on such a transaction—but this depends on the country. In Austria, for example, American Express must charge a small commission. Optima card holders, too, qualify for this service. Ask American Express to send you their booklet that lists all their offices worldwide. Write or call American Express International, 165 Broadway, New York, NY 10006, tel. 800 227 4669.

Make purchases with a credit or charge card if possible. Visa, MasterCard, American Express, Diners Club and Carte Blanche are widely accepted in Europe. Visa is top dog everywhere but Switzerland, Austria and Germany, where MasterCard is much more popular. (Note that non-European *fuel company* credit cards are not accepted at European service stations.) I recommend taking at least the first three cards listed above. No commission or foreign transaction fee is associated with using these cards for purchases, and you get a good exchange rate as well. Furthermore,

you get the leverage of the credit card company to back you up if there's a subsequent problem with a merchant (such as a problem getting a VAT refund).

The exchange rate applied to a credit or charge card purchase is calculated on the date the card network receives the merchant's receipts for payment—the "clearing" date. However, it's the "posting" date—the date the purchase is charged to your account—that's listed on monthly statements. Although the two dates are often the same, the posting date tends to lag behind. If the dollar is plunging, you may wanna do everything in your power to make a transaction *clear* fast. If, on the other hand, the dollar is rising, you may want to press for a delay. As such, it may help you to know the typical time it takes the leading card companies to clear a transaction.

	Days to Clear	Exchange Rate
AMEX	0–7	Reuters
Diners Club	2–5	Wall St. Journal
MasterCard	0–3	Telerate, Reuters
Visa	3–6	Citibank, Barclays

Credit cards and ATM cards are quickly making traveler's checks obsolete. Indeed, many merchants are reluctant to accept traveler's checks; most will ask you to go to a bank and cash the check instead. Traveler's checks are now necessary only in small amounts to assure that loss or theft of all your possessions doesn't leave you stranded and without any way to get money. But if you plan to buy a vehicle in Europe, it may be best to use traveler's checks to pay for it. No one will accept a personal check, and you don't wanna be walking around with a lot of cash; a traveler's check gives you the same credibility as a certified check. If you do get traveler's checks, get half in your nation's currency and the other half in a strong European currency, such as Deutsch Marks or Swiss Francs: if the dollar drops significantly, you can change the stronger foreign currency checks into the currency of the country you're in. If you don't already own an American Express card, you may wanna get a few American Express traveler's checks so you can use their free mail-holding service. (See the *Receiving Mail* section later in this chapter.)

Even if all your possessions become lost or are stolen in Europe, you can always have money wired if you have reliable contacts back home. A friend or relative can wire money via Western Union, tel.

800 225 5227, or American Express, tel. 800 543 4080 (800 933 3278 in Canada), by either visiting one of the offices or calling and charging the transaction to a credit card. Within minutes you can pick up the cash at the nearest overseas office. Note, however, that the fee charged for such service is about $30 if you send $250, and about $70 if you send $1000.

If a US citizen is *really* down and out while abroad, the US Department of State's Citizens Emergency Center, tel. 202 647 5225, will extend a repatriation loan to pay for his or her direct return to the US.

When it comes to exchanging money, it's best to do it at a bank. Banks consistently offer the best exchange rates. Post offices in Denmark, Germany and Norway offer good rates as well. Banks and exchange booths at airports, train stations or border entry points employ worse rates than their city counterparts. As such, change only a modicum of money when you first arrive in a country. Also, consider bypassing the exchange shops set up at borders. The following exchange shops, however, are government regulated and reliable: *Change, Wechsel, Cambio, Växel*. Increasingly conspicuous are machines in which you insert a foreign currency—dollars,

pounds, francs, whatever—and receive local money in return; exchange rates tend to be poor, however. Regardless, don't run yourself ragged trying to find the best exchange rates. You're in Europe to have a good time; if you have to pay a few extra dollars to avoid traveling across town to the American Express office or to avoid checking the exchange rates in five different banks, so be it. Be careful of black marketeers in Eastern Europe: they may offer excellent exchange rates, but the money they give you may be counterfeit. Real money is characterized by a watermark stamp (a very subtle and monotone picture, of a person usually) and a metallic band running around the short dimension of the bill.

Driving

The *Fédération Internationale de l'Automobile (FIA)* and the *Alliance Internationale de Tourisme (AIT)* each sponsor alliances of various national motoring clubs—including the AA, AAA, CAA, and NAC—such that participating clubs reciprocate their benefits to members of allied clubs. Depending on its affiliation, your club will give you an *FIA* and/or *AIT* booklet as your entitlement to these benefits. In the *Country-by-Country Information* chapter, I note and provide the address and telephone number of all European clubs; still, AAA members might as well ask for the brochure "Offices to Serve You Abroad". In additon to assuring your reciprocal membership in dozens of European motoring clubs, the *FIA* and *AIT* booklets contain letters of credit which help cover such costs as vehicle repair and medical and legal fees. If you don't belong to an *FIA* or *AIT*-affiliated club, you can effect the above coverage by paying fees—some low, some relatively high—for temporary membership in foreign clubs.

Some of these clubs sell separate breakdown coverage. For instance, you can buy Europe-wide breakdown coverage from either of Britain's automobile clubs—the Automobile Association (AA), tel. 01256 21023, or the Royal Automobile Club (RAC), tel. 01800 678000—but you must first buy a membership, an expensive proposition. A cheaper and adequate alternative is the coverage offered by the London-based outfit National Breakdown, tel. 0171 499 0039.

As I said in the *Why Drive?* chapter, your domestic license is, in most cases, all you need to legally drive in a European country. However, the Commonwealth of Independent States, Greece, Hungary and Spain require you to carry an International Driving Permit (IDP); and Austria, Germany and Italy require you to carry either the IDP or a translation of your license. Moreover, Italy requires drivers of rental cars to carry an International Driving Permit or to purchase for a nominal fee a declaration from an Automobile Club d'Italia (ACI) frontier or city office. Since several other European countries recommend carrying an IDP, you should strongly consider getting one regardless of what country or countries you'll be driving in. The local office of your auto club sells IDPs for a scant $10. If you need an IDP, take your license, two passport-sized photos and $10 to the club office. (Though for $6 the club will snap and develop the photos for you.) Ten minutes later you'll be able to legally drive on any European road—assuming you're at least 18 years of age. If you plan to operate a motorcycle in Europe, be sure to have the auto club certify your qualification to do so.

Whether you rent, lease, buy or ship a vehicle, you'll probably get Green Card auto insurance, the kind that explicitly covers you in several countries instead of just one. However, as I described in the *Buying* chapter, even Green Card insurance excludes certain European countries from the domain of its coverage. And if you buy your own insurance to cover a vehicle you ship to or buy in Europe, you'll have to buy it in minimum one-month increments. Fortunately, certain non-Green Card auto-insurance policies—designed specifically for foreign motorists, sponsored by one European country or another, and effective in that country only—allow you to augment Green Card insurance so you can drive in more countries and/or be insured over periods that are not multiples of one month. A country may make such insurance available through its embassies or consulates or through offices located at points of entry. Italy, for example, sells auto insurance—good in Italy only—that covers fifteen, thirty or forty-five day periods; but if you wanna buy this insurance, you must do so before you arrive in Italy. Finland, Norway, and Sweden, on the other hand, form a common border insurance area: insurance that does or doesn't cover you in one of these countries does or doesn't cover you in the others. Scandinavian regional insurance is sold at border entry points of each Scandinavian country; minimum validity 30 days, maximum 1 year.

It used to be that Green Card insurance was the only true blanket coverage available, but besides the Scandinavian agreement, many other countries have recently agreed to join one alliance which recognizes as valid in any member state the auto insurance sold in such states. Countries not party to this agreement are Albania, Andorra, Bulgaria, Croatia, Estonia, Gibraltar, Greece, Iceland, Malta, Poland, Romania, Slovenia and Turkey. A Green Card is compulsory in Andorra, Bulgaria, Poland and Romania; and it's strongly recommended for travel in Greece, Italy, Portugal and Spain. A Green Card covering Turkey should be valid for both the European and Asian sectors.

Despite all the other insurance options, good 'ol fashioned Green Card insurance is still preferable: the documents that come with it are familiar to officials Europe wide and are very useful when reporting a traffic accident.

Many people have trouble finding auto insurance that covers the newly independent Eastern states. You can arrange such insurance for vehicles (except motorcycles) registered in the UK by contacting Black

Sea & Baltic General Insurance Co., Ltd., 65 Fenchurch Street, London EC3, England, tel. 0171 709 9202 or 0171 709 9292. Auto insurance for only the CIS is available through the agency *Ingosstrakh* (offices in several European countries) or at the border posts at Brest (on the Polish border) and Uzhgorod (on the Czech border). Insurance for Croatia and/or Slovenia can be purchased from Dalmatian and Istrian Travel Ltd., 28 Denmark St., London WC2H 8NJ, tel. 0171 379 6249. Contact embassies, consulates or tourist information offices for more information. (See the *Resources* chapter.)

If you plan to buy auto insurance in Europe, you should, if possible, secure from your auto-insurance provider a statement of accident-free driving. By presenting such a statement when you buy your insurance, you can qualify for substantial discounts.

As discussed in the *Renting* chapter, vehicles using Swiss expressways must be graced by a special sticker or *vignette*. You can buy this *vignette* for 30 SwF (about $22) at Swiss National Tourist offices, Swiss Customs posts, Swiss post offices, or Swiss garages. The *vignette* is valid for one calendar year, is non transferable, and

should be applied to the windshield. You must obtain a separate *vignette* for a trailer or caravan. If your vehicle doesn't bear a *vignette* and the Swiss police catch you driving on an expressway, you'll be subject to a 100 SwF fine—on top of the *vignette's* cost. Expressways offer the only hope for speedy and level motor travel through mountainous Switzerland. Still, it's not absolutely necessary to use the expressways there; I didn't. You have to ask yourself this: Why do I wanna travel quickly and horizontally through Switzerland? Carefully study your map and the Switzerland portion of the *Country-by-Country Information* chapter to determine if you want a *vignette*.

If you're renting or leasing a vehicle or buying one direct from the factory, bring any vouchers and copies of any agreements or other contracts. And of course if you're shipping and importing, you'll need the proper documents for Customs, etc.

Never leave the ownership papers (called a "Grey Card") or the insurance papers alone in the vehicle. In fact, you should make photocopies of these papers and of your domestic driver's license and IDP and then stash them in the same safe place (a neck pouch or money belt, for example) you keep the copies of your passport and birth certificate. If you're missing one of these documents when police pull you over, you'll be fined on the spot.

If you'll be driving someone else's vehicle, you should get written permission from the owner. In Portugal, however, you must obtain an *Autorizacao* certificate also; to get one, contact your local motoring club or a Portuguese tourist office or embassy, or stop in a European vehicle-registration office. Again, make and stash photocopies of these documents.

Health and Security

Buying travel insurance is the closest thing to buying a guarantee for a hassle-free trip. Such coverage can include personal liability, personal accident, hospital benefit, medical expenses, evacuation, money loss, baggage loss or damage, travel delay or interruption, cancellation, legal expenses, and loss of passport expenses. A friend of mine took ill on her trip and spent ten days in a British hospital; besides the fact that her regular health insurance covered the bills, she got about $150 a day from her travel insurance. Of course you must determine for yourself if the risks justify the costs.

Beware of package travel insurance plans that span health, baggage, autos and the like: they usually duplicate insurance that you already have and contain too many exclusions. Check if your current health care covers you abroad, and bring along any medical insurance claim forms you may need. Also check how your credit cards may cover you. Baggage insurance benefits for lost or stolen articles tend to be lousy—covering up to $1000 only and excluding items like cameras, jewelry and currency. Airlines automatically cover each passenger's luggage for roughly $1250 on domestic and $650 on international flights. Motor vehicle rental and leasing companies also offer baggage insurance. As such, develop a list of the areas in which you are now not adequately covered. Next, call the travel insurance companies I list below. Determine if these companies can offer a piecemeal, customized package. I recommend that you consider purchasing the insurance from a company that's underwritten by an insurance company in your home country: this will ease the settling of any claims when you return home and, sorry to add, will cover the costs of transporting your body home if you meet your end abroad. Regardless, determine (1) if you're covered for personal effects left unattended in a locked motor vehicle (specify if you'll be traveling in a camper van), (2) the maximum coverage of any single article, and (3) if sports activities such as skiing or hanggliding are covered.

The AAA offers several different travel insurance plans. Contact your local club office.

Access America, tel. 800 284 8300 or 212 490 5345, FAX 212 808 5626, provides two weeks of $10,000 medical coverage for $49, as well as two weeks of $20,000 medical coverage for a family at a cost of $99.

Amex Assurance Co., tel. 800 541 3522.

Carefree, tel. 800 323 3149 or 516 294 0220, FAX 516 294 0268. Underwritten by Hartford Insurance and headquartered in Mineola, New York.

Corporate Assist, tel. 800 756 5900.

Council Travel, tel. 415 693 8761.

Europe Assistance Worldwide Services, tel. 800 821 5309.

Tele-Trip, tel. 800 228 9792. Affiliated with Mutual of Omaha and stationed in Omaha.

Travel Assistance International, tel. 800 821 2828 or 202 347 2025, FAX 202 393 2459. US only.

Travel Guard International, tel. 800 826 5850 or 715 345 0505. Underwritten by TransAmerica.

Travel Med/Medex Assistance, tel. 800 732 5309.

Travel Insurance Pak, tel. 800 243 3174. Underwritten by The Travelers.

Traveler's Emergency Network, P.O. Box 238, Hyattsville, MD 20797–8108, tel. 800 ASK 4TEN.

Voyage Assistance International, tel. 514 284 3230, FAX 514 284 3203. Canada only.

Wallach and Company, Inc., tel. 800 237 6615 or 703 281 9500 in the US, tel. 800 446 5166 in Canada. FAX 703 687 3172.

WorldCare Travel Assistance Association, Inc., tel. 415 541 4991, FAX 415 541 7950. US only.

The International Association for Medical Assistance to Travelers will send a worldwide list of approved member doctors, along with current information concerning diseases and inoculations. Membership is free. Write to IAMAT.

417 Center St., Lewiston, NY 14092.

40 Regal Road, Guelph, ON N1K 1B5.

P.O. Box 5049, Christchurch, New Zealand 5.

57 Voirets, 1212 Grand-Lancy, Geneva, Switzerland.

Intermedic, 777 Third Ave., New York, NY 10017, will provide a list of qualified, English-speaking doctors who respond to emergency calls and charge reasonable fees.

The International SOS Medical Service Program, Neshaminy International, Trevose, PA 19407, tel. 800 523 8930, will guarantee your hospital costs and arrange an ambulance plane in case of emergency.

Probe Medi-Guard Corporation, P.O. Box 77, Clarksburg, NJ, will convert your medical data to microfilm, which can be read through a collapsible viewer the size of a credit card.

Medic Alert, 2323 Colorado Ave., Turlock, CA 95380, tel. 209 668 3333, sells ID bracelets and necklaces which specify the wearer has a medical condition that might not be apparent and which provide a 24-hour number to call for the patient's medical history.

The Centers for Disease Control International Travelers Hotline, tel. 404 332 4559 will tell you what inoculations you may need for a particular destination. For a FAXed index of current health risks, suggested immunizations, and food and water precautions covering sixteen regions, call 404 332 4562. Be especially careful if going to the former Soviet Union: typhoid incidence and the incidence of other diseases is high there; recently, several tourists have died as a result—get the appropriate shots! Regardless, consider bringing a record of all your inoculations in case you decide to continue on to less developed areas of the world.

Health Information for International Travelers, Superintendent of Documents, US Government Printing Office, Washington, DC 20402, tel. 202 512 1800.

Citizens of the US may wanna solicit State Department Advisories concerning civil unrest; call 202 647 5225. Trip-planning publications are also available from the State Department..

Bring your eyeglasses prescription: it's possible you'll lose your glasses. My old glasses are probably still on the shore of the Geirangerfjord in Norway; if you find 'em, let me know.

Hostellers and/or Students

To stay in hostels that are affiliated with the Hostelling International (HI) organization, you should have an HI membership card. The card costs $10 for persons under 18 years of age, $25 for adults 18–54 years of age, $15 for persons at least 55 years of age, $35 for families with children under 16 years of age, or $250 for life. Adults and families can save 20 or 30 percent respectively on the renewal of a membership if they renew before the old membership expires.

For $13.95 each, you can order guides to HI hostels in (1) Europe and the Mediterranean and (2) Africa, America, Asia, Australia, and New Zealand; and for $5.95 you can order *Hostelling North America: The Official Guide to Hostels in Canada and the United States*. However, the combination of word of mouth, a good budget guidebook, and some ancillary maps and other materials distributed by tourist offices and hostels should provide you with plenty of information about the locations and offerings of Europe's hostels.

The following are national offices of Hostelling International. If requesting a membership by mail, you must include your name, address, city, state or province or territory, postal code, daytime phone, and birth date—along with a check for the proper amount. Or you can call and charge your membership to a Visa or MasterCard.

Australian Youth Hostel Association, P.O. Box 61, Strawberry Hills, Sydney, NSW 2011, tel. 01 212 1266.

In Canada, tel. 800 663 5777.

YHA New Zealand Inc., P.O. Box 346, Christchurch 1, tel. 03 799 970.

Hostelling International-American Youth Hostels, Membership Services, 733 15th Street, NW, Suite 840, Washington, DC 20013-7613, tel. 800 444 6111, 202 783 0717, or 202 783 6161.

The International Student Identification Card (ISIC) entitles students under 26 years of age to big discounts on everything from museum entry to ferry passage; it may also provide limited travel insurance.

Be sure to get this card if you qualify. Write or call one of the agencies listed below. To get an ISIC, you need proof of your current status as a full-time student, a 1 1/2-inch by 2-inch photo with your name printed on the back, proof of your age and nationality, your name and address, and a check for $14.

Council Travel operates thirty-four offices across the US, Europe and Asia. They sell railpasses, guidebooks, HI cards, ISICs, and budget airfares. Contact one of the following to find the office nearest you.

530 Bush St., Ground Floor, San Francisco, CA 94108, tel. 415 421 3473.

1138 13th Street, Boulder, CO 80302, tel. 303 447 8101.

1153 N. Dearborn St., 2nd Floor, Chicago, IL 60610, tel. 312 951 0585.

1384 Massachusetts Ave., Suite 201, Cambridge, MA 02138, tel. 617 497 1497.

Travel CUTS (Canadian Universities Travel Services) offers discount travel services, railpasses, HI cards, ISICs, and the Student Work Abroad Programme (SWAP).

187 College St., Toronto, ON M5T 1P7, tel. 416 979 2406.

295A Regent St., London W1R 7YA, tel. 071 637 3161.

STA Travel offers bargain flights, accommodation reservations, tours, railpasses, insurance, and ISICs.

17 E. 45th St., New York, NY 10017, tel. 800 777 0112.

7202 Melrose Ave., Los Angeles, CA 90046, tel. 213 934 8722.

74 Old Brompton Rd., London SW7 3LQ, tel. 071 937 9962.

222 Faraday St., Carlton, Melbourne, Victoria 3050, Australia, tel. 03 34 69 11.

10 High St., Auckland, New Zealand, tel. 09 309 99 95.

Senior Citizens

Membership in the American Association of Retired Persons (AARP), 601 E St. NW, Washington, DC 20049, tel. 202 434 2277, entitles US citizens to discounts on everything from car rental to sightseeing. Any citizen of the US who is over 50 years of age qualifies for membership. The annual fee is $8. Call 800 927 0111 for information.

Membership in the National Council of Senior Citizens, 1331 F St. NW, Washington, DC 20004, tel. 202 347 8800, entitles US citizens to discounts on car rentals, among other things. The annual fee is $12.

Phoning

Call your long distance telephone company (AT&T, MCI, Sprint, etc.) and ask them to send to you a card listing their overseas access numbers. By dialing a certain number from a certain country, you can be instantly connected to an operator at home. Charges can be billed collect (surcharge of about $6) or to a calling card (surcharge of about $2.50). Expect to pay about $1.50 per minute (including surcharge) for calls to North America that are billed to a calling card. Citizens of the US should call 800 874 4000 ext. 223 for info on AT&T USA Direct, 800 444 3333 for info on the MCI CALL USA service, and 800 347 8989 for info on the Sprint service. Australia Direct, Canada Direct and New Zealand Direct services are similar but not as extensive. For information on these services, call 0102 in Australia, 800 561 8868 in Canada, and 018 in New Zealand.

Receiving Mail

People can send mail to you in any city or town by general delivery. The envelope should be marked "Hold" and addressed, for example, as follows.

Eric **BREDESEN**, Post Restante, City, Country.

Unless the sender specifies a certain post office by street address, your mail will be sent to the central post office. In Eastern Europe a *1* must be placed after the city name to make sure the mail arrives at the central post office. *Post Restante* is the international term for this service; at least it's understood in every country. In Spain the term is *Lista de Correos;* in German-speaking lands it's *Postlagernde Briefe*. Bring your passport or other ID with you to pick up your mail. If the clerk insists that there is no mail for you, ask him or her to check under your first name. Some countries charge a small fee for mail received this way.

If you own an American Express card or traveler's checks, you can request that people send your mail or take messages intended for you to certain American Express offices. American Express will hold the mail or messages for one month unless the envelope stipulates a longer period. The American Express brochure I mentioned earlier in this chapter lists those offices which hold mail.

Miscellaneous

Campers should consider getting a Camping Card Internationale (CCI) — sponsored by the *FIA,* the *AIT* and the International Federation of Camping and Caravaning (FICC) and commonly called a "Camping Carnet". Some campgrounds require that one CCI per campsite be deposited with the office. Some demand either a CCI or a passport. (Though you should carry your passport with you at all times.) For campground managers, the CCI amounts to a guarantee of payment: if you damage anything and/or leave without paying, the campground will turn in your card and eventually receive compensation. For you, the Carnet provides 2.5 million SwF worth of insurance against any damages you might accidentally cause to the campground; and in some cases it entitles you to discounts. The following organizations sell the CCI for about $25.

The National Campers & Hikers Association, Inc., 4804 Transit Road, Building 2, Depew, NY 14043-4704, tel. 716 668 6242.

National Campers & Hikers Association, 51 West 22nd Street, Hamilton, ON L9C 4N5, tel. 416 385 1866.

But *FIA-* and *AIT*-affiliated European motoring clubs, campgrounds belonging to the FICC, and the FICC office at rue de Rivoli, Paris, sell carnets for about half the price you'd pay at home.

If you'll be hostelling, camping, or staying with families or friends, consider bringing some of your favorite recipes, or researching recipes that are representative of the areas you'll be traveling to.

If bicycling, write down the make, model, and serial number of the bicycle. Do the same with the address of the lock insurer.

If you're bringing an expensive, foreign-made item such as a camera or camcorder, you should either take the sales receipt with you or register the item with Customs before you leave your home country. Such documentation allows you to prove upon return that you didn't buy the item abroad, and thus ensures that you don't have to pay duty on it.

Don't forget a list of contacts in Europe and addresses and phone numbers of people who you want to write to or call back home.

Business or calling cards are especially respected in Europe; they'll open many doors.

If you plan to land a job in Europe, don't forget your résumé and letters of recommendation.

Summary

airline or boat ticket

any railpasses you've bought

passport

eight passport-sized photos

copy of passport

copy of birth certificate

necessary visas

AMEX, Visa, MasterCard, Diners Club, Carte Blanche

1-800 numbers of credit card companies

description of the benefits associated with your credit or charge cards

personal checks

a few traveler's checks

list of the numbers of any traveler's checks you have

documents

savings and checking and investment account numbers

FIA and/or *AIT* booklets from your motoring club

driver's license

copy of driver's license

international driving permit

copy of international driving permit

documents associated with a vehicle rental, lease, or purchase

documents associated with shipping and importing a vehicle

statement of good driving

travel insurance information

eyeglass prescription

prescriptions for medicine

immunization record

medical insurance forms

IMAT information

Hostelling International card

ISIC card

phone card with international dialing instructions

proof of membership in any national organizations

Camping Carnet

recipes

bicycle information: serial number, insurance, etc.

customs registration or receipt of expensive foreign-made items

list of contacts in Europe

addresses to send post cards to back home

business or calling cards

résumé and letters of recommendation

Leave copies of all the above with some reliable person back home, and bring a second set of copies with you. Also, consider leaving signed checks and deposit slips so that this person can take care of your finances. If you'll be gone a long time, consider giving someone power of attorney over your affairs.

Make copies of your vehicle registration and insurance papers as soon as you get them.

12. packing

Electronics

Most European countries maintain a standard electricity supply of 50 Hertz AC frequency at 220 Volts. However, areas of Greece and Sweden use 110 Volts; parts of Italy, 115 Volts; parts of Spain 120, Volts; parts of the Netherlands, 127 Volts; parts of Portugal, 210 Volts; and the British Isles, 240 Volts. Most of Europe employs a standard two-pin plug; in the British Isles, however, a three-pin plug is standard.

Unfortunately most North American appliances are designed to operate on 60 Hertz AC at 110 Volts and with plugs that don't fit in European sockets. Check whether the appliances (shaver, hair dryer, camcorder, laptop computer, etc.) you plan to take can accept the necessary voltages and frequency; if they can't, you may need to buy a transformer. Most camcorder battery rechargers are designed to accommodate world travelers and thus accept a wide range of voltages and frequencies (in other words, they are "autosensing") and come with a two-pin plug adapter. Newer-model laptop computers autosense as well. Many hotels provide electric razor and toothbrush sockets that supply the North American standard 110 Volts, but they're intended for these low-wattage items only—don't plug a high-wattage appliance, such as a hair dryer, into one of these sockets. If you need a transformer or plug adapter, try contacting Magellan's Travel Essentials or Franzus. (See the *Resources* chapter.) You can purchase two- and three-pin plug adapters abroad as well.

Instead of the NTSC system used in North America to encode televison and VCR signals, Europe uses the PAL system. Despite this difference, blank tapes bought in Europe *will* work on your NTSC machine; only the length of the tapes is different (in order to achieve an even playing time, such as two hours, in the system they're designed for). However, Americans will find that tapes cost much more in Europe than they do at home. Of course the camcorders *themselves* are designed to decode either NTSC- or PAL-encoded signals—not both. Naturally, European merchants sell PAL-based camcorders. Thus, don't expect to buy a camcorder in Europe that'll produce recordings you can play at home. Of course this rule goes for televisions and VCRs too.

Some camcorder tips . . .

- Keep the sun at your back in most situations.

- Don't zoom in and out too much.

- Pan slowly and zoom consistently.

- Don't shoot too long; keep it short and sweet.

- Don't start a scene with a pan. Establish the scene first and then, if you must, pan. Change the pace of the filming. Begin scenes differently: fade in and fade out, but not every time; begin with a zoomed shot, then increase the angle (and vice versa). Don't overlook the details of a place: flowers, food, signs, vehicles, faces. Mix in staccato shots of minutiae with the hackneyed and unimaginative slow-pan. Occasionally interview the participants in the video as to their impressions of the place. Ask what surprised them most: this'll preserve first impressions that are naturally telling but too often forgotten.

- Some people don't like to be filmed. You must strike a balance between getting the shot, not offending the subjects, and not compromising your own experience. Try not to let the camera affect the shot. The most poignant and truthful videos are shot when the subject is unaffected by the recording device. Although at times it's great fun to get people playing to the camera, this quickly becomes tiring when watching two hours of video—assuming you're not working with great talent. I once missed filming an Aussie girl during a dusk wine-drinking fest on the Spanish coast of the Mediterranean; she was perhaps one of the most brilliant gabs I'll ever meet, and I missed recording her.

- If you haven't bought a camcorder yet but want to, I suggest the 8 mm format. Sure, the tapes don't play in your VHS VCR,

but it's easy to plug in the camcorder; and because the camcorder basically acts as a second VCR, you don't need another VHS VCR to make copies of your all-important original tapes. And you'll wanna make copies in order to preserve the original tapes, diminish the chances of losing the record of your trip, and to send them to friends and relatives. What's more, the small 8 mm tapes play for two hours, as opposed to the mini VHS tapes which play for only one-half hour. Either way, get a palm-sized camcorder and carry it with you in a waste pack; you won't even know it's there—and neither will thieves. Furthermore, you can sleep with it in hostels and hotels to prevent its theft.

- If you'll be in Europe for quite a while, consider mailing tapes home. The mail is remarkably trustworthy, but label the tape and case anyway.

- Label the camcorder with your name and address, and label the tapes themselves. If one or both items are lost, at least there's hope that some nice person will return them.

- Consider bringing a backup battery.

Some camera tips . . .

- Keep the sun at your back in most situations.

- Use the rule of thirds when taking landscapes: avoid aligning the horizon across the middle of the picture; align it across the bottom or top third.

- Incorporate people into most of your pictures. It makes the pictures more interesting. And unless you photograph them, you *will* forget the faces of people you'd swear you'll never forget.

- Mix in some close-ups with the wide-angle shots.

- Buy your film at home, but have it developed quickly to minimize its deterioration.

- Consider buying a disposable, wide-angle (17 mm) camera. The pictures these things take are incredible, excellent for capturing sweeping landscapes that a 35 mm simply can't relate.

- Consider using some black and white film.

- Label the camera with your name and address. If it's lost, at least there's hope that some nice person will return it and the precious film inside.

Although most individual X-ray machines at airports won't damage film, there is a cumulative effect. US federal agencies are said to be the principal purchasers of lead film shields. Indeed, certain airports in Eastern Europe use antiquated X-ray machines that can inflict serious damage to film—even if the film is protected by a standard lead shield. As such, you should either carry all your film in lead-laminated pouches (available at camera shops or from Magellan's) or remove film from your carry-on bags and request a hand inspection of it at the airport. If it's necessary to leave film in checked baggage or mail it across international borders, mark the outside of the container "Unprocessed Photographic Film. Please Do Not X-ray."

Always keep your camera and film out of the sun. In hot weather keep the film wrapped in foil or store it in an insulated bag. If mailing a roll of film, never deposit it in an outside mailbox.

Moisture is a problem in cold weather. Keep the camera warm by carrying it close to your body. And carry it in a plastic bag from which you've sucked all the air: this way, whatever condensation forms after you bring the camera into a warm room will form on the outside of the bag, not the camera. You should load and unload, however, outdoors in the cold: the film gets

tacky if loaded in a warm room and then taken out. To keep the sun from streaking your film when you change it, do the changing in a shady spot or in a special changing bag.

If you plan to sell your photos to a publication, take *slides,* rather than prints, for color shots. Editors call slides "transparencies" and use them because they cost a third less and can be duplicated or copied in color or black and white.

A waist pouch works great for carrying both palm-sized camcorders and cameras, among other things. Beware, however: the pouch is an instant signal that you're a tourist. This signal is bad if you're trying to be hip, but it's also bad if you don't wanna be singled out by thieves. Trouble is, it's pretty hard not to look like a tourist—no matter what you do. (Baseball hats, shorts and tennis shoes are other giveaways.) But who are you trying to fool? I wouldn't worry about it. During one trip, I wore a waist pack containing my camcorder and some money and credit cards wherever I went—not too cool, but great for getting good shots. Just be careful in crowds. By applying some tape around the clip or tying the loose end of the strap

to a belt loop, you'll thwart most thieves. A hint for North Americans: don't call it a "fanny" pack; trust me on this one.

Consider bringing a voice recorder to record your impressions. If you're traveling alone, a voice recorder is easier to operate while driving than is a camcorder. Don't forget extra tapes and batteries. Also bring some music tapes for the car stereo.

If if if you absolutely must, bring an alarm clock. Magellan's sells tiny alarm clocks designed for travelers.

Things for the Vehicle

Bring the maps and brochures that the tourist offices sent you, or maps you bought yourself. But remember, maps are cheaper in Europe.

If you're handicapped and have a wheel chair placard, bring it along. You'll be afforded the same rights in Europe that you are at home.

Bring booster cables, a flashlight, pliers, screwdrivers (both flat- and Phillips-head), open-end wrenches, electrical tape, duct tape, a wire hanger, and a pocket knife. Also bring chalk: if you get in an accident and have to move your vehicle, you can mark the position of the tires before you move it.

Consider bringing spare parts if you plan to travel in Romania: spare parts are scarce there and, as such, are prized.

You might wanna bring a magnetic box in which you can place an extra set of vehicle keys and stick somewhere on the underside of the vehicle.

A compass might come in handy.

Bring some clear plastic to use as a temporary window in the event that one gets broken. Duct tape will work to fasten the plastic to the vehicle. In fact, duct tape will prove useful in many an emergency.

Consider bringing a container and si-phon to siphon gasoline in case you run out. But don't worry; there's no lack of fuel stations in Europe.

Consider bringing a rubber tarantula or rubber snake. You can leave one of these on the front passenger seat to repel thieves. Who knows? It might work.

The incidence of vehicle theft is high in the city of Prague and in Poland. Con-sider bringing a car-theft deterrent like "The Club" if you have one. Whether you buy such a device specifically for your trip depends on the insurance and vehicle you'll

have. Usually, renters and leasers are ad-equately covered by theft insurance; others may have to purchase auto-theft insurance at a substantial cost.

Some countries require motor vehicles (except motorcycles) to carry certain safety-promoting items. Vehicles rented in a par-ticular country should come with such equipment. When leasing, buying or ship-ping a vehicle, the responsibility for ob-taining the proper accouterments lies with you. See the end of the *Why Drive?* chapter for a list of these items.

Motorcyclists too should see the end of the *Why Drive?* chapter for a list of motorcycle accessories.

Van-trippers and motorhomers, you should buy a large airtight container, fill it with water, soap, and dirty clothes, and let the motion of your vehicle do your wash-ing for you. Laundromats are quite expen-sive in Europe. And don't forget lengths of hose and electrical cable as described in the *Alternative Accommodations* chapter.

Luggage

Airline baggage allowances for interna-tional flights depend on the carrier, the route, and your ticket class. Generally,

you're allowed to check two bags—the sum of each piece's length, width, and height not exceeding 62 inches (158 centi-meters) or weighing more than 70 pounds (32 kilograms). A third piece may be car-ried on, the sum of its dimensions being less than 45 inches (114 centimeters). In practice, only the spirit of these regulations is enforced.

If you're flying between two foreign destinations, the piece method may be re-placed by the weight method. Under this method, luggage should not exceed 44-pounds (20-kilograms) for economy class, 66-pounds (30-kilograms) for business class, or 88-pounds (40-kilograms) for first class. If such a flight connects with an international flight, the piece method will be in effect.

Security

Always split your valuables into two sepa-rate places, such as a neck pouch and a waist pack. A neck pouch is more comfort-able and accessible than the admittedly more secure money belt. Keep one or more credit cards in each of these carrying de-vices: if one of the carriers is stolen, you can use the other card. You can order neck pouches and money belts from Europe Through the Back Door. (See the *Resources* chapter.) If you have traveler's checks, keep the bulk of them in one place and a list of the check numbers in the other. Don't use a billfold unless it's absolutely necessary. But consider bringing an old billfold filled with worthless cards, little money, and a note telling potential robbers what you think of 'em: in case of a robbery, you can hand over the trick billfold. If you wanna use a shoulder bag, get one with a long strap so you can put it securely across your opposite shoulder. You might even wanna use safety pins to pin your pockets and pack zippers shut. A rubber wedge can function as a door lock where the latter is absent or insufficient.

Budget travelers, why make your backpack the most expensive thing you have and the biggest target for theft? Backpacks are made for hiking miles and miles of rough terrain. You probably won't be doing much of that, especially if you drive. The pack will spend most of its time at your feet or locked away at a hostel or pension. Consider getting a canvas backpack, sea sack or duffle bag instead. You can find these at your local Army Surplus store. Not only is such luggage cheaper, it gives you the aura of a salty sea-dog. Sure it'll require you to pack light, but note the virtues of light packing that I describe later.

Miscellaneous

Bring your favorite toiletries: you probably won't be able to find them in Europe.

Don't forget any medication you may need, including aspirin.

Along with your prescription, consider bringing an extra pair of glasses or contacts—espcially if you'll be driving in Spain, where drivers are required to have a backup pair in the vehicle.

Bring a journal to record your experiences and thoughts and the addresses of people you'll meet. This is very important.

Phrasebooks work best as an icebreaker. The natives think it's hilarious to see their language condensed as such, and they appreciate your effort to learn. Open it up, hand it over, and listen to 'em roar; you'll be off to a good start.

A book of poetry might be apt. It's amazing how inspiring a group of friends, a bottle of wine, and the Swiss Alps can be.

Bring along a good paperback, preferably one with a travel theme.

To push the budget-travel envelope consider making your own postcards using tourist brochures obtained in Europe, thin cardboard, knife or scissors, and glue. The results are amazingly professional-looking. But sure the cardboard isn't thicker than the normal postcard material, or you may end up paying more in extra postage than you save by not buying postcards. By the way, postcards cost only $0.30 or so.

Bring a cheap solar calculator to calculate exchange rates, fuel efficiency, etc.

Campers, you can exchange empty propane cylinders at campground or sporting goods stores. Propane refills are available all over at stores, service stations and campgrounds.

Consider bringing a Nerf football, a baseball and gloves, or a frisbee. Foreign passtimes intrigue Europeans and thus serve as great icebreakers. And if you can make balloon animals, you can be a star street performer wherever you go.

Two small narrow cups, one for you and one for a friend, will add class to vagabond wine drinking.

Dental floss can also function as a cheese slicer and as emergency thread.

A Palestinian-style scarf, 1 x 1 meters, can function as a sun hat, a rain hood, a table cloth, a towel, a sling, padding, a pillow, a laundry bag, a rope, etc.

A small plastic hook with a suction cup will be handy in bathrooms where hooks are absent—an all too common case.

Bungee cords are handy for attaching micellany to your pack.

Consider bringing a fishing pole. Some great streams and lakes exist in Europe. Furthermore, a fishing pole gives a traveler instant credibility with natives everywhere across the globe.

You'd better leave the family pet at home. An imported animal must be put under quarantine for six months in some countries.

If you want a knife for protection (though I don't recommend carrying one), make it a dive knife: Customs officials are used to seeing these.

Light Packing

You may wanna consider "traveling light". The less you have the less you have to carry and worry about and the less you have to lose. And to reduce your belongings to the essential is one of travel's most sublime and surprising pleasures; the old nomad in you will well up and grin. Below is a list of items that are widely considered necessary.

all the documents mentioned in the *Documents* chapter

guidebooks

multi-language phrasebook

paperback book

journal and a mechanical pencil (a pen might explode; mine once did)

eyeglasses, contact lenses, cleaning solution

sunglasses

earplugs (and perhaps an eye mask)

pocket knife with can opener and corkscrew

camera or small camcorder and some film

waist pack for camera or camcorder, credit cards, etc.

neck pouch and/or money belt for valuables

chain or steel wire and padlock

heavy-duty garbage bag for stuffing/rain protection

small tent (if you plan to camp)

plastic ground cloth for the tent

sleeping mattress for the tent

sleeping bag, down insulated

thin nylon rope or string to tie things to metal loops on sack or backpack

bungee cords

waterproof hiking boots

two pair cotton socks

two pair wool socks

one pair of walking shoes

(When it comes to clothes, go old; those that look good even though they're about to fall apart are best.)

one x-large wool shirt: can function as coat, rain coat and pillow, and doesn't need washing often.

one pair of jeans

swimming trunks that triple as shorts and towel: these dry quick and come clean in the shower.

one pair of khaki pants: they don't show dirt, and they pass for dress-up.

three non-white, collared shirts: they don't show dirt, their open neck makes them cooler and faster to dry, and they look nice.

Palestinian scarf

duct tape

lighter

biodegradable liquid dishwashing soap: for washing dishes, clothes, and yourself. Hey, soap is soap. Bring a small container and refill it as you go.

prescription medicines

toothbrush, dental floss, deodorant, comb or brush, aspirin, chap stick, contraceptives, tampons, razor, sunscreen

sewing kit with buttons and safety pins

rope for clothesline or whatever: washing machines and dryers are very expensive.

rubber door wedge

two small narrow cups for wine

squash ball to plug sinks for washin; a film container wrapped in plastic does almost as well.

lengths of hose and electrical cord if you're a motorhomer

Here are some items you may think you need but likely don't.

underwear (Yes!)

alarm clock

pillow

flashlight

bug repellent

water purifier

clothes soap

cooking equipment

You'll be a proud and admired paragon of wisdom on the budget travel circuit if you follow this list faithfully. Virtually everybody over-packs and ends up complaining about it.

Bicycles

Usually you can bring a bicycle on a plane free of charge. Go to a bike shop and get a used bike box for free. To get the bike in the box, you'll have to remove the handle bars, pedals, and rear wheel. So you can reassemble the bike when you arrive and disassemble the bike when you leave again, bring along the tool you used to disassemble the bike. Throw away the bike box when you arrive; you can pick up another from a bike shop just before you leave.

Here's what you need for long distance bicycling.

hybrid bike: 2-inch clearance with crotch when standing.

or a touring bike: 1-inch clearance with crotch when standing.

helmet: roads are narrow, usually without bike lanes.

toe clips: these add about 30 percent to your efficiency.

water bottle and holder

rack over the tire: if you have panniers, be sure they can attach; is there enough clearance for mud guards?

sea sack (if you don't have panniers)

5 or 6 bungees (if you don't have panniers)

lock: motorcycle-type revolver lock with insurance

garbage bag cut to drape over sea sack in the rain (if you don't have panniers)

rain gear

map with at least four miles to an inch and showing every road

pump with pressure gage

tire-repair kit

maintenance manual

the following tools or a multi-purpose tool that can perform their functions:

adjustable wrench
Allen wrenches
spoke wrench
pliers
Phillips screwdriver
regular screwdriver
chain link removal tool
free wheel tool

the following replacement parts:

lubricant
brake pads
2–3 cables for front and back
tire
3–4 spokes
1–2 tubes
tire irons

Note that in the absence of panniers — and by employing the light packing approach described previously — you can save about $80 by purchasing a simple canvas sea sack instead of panniers. Four or five bungy cords can secure a properly packed sea sack to the rack over the rear tire; but get at least one extra, just in case. A large plastic garbage bag can protect the sack from rain.

If you currently have bike insurance (such as that associated with a lock guarantee), check if it applies abroad.

Jet Lag

The most reasonable advice I can give you about avoiding jet lag is this: Don't try too hard, at least not until you get to your destination. Your body is a very smart machine and is not easily tricked. As such, there is no sure-fire, esoteric formula for beating jet lag. Forget the eating and sleeping changes that some people preach you should practice the week before you go; just get excited and enjoy your flight — that's what it's all about. There are some reasonable measures to take during the flight, however: drink lots of liquids, eat lightly, don't drink coffee or alcohol, eat little or no sugar, and try to cop a two- or three-hour nap. Maybe that blows your idea of fun, eh?

When you land in Europe, not only will you be displaced in space and time, but an unpredictable combination of fatigue and adrenaline will create a sense of unreality that may be interesting enough in itself to keep you awake. And this is exactly what you must do: stay awake. You can help matters by immediately spending two hours outdoors: the natural light will begin re-tuning your body clock. If you make it to the local bedtime, chances are you'll have beat the jet lag; you'll wake the next day and be back in phase. Besides, with Europe at your feet, you'll never have a better reason to stay awake.

There is, however, at least one good book on the subject. *Overcoming Jet Lag,* by Charles F. Ehret and Lynne Waller Scanlon, offers a three-step program (used by the US Army) to counter jet lag. Berkeley Books; $8.

By the way, non smokers should not agree to sit in the smoking section on international flights. Within seconds after the *No Smoking* light is turned off, dozens of smokers will light up, making the section at least twice as smoky as the smokiest bar you've ever been in.

part 2
·········
on the road

13. country-by-country information

O highway I travel, do you say to me Do not leave me?/*Do you say* Venture not—if you leave me you are lost?/*Do you say* I am already prepared, I am well-beaten and undenied, adhere to me?/*O public road, I say back I am not afraid to leave you, yet I love you/You express me better than I can express myself.*

—Walt Whitman, *Song of the Open Road*

I begin this chapter by presenting several pages of general information before switching to a country-by-country format. Throughout, as I related in the *Itinerary Suggestions* chapter, I include virtually no topographical or road-condition information. I don't wanna waste your time with verbal descriptions of landscapes when *maps* can give you such info much more precisely, thoroughly, and immediately.

And as for road conditions, virtually none of the roads in 1990s Europe are prohibitively bad. I do, however, address toll roads, toll tunnels, and mountain passes on a country-by-country basis.

Borders

As I described in the *Why Drive?* chapter, in most cases border-crossing is a quick and hassle-free process. Although potentially you're subject to passport checks and searches of your person and vehicle upon crossing a border, often you can zip across the borders of Northern European countries without even slowing down. Sometimes you'll be required to slow down and stop before the guards simply wave you through. A circular sign reading *"Douane Zoll"* is a signal that you must stop. Most likely you'll just queue-up in your vehicle, wait a minute or two, hand each passenger's passport to the guard when you reach the station, flash a smile, wait a moment until the guard returns the passports, and proceed forward a couple hundred meters to the border station of the next country (where you'll repeat the process). Sometimes the guards will wanna see your vehicle's registration and proof of insurance. Sometimes, even, your vehicle will be searched. If you're chosen for a search, follow the Customs officers' directions and chalk it all up to experience; it's not too time consuming or nerve-wracking—unless, of course, you've got illegal substances or items with you. It goes without saying that you should never bring illicit drugs or weapons across borders. If you're transporting hitchhikers or others who haven't had the opportunity to gain your trust, politely and up front make it known to them that they must get out at the border and lug their things across on foot. If your vehicle has significant cosmetic damage to it, point it out to the Customs officials and have them note it on your passport; otherwise upon exiting the country you might be suspected of having been in an accident in that country and fleeing your associated responsibilities. If a country requires you to declare your vehicle with Customs, you'll probably be obliged to pay customs duty and tax if you leave the country without the vehicle.

Here's one trick to be aware of: if several fuel stations are clustered on your side of a border, fuel is probably more expensive in the next country; fill up before crossing.

The auto clubs of many countries maintain offices at the borders. These offices may sell everything from auto insurance to maps to guidebooks.

In the country-by-country descriptions, I delineate the duty-free customs allowances of each country. In relation to those allowances, you should know that the following countries comprise the European Community (EC): Belgium, Denmark, France, Germany, Great Britain, Ireland, Italy, Luxembourg, the Netherlands, Portugal, and Spain.

Finally, note that many border crossings close overnight, from, say, 8:00 or 9:00 P.M. to 7:00 or 8:00 A.M.; but most stay open until 10:00, 11:00, or 12:00 P.M. in the summer.

Concessions for Hostellers

Membership in Hostelling International (HI) entitles you to various concessions, concessions which differ from country to country. As such, I list motoring-related HI concessions on a country-by-country basis in this chapter. Always ask at museums and other attractions if your HI membership qualifies you for a discount.

Signals and Signs

The *STOP* sign is used throughout Europe—and it even reads "STOP" in English. Europe also uses the same *Yield* sign as North America. The *Red light = stop, green light = go* convention is used everywhere as well. A solid or flashing amber light precedes the red light and green light in most areas. This light signals that a red or green light is imminent. If you have the option to eventually turn right (or left in the British Isles) at a stop, a green arrow that points right may light simultaneously with the main red light that's stopping traffic from moving straight ahead. This green arrow means you can make a yielding right turn. Turning right when both these lights

show red is against the law. In other words, *no right turn on red*.

The same set of standardized road signs are used all over Europe. These signs are essentially graphic rather than linguistic in nature. As such, their meaning tends to be easy to understand. Of course the meaning of some signs is less obvious than the meaning of others. In Figure 13.1, I illustrate the more confusing signs. Note the sign that means *No bicycles*. The border of this sign is red. The color red on a European road sign signals negative information such as a prohibition or warning. You may encounter a similar circular sign showing a bicycle on a *blue* background. This sign designates a bicycle trail. As used on the road signs the color blue is positive in that it signals an obligatory action or some feature—such as a bicycle lane, a rest stop or a parking garage—that you can take advantage of; in other words, it says *do consider* rather than *don't consider*.

As in North America, dashed center lines mark passing zones; while solid center lines denote no-passing zones. Sometimes painted in regular succession amidst the dashed lines are fat arrows which curve slightly and point toward one lane while

Figure 13.1

Some Standard Road Signs.

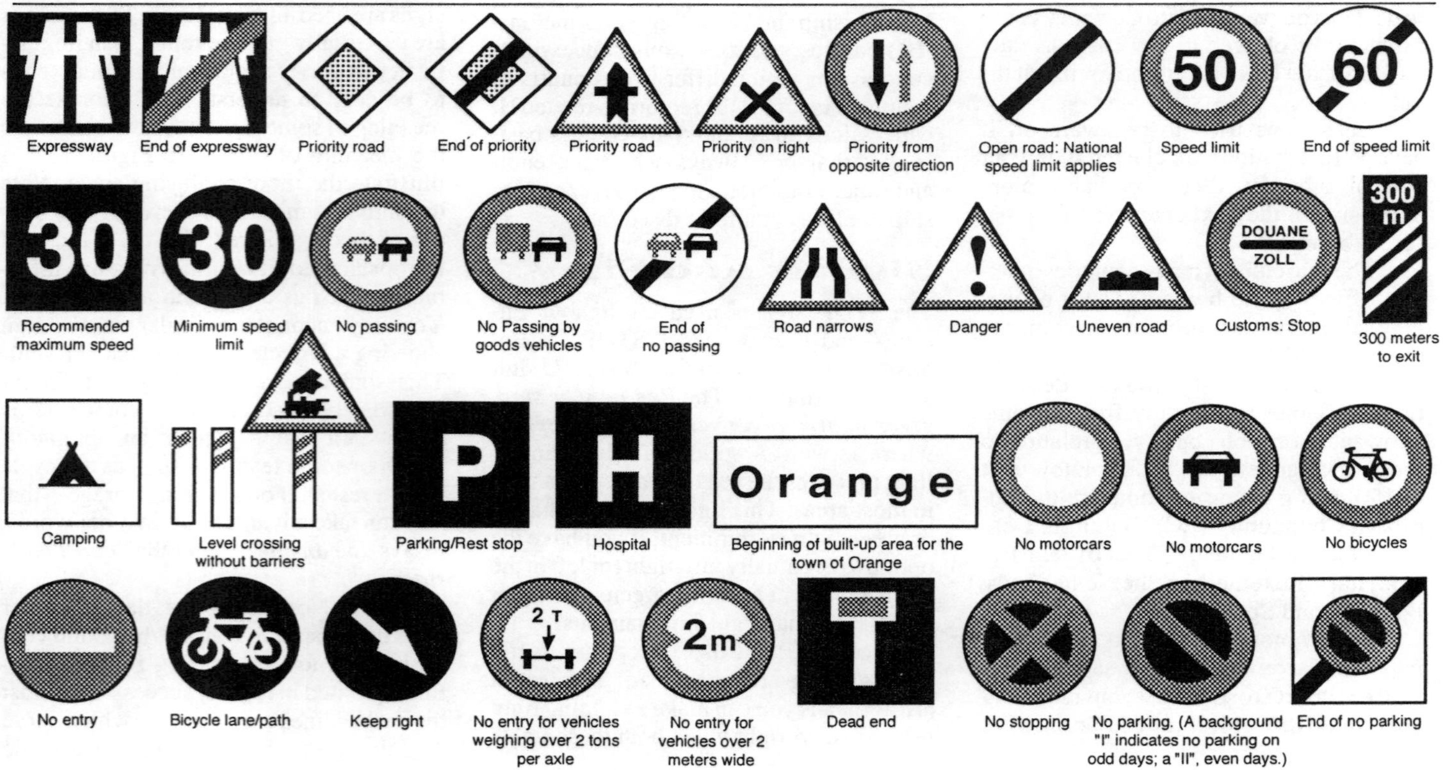

Expressway
End of expressway
Priority road
End of priority
Priority road
Priority on right
Priority from opposite direction
Open road: National speed limit applies
50
Speed limit
60
End of speed limit
30
Recommended maximum speed
30
Minimum speed limit
No passing
No Passing by goods vehicles
End of no passing
Road narrows
Danger
Uneven road
DOUANE
ZOLL
Customs: Stop
300 m
300 meters to exit
Camping
Level crossing without barriers
P
Parking/Rest stop
H
Hospital
Orange
Beginning of built-up area for the town of Orange
No motorcars
No motorcars
No bicycles
No entry
Bicycle lane/path
Keep right
2 T
No entry for vehicles weighing over 2 tons per axle
2m
No entry for vehicles over 2 meters wide
Dead end
No stopping
No parking. (A background "I" indicates no parking on odd days; a "II", even days.)
End of no parking

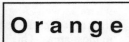

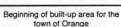

otherwise pointing almost straight ahead in the direction of that same lane. These arrows tell vehicles traveling in that lane that their passing zone will soon come to an end.

Cities usually post street signs not on poles at the corners but on placards attached one story up on buildings. Note that street names in some areas are apt to change frequently along an otherwise continuous avenue of concrete, and main routes may go unsigned while the intersecting and relatively minor cross streets are religiously labeled.

Fuel

In Table 13.1, I list the average gasoline prices for most of Europe's countries. Despite the fact that Norway's gasoline prices are the highest, the price of *diesel* fuel in Norway is a full *one-half* that of gasoline; and despite Britain's and Ireland's gasoline being some of the cheapest, the price of diesel in both countries is virtually the same as the price of gasoline. Both of these cases contrast with the usual price of diesel being two-thirds that of gasoline.

Note how cheap gas is in Switzerland, Spain and Denmark relative to surrounding countries. Although not listed, fuel in

Table 13.1

Recent Average *Gasoline* Prices in Various Countries.

	Foreign Price	US Dollars per Gallon
Cyprus	C£0.67/liter	$1.18
Bulgaria	8.85 leva/liter	$1.45
Poland	zl 12 266 /liter	$2.29
Switzerland	0.98 SwF/liter	$2.74
Ireland	IR£0.50/liter	$2.93
Great Britain	£0.49/liter	$2.95
Spain	97 ptas/liter	$2.96
Greece	195 dr./liter	$2.97
Portugal	130 Esc/liter	$2.97
Czech Republic	23.15 Kcs/liter	$3.00
Slovak Republic	22.50 Sk/liter	$3.00
Austria	AS 9.5/liter	$3.33
Italy	1500 lire/liter	$3.43
Denmark	5.90 kr./liter	$3.62
Germany	DM1.55/liter	$3.82
Netherlands	Fl. 1.73/liter	$3.84
Sweden	SEK 7.80/liter	$3.89
Hungary	104 Ft/liter	$4.00
France	5.75 FF/liter	$4.03
Norway	NOK 7.50/liter	$4.23

Average = $3.82/gallon, $1/liter (Bulgaria, Cyprus, Greece, Poland excepted)

Average = $3.55/gallon, $0.93/liter (Cyprus excepted)

Andorra is much cheaper than fuel in either Spain or France.

Fuel is much more expensive at stations along the expressways. Supermarkets along main roads at the edges of towns sell the cheapest fuel in France, Belgium, Germany, and the Netherlands. In France the main supermarket chain is *Mammoth;* in Germany the main chain is *Spar;* in the Netherlands it's *Mamoet.* The governments of Italy and Spain and Eastern Europe regulate fuel prices; all stations have the same price, so don't waste your time shopping for fuel in these countries.

Pump your own gas, or make it a habit to check that the attendant didn't cheat you. If you pay with a credit card, make sure the receipt is accurate. Some stations require that you pay not inside at a counter but outside at a booth upon driving out of the station area. If this is the case and a line of vehicles forms at the pay booth, you may have to wait to pump your fuel until the person who preceded you at the pump pays for theirs. Especially when dealing with such setups, note the total fuel charge on the pump so the attendant at the booth can't overcharge you; sometimes the attendants depend on your honesty and let you quote the total to them at the booth. In hot weather, fill up early in the morning or late in the evening when the air is cooler: the fuel will be more dense then, and thus you'll get more fuel for your Franc (or whatever). If a pump's nozzle won't fit in your tank, you're mistakenly trying to put leaded gas into a vehicle that requires unleaded. A pump with a green stripe holds unleaded fuel. LPG pumps always occupy their own island.

I make it policy to fill up when the fuel level dips to a quarter of a tank, but fuel stations are so plentiful that the chances of unexpectedly finding yourself low on fuel and far from a station are very low. If, however, you're careless enough to come close to running out of fuel, try the following technique: accelerate very slowly to 33 kph; turn off the ignition and move the gear to neutral; let the vehicle slow to 8 kph; start the engine; and repeat. This trick can double or even triple fuel efficiency; but it's a trick that won't work if your steering wheel locks when the ignition is off, and it can be illegal and dangerous.

Driving

Later I go into great detail about the rules of the road for each country. You should familiarize yourself with and try to adhere to these rules, but don't sacrifice the proper state of mind in the process. As to the proper state of mind, I think it's best described as bridled joy, with you riding high in the saddle and coolly commanding the reins. The best way to nurture this attitude is to tone down your dependence on memory, to let the environmental stimuli flow into you unimpeded, to react natu-

rally and to trust your reactions, to make mistakes and—because you know you'll learn from your mistakes and because you celebrate the fecundity of the unexpected—not to give a damn, to throw off the great weight of fastidiousness, to make the conceptual leap from the mundane to the invigorating, to exercise the old adage: When in Rome, do as the Romans do. In other words, go with the flow; be cool; blend in with traffic; and revel in the fact that you're truly participating in a different culture, that you've effectively become, for a short time at least, a citizen of Europe. When in Paris do as the Parisians and park on the sidewalk. When in Scandinavia, if you notice everybody else driving with their lights on—even in bright sun—you'd better too. It's easy.

OK, but now you're on the road in, say, France, and you think you may be on the *wrong* road. You're getting nervous because you wanna stay off the toll roads. After reading the France section of this chapter you know that blue signs marked with the letter *"A"* indicate *Autoroute péage* (toll) roads; while green signs with the letter *"N"* indicate non-toll *Route National* highways. No problem: just follow the signs in green, the signs that indicate the non-toll highways. At times, you'll note, the signals seem ambiguous because one sign bears both blue and green sections listing *A* and *N* roads respectively. "How can I be on both an *A* and an *N* road at the same time?" you'll ask yourself. Such signage means only that you're on your way to both types of road, that the road the sign marks is not a toll road; eventually you'll have the option to enter either the toll road or a non-toll road. Sometimes after following a green-only or a blue/green sign, a blue-only sign will appear unaccompanied by possible turn-offs. Don't worry: eventually another green sign will direct you to a non-toll road before you have to pay. This all sounds simple, and it is. *Just keep following the last sign you saw. Keep following the last sign you saw. Keep following the last sign you saw . . .* Sorry, but I feel the redundancy is necessary. It's easy to get flustered and worry that you missed an important turn. But the keen state of mind that you'll be in, coupled with the excellent nature of the roads and signage, will render quite small the chances of actually missing such a turn-off. Be astute, but trust yourself and the road design and signage. In a word, *relax;* usually it all comes together in the end. The wis-

dom of this simple approach has been apparent to me time after time throughout my travels. I've slowly learned not to get flustered when there isn't a meaningful sign placed every one kilometer. This is more than a prudent approach to driving; it's an attitude, an attitude that will greatly increase the pleasure you draw from your trip. You are, after all, on the road; you should be singing songs and talking like Kerouac.

And, as I first described in the *Why Drive?* chapter, history has assured that navigating to the cities and towns and sights is much more of a song than you might expect. First, most of the European languages you'll encounter are cognate with English; so it tends to be quite easy to read signs which give directions. What's more, each city and town grew from an old town center. In this center, of course, lie most of a town's attractive sites and accommodations. Everything falls into place if you follow the ubiquitous signs to the town center or simply head toward the tallest church spire. Most of the signs denoting town centers bear variations of the word *center,* such as *"Centro"*, *"Centrum"*, *"Centre Ville"*, *"Centro Città"*, or *"Zentrum";* in many parts of Germany the

word is *"Stadtmitte"*. Furthermore, on the way to the center of town you'll see tourist information boards or signs indicating the direction to the tourist office. Most such signs read *"i"* for information; in France, however, they read *"Office du Tourisme"* or *"Syndicat d'Initiative";* in the Netherlands they read *"VVV";* sometimes they bear a lone *"?"*.

Another way to get your bearings when entering a town is to follow the signs that point to the train station. Both the signs and the stations they point to are ubiquitous in Europe. Look for signs reading *"Gare"*, *"Estacion"*, or some variation of the word *station.* Many guidebooks use the train station as the origin for their directions to sights and accommodations. Furthermore, the famous and (here we go again) *ubiquitous* Hostelling International sign (see the *Alternative Accommodations* chapter) tends to be nearby, pointing the way to the nearest hostel. In most cases hostel proprietors have placed these signs in a series and with a frequency designed to lead all but the most clueless along the best route to the hostel door. Often, a tourist office operates out of the local train station. At the very least you'll find city maps dispensed inside or a single city map displayed on a large public board just outside. Perhaps what's more important, many of your fellow travelers at the station will be more than happy to give you the scoop on the best places to stay, the best sights, and the best places to hang out. Moreover, the parking lot will be at your disposal—often free of charge: you can just leave your vehicle in the lot and continue on foot or by metro, bus, or taxi. Since governments tend to build train stations near places of interest and since business people who cater to travelers tend to locate their establishments around either train stations or places of interest, you probably won't feel compelled to stray too far from the station.

To leave a city either follow the signs that indicate the road or the city you wanna travel on or to or follow the signs that bear words meaning "all directions" or "other directions". For translations of these phrases, see the "Road Signs" portions in the France, Germany, Italy, the Netherlands, and Spain sections of this chapter.

European police don't seem to enforce speed limits with the same gusto as do North American police. The fast lane is usually just that—fast. The countries hungriest for speed are Germany and Great Britain, where fast-lane speeds of 120 mph

(200 kph) and 100 mph (166 kph), respectively, are common. As I'm sure you've heard, no speed limit exists on many sections of the famous German *autobahns*. In contrast to Germany and Britain, traffic in Norway seems to crawl along. Generally, traffic flows about 10 mph (17 kph) faster than traffic in North America. The roads are good enough to handle the high speeds, but if you don't fancy yourself a Euro Speed Racer or if your vehicle simply can't keep up, you won't be alone: plenty of Europeans drive 55 mph in the slow lanes or amicably signal or pull onto the shoulder so speedier drivers can pass. Many countries define speed limits in terms of "built-up" areas. A built-up area is indicated by a sign, placed along the road at the community boundary, that bears the name of the community. The end of a built-up area is indicated by a black slash across a twin of this sign. If when outside a built-up area the police nail you for speeding, they won't pull you over immediately; instead, they'll radio one of their colleagues who'll pull you over at a convenient spot down the road.

You need to familiarize yourself with the ways drivers may signal to you. If someone driving in the opposite direction

blinks their vehicle's headlights, it means that police are lying in wait ahead. On the open road someone who wants to pass will come up behind you with their vehicle's left blinker (right blinker where driving is on the left) and/or headlights flashing; if you're on a single-lane highway, signal with your vehicle's right directional (left directional where driving is on the left) when you think it's safe for them to pass. European truckers use the same blinker signal to let you know it's safe to pass them. If the truck driver sees danger ahead he'll engage his truck's left blinker (right blinker where driving is on the left). Although these signals aren't fool proof, you may soon come to trust them. Two quick beeps on the horn means "Thank you." You're also expected to sound your horn before taking a blind curve on a narrow rural or mountain road. Otherwise, use the horn as a last resort.

You'll encounter tunnels in mountainous areas. Be sure to turn on your vehicle's headlights before entering a tunnel; police tend to lie in wait on the other end, nailing driver's who haven't lit up. Norway's tunnels are so long they're unnerving; you'll feel like Starbuck being shot out of the Battlestar Gallactica, and you'll think to yourself, "Gee, even Superman woulda had a hard time digging these tunnels."

By the way, driving with headlights on decreases by 30 percent your chances of being in a collison with another vehicle — that's why it's required at all times in Scandinavia. And cops are bound to go easier on drivers thoughtful enough to light up.

To use toll roads, you must, upon entering the system, pay at a booth or else get a ticket by pushing a red button on a driver's-side ticketing machine. Sometimes the ticketing machine controls a barrier; other times there's no barrier. If you go through an unbarred control point without getting a ticket, you'll be charged the maximum toll at the next exit. So they can further prosecute violaters, many toll stations use automatic cameras to photograph any vehicle that passes through a pay booth without paying.

If you travel through mountain tunnels or over passes which charge a toll, note that many offer discounted return fares for travelers who'll return within a certain period, usually 72 hours.

Where two roads of equal priority intersect, you must give way to traffic coming from your right. In France this rule once applied to all roads, thus supplanting any notion of a priority road; fortunately this is no longer the case. These days long stretches of European roadway are clearly marked as priority roads, and/or the approaches to and intersections with priority roads are clearly marked with warning signs and with *Yield* and *STOP* signs. Since they don't really *intersect* with other roads, all expressways (variously called *autoroutes, autobahns,* motorways, etc.) have priority. Only on occasion will two roads of equal (unmarked) priority intersect and oblige you to methodically exercise your knowledge of what in France is called *"priorité à droite"* or "priority on the right".

"Hey, look kids. There's Big Ben, and there's Parliament," exclaims driver Chevy Chase — starring as Clark Griswald, the well-meaning but bumbling patriarch of the pathetic Griswald clan — in a scene from the 1985 movie *European Vacation.* The scene unfolds early one day in the family's rented car as Clark attempts to navigate a London roundabout. "Kids. Big Ben, Parliament, (again)," he repeats the second time around. "Kids." "We know," they retort in unison. *"...Big Ben, Parlia-ment."* Dusk finds the Griswald's little car circling on the same roundabout, all passengers but Clark fast asleep. "It's amazing," Clark says to himself in hysterical disbelief. "I cannot get left."

Roundabouts: those circular intersections where stop signs are nonexistent, and everyone's at everyone else's mercy, and you have to join the flow if you wanna go — and you could, in theory, go around forever. To many of us North Americans, roundabouts epitomize European motoring. The popular American imagination elevates few elements of civil engineering to the level of enigma, but it has done so with roundabouts. Many non Europeans assume that if roundabouts are such a puzzle, so must be the rest of European motoring. You know by now that this assumption is unsound. But what *is* the deal with roundabouts anyway? Although in most cases you don't need to stop when entering a roundabout, you must yield to traffic that's already on it. A red-bordered, triangular sign bearing a circle of arrows — and, perhaps, a country-specific legend — indicates such a roundabout. Though increasingly rare, some roundabouts in France aren't graced by such a sign and thus make it incumbent for you to exercise the aforementioned *priorité à droite* rule; in other words, traffic on these roundabouts must yield to traffic entering. Regardless of signage, it should be immediately obvious if the traffic on or entering the roundabout is or is not waiting for you to enter. Once on the circle, you can go around indefinitely until you figure out which exit you wanna take. You'll get the impression that you're skating around that old roller rink you used to go to as a kid. Indeed, you'll become a bit giddy. You'll quickly come to like these little rinks: they allow you to make unhurried decisions as your vehicle is moving, and they reduce the number of stops you must make. If two lanes enter a roundabout, you should stay in the inside lane, engaging your vehicle's inside blinker until you identify the exit you wish to take and until you pass the exit immediately before that one. Once you reach this point you should engage your vehicle's outside blinker, move into the outside lane, and exit the roundabout. England and France employ the most roundabouts.

A level train crossing without barriers is indicated by the three signs illustrated in Figure 13.1 set at 80 meter intervals before the crossing. A flashing red beacon and/or continuous bell warns of an approaching train. When the way is clear, the beacon changes to white or amber, and/or the bell ceases. You must turn off your vehicle's headlights when waiting at a crossing.

Let's hope that all your stops are pleasant, but you should note the places where they're less likely to be so. Geneva's International Road Federation has declared Turkey and Latvia the most dangerous European countries in which to drive; Portugal is close behind. The safest countries for drivers are the Netherlands, Denmark, Finland, and Germany. The Federation's comments generally agree with the data in Table 13.2.

Most countries empower their police to collect fines on the spot from violators. If the police require that you pay them, make sure you get a receipt; and if possible, make sure the nature of the offense and the amount of the fine as described on the receipt match the actual offense and the amount you paid. Police in France and Italy use roadblocks to conduct random checks of vehicles and drivers. Blood alcohol limits in Europe are given in milligrams (mg), so that's how I list them for each country. Note that a blood alcohol limit of, say, 80 mg is equal to a limit of 0.08 percent or 0.8 grams per liter.

Table 13.2
Vehicle Fatalities.

Country	Average number of deaths per million registered vehicles.
Great Britain	207
Netherlands	223
Germany	239
Italy	255
United States	**257**
Denmark	332
Luxembourg	348
France	394
Belgium	460
Ireland	496
Spain	624
Greece	771
Portugal	1008

Parking

As I enthusiastically related in the *Why Drive?* chapter, you should be able to find free parking all over Europe. Some neighborhoods, however, reserve free parking—or *all* parking—for residents. In such areas the residents' vehicles bear an official sticker. Check the other vehicles around yours to see if they all bear the same sort of sticker in the same place on one of the windows.

Parking meters and "pay-and-display" schemes are common. A pay-and-display scheme requires you to pay at a central machine (some machines ask you to punch in your vehicle's license plate number too), press a button (usually the green one, the others are for local residents whose vehicle's bear special permits), receive a ticket that lists a time-of-day limit commensurate with the amount you paid, and display the ticket on the side of your vehicle's dashboard closest to the curb. Most of these machines account for periods of the day when parking is free, so you can pay at night for the first hour or two after 8:00 or 9:00 A.M. the next day.

Many cities in Austria, Belgium, Denmark, France, Italy, Luxembourg, the Netherlands, Portugal, Spain, and Switzerland enforce *Blue Zones* or short-term parking areas. The marking of these zones varies from country to country. Before parking in a *Blue Zone* you must obtain special tickets or a disc from a tourist office, police station, or tobacconist. Sometimes you must buy the tickets or disc, but usually they're

given free of charge. In fact, many rental companies include a disc or "blue card" in their vehicles. When using a ticket, you write on it the date and time of your arrival (Europeans write the day number before the month number and use the military convention for noting times) and then display it on the side of your vehicle's dashboard closest to the curb. Discs, on the other hand, either bear a clock face and a set of unmechanized clock hands which you can set to show the time of your arrival, or they actually function as timers. In lieu of these items a simple note left on your dashboard may suffice. It's worth noting that during my first extended motor tour of Europe I was unaware of such zones; I never bought tickets or obtained a disc, and I never suffered a penalty—and I parked in many cities and towns which supposedly enforce *Blue Zones*. Maybe I was lucky. If you're unsure about whether you should obtain a ticket or disc, check the dashboards of the other vehicles in the area to determine if other drivers feel it's necessary.

If you do get a parking ticket and you do feel compelled to pay it, most countries offer a rather ingenious way to do so. Take the ticket to a tobacconist, purchase a tax

stamp (called a *"timbre fiscal"* in France) in the proper amount, afix the larger of the tax stamp's two sections to the ticket, and, using a regular stamp, mail the tax-stamped ticket to the address indicated on the ticket. Note that wheel clamps are coming into wider use.

Most parking garages and lots employ one rather clever pay-for-parking scheme. Upon entering, you receive a ticket. Just before you leave, you take the ticket to a central processing machine and place it in a slot. The machine then prompts you to insert the appropriate amount of cash. Insert the cash and the machine returns any change along with the ticket, which now bears the time and a certification of payment. Finally, you must present the ticket to the attendant when you leave.

As I mentioned in the *Why Drive?* chapter, Barcelona harbors amazing car parks. When you drive in, an attendant directs you to continue into a chamber. Once you properly align the vehicle in the chamber, you exit both the vehicle and the chamber. Finally, the attendant closes the chamber, and the vehicle is hydraulically moved to some secret, subterranean vault. Be sure to remove your luggage when you remove yourself from the chamber: I once didn't and had to recall my car, drive it out, and pay before being able to re-park it.

Theft and Safety

Most theft in Europe is of the petty variety, rarely involving assault: the thief does not want a confrontation. Thus, by using your head you can prevent almost every potential crime.

For example, don't let people listen in or somehow note your phone card or credit card number. Watch your credit card after giving it to a clerk: you don't want the clerk to make extra imprints. Review all charge slips before you sign them. And be careful with your charge card receipts: they have the card number on them too. In fact, you should destroy old carbons, billing statements, and other records that bear your account number.

Don't flaunt your money or act too much like a tourist. You know how foreigners stand out as targets for crime. Don't compromise your trip, but don't unnecessarily make yourself a bigger target. Be discreet when doing your thing in banks, at ATM machines, or at exchange booths. Take note of the people around you. Try to blend in and look confident. If you have a

shoulder bag, wear the strap across the shoulder opposite the side on which the bag hangs. Be careful in crowded places such as those around street performers and on metros and buses: pick-pockets love crowds—especially crowds ripe with tourists. Beware at beaches. If two people approach you, one speaking to you and the other hovering around, go on red alert: the speaker may be trying to distract you while the other person nabs an item. And never fall asleep with a valuable next to you. Move in groups when it's convenient. In no way is the danger great enough that you should modify your itinerary; just be smart, that's all.

The further south you go the more you need to be aware of your possessions and personal space. Beware of young vagrant children and their adult cohorts who hover around and pick-pocket travelers. Such thieves may walk into you with an open newspaper or large flat box held extended from their waste, wave a newspaper in your face, or throw a baby doll into your arms to distract you while their accomplices rifle through your pockets. Other thieves may approach you with flowers or some other triviality to sell; simply brush them off—and don't feel bad about it. I've even heard

of tourists being glopped with mustard then "assisted" by ostensibly helpful bystanders who in fact did the glopping and who point to the sky and claim the stuff is bird doo while they wipe it off and swipe what they can. No matter, if you're aware of their presence and have taken simple security precautions, thieves will leave you alone.

Thefts *from* vehicles occur with alarming frequency in Spain and Southern Italy. Regardless of where you are, leave nothing of value in the vehicle. Leave the glove compartment open and emptied. If a rear seat pulls down to offer access to the trunk, pull it down—and leave the trunk empty. If your vehicle has a hatchback, remove the shield that conceals the empty trunk. Consider leaving the front passenger door open to allow thieves easy access: otherwise, they'll break a lock or window. Essentially, make the scene look as if some other thief has been there already. If you drive into the larger cities, consider parking in front of embassies and banks where security may be better, or in an area where traffic police are working. Throughout Europe, parking ramps offer safer haven than the streets; but they may not be worth the cost.

The rate of theft of vehicles *themselves* is high in the city of Prague and in Poland. Consider parking in small towns outlying the larger cities. You can take the extremely cheap trains into the metro area. Thieves concentrate where the tourists are, and the tourists usually aren't in the small towns. Turning your wheels all the way to the curb may also help.

Some thieves are more aggressive than those I've mentioned so far. Keep your vehicle's doors locked when driving, and keep the vehicle in gear at a stop. If someone points to your tires as if indicating that the tires are flat, don't get out to look. If someone bumps you—especially if they bump you repeatedly—think twice before unlocking the doors and getting out of the vehicle. Rather, turn on your vehicle's hazard lights to signal that you're not fleeing, and drive slowly to a well-populated and well-lit place. Beware if you pick up a rental car at Madrid's airport. The rental companies there park their vehicles in unprotected and unsupervised areas. As a result, thieves have learned to puncture the tires, wait outside, follow exiting vehicles, and rob them when the unsuspecting driver pulls over with a flat. Always be wary of an offer of roadside help extended by anyone

other than a uniformed police officer or civil guard. If a person stops to help, ask them to call the police. Conversely, don't *you* stop to help a stranded motorist: in the more marginal parts of Europe, roadside brigands are known to feign car trouble then steal your vehicle and/or rob you when you stop to help.

Lock away your baggage overnight, and lock the door to your room as well. When staying in a hostel, take a hint from nature and sleep with your valuables between your legs. Out of sight is out of mind; don't unnecessarily tempt thieves. Passports are a valuable commodity on the black market—keep yours secure. If you travel in a *couchette* on an overnight train, tie the door shut: thieves pay-off conductors, put sleeping gas into compartments, and proceed to pilfer the unconscious occupants' possessions; if you're not careful, you'll wake up minus one suitcase or backpack but plus one big head ache. Italian trains have become infamous for such robberies. If something of yours does get stolen from your person, vehicle, or room and if you have some form of insurance to cover the theft of the item, make sure you get a police report at the next convenient opportunity, if you know what I mean.

Mail

In Table 13.3, I list the various costs of sending a postcard to North America. The table serves to relate the general cost of postage in each country.

Overheating

In hot weather check the radiator's water level frequently. If the water level is low but not below the bottom of the header tank, you can immediately add water. If, however, the water is below this level, you should allow the engine to cool before adding water: otherwise you may damage the cylinder block. If the radiator is overheating, let it cool before very carefully and slowly opening the radiator cap. If you aren't careful, a rush of steam from the radiator may severely burn you. High engine temperatures resulting from some combination of a high ambient temperature, an ineffective cooling system, and extreme strain on the engine from, say, a steep ascent, can vaporize fuel in the lines, the pump, or the carburetor, causing the engine to stop. If such a stall occurs, let the engine cool off before trying to restart it.

Table 13.3

Recent Cost of a Mailing a Postcard to North America.

Austria	AS 8.50	$0.70
Belgium	BF 32	$0.96
Bulgaria	10 leva	$0.43
Cyprus	C£0.56	$0.26
Czech Republic	6 Kc	$0.20
Denmark	5 kr.	$0.80
Finland	FIM 3.40	$0.59
France	3.70 frs.	$0.68
Germany	DM0.80	$0.52
Great Britain	£0.33	$0.52
Greece	120 dr.	$0.48
Netherlands	Fl. 0.75	$0.44
Hungary	34 Ft.	$0.34
Ireland	IR£0.38	$0.59
Italy	950 lire	$0.57
Luxembourg	22 fr.L	$0.70
Norway	NOK 5.50	$0.81
Poland	zl 3500	$0.17
Slovak Republic	6 Sk	$0.18
Spain	83 ptas	$0.66
Sweden	SEK 6	$0.79
Switzerland	1.80 Fr.	$1.32

Breakdowns & Accidents

If you've rented or leased a vehicle, your contract should entitle you to some form of roadside service. Regardless, chances are that the local motoring club will come to your aid. As I detailed in the *Documents* chapter, most of the European clubs belong to one of the two international touring organizations, either the *Fédération Internationale de l'Automobile* (*FIA*) or the *Alliance Internationale de Tourisme* (*AIT*) and thus are obligated to reciprocate their benefits to members of likewise-affiliated clubs. If you don't belong to an affiliated club, you can buy temporary membership in any number of European clubs. Even if you aren't reciprocally or directly a member of these clubs, they'll still come to your aid—for a charge. In the country-by-country descriptions, I include the address and phone number of all automobile clubs, and I note if they're affiliated with the *FIA* and/or *AIT*.

Get a receipt for any service you must pay for: your automobile club, rental or leasing company, or dealer may reimburse you if you do. *Always* secure a cost esti-mate before submitting your vehicle for maintenance.

Besides the information about automobile clubs, I include in each country's description the local telephone numbers for the police, fire, and ambulance services. In many areas, emergency phones are in place along major roads. Laws, unless I note otherwise in a country's description, require you to call police to the scene of any accident that involves you and that results in damage to a vehicle or person. However, sometimes—especially in the South—the parties involved can settle such damages on the spot. Such settlements are facilitated by the European Accident Statement. This form—found in the glove compartment or in the pocket on the driver's side door of most rental vehicles—provides a standard format on which to draw a diagram of the accident, note the information about the vehicles and drivers involved, and note other important facts about the accident. All drivers involved sign the form and receive a carbon copy; they then send a copy of their copy to their rental or leasing or insurance company. Of course you should carefully consider your insurance coverage before settling accidents without involving the police. In *Appendix*

Table 13.4

Appropriate Placement of Warning Triangles.

	Distance in Meters Behind the Vehicle	Minimum Visible Distance in Meters
Austria	—	100
Belgium	30 (road)	50
	100 (expressway)	
Finland	50 (road)	110
	150 (expressway)	
France	30	100
Germany	100 (road)	100
	150 (expressway)	
Greece	100	110
Great Britain	50	110
Italy	50 (road)	110
	150 (expressway)	
Luxembourg	30	100
Netherlands	30	100
Norway	30	100
Portugal	30	100
Spain	30	100
Sweden	30	100
Switzerland	50 (road)	110
	150 (expressway)	
Sweden	30	100

place one or two warning triangles along the roadside behind the vehicle. (Motorcycles are exempt from this requirement.) You should also turn on the vehicle's hazard lights. In Table 13.4, I list the appropriate distances at which you should place the triangle or triangles behind the vehicle.

Miscellaneous

I provide metric conversion charts in *Appendix E*. But if you wanna perform a quick conversion of kilometers to miles, simply divide the kilometer figure by ten (in other words, move the decimal point one place to the left) and multiply by six. You can invert the process to convert miles to kilometers: multiply by six and divide by ten.

You'll have to do some more math in your role as a consumer. A good way to exercise this role is by patronizing—in the best sense of the word—the local baker or grocer. Such interactions will give you a greater understanding of everyday life in Europe. Note that in many parts of Europe it's considered rude for a customer to carefully inspect produce for flaws—especially by handling it. When asking for a certain number of items, indicate the number with your fingers—using your thumb as num-

F, I detail the issues you should in that case address; and in the *Appendix G*, I provide several phrases which will be useful in the event of an accident. Note that you should never sign a statement that you can't read; insist on a translation.

If you stop your car or van or caravan on the shoulder of a highway, you must

ber *one*. Do the same to indicate weight in kilograms. When ordering items that must be sliced, however, pantomime the number of slices by making slicing motions, not by holding up fingers. Large stores employ an ingenious scheme to properly price produce. The customer picks out a particular fruit or vegetable and places it on a central electronic scale. After referencing a numbered array of pictures pasted on the scale, the customer punches the numbers on the scale's keyboard that correspond to the produce. The machine then spits out a sticker with the proper price for the amount and type of produce. Finally, the customer places the sticker on the clear plastic bag containing the produce. The sticker bears the name of the produce, so cheating is impossible without the help of the clerk. It's unwise to frequent grocery or convenience stores along expressways or at campgrounds: such stores elevate prices. The cheapest groceries are sold where the cheapest fuel is sold, along major roads exiting towns.

Many shops close from about noon to 2:00 P.M., and many restaurants don't open their kitchens until later in the afternoon. To avoid a lunchtime hassle, keep a little extra food in your vehicle. Better yet, try to get into the European pattern of eating a late and large lunch and a late and lighter supper. If you don't fall into this pattern, you'll be missing out on two of Europe's most significant rituals. Also, don't let Sunday closings catch you off guard. Most shops and all banks do not open on Sundays, and banks rarely open on Saturday.

When playing the role of consumer in a foreign land, you should endeavor to employ at least a few of the local phrases. Yet many tourists claim that Europeans become haughty or irritated if you awkwardly attempt to communicate with them in their language. Of course *some* Europeans *do* react this way. However, such a reaction can become chronic only in areas where you should expect people to be jaded from suffering huge volumes of fumbling tourists. No, in the vast majority of cases Europeans amiably endure even the most faltering attempts by foreigners to exercise the local language. Indeed, saying "please" and "thank you" in their language—and smiling sincerely—will almost guarantee good relations. And it's amazing how much you can communicate using facial expressions and bodily gestures.

Speaking of gestures, people are really quite simple and similar in that they all want respect. The definition of respectful behavior, however, varies somewhat. In America a waitress is being respectful if she attends her tables in a fashion that approximates a hummingbird in a flower patch. Europeans, however, consider such service disrespectful of the customers' right to enjoy a meal in a relaxed and semi-private environment. (I've come to revel in this more civilized approach to dining.) It's true, however, that the customer simply doesn't command the same high and mighty seat in Europe that he does in the US.

Finally, let's consider the word *mien*. *Webster's* says that "one's appearance, bearing, or manner" constitute one's *mien*. Of course most people are virtually occupied with concerns about their appearance, bearing, and manner. Yet of these characteristics the word *mien* connotes the aspects that are the most difficult for us to control. Because it's so defining of your personality yet so hard for you to control, your *mien* makes it virtually impossible for you, as a foreigner, to "fit in" abroad. Fitting in may be important in *every* sense of the word *mien* if you're an immigrant or otherwise plan to be assimilated into the culture, but as a traveler you cannot—and you should not—strive for this end. As a traveler (no matter how trite this sounds) you're an unofficial ambassador of your land, and it's your duty to represent it with integrity. As such, it's your duty to maintain much of your *mien,* your duty to be yourself. Yet we all sense that a traveler should modulate his or her *mien.*

Let's take a closer look at *Webster's* definition. Of the words *appearance, bearing* and *manner,* the word *bearing* is the one that suggests force, the one with threatening connotations. Indeed, of the type of American who inveterately offends the sensibilities of the hosts in, say, the contemplative air of a small Paris art museum, it's not so much their appearance or manner that offends (Paris is an incredibly polyglot city) but their *bearing;* it's that they can be heard and almost felt *bearing* down on this or that room with the stentorian and momentous presence of people who somehow assume a certain ownership of the place, as if they were, with all the earnestness of a well-intentioned parvenu, taking the obligatory inventory of some inheritance. It's this good-natured but tangential *bearing,* carrying the collective energy of the idealistic angels who alighted for the spiritual and temporal riches of America and left what remained of Europe's

optimism to create and suffer two world wars, that Europeans immediately sense and associate with what's commonly called the "Ugly American"; it's an energy now blithely channeled through a confidence in both position and progress and so unswerving as to be largely insensate to the ironical, a paradoxical and obtuse confidence no post-modern European can embrace without feeling the fool. Indeed, the quintessential fatalism in today's European spirit is the antithesis of the American élan; yet the future of both continents lies in a reunification of these daemons, in some robust middle ground. And so I suggest that you pay special attention to your bearing when you travel in Europe, that you explore and help create this rich middle ground, this future.

Andorra

Customs

Extremely lax.

Non-toll Mountain Passes

N22's Envalira Pass, L'Hospitalet to Andorra. At 2,407 meters, this is the highest pass in the Pyrénées; it's closed occasionally in the winter. Maximum grade is 12.4 per cent; minimum width is 6.2 meters (20 ft.); maximum vehicle height is 3.56 meters (11.5 ft.); OK for caravans.

Fuel

Unleaded gasoline is known as either *essence sans plomb* or *gasolina sin plomb.* Diesel fuel is known as *diesel.* LPG is known as *Gaz de pétrole liquéfié (GPL).* Fuel is much cheaper in Andorra than in France or Spain.

Driving

Snow tires or chains are essential in the winter. Police are empowered to collect fines on the spot. Speed limits: 40 kph (25 mph) in built-up areas, 70 kph (44 mph) outside built-up areas. Other regulations approximate those of France.

Banks

Open on weekdays from 9:00 A.M. to 1:00 P.M. and from 3:00 P.M. to 5:00 P.M. and on Saturday from 9:00 A.M. to noon.

Shops

Open daily from 9:00 A.M. to 8:00 P.M.

National Holidays

Third Sat in July; last Sun in July and following Mon and Tues; July 25, 26, 27; first Sat in Aug, and following Sun and Mon; Aug 15, 16, 17; Sep 8, 16, 17.

Breakdown, Accident or Emergency

Police, tel. 17; Fire and Ambulance, tel. 18. Automobil Club d'Andorra, *FIA* member, Babet Camp 4, Andorra-la-Vella, tel. 20 8 90.

Austria

Customs

Persons at least 18 years of age who arrive from other European countries may import the following free of duty: 200 cigarettes or 100 cigars or 250 grams of tobacco, 2 liters of wine and 1 liter of spirits, 1 bottle of toilet water (about 300 milliliter size), and 50 milliliters of perfume. Persons arriving directly from non-European points may import twice the above free of duty. You may import 10 liters of spare fuel free of duty.

Tolls

The major Austrian toll companies sell passes which, compared to paying each individual toll, can substantially reduce the average cost of tolls. Tolls are not charged as a rule on Austrian expressways, but, rather, only where construction of an expressway or road entailed an especially large expense—as in the cases of tunnels and of routes traversing mountain passes. Credit cards are *not* accepted.

Toll Roads and Passes:

A10 from Salzburg to Carinthia: AS 190 for a car or van having up to 9 seats and traveling during May through October, AS 120 for a car or van having up to 9 seats and traveling during November through April, AS 40 for a trailer, AS 100 for a motorcycle.

A13/A22's Brenner Pass from the Tyrol to Italy: AS 130 for car, van or caravan having up to 9 seats; AS 170 for a car towing a trailer or caravan; AS 100 for a motorcycle.

B107's Grossglockner Pass from Bruck to Lienz: AS 330 for a car with or without a trailer, AS 220 for a motorcycle. 2505 meters; closed from late October to early May; maximum grade is 12.5 percent; minimum width is 5 meters (16 ft.); extremely scenic; OK for powerful caravans.

B186/SS44B's Timmelsjoch Pass from Ötz to Merano, Italy: AS 80 for a car single, AS 120 for a car return, AS 50 for a motorcycle single, AS 70

for a motorcycle return. 2509 meters; closed from early October to late June; maximum grade is 14.3 percent, minimum width is 3.72 meters (12 ft.); very difficult; only open to private cars not towing trailers or caravans.

B188's Silvretta/Bielerhöhe Pass from Bludenz to Landeck: AS 40 for single, AS 15 for same day return, AS 15 for a child aged 6 to 16, free for a child under 6. 2032 meters; closed from late October to early June; maximum grade is 11 percent; minimum width is 5 meters (16 ft.); 32 hairpin turns; no caravans allowed.

B108 Felber Tauern road from Kitzbühel to the East Tyrol: AS 190 for a car during the summer, AS 110 for a car during the winter, AS 40 for a trailer, AS 100 for a motorcycle.

B165's Gerlos Platte Pass, Zell am Ziller to Mittersill. AS 90 for a car with or without trailer, AS 50 for motorcycle. 1627 meters; usually open in winter; maximum grade is 8.3 percent; minimum width is 4 meters (13 ft.); caravans are not allowed.

Several tunnels require tolls:

A9's Bosruck Tunnel between Spital am Pyhrn and Selzthal: AS 70 for a car or van having up to 9 seats, AS 30 for a trailer, AS 60 for a motorcycle.

A9's Gleinalm Tunnel between St. Michael and Friesach: AS 130 for a car or van having up to 9 seats, AS 30 for a trailer, AS 100 for a motorcycle.

A10's Katschberg Tunnel between Salzburg and Carinthia: AS 95 for a car or van having up to 9 seats and traveling during May through October,

AS 60 for a car or van having up to 9 seats and traveling during November through April, AS 20 for a trailer, AS 50 for a motorcycle.

A10's Radstädter Tunnel between Salzburg and Carinthia: AS 95 for a car or van having up to 9 seats and traveling during May through October, AS 60 for a car or van having up to 9 seats and traveling during November through April, AS 20 for a trailer, AS 50 for a motorcycle.

A11's Karawanken Tunnel runs between Austria and Slovenia, linking St. Jakob and Jesenice: AS 90 for a car whose height as measured vertically from the front axle is less than 1.3 meters, AS 135 for a car towing a trailer or caravan, AS 135 for a caravan, AS 90 for a motorcycle.

S16's Arlberg Tunnel south of the Arlberg Pass: AS 150 for car, van or caravan having up to 9 seats; AS 210 for a car towing a trailer or caravan; AS 100 for motorcycles. Usually open all year. When it is closed, however, vehicles and trailers can use the rail tunnel between Langen and St. Anton. (Make reservations 3 hours in advance: Langen, tel. 05582 201; St. Anton, tel. 05446 2242).

B167-B105's Tauern Rail Tunnel conveys vehicles between Bockstein and Mallnitz. As many as 47 trains make the 10 minute journey each day. Vehicles must be loaded at least 30 minutes prior to departure. AS 190 for cars traveling during May through October, AS 120 for cars traveling during November through April, AS 40 for a trailer, AS 100 for a motorcycle.

Non-toll Mountain Passes

Non-toll mountain passes tend to be much more difficult to negotiate than the passes which charge a toll. If you're driving a vehicle, such as a caravan, that is not allowed on or recommended for some of the following passes, or if you wanna travel quickly across or through the mountains, note that a mountain pass or tunnel which charges a toll tends to be close by.

B20's Annaberg Pass, St. Polten to Mariazell. 976 meters; usually open in the winter; maximum grade is 12.4 percent; minimum width is 4 meters (13 ft.); especially scenic; lightly traveled; OK for caravans.

B82's Seeberg Pass, Völkermarkt to Ljubljana, Slovenia. 1218 meters; usually open in the winter; maximum grade is 12.4 percent; minimum width is 5 meters (16 ft.); good alternative to the Loibl and Wurzen passes; not recommended for caravans.

B95's Turracher Höhe Pass, Predlitz to Feldkirchen. 1762 meters; usually open in the winter; maximum grade is 22.2 percent; minimum width is 4 meters (13 ft.); not recommended for caravans.

B99's Katschberg Pass, Spittal to Radstadt. 1640 meters; usually open in the winter; maximum grade is 20 percent; minimum width is 6.2 meters (20 ft.); not recommended for caravans.

B99's Radstädter-Tauern Pass, Radstädter to Spittal. 1740 meters; occasionally closed from January to March; maximum grade is 16.6 percent;

minimum width is 5 meters (16 ft.); not recommended for caravans.

B109's Wurzen Pass, Villach to Kranjska Gora, Slovenia. 1072 meters; usually open in winter; maximum grade is 18.2 percent; minimum width is 4 meters (13 ft.); no caravans allowed; very difficult for other vehicles.

B110/SS52B's Plöcken Pass from Kötschach-Mauthen to Tolmezzo, Italy. 1363 meters; occasionally closed during December to April; maximum grade is 14.3 percent; minimum width is 4.8 meters (16 ft.); on summer weekends expect delays resulting from heavy traffic; marginally negotiable by caravans.

B138's Pyhrn Pass, Windischgarsten to Liezen. 945 meters; usually open in winter; maximum grade is 10 percent; minimum width is 4 meters (13 ft.); OK for caravans.

B145's Pötschen Pass, Bad Ischl to Bad Aussee. 972 meters; usually open in winter; maximum grade is 9 percent; minimum width is 7.1 meters (23 ft.); good views of the Dachstein; OK for caravans.

B161's Thurn Pass, Kitzbühel to Mittersill. 1275 meters; usually open in winter; maximum grade is 8.3 percent; minimum width is 5 meters (16 ft.); especially scenic; OK for caravans.

B181/B307's Aachen Pass, Jenbach to Tegernsee, Germany. 941 meters; usually open in winter; maximum grade is 14.3 percent; minimum width is

5.9 meters (19 ft.); especially scenic; not recommended for caravans.

B182/SS12's Brenner Pass, Innsbruck to Bolzano, Italy. 1375 meters; usually open in winter; tire chains are sometimes necessary in winter; maximum grade is 14.3 percent; minimum width is 6.2 meters (20 ft.); especially scenic; busiest transalpine pass; closed to vehicles towing anything but a luggage trailer; not recommended for caravans.

B197's Arlberg Pass, Feldkirch to Innsbruck. 1793 meters; occasionally closed from December to April; maximum grade is 13.3 percent; minimum width is 6.2 meters (20 ft.); especially scenic; closed to vehicles that are towing other vehicles.

B198's Flexen Pass, Stuben to Reutte. 1772 meters; usually open but the road north of the pass, from Lech to Warth, is usually closed November through April; maximum grade is 10 percent; minimum width is 5.9 meters (18 ft.); especially scenic; not recommended for caravans.

B200's Hochtannberg Pass, Egg to Warth. 1679 meters; occasionally closed from late December to late March; maximum grade is 14.3 percent; minimum width is 4 meters (13 ft.); not recommended for caravans.

B306's Semmering Pass, Gloggnitz to Mürzzuschlag. 984 meters; usually open; maximum grade is 6 percent; minimum width is 6.2 meters (20 ft.); especially scenic; OK for caravans.

B314's Fern Pass, Imst to Reutte. 1210 meters; usually open; maximum grade is 10 percent; minimum width is 6.2 meters (20 ft.); OK for caravans.

B315/SS40's Resia Pass, Landeck to Malles, Italy. 1504 meters; usually open; maximum grade is 10 percent; minimum width is 6.2 meters (20 ft.); especially scenic; OK for caravans.

Road Signs

Road signs unique to Austria include the following.

Anhänger Verboten	No trailers
Ausweiche	Detour
Beschränkung für Halten oder Parken	Stopping or parking restricted
Halten Verboten	No waiting
Hupverbot	Do not use horn
Lawinen Gefahr	Avalanche danger
Querstraße	Crossroads
Steinschlag	Falling rocks
Straße Gesperrt	Road closed
Umleitung	Diversion

The word *bahnhof*, whether alone or incorporated in another word, indicates a train station. The expressways are called *autobahnen;* one step down are the national *schnellstraßen* highways, followed by the national *bundestraßen* highways; the provincial *landestraßen* are next in order, followed by the community roads or *gemeindestraßen*. The *autobahnen* are denoted by green signs with white characters. The *schnellstraßen* are indicated by blue signs with white numbers and are the one type of intersecting road that automatically has priority over all other roads. The *bundestraßen* are noted by circular yellow signs with black numbers.

Fuel

AS9-AS10 per liter for gasoline. Most fuel stations are open 8:00 A.M. to 8:00 P.M.; stations in large cities may operate 24 hours. Generally, major credit cards are *not* accepted. Regular unleaded has an octane rating of 98. Unleaded gasoline is known as *essence sans plomb* or *gasolina sin plomo*. Regular unleaded gasoline has an octane rating of 91; the octane rating of super is 98. As for leaded gasoline, super is no longer sold; super plus (98 octane), containing a lead additive, should be used instead. Diesel goes by its English name. LPG is called *autogas*.

Driving

The minimum age of a driver is 18 years. Children must be at least 12 years of age to sit in the front seat (unless a special seat or seat belt is fitted or unless they're over 1.5 meters tall). The use of seat belts is compulsory for front- and rear-seat passengers. Helmets are compulsory for motorcyclists and their passengers. The legal blood alcohol limit is 80 mg. Speed limits are as follows: 50 kph (30 mph) in built-up areas, 100 kph (62 mph) outside built-up areas, 130 kph (81 mph) on expressways, and 100 kph (62 mph) for cars with a caravan or trailer under 750 kg traveling on expressways. If the trailer or caravan is larger, contact a national motoring club for more information. In the Vorarlberg and the Tyrol, maximum speed limit is 80 kph (50 mph). Expressway speed limits are only 100 kph (62 mph) on the following: A8 (Innkreis), A9 (Pyhrn), A10 (Tauern), A12 (Inntal), A13 (Brenner), A14 (Rheintal).

In exception to the priority-on-your-right rule, trams coming from your left have priority. Ascending vehicles have priority on mountain roads.

Headlights must be on at all times in built-up areas. Parking lights are not necessary if your vehicle is visible from at least 50 meters away. Motorcycles must be operated with headlights on — night and day. Horns cannot be used in Vienna and are prohibited elsewhere as indicated by signs.

Passing on the right is allowed only on one-way streets or when passing trams or when passing a vehicle that is indicating a left turn. You are not allowed to cross a solid yellow center line. Give warning of your approach by flashing your lights.

Police are empowered to collect fines of up to AS 500 on the spot. The officer must issue an official receipt. You'll have two weeks to pay. You can request to bring the case before a court instead, but you may be asked to make a security deposit.

Parking

Except for when quickly loading and unloading, don't park in the following areas: where you see a sign saying *Halten Verboten*, where you see crosses on the road in front of houses, within 15 meters of pedestrian crossings or public transportation stops, in front of fuel stations or any entrances, on narrow roads, on the left of one-way streets, or on priority roads outside built-up areas during conditions which significantly reduce visibility. In Vienna it's illegal to park between 8:00 P.M. and 5:00 A.M. from December 15 to March 31 on roads with tram rails; this rule allows for snow removal. *Blue Zones* exist in many cities and are marked on their boundary by the *No Parking* sign bearing the word *Kurzparkzone* (short-term parking) or *zone;* blue road markings may mark the zone. Fees are associated with *Blue Zones* in Baden, Bludenz, Bregenz, Feldkirch, Graz, Innsbruck, Klagenfurt, Krems, Linz, St. Pölten, St. Veit/Glan, Salzburg, Schwaz, Vienna, Villach, Völkermarkt, Wiener Neustadt and Wolfsberg. Tickets for the *Blue Zones* in the above cities can be purchased at machines in the parking area or at banks or tobacconists. Unless otherwise indicated by a sign, parking in *Blue Zones* is allowed for 3 hours. In the *Blue Zones* of other towns, free parking is allowed for 90 minutes. Parking tickets are not required in these other towns, but you must obtain a parking *disc* free of charge from tobacconists. Even motorcycles need to display such a disc.

Don't leave an unhitched trailer in a public parking place. In Salzburg, the Tyrol, and Upper Austria, it's illegal to park caravans outside special parking lots or within 500 meters of a lake. And don't park a caravan within 200 meters of the Grossglockner High Alpine Road or on the expressway in Salzburg. Violaters are subject to heavy fines and the towing of the vehicle.

Camping

An International Camping Carnet is not required by the campgrounds. Free-camping without appropriate permission is illegal; but note that it's commonly practiced in state forests with permission of the park authorities. Overnight parking and sleeping is allowed at highway rest areas and on most city streets, except in Vienna and except where otherwise posted; but campng equipment may not be set up outside the vehicle.

Banks

Open on weekdays from 8:00 A.M. to noon or 12:30 P.M. and from 1:30 P.M. to 3:00 or 4:00 P.M.

Shops

Open on weekdays from 8:00 A.M. to 6:00 P.M. and on Saturday morning; smaller shops may close from noon to 2:00 P.M.

National Holidays

Jan 1; Epiphany; Easter Mon; Labor Day; Ascension; Whit Monday; Corpus Christi; Assumption; Aug 15; Oct 26; Nov 1; Dec 8, 25, 26.

BBC Radio Hours and Corresponding Frequencies

5:00 A.M. to 7:30 A.M.: 9410, 12095 and 15070 kHz

7:30 A.M. to 4:00 P.M.: 9660, 15070 and 17640 kHz

4:00 P.M. to 10:30 P.M.: 9410, 12095 and 15070 kHz

Breakdown, Accident or Emergency

Police, tel. 133; Fire, tel. 122; Ambulance, tel. 144. Emergency road service and technical assistance is available from ARBÖ, tel. 123; or ÖAMTC, tel. 120. The local prefix must be added to these numbers. Note that emergency phones are placed along major roads. Österreichischer Automobil Motorrad-und Touring Club (ÖAMTC), *FIA* and *AIT* member, Schubertring 1-3, 1010 Vienna 1, tel. 0222 711 99, office hours from 8:00 A.M. to 5:00 P.M. on weekdays.

The Baltic States: Estonia, Latvia, and Lithuania

Customs

Upon arrival you must sign an agreement to export your vehicle at the end of your visit; you must present this document when leaving the country. You may be given a customs declaration to fill out. List your money and valuables so you can avoid paying duty on them when you leave. You may import spare fuel free of duty. **Estonia** allows the following free of duty: 1 liter of beverage consisting of up to 58 percent alcohol by volume, 1 liter of beverage up to 21 percent alcohol by volume or 2 liters of mild alcohol or 10 liters of beer, 200 cigarettes or 20 cigars or 250 grams of tobacco, and $1000. Limits also exist on the value of purchases which may be exported free of duty. **Latvia** allows the following free of duty: 1 liter of spirits and 2 liters of wine (for persons over 16 years of age). Up to 100 percent duty can be levied on antiques of artistic value. **Lithuania** places limits on the amount of amber that can be exported. You are supposed to obtain a permit from the Culture of Ministry and pay duty to export artworks of special value—this process takes about three days. There are two entry points between Poland and Lithuania: Ogrodniki to Lazkijai, and Szyplszki to Kalvarije (on the Swalki to Marijampole Road). Up to 20 liters of spare fuel may be imported.

Long lines of local traffic with goods to declare often form. Visiting motorists may by-pass such lines and go straight to a Customs check point.

Fuel

A new chain of Neste Oy stations service the M-12 ("Via Baltica") expressway. These eleven stations are located every 150 km, open 24 hours, and accept Visa and Diners Club. Away from this road there is a dearth of stations, and though the fuel is of poor quality long lines often form for it. Manytimes you'll encounter tankers selling fuel alongside the main highways. Tallin, Riga and Vilnius each boast two stations; Parnu, Savikrasti, Kekava, Panevezys, and Marijampole, one. Since central European diesel fuel congeals in winter, a special winter blend with a high congealing point is offered by Neste or Kesoil stations.

Driving

Persons in the front seat must wear seatbelts. The legal blood alcohol limit is 0 mg. Speed limits are as follows: 60 kph (37 mph) in built-up areas (50 kph in Estonia), 90 kph (56 mph) outside built-up areas; vehicles over 3.5 metric tons (3500 kg) are limited to 70 kph (44 mph). Fines are levied for relatively minor excesses of these limits.

In towns the roads are full of potholes. Main roads outside towns are in good condition, but secondary roads are surfaced with gravel or sand. Driving at night is dangerous: locals often use sidelights only, slow-moving vehicles abound, and goods fallen from vehicles often clutter the roads.

Police in Lithuania are empowered to levy fines on the spot.

Parking

Be careful not to park on tram lines. Due to high incidence of vehicle theft and pilfering, guarded parking facilities should be used. Tallin harbors some zones requiring parking tickets, and wheel camps are used. In Lithuania, parking is prohibited within 15 meters of bus stops and within 5 meters of intersections; wheel clamps are not used.

Shops

Open 8:00 A.M. to 2:00 P.M. and from 3:00 to 5:00 P.M. (7:00 to 8:00 P.M. in Lithuania) on weekdays, 9:00 A.M. to 3:00 P.M. (6:00 P.M. in Lithuania) on Saturday. Department stores in Lithuania are open from 10:00 A.M. to 6:00 P.M. on Saturday.

National Holidays

Estonia: Jan 1; Feb 24; Good Fri; Easter Mon; May 1; June 23; Dec 25, 26.

Latvia: Jan 1; Good Fri; Easter Mon; May 1; June 23; Nov 18; Dec 25, 26.

Lithuania: Jan 1; Feb 16; Good Fri; Easter Mon; May 1; July 6; Dec 25, 26.

BBC Radio Hours and Corresponding Frequencies

5:00 A.M. to 7:30 A.M.: 9410, 12095 and 15070 kHz

7:30 A.M. to 4:00 P.M.: 12095, 15070 and 17640 kHz

4:00 P.M. to 10:30 P.M.: 9410, 12095 and 15070 kHz

Breakdown, Accident or Emergency

Spare parts for western vehicles are not available. Police, tel. 02; Fire, tel. 01; Ambulance, tel. 03. The national motoring clubs are the following.

Estonian Auto-Moto Union (AUTOM), *FIA* and *AIT* member, Pikk 41, 200002 Tallinn, tel. 7 014 260 12 15.

Auto-Moto Society of Latvia (LR AMB), *FIA* and *AIT* member, Raunas 16 B, 226039 Riga, tel. 7 0132 56 83 39 or 7 0132 56 62 22, FAX 7 0132 33 19 20.

Lietuvos Automobilininku Sajunga (LAS), *FIA* and *AIT* member, Lvovo 9, 232005 Vilnius, tel. 7 0122 35 12 73 or 7 0122 35 89 12, FAX 7 0122 35 89 19.

Belgium

Customs

Non-EC citizens may import the following free of duty: 200 cigarettes or 50 cigars or 250 grams of tobacco, 2 liters of still wine, 1 liter of spirits or 2 liters of aperitif wine, 50 grams of perfume. Other imported goods from non-EC countries cannot exceed BF 2000 in value. There are no restrictions on the import and export of currency. You can import 10 liters of spare fuel free of duty.

Tolls

There is a toll for the use of Antwerp's Liefenhoeks Tunnel.

Concessions for Hostellers

North Sea Ferries offers discounts on their service between Hull, England, and Zeebrugge, Belgium.

Sealink Stena Line grants a 20 percent discount on standard fares for foot passengers or motor vehicles plus up to five passengers between Belgium and England.

Road Signs

Note that there are two languages generally spoken in Belgium: Flemish in the northern half, and French in Brussels and in the southern half. Antwerpen (Flemish) is Anvers (French); Brugge is Bruges; Bruxelles is Brussel; Ghent is Gand; Luik is Liège; Leuven is Louvain; Namen is Namur; Bergen is Mons; and Doornik is Tournai. The words *"Passage Difficile"* and *"Moeilijke Doorgang"* indicate a difficult section. The word *station* in Flemish indicates a train station; while the word in French is *gare*. International expressways are signified by green signs with white characters preceded by the letter *E;* national highways are noted by black signs with white letters preceded by the letter *A*. As part of a new naming convention, lesser highways may have two road numbers—both the old and the new—preceded by an *N*.

Fuel

BF 32 per liter for gasoline. Most fuel stations are closed from 8:00 P.M. to 8:00 A.M., and all day Sunday, but stations along expressways are open 24 hours, seven days a week. Major credit cards are accepted at stations in large towns and along the expressways. Leaded super gasoline has an octane rating of 98 or 99. Unleaded gasoline is known as *normale sans plomb, onglood, unverbleit,* or *bodvrije benzine*. Unleaded regular has an octane rating of 92; the octane rating of super is 95.

Driving

The minimum age of a driver is 18 years. Children must be at least 12 years of age to sit in the front seat (unless a safety seat is fitted). The use of seat belts is compulsory for front- and rear-seat passengers. Helmets are compulsory for motorcyclists and their passengers. The legal blood alcohol limit is 80 mg. Speed limits are as follows: 50 kph (30 mph) in built-up areas, 90 kph (56 mph) outside built-up areas, and 120 kph (74 mph) on expressways.

In exception to the priority-on-your right rule, trams always have priority.

Headlights must be on between dusk and dawn and during inclement weather. Motorcycles must be operated with headlights on—night and day. The horn should only be used outside built-up areas.

Police are empowered to impose and collect fines on the spot. Fines range from BF 750 to BF 4000. You must place a security deposit if you refuse to pay. Police may request that you take a blood alcohol test; although you can by law refuse, you might as a result be arrested.

Parking

Blue Zone parking areas—indicated by signs placed at their periphery—exist in Antwerp, Bruges, Brussels, Ghent, Liège, and Öostend. However, where meters or the like are in place in the zones, discs are not required or sufficient. You can obtain a parking disc from police or service stations, some merchants, or offices of the RACB motoring club. Outside these zones a parking disc must be used where the parking sign includes an extra panel bearing the image of a disc or where the words *"Disque Obligatoire"* or *"Schisf Verplicht"* indicate the beginning of a *Blue Zone*. Don't park within 15 meters of a tram, bus or rail stop or near where tram or rail lines cross the road. Some parking garages are not manned on weekends and holidays; operate the barrier automatically with the proper coins. Wheel clamps are used in Antwerp and Ghent.

No parking from 1st to 15th of the month

No parking from 16th to end of the month

End of Blue Zone parking area

Camping

The government classifies registered sites on a four-star basis; one- and two-star sites don't have showers. Since many campgrounds play host to virtually permanent trailer-living residents, it can be hard to find a spot in high season. An International Camping Carnet is not required. Apart from overnight stays at highway rest areas, free-camping without appropriate permission is not legal.

Banks

Open on weekdays from 9:00 A.M. to noon and from 2:00 to 4:00 P.M.

Shops

Open from 9:00 A.M. to noon and from 2:00 P.M. to 6:00 P.M. (supermarkets stay open until 8:00 P.M., and on Friday most shops are open until 9:00 P.M.) every day but Sunday.

National Holidays

Jan 1; Easter Mon; Labor Day; Ascension; Whit Mon; July 21; Aug 15; Nov 1, 11; Dec 25.

BBC Radio Hours and Corresponding Frequencies

5:00 A.M. to 7:30 A.M.: 648, 9410 and 15575 kHz

7:30 A.M. to 4:00 P.M.: 648, 9750 and 12095 kHz

4:00 P.M. to 10:30 P.M.: 6195, 9410 and 12095 kHz

Breakdown, Accident or Emergency

Police, tel. 101; Fire & Ambulance, tel. 100. If you are in an accident, you must—unless people are injured—move your vehicle off the road so that traffic is not obstructed. Before you do this be sure to properly note the post-accident position of the vehicles; this includes marking the tire position with chalk, and taking photographs.

Royal Automobile Club de Belgique (RACB), *FIA* member, 53 rue d'Arlon, 1040 Brussels, tel. 02 2300810; office hours from 8:30 A.M. to 5:00 P.M. on weekdays. Touring Club Royal de Belgique (TCB), *AIT* member, 44 rue de la Loi, 1040 Brussels, tel. 02 2332211; office hours from 9:00 A.M. to 6:00 P.M. on weekdays and from 9:00 A.M. to noon on Saturday.

Bulgaria

Customs

You may import the following free of duty: 250 grams of tobacco, 1 liter of hard liquor, and 2 liters of wine. Items for personal use are also free of duty. Visitors should declare expensive items such as cameras. You can import 20 liters of spare fuel free of duty.

Tolls

Foreign-registered vehicles using expressways or four-lane rods must pay tolls: 2 leva per km for a private car, 3 leva per km for a van with less than 12 seats, and 4 leva per km for a bus. There's also a toll to cross the bridge over the Danube between Rousse, Bulgaria, and Gjourguevo (Giurgia), Romania: 210 leva plus a $1 tax for a private car, 390 leva plus a $2 tax for a van with less than 12 seats, 60 leva for a motorcycle.

Road Signs

Town names are given in both Bulgarian and French.

Fuel

Fuel stations are located in large towns and every 35 km or so along main roads. Most stations operate from 6:00 A.M. to 9:30 P.M., but some are open 24 hours. Fuel in blue pumps is of much better quality. Regular leaded gasoline costs about 8.85 leva per liter. Leaded regular has an octane rating of 86; the octane rating of super is 96. Unleaded gasoline is known as *bes olovo bleifrei;* the super variety has an octane rating of 93.

Driving

The minimum age of a driver is 18 years. Children must be at least 10 years of age to sit in the front seat. The use of seat belts is compulsory for front-seat passengers. Helmets are compulsory for motorcyclists and their passengers. The legal blood alcohol limit is 0 mg. Speed limits are as follows: 60 kph (37 mph) in built-up areas (50 kph for motorcycles and for cars towing a trailer), 80 kph (50 mph) outside built-up areas (70 kph for motorcycles and for cars

towing a trailer), and 120 kph (74 mph) on expressways (100 kph for motorcycles and for cars towing a trailer).

In exception to the priority-on-your-right rule, trams always have priority. Pedestrians on banded cross walks have priority over all vehicles except trams.

In towns drivers must use headlights where lighting is not good. Fog lights or headlights should be used when weather significantly reduces visibility. Unless otherwise indicated, horns can be used outside built-up areas.

Police are empowered to collect fines on the spot; they should issue a receipt.

Camping

Camping is quite popular in Bulgaria. Campgrounds along the Black Sea—especially those which are part of a larger vacation complex—tend to fill up quickly. Motorhomes are a novelty; sites with electrical connections are offered, but don't plan to fill up on propane. An International Camping Carnet is not required. Free-camping without appropriate permission is not legal.

Banks

In main towns, open on weekdays from 8:00 A.M. to 12:30 P.M. and from 1:00 P.M. to 3:00 P.M., and on Saturday from 8:00 A.M. to 2:00 P.M.

Shops

In main towns most are open from 8:00 A.M. to 1:00 P.M. and from 2:00 to 7:00 P.M. on weekdays, and from 8:00 A.M. to 2:00 P.M. on Saturday.

National Holidays

Jan 1; May 1, 2, 24; Sep 9, 10, Nov 7; Dec 24, 25.

BBC Radio Hours and Corresponding Frequencies

5:00 A.M. to 7:30 A.M.: 9410, 12095 and 15070 kHz

7:30 A.M. to 4:00 P.M.: 9660, 15070 and 17640 kHz

4:00 P.M. to 10:30 P.M.: 9410, 12095 and 15070 kHz

Breakdown, Accident or Emergency

Police, tel. 166; Fire, tel. 160; Ambulance, tel. 150. For emergency motoring assistance, telephone 146. In case of an accident which results in only minor damages to the vehicles and no injury to the occupants, the vehicle owners are not required to involve the police. But if the other driver is not insured, you should contact the police so they'll create a proper report which you you can present to your insurance company. Union of Bulgarian Motorists (SBA), *FIA* and *AIT* member, 3 Place Positano, 1000

Sofia, tel. 87 88 01 or 87 88 02, office hours from 9:00 A.M. to 6:00 P.M. on weekdays.

CIS

Customs

The Commonwealth of Independent States consists of Armenia, Azerbaijan, Belarus, Kazakhstan, Kirkghiza, Moldova, Russia, Tajikistan, Turkmenistan, Ukraine, and Uzbekistan.

To obtain a visa, you must present proof that you've delineated your itinerary and booked accommodation before your departure. Moreover, visas are rarely issued to individuals who have not booked through a recognized tour company. And motorists limited to 300 miles per day and must secure an itinerary card and special "Autotourist" visa. Arrange itineraries through Intourist.

Fuel

Fuel stations are rare, with one every 100 km or so on average. Therefore you should carry some spare fuel. Since western oil and antifreeze are also rare, carry a spare supply of these as well. The most widely available fuel is gasoline with an octane rating of 75, but 95 octane and diesel can be found.

Driving

The use of seat belts is compulsory for front- and rear-seat passengers. The legal blood alcohol limit is 0 mg. Speed limits are as follows: 60 kph (37 mph) in built-up areas, 110 kph (68 mph) outside built-up areas.

Avoid driving at night. Use your horn only in cases of immediate and extreme danger. It's an offence to drive a dirty vehicle.

Police are empowered to collect fines on the spot.

BBC Radio Hours and Corresponding Frequencies

5:00 A.M. to 7:30 A.M.: 9410, 12095 and 15070 kHz

7:30 A.M. to 4:00 P.M.: 12095, 15070 and 17640 kHz

4:00 P.M. to 10:30 P.M.: 9410, 12095 and 15070 kHz

Breakdown, Accident or Emergency

Obtain help from traffic police or an Intourist office. If your vehicle is damaged, be sure to secure an official accident report (spravka) to ease its export. Spare parts are rare; consider bringing some along.

Croatia

Fuel

Most stations are open from 6:00 A.M. to 8:00 P.M., but some along major roads stay open 24 hours. Leaded super has an octane rating of 98; unleaded super, 91 or 95.

Tolls

Charged on the E59 and the E70 out of Zagreb.

Driving

Children must be at least 12 years of age to sit in the front seat. The use of seat belts is compulsory for front- and rear-seat passengers. Helmets must be worn by motorcyclists and their passengers. The legal blood alcohol limit is 50 mg. Random breath tests are legal. Speed limits are as follows: 60 kph (37 mph) in built-up areas, 90–100 kph (56–62 mph) outside built-up areas; and 130 kph (81 mph) on expressways. Caravans and cars towing a trailer are limited to 80 kph (50 mph).

Vehicles entering a roundabout have right of way. School buses and vehicles of public transport have right of way when they're leaving a stop. Do not drive on tram lines. Don't pass a bus when passengers are getting on or off.

Motorcyclists must use headlights day and night. Other motorists must use headlights in built-up areas when visibility is less than 100 meters, and outside built-up areas when visibility is less than 200 meters. Use your horn only in cases of immediate and extreme danger.

Police are empowered to collect fines on the spot.

Road traffic info is privded 24 hours a day by Hrvatski Auto-Klub, tel. 041 415 800.

Banks

Open on weekdays from 8:00 A.M. to 7:00 P.M., and on Saturday till to noon.

Shops

Open on weekdays from 8:00 A.M. to 8:00 P.M., and on Saturday till noon. Food shops are open Monday–Saturday from 6:00 A.M. to 7:30 P.M.

National Holidays

Jan 1, 6; May 1, 30; June 22; Aug 15, Dec 25, 26.

Breakdown, Accident or Emergency

Police, tel. 92; Ambulance, tel. 94; Fire, tel. 93. The police must be called to the scene of an accident. They'll issue a certificate detailing any damage to your vehicle. This certificate will ease export of the vehicle. The national motoring club is the Hrvatski Auto-Klub, *AIT* and *FIA* member, Draskoviceva 25, 41000 Zagreb, tel. 41 454 433, office hours on week-

days from 7:30 A.M. to 3:30 P.M. (5:30 P.M. on Tuesday).

Cyprus

Customs

You may import the following free of duty: 250 grams of tobacco, 1 liter of spirits, 750 ml of wine, 300 ml of perfume, and up to C£50 worth of other goods. The export of antiques and historical artifacts is forbidden unless special permission is obtained from the Ministry of Tourism in Nicosia.

Fuel

Gasoline costs about C£0.56 per liter. Available 24 hours in larger towns. Leaded regular has an octane rating of 87; the octane rating of super is 98. Unleaded fuel is available in major towns only. It's illegal to carry spare fuel.

Driving

Driving is on the left. The minimum age of a driver is 18 years. Children must be at least 5 years of age to sit in the front seat. The use of seat belts is compulsory for front-seat passengers. Speed limits are as follows: 50 kph (30 mph) in built-up areas, 60–100 kph (37–62 mph) outside built-up areas.

Headlights must be used between half an hour after sunset and half an hour before sun-

rise. Horn use is discouraged, especially between 10:00 P.M. and 6:00 A.M. and especially near hospitals.

Banks

Open on weekdays from 8:15 A.M. to 12:30 P.M. Some banks have tourist services on weekdays in winter from 3:00 P.M. to 6:00 P.M., on weekdays in summer from 4:00 P.M. to 7:00 P.M., and on Saturday from 8:30 A.M. to noon.

Shops

Open on weekdays from 8:00 A.M. to 1:00 P.M. and from 4:00 P.M. to 7:00 P.M. (2:30 P.M. to 5:30 P.M. in winter). Open until 1:00 P.M. on Wednesday and Saturday.

National Holidays

Jan 1, 6; Mar 25; Easter according to Greek Orthodox Calendar; Apr 1; Oct 28, 29; Dec 24, 25, 26.

Breakdown, Accident or Emergency

Dial 199 for Ambulance and Police. The national motoring club is the Cyprus Automobile Association, 12 Chr. Mylonas Street, Nicosia 141, tel. 02 313233. The club's office hours are effective June through September and run from 8:00 A.M. to 1:00 P.M. and from 3:00 P.M. to 7:00 P.M. on weekdays except Wednesday, and from

8:00 A.M. to 1:00 P.M. on Wednesday and Saturday.

Czech Republic

Customs

You may import the following free of duty: 250 cigarettes or their equivalent in tobacco, 1 liter of spirits, 2 liters of wine, 0.5 liters of eau de cologne, and gifts up to a total of 1000 Kc in value. Declare valuable items. Note that upon departure, crystal purchased with cash may be subject to a tax equal to 100 percent of its retail price. Keep all receipts. Only antiques purchased at government-appointed shops may be exported. You may import 20 liters of spare fuel free of duty. A map showing the locations of fuel stations which sell unleaded gasoline is available at the border.

Tolls

Vehicles using the expressways must buy a sticker valid for one year and display it on their vehicle's windshield. For cars the sticker costs 400 Kc.

Road Signs

The following signs are unique to the Czech and Slovak Republics.

CHODTE VLEVO	Pedestrians walk on the left
DALKOVY PROVOZ	Bypass
H NEMOCNICE	Hospital
JEDNOSMERNY PROVOZ	One-way traffic
OBJÌZDKA	Detour
PRUJEZD ZAKÁZÁB	Closed to vehicles

The Czech word *nádrazí* indicates a train station.

Fuel

Gasoline costs about 6 Kcs per liter. Fuel stations are usually located on the edge of towns. Stations on international roads and in large towns are open 24 hours. Credit cards are accepted in main towns and in popular tourist areas. Finding a station in Prague is difficult. Leaded regular gasoline has an octane rating of 90; the octane rating of super is 96. Lead-free gasoline is known as *natural* and is available at select stations only; its octane rating is 96. Diesel is designated by a sign that reads *TT Diesel*.

Driving

The minimum age of a driver is 18 years. Children must be at least 12 years of age to sit in the front seat. The use of seat belts is compulsory for front- and rear-seat passengers. Helmets are compulsory for motorcyclists and their passengers. Goggles are compulsory for motorcyclists riding a machine with a 50 cc or larger engine. The legal blood alcohol limit is 0 mg. Speed limits are as follows: 60 kph (37 mph) in built-up areas between 5:00 A.M. and 11:00 P.M., 90 kph (56 mph) in built-up areas between 11:00 P.M. and 5:00 A.M., 90 kph (56 mph) outside built-up areas, 110 kph (68 mph) on expressways, 80 kph (50 mph) for a car with a caravan or trailer traveling outside built-up areas or on expressways, and 90 kph (56 mph) for motorcycles outside built-up areas.

Headlights must be on when weather impairs visibility. Motorcyclists must use low beams at all times. When waiting at level train crossings use sidelights only. Horns can be used only to warn of danger or to signal that you are about to pass. Horns are prohibited in central Prague between 9:00 P.M. and 5:00 A.M., from March 15 to October 15, and from 8:00 P.M. to 6:00 A.M. the rest of the year.

Trams should be passed on the right; if there is no room on the right, trams can be passed on the left. It's illegal in Prague to pass trams on the left.

Police are empowered to collect fines on the spot. Laws and regulations are enforced with vigor in the Czech Republic—follow the rules.

Parking

Parking is only allowed on the right side of the road, but this restriction does not apply to one-way roads. Parking along a tram line is prohibited unless a 3.5-meter wide lane is left between the vehicle and the tram lane. Don't park within 5 meters of an intersection, pedestrian crossing, or public transportation stop. Don't park within 15 meters of a train crossing.

Your vehicle is banned from the Prague city center unless you're staying in a hotel there. But don't worry, the true city center is really a quite small area. If you're staying in a private room near Wenceslas Square (Vacavske namesti), try parking on one of the streets behind the National Museum; parking on these streets is unrestricted and free of charge. Illegally parked vehicles may be towed or clamped.

Camping

Camping is very popular. Most campgrounds, called *Autocamps*, are open from June 15 to September 15. Some rent cabins and stay open all year. An International Camping Carnet is not required. Free-camping without appropriate permission is not legal, and it's less likely to be tolerated in forested areas.

Banks

Open on weekdays from 8:00 A.M. to 3:00 P.M.

Shops

Open on weekdays from 9:00 A.M. to 6:00 P.M. Some close from noon to 2:00 A.M.; some open until noon on Saturday.

National Holidays

Jan 1; Easter Monday; May Day; May 9; Dec 25, 26.

BBC Radio Hours and Corresponding Frequencies

5:00 A.M. to 7:30 A.M.: 6195, 9410 and 15575 kHz

7:30 A.M. to 4:00 P.M.: 9410, 12095 and 15070 kHz

4:00 P.M. to 10:30 P.M.: 6195, 9410 and 12095 kHz

Breakdown, Accident or Emergency

The emergency telephone number for motorists is 154; Police, tel. 158; Fire, tel. 150; Ambulance, tel. 155. Any accident resulting in injury or causing damages in excess of 1000 Kcs must be immediately reported to police. If you plan to export the vehicle, it's advisable to contact the police even if damages are slight: the police will give you a certificate to ease the exporting process. Ustredni Automotoklub CSFR (UAMK), *FIA* and *AIT* member, Na Rybnicku 16, 120 76 Prague 2, tel. 22491 1843; office hours from 7:45 A.M. to 4:45 P.M. on weekdays. The CSFR operates a breakdown service; in Prague, tel. 7734555. Another club is Autoklub Ceské Republiky (ACR), *FIA* member, Opletalova 29, 110 00 Prague 1, tel. 22421 0266; office hours from 7:30 A.M. to 4:00 P.M. on weekdays. Autoturist, Na Rybnicku 16, 120 76 Prague 2, tel. 2 203 355, office hours from 7:30 A.M. to 4:00 P.M. on weekdays, is an information service for motoring tourists.

Denmark

Customs

Arriving from a non-EC country or with goods that were *not* taxed in the EC, you must pay Danish taxes on all alcoholic beverages greater than 1 liter of liquor or 2 liters of strong wine and on amounts greater than 2 liters of other wine; and you may import the following free of duty: 200 cigarettes or 100 cigarillos or 50 cigars or 250 grams of tobacco, 50 grams of perfume, and other items—including beer—up to a total monetary value of 350 kr. Arriving from another EC country, you may import the following free of duty if it *was* taxed in the EC: 1.5 liters of liquor or 3 liters of strong wine consisting of under 22 per cent alcohol by volume, 5 liters of other wine, 300 cigarettes or

150 cigarillos or 75 cigars or 400 grams of tobacco, 75 grams of perfume, and other items up to a total of 2800 kr. You may import 10 liters of spare fuel free of duty if arriving from an EC country.

Concessions for Hostellers

Color Line offers 10 percent discounts on fares for persons under 26 years of age on its ferry services between Kristiansand, Norway, and Hirtshals, Denmark, and between Oslo, Norway, and Hirtshals, Denmark.

Larvik Line offers a 10 percent discount on fares between Larvik, Norway, and Fredrikshavn, Denmark.

Scandinavian Seaways offers discounts on their ferry service between Newcastle, England, and Esbjerg, Denmark.

Stena Line offers a 10 percent discount off fares on the services below (tickets are obtainable only at Terra Nova Travel Sections and valid for Monday through Thursday travel from June through August).

Oslo, Norway— —Fredrikshavn, Denmark.
Moss, Norway— —Fredrikshavn, Denmark.
Göteborg, Sweden— —Fredrikshavn, Denmark.

The ferry service between Luxhaven, Germany, and Helgoland (a Danish Island) is discounted for groups of 6 or more, members being under 23 years of age.

Fuel

Gasoline costs about 5.90 kr. per liter. Fuel stations that are not in large towns often close at night; many, however, offer self-service pumps which accept 100 Kr notes 24 hours a day. Major credit cards are generally accepted. Leaded super gasoline has an octane rating of 98. Unleaded Gasoline is known as *blyfri benzin*. Regular unleaded has an octane rating of 92; the octane rating of super is 95 or 98. Diesel is called *dieselolie*. LPG goes by its English name.

Road Signs

Ensrettet kørsel	One-way Street
Fare	Danger
Farligt sving	Dangerous curve
Fodgaengerovergang	Pedestrian crossing
Gennemkørsel forbudt	No through road
Hold til højre	Keep to the right
Hold till venstre	Keep to the left
Indkørsel forbudt	Do not enter
Korsvej	Crossroads
Omkørsel	Detour
Vejarbejde	Road in repair
Vejen er spaerret	Road closed

The word *banegården* indicates a train station.

Sightseeing

Compulsory slow lane

Driving

The minimum age of a driver is 18 years. Children under 3 years of age must be seated in a special child restraint. The use of seat belts is compulsory for front-seat passengers. Helmets are compulsory for motorcyclists and their passengers. The legal blood alcohol limit is 80 mg. Speed limits are as follows: 50 kph (30 mph) in built-up areas, 80 kph (50 mph) outside built-up areas, 110 kph (68 mph) on expressways, and

70 kph (44 mph) for cars with a caravan or trailer traveling outside built-up areas or on expressways.

If a line of triangles is painted across the road, it means you must yield. You must also yield to buses. Beware of bicyclists.

Headlights must be used at all times. Use your lights instead of your horn to signal warning in circumstances not involving immediate and extreme danger. When wiaitng at a level train crossing use only sidelights, headlights should be off.

Police are empowered to collect fines on the spot.

Parking

Parkering/Standsning/Stop Forbudt means *no parking/no stopping;* you are, however, allowed a three-minute grace period for loading and unloading when in such a zone. Parking discs allow parking for usually one hour and are required where no parking meters are in place in central Copenhagen. Discs are available at banks, fuel stations, post offices, tourist offices, and the motoring club (FDM) offices. Parking meters usually allow up to 3 hours of parking. Meters are checked on weekdays from 9:00 A.M. to 6:00 P.M. and on Saturday from 9:00 A.M. to 1:00 P.M., they accept 1 Kr and 25 øre coins. In other large towns, parking on the street is often restricted to one hour; this is indicated by the standard No Parking sign bearing the words *"1-times zone"*. (A series of slashes across this sign indicates the end of the restriction.)

Camping

Denmark's campgrounds are outstanding. and though most are open from May 1 to early September, some stay open all year. Camping parties without an International Camping Carnet must purchase Danish Camping Pass. Free-camping without appropriate permission is not legal, and it's not tolerated on beaches or dunes.

Banks

Banks in Copenhagen are open on weekdays from 9:30 A.M. to 3:00 P.M. and on Thursdays until 6:00 P.M. Outside Copenhagen the banking hours vary. ATM machines are often out of service in Denmark; if you find one that works for you, consider withdrawing more cash than you usually do.

Shops

Open on weekdays from 9:00 A.M. to 5:30 P.M. and on Saturday until noon.

National Holidays

Jan 1; Maunday Thur; Good Fri; Easter Mon; June 5; Ascension; Whit Mon; Dec 24, 25, 26, 31.

BBC Radio Hours and Corresponding Frequencies

5:00 A.M. to 7:30 A.M.: 6195 and 9410 kHz

7:30 A.M. to 4:00 P.M.: 9410 and 12095 kHz

4:00 P.M. to 10:30 P.M.: 6195, 9410 and 12095 kHz

Breakdown, Accident or Emergency

Police, Fire, and Ambulance, tel. 112. All highways have emergency phones. The rescue corps, Falck, tel. 33 14 22 22, can help 24 hours a day. The national motoring club is Forende Danske Motorejere (FDM), *AIT* member, FDM-Huset, Firskovvej 32, Lyngby, Copenhagen, tel. 02 93 08 00, office hours on weekdays from 9:00 A.M. to 5:00 P.M. and on Saturday from 9:00 A.M. to noon.

Finland

Customs

Europeans age 16 and up may import 200 cigarettes or 250 grams of tobacco free of duty; non-Europeans can import twice as much free of duty. Anyone age 20 and up may import the following free of duty: 2 liters of beer, 1 liter of alcohol consisting of under 22 percent alcohol by volume, and 1 liter consisting of over 22 percent alcohol by volume. Anyone 18 years and up may import the following free of duty: 2 liters of beer and 2 liters of beverages consisting of under 22 percent alcohol by volume. The maximum value of imported goods is FIM 1500. You must declare any spare fuel.

Concessions for Hostellers

Europcar and Inter Rent grant a 10 percent discount.

Fuel

Fuel stations are usually open on weekdays from 7:00 A.M. to 9:00 P.M., with far fewer open hours on the weekend. Some stations are open 24 hours, and some have automatic pumps that accept cash. Major credit cards are widely accepted. Leaded gasoline may not be available in some places; but if not, an unleaded substitute with a special additive will be. Unleaded regular gasoline has an octane rating of 92; the octane rating of super is 99. Unleaded gasoline is known as *lyijyton polttaine*. The octane rating for unleaded regular is 95; the octane rating of super is 98.

Road Signs

Aja hitaasti	Drive slowly
Ajo sallittu omallo vastuulla	Proceed at your own risk
Aluerajoitus	Local speed limit
Kelirikko	Frost damage
Kokeile jaruja	Test your brakes
Kunnossapitotyö	Road in repair
Lossi-farja	Ferry
Päällystetyötä	Road being resurfaced
Tie rakenteilla	Road construction
Tulli	Customs
Varo irtokivia	Loose gravel

Expressways are denoted by the characters M1 to M999. First class main roads take the numbers 1 to 39; second class main roads take 40 to 99; other highways take 100 to 999; lesser main roads take 1000 to 2999; and local roads take the numbers 11,000 to 19,999.

Detour due to road work

Prohibiton applies between 8 A.M. and 6 P.M.

Driving

The minimum age of a driver is 18 years. The use of seat belts is compulsory for front-seat passengers. Children must be constrained either by seatbelts or in a child seat. Helmets are compulsory for motorcyclists and their passengers. The legal blood alcohol limit is 50 mg. Speed limits are as follows: 50 kph (30 mph) in built-up areas, 80 kph (50 mph) or 100 kph (62 mph) outside built-up areas, 120 kph (74 mph) on expressways, and 80 kph (50 mph) for cars with a caravan or trailer traveling outside built-up areas or on expressways.

Approaches to priority roads are denoted by a sign showing a red triangle on a yellow background. In another exception to the priority-on-the-right rule, trams always have priority.

Headlights must be used at all times outside built-up areas. Use of horns in towns and villages is illegal except in the case of immediate and extreme danger. Otherwise, horns and headlights should be used when poor visibility demands them.

Passing is allowed on the right if you are traveling a multi-lane road, but be careful not to cross the white line which indicates the bicycle and pedestrian lane.

Police are *not* empowered to collect fines on the spot; but the fines are extremely steep, the minimum being 150 FIM. You pay up at a bank or post office.

Parking

Parking lights must be on if you're parked in a dimly lit public spot. Wheel clamps aren't used, but illegally parked vehicles may be towed.

Camping

Though most campgrounds are open from June 1 to September 1, many stay open all year. Grounds are rated from one to three stars. One-star grounds are devoid of showers and electrical hookups, and even three-stars doesn't guarantee a campstore or restaurant. Parties without an International Camping Carnet will probably have to purchase a Finnish Camping Pass. Free-camping without appropriate permission is not legal.

Banks

Open on weekdays from 9:15 A.M. to 4:15 P.M.

Shops

Open on weekdays from 9:00 A.M. to 5:00 P.M. and on Saturday until 2:00 or 4:00 P.M.

BBC Radio Hours and Corresponding Frequencies

5:00 A.M. to 7:30 A.M.: 9410 and 12095 kHz

7:30 A.M. to 4:00 P.M.: 12095 and 15070 kHz

4:00 P.M. to 10:30 P.M.: 9410, 12095 and 15070 kHz

National Holidays

Jan 1; Epiphany; Good Fri; Easter Mon; May Day; first Sat after Ascension; Whit Sat; first Sat in Nov; Dec 6, 25; St. Stephen's Day.

Breakdown, Accident or Emergency

In Helsinki, telephone 000 for Police, Fire, or Ambulance; elsewhere call 10022 for Police, 112 for Fire or Ambulance; check telephone boxes for contrary instructions. The Automobile and Touring Club of Finland patrols the roads from Friday evening to Sunday night; in Helsinki, tel. 9 0 694 0022; outside Helsinki, tel. 9 700 8080. Immediately report any accidents to the Finnish Motor Insurers' Bureau, tel. 9 0 680 401 or 9 019251, FAX 6804 0368, and to the police. The bureau's Finnish name is Liikennevakuutusyhdistys, and its head office is at Bulevardi 28, 00120 Helsinki 12. The national motoring club is Autoliitto Automobile and Touring-Club of Finland (ATCF), *FIA* and *AIT* member, Hämeentie 105 A, 00550 Helsinki 0050, tel. 9 0 774 761, FAX 7747 6444, office hours from 8:30 A.M. to 3:30 P.M. on weekdays during June through August and from 8:30 A.M. to 5:30 P.M. on weekdays during September through May.

France

Customs

Arriving from a non-EC country, you may import the following free of duty: 400 cigarettes or 100 cigars or 100 grams of tobacco, 1 liter of liquor consisting of over 22 percent alcohol by volume, 2 liters of wine, 0.50 liters of perfume, 0.25 liters of toilet water, and other goods to a value of 300 FF. Arriving from an EC country, you may import the following free of duty: 300 cigarettes or 150 cigarillos or 75 cigars or 400 grams of tobacco, 1.5 liters of liquor consisting of over 22 percent alcohol by volume or 3 liters of liquor consisting of under 22 percent alcohol by volume or 3 liters of fortified or sparkling wine, 4 liters of still wine, 0.9 liters of perfume, 0.375 liters of toilet water, and other goods to a value of 2400 FF.

Concessions for Hostellers

Irish Ferries offers discounts on their service between Le Havre, France, and Rosslare, Ireland, and between Cherbourg, France, and Rosslare, Ireland.

Stena Sealink Line grants a 20 percent discount on standard fares for foot passengers or cars plus up to five passengers between France and England.

Tolls

An *autoroute* on which tolls are charged is indicated by a sign, usually blue, reading *péage*. Green signs indicate non-toll expressways. On sections of *autoroute* in the proximity of large cities no toll is charged. Visa and MasterCard are accepted. Vehicles are classified as belonging to one of three groups.

(1)   Private car or van with 2 axles, up to 9 seats, and with a height less than 1.3 meters as measured vertically from the front axle.

(2)   Vehicle or combination of vehicles with more than 2 axles and with a height of less than 1.3 meters as measured vertically from the front axle. Tolls for these vehicles are, on average, 50 percent more expensive than tolls for category-1 vehicles.

(3)   Caravans and vans having more than 9 seats, buses with two axles, commercial vehicles with two axles and a height greater than 1.3 meters as measured from the front axle. Tolls for these vehicles are, on average, 66 percent more expensive than tolls for category-1 vehicles.

(4)   Motorcycles. Tolls for motorcycles are, on average, 30 percent cheaper than tolls for category-1 vehicles.

Road	Toll for a Category-1 Vehicle
A1 Paris to Lille	54 FF
A1 Paris to Roye (Amiens)	31
A1 & A2 Paris to Belgium	55
A2 Bapaume to Hordain	24
A4 Calais to Strasbourge	207
A4 Paris to Reims	45*
A4 Reims to Metz	60
A4 Metz to Strasbourg	52*
A5 Troyes to Langres	25
A6 Calais to Lyon	250
A6 Paris to Beaune	82
A6 Paris to Lyon	128
A6 & A36 Paris to Mulhouse	147
A6 & A40 Paris to Geneva	165
A7 Calais to Marseille	352
A7 Lyon to Aix-en-Provence	102
A7 & A9 Lyon to Montpellier	97
A8 Aix-en-Provence to Cannes	59
A8 Calais to Cannes	412
A9 Calais to Le Perthus	427
A8 Cannes to Italy	29*
A9 Orange to Le Perthus	101
A9 Orange to Narbonne sud	68
A9 & A55 Montpellier to Arles	23
A10 Paris to Tours	82
A10 Tours to Bordeaux	121
A10 & A71 Paris to Clermont-Ferrand	141
A11 Paris to Angers	101
A11 Angers to Nantes	29*
A11 & A81 Paris to Rennes	107
A13 Paris to Tancarville (Le Havre)	31*
A13 Paris to Caen	55*
A26 Calais to Reims	88
A26 Reims to Troyes	41
A26 & A31 & A6 Reims to Lyon	153
A26 & A31 & A6 & A40 Reims to Geneva	200
A31 Beaune to Dijon	6
A31 Langres nord to Toul (Gyc)	33
A31 & A6 Nancy to Lyon	109
A31 & A6 & A40 Nancy to Geneva	157
A36 Beaune to Besançon Center	25
A36 Paris to Mulhouse	157
A36 & A6 Mulhouse to Lyon	114*
A36 & A6 & A40 Mulhouse to Geneva	162*
A40 Calais to Genève	296
A40 Calais to LeFayet	321
A40 Geneva to Chamonix	24*
A41 Annecy to Chambéry	38
A41 Annecy to Chamonix	16*
A41 Chambéry to Grenoble	47
A41 Chambéry to Scentier	41
A42 Pont d'Ain to Lyon	18
A43 Lyon to Chambéry	46
A43 & A48 Lyon to Grenoble	41
A43/431 Lyon to Les Abrets	29
A43/431 Lyon to Albertville	71

A48/43 Bourgoin to Grenoble	26
A48/43 Calais to Grenoble	295
A49 Grenoble to Valence	40
A50 Marseille to Toulon	18.5
A51 Sisteron to Aix-en-Provence	42.5
A52 Aix-en-Provence to Aubagne	14.5*
A54 Arles to Nimes ouest	9
A55 Arles to Nimes	9
A57 & A8 Toulon to Cannes	45
A61 Toulouse to Narbonne sud	56
A61 & A9 Toulouse to Le Perthus	85
A61 & A9 Toulouse to Montpellier	90
A62 Bordeaux to Toulouse	84
A63 St. Geours-de-Maremme to Spain	49*
A64 Sames to Tarbes est	32
A71 Orléans center to Bourges	45
A71 Bourges to Clermont Ferrand	61
A71 Calais to Clermont Ferrand	244
A72 Clermont-Ferrand to St. Etienne	49
A81 Paris to La Gravelle	115
N937 Nantes to Montaigu	9*

Some toll barriers on route are operated automatically by your deposit of the exact toll in coins.

Several tunnels require tolls.

A40-N205/SS26D's (E25's) Mont Blanc Tunnel between Chamonix and Entrèves, Italy: 90–175 FF for a car (depending on wheel base), 175 FF for a car towing a trailer or caravan, 90 FF for a motorcycle. Special rate for those making roundtrip within 72 hours. Customs are on the Italian side.

N6/SS35's (E70's) Frèjus Tunnel between Modane and Bardonecchia, Italy is open all year: 90–175 FF for a car (depending on wheel base), 175 FF for a car towing a trailer or caravan, 90 FF for a motorcycle. Minimum speed of 60 kph, maximum of 80 kph.

N20's Col du Puymorans Tunnel between Toulouse and Bracelona, Spain. Saves 20-minute climb over twisting 1.2-mile pass that's often snowbound in winter. 40 FF for cars.

D929/C138's Bielsa Tunnel runs through the Pyrénées between Bielsa and Aragnouet, France; usually open all year, but closes from 10:00 P.M. to 6:00 A.M. from November through April.

During daylight hours vehicle ferries run across the Gironde estuary between Royan and Le Verdon, and in the south between Blage and Lamasque. Crossing times are 30 and 25 minutes, respectively, and the ferries make one roundtrip per hour.

Tolls are charged on the following bridges.

N178-N182's Tancarville Bridge: car, 12 FF minimum (according to hp); motorcycle, 1 FF.

D77-D231's St. Nazaire Bridge: car, 22–30 FF (according to hp); motorcycle, 2–5 FF.

From the west coast to Ile de Ré and to Ile de Noirmoutier.

Pont de Martrou.

Rochefort (Charente Maritime).

Pont de St, Nazaire (Loire Atlantique).

Pont de Brotonne (Seine Maritime).

Non-toll Mountain Passes

Non-toll mountain passes tend to be much more difficult to negotiate than the passes which charge a toll. If you're driving a vehicle, such as a caravan, that is not allowed on or recommended for some of the following passes or if you wanna travel quickly across or through the mountains, note that a mountain pass or tunnel which charges a toll tends to be close by.

N5's (E2's) Faucille Pass, Morez to Geneva, Switzerland. 1322 meters; usually open in the winter; maximum grade is 10 percent; minimum width is 5 meters (16 ft.); scenic view of Mont Blanc; difficult; not recommended for caravans.

N6/SS35's Mt. Cenis Pass, Chambéry to Turin, Italy. 2083 meters; closed from early November to mid May; maximum grade is 12.5 percent; minimum width is 5 meters (16 ft.); OK for caravans.

N20's Puymorens Pass, Toulouse to Bourg-Madame. 1913 meters; closed occasionally from November to April; maximum grade is 10 percent; minimum width is 5.5 meters (18 ft.); maximum vehicle height of 3.56 meters (11.5 ft.); OK for caravans.

N75's Croix-Haute Pass, Grenoble to Sisteron. 1176 meters; usually open; maximum grade is 14.3 percent; minimum width is 5.5 meters (18 ft.); OK for caravans.

N85's Bayard Pass, Grenoble to Gap. 1247 meters; usually open; maximum grade is 14.3 percent; minimum width is 6.2 meters (20 ft.); marginally negotiable for caravans.

N90/SS26's Petit St. Bernard Pass, Bourg-St.-Maurice and Aosta, Italy. 2188 meters; closed from mid October to mid June; maximum grade is 8.3 percent; minimum width is 5 meters (16 ft.); no vehicles over 15 metric tons (15 000 kg); not recommended for caravans.

N91's Lautaret/Altareto Pass, Briançon to Vizille. 2057 meters; closed occasionally from December through March; maximum grade is 12.5 percent; minimum width is 4.34 meters (14 ft.); especially scenic; OK for caravans; not recommended for buses.

N94/SS24's Montgenevre Pass, Briançon to Turin, Italy. 1850 meters; usually open; maximum grade is 9 percent; minimum width is 5 meters (16 ft.); tire chains required in winter; especially scenic; OK for caravans.

N134/N330's Somport Pass, Pau to Huesca, Spain. 1632 meters; usually open; maximum grade is 10 percent; minimum width is 3.72 meters (12 ft.); OK for caravans.

N204/SS20's Col de Tende Pass, La Giandola to Borgo San Dalmazzo, Italy. 1320 meters; usually open, but closed from 9:00 P.M. to 6:00 A.M.; maximum grade is 9 percent; minimum width is 5.58 meters (18 ft.); no caravans allowed in the winter.

N506/A203-A9-A21's Col de Montes Pass, Chamonix to Martigny, Switzerland. 1460 meters; closed occasionally from December through early April; maximum grade is 12.5 percent; minimum width is 3.1 meters (10 ft.); OK for small caravans.

D64's Restefond Pass, Juasiers to St. Etienne-de-Tinée. 2802 meters; closed October through June; maximum grade is 11 percent; minimum width is 3.1 meters (10 ft.); highest Alpine pass; not recommended for caravans.

D118's Quillanne Pass, Carcasonne to Mont-Louis. 1715 meters; closed occasionally from November through March; maximum grade is 8.3 percent; minimum width is 5 meters (16 ft.); OK for caravans.

D465's Ballon d'Alsace Pass, St. Maurice-sur-Moselle to Belfort. 1178 meters; closed occasionally from December through March; maximum grade is 11 percent; minimum width is 4 meters (13 ft.); OK for caravans.

D618's Peyresourde Pass, Arreau to Bagnères-de-Luchon. 1563 meters; usually open; maximum grade is 10 percent; minimum width is 4 meters (13 ft.); not recommended for caravans.

D618's Port Pass, St.-Girons to Tarascon-sur-Ariège. 1250 meters; closed occasionally from November through March; maximum grade is 10 percent; minimum width is 4.34 meters (14 ft.); especially scenic; not recommended for large caravans.

D900/SS21's Larche/Argentera Pass, Barcelonnette to Cuneo, Italy. 1994 meters; closed occasionally from December through March; maximum grade is 8.3 percent; minimum width is 3.1 meters (10 ft.); OK for caravans.

D902's Galibier Pass, St. Michel-de-Maurienne to Lautaret Saddle. 2645 meters; closed from October through June; maximum grade is 12.5 percent; minimum width is 3.1 meters (10 ft.); not recommended for caravans. The tunnel that once allowed traffic under the summit has been closed.

D902's Iseran Pass, Lanslebourg to Bourg-St.-Maurice. 2770 meters; closed from mid October to late June; maximum grade is 11 percent; minimum width is 4 meters (13 ft.); not recommended for caravans.

D902's Izoard Pass, Briançon to Guillestre. 2360 meters; closed from late October through mid June; maximum grade is 12.5 percent; minimum width is 5 meters (16 ft.); not recommended for caravans.

D902's Vars Pass, Barcelonnette to Guillestre. 2110 meters; closed occasionally from December through March; maximum grade is 10 percent; minimum width is 6 meters (16 ft.); not recommended for caravans.

D908's Allos Pass, Barcelonnette to Entrevaux. 2250 meters; closed from early November through early June; maximum grade is 10 percent; minimum width is 4 meters (13 ft.); especially scenic; maximum vehicle width of 1.83 meters (5 feet 11 inches); not recommended for caravans.

D909's Aravis Pass, Annecy to Chamonix. 1499 meters; closed occasionally from December through March; maximum grade is 9 percent; minimum width is 4 meters (13 ft.); especially scenic; not recommended for caravans.

D918's Aspin Pass, Arreau to Luz-St.-Sauveur. 1490 meters; closed from December through April; maximum grade is 12.5 percent; minimum width is 4 meters (13 ft.); especially scenic; OK for caravans.

D918's Aubisque Pass, Laruns to Argelès-Gazost. 1710 meters; closed from mid October through June; maximum grade is 10 percent; minimum width is 3.4 meters (11 ft.); especially scenic; not recommended for caravans.

D918's Tourmalet Pass, Luz-St.-Sauveur to Arreau. 2115 meters; closed from October through mid June; maximum grade is 12.5 percent; minimum width is 4.34 meters (14 ft.); not recommended for caravans.

C135's Ibaneta Pass, St.-Jean-Pied-de-Port to Pamplona, Spain. 1058 meters; usually open; maximum grade is 10 percent; minimum width is 4 meters (13 ft.); especially scenic; OK for caravans.

D933/C135's Ibaneta Pass, Pamplona to St.-Jean-Pied-de-Port, France. 1058 meters; usually open; maximum grade is 10 percent; minimum width is 4 meters (13 ft.); especially scenic; OK for caravans.

D934/C136's Pourtalet Pass, Pau to Huesca, Spain. 1791 meters; closed from late October to early June; maximum grade is 10 percent; minimum width is 3.4 meters (11 ft.); not recommended for caravans.

D2202's Cayolle Pass, Barcelonnette to Nice. 2327 meters; closed from early November to early June; maximum grade is 10 percent; minimum width is 4 meters (13 ft.); not recommended for caravans.

A203's Forclaz Pass, Chamonix to Martigny, Switzerland. 1527 meters; usually open; maximum grade is 8.3 percent; minimum width is 5 meters (16 ft.); no vehicles over 2.54 meters (8 feet 2 1/2 inches) wide; no trailers over 5 metric tons; especially scenic; marginally negotiable by caravans.

Fuel

Gasoline costs between 5.30 and 6.10 FF per liter. Fuel is more expensive along the super-highways than at supermarkets; look to fill up at supermarkets on main roads exiting towns. Major credit cards are accepted. Many stations require that you pay at a booth upon driving out of the station area. If this is the case and a line of vehicles forms at the pay booth, you may have to wait to pump your fuel until the person who preceded you at the pump pays for their fuel. Especially in dealing with such setups, note the total fuel charge on the pump so you won't be overcharged at the booth; sometimes the operator may depend on your honesty and let you quote the total at the booth. Vehicles equipped with a catalytic converter may carry 10 liters of spare fuel but may not carry it on ferries to Corsica.

Leaded regular gasoline has an octane rating of 90; the octane rating of super is 98. Unleaded gasoline is known as *essence sans plomb*. Super unleaded gasoline has an octane rating of 95 or 98. Often, diesel fuel is called by its English name; otherwise, diesel is called *gas-oil* or *gaz-oil*. LPG is called *Gaz de pétrole liquéfié (GPL)*.

Road Signs

Aire de repos	Rest stops
Allumez vos lanternes (or *feux*)	Turn on your lights
Attention au feu	Fire hazard
Attention travaux	Beware roadworks
Autre directions	Other directions

Barrière de dègel	Trucks not allowed
Chaussèe dèformèe	Bumpy road ahead
Centre Ville	Town center
Gendarmerie	Police station
Gravillons	Loose chippings
Haute tension	Electric line
Interdit aux piètons	No pedestrians
Nids de poules	Potholes
Rappel	Remember
Route barrèe	Road closed
Sens-unique	One-way
Serrez a Droite	Keep to the right
Sortie	Exit
Toutes Directions	All directions
Voie unique	One lane road

Blue signs and the letter *A* indicate *Autoroute pèage* or toll roads, while green signs and the letter *N* (*RN* on older maps) indicate non-toll *Route National* highways. *D* roads are provincial or *routes dèpartementals*. Just follow the signs in green if you wanna avoid tolls but still make good time. To exit a metropolitan area follow the signs that read *"Toutes Directions"* (All Directions) or *"Autre Directions"* (Other Directions). Exits or *sorties* off the *autoroutes* are sometimes embellished by an orange panel marked *"Bis";* these signs indicate alternate routes which avoid areas prone to congestion at peak driving times. A free map of *Bis* routes is published in June each year by the French Government; check for this map at tourist offices in France if you haven't already obtained it. *Itineraires de dèlestage* are routes that avoid the cities; these are signified by blue signs with yellow arrows. To avoid rush hour in large cities don't drive between 7:00 A.M. and 9:30 A.M. or between 4:30 P.M. and 7:30 P.M. The word *gare* indicates a train station.

No parking from 1st to 15th of the month

No parking from 16th to end of the month

Parking alternates sides every two weeks

Driving

The minimum age of a driver is 18 years. Children must be at least 10 years of age to sit in the front seat. Children under 10 years of age must be seated in the rear and in an approved child seat or restraint. The use of seat belts is compulsory for front- and rear-seat passengers. Helmets are compulsory for motorcyclists and their passengers. The legal blood alcohol limit is 80 mg. Generally, speed limits are as follows: 50 kph (30 mph) in built-up areas, 90 kph (56 mph) or 110 kph (68 mph) outside built-up areas, and 130 kph (81 mph) on expressways. During good weather the minimum speed in the far left lane of expressways is 80 kph (49 mph). In bad weather, limits are lowered to 80 kph (50 mph) outside built-up areas, 100 kph (62 mph) when multiple lanes are provided in each direction, and 110 kph (68 mph) on expressways. Visitors who've held their license for less than one year must always observe a 90 kph (56 mph) speed limit. The speed limit on Paris's *Pèriphèrique* (ring road) is 80 kph (49 mph). This same 80 kph limit applies to cars towing a trailer that's not as heavy as the car. If the trailer is less than 30 percent heavier than the car, the limit is 65 kph (39 mph); if the trailer is more than 30 percent heavier, the limit is 45 kph (28 mph). In both cases a plate showing the maximum speed must be displayed on the back of the trailer, and the vehicle-trailer combination is not allowed in the far left lane of expressways.

A flashing red traffic light means *Do not enter;* flashing amber means *Caution;* flashing yellow arrows mean *Yield.* A sign reading *"Danger Priorité à Droite"* reminds you that traffic on the right has priority at intersections. A sign reading *"Passage protégé"* indicates that you're approaching a road that has priority. When traffic on a roundabout has priority, this is indicated by a red-bordered triangular sign bearing the roundabout symbol and the words *"vouz n'avez pas la priorité"* (you do not have right of way) or *"cedez le passage"* (give way).

Motorcycles must be operated with the headlights on—night and day. Vehicles parked in dimly lit public places must have their parking lights on. Horns should only be used in cases of immediate and extreme danger. If a driver coms up behind and flashes you, he's communicating that he wants to pass.

Broken center lines indicate a section of road where passing is allowed. A moving tram on a two-way street may be passed on the right only. A moving tram on a one-way street, however, may be passed on the left. Do not pass a stopped tram which passengers are boarding or disembarking.

Some police are empowered to collect fines of up to 2500 FF on the spot. For minor offences a fine is payable within 30 days. A deposit might be required if a serious offence is committed by a non resident.

Parking

Follow the local parking customs. Often you'll see cars parked half-on and half-off the sidewalk. If this practice seems to be the norm in an area, go ahead and do it. I've had no problem consistently finding free and well-located parking spots in downtown Paris.

Don't park where the curb is painted yellow. If, based on whether the date is even or odd, parking is allowed on one side of the street or the other, signs reading *"Coté du Stationnement, jour pairs"* (even) or *"impairs"* (odd) are in place. Parking on the left side of a street is allowed along one-way streets only. The end of a no parking zone is indicated by a sign reading *"Fin d'interdiction de stationner."* On dark streets, parking lights must be left on. In Paris, parking is not allowed along two main *axes rouges* or red routes: the north-south route includes the Ave. du Général Leclerc, a portion of the Blvd. St. Michel, the rue de Rivoli, Blvd. Sébastopol, Blvd. Strasbourg, Blvd. Barbès, Blvd. Ornano, rue Lafayette, and Ave. Jean

Jaurès; the east-west route includes the left banks of the Seine and the Quai de la Mégisserie. Do not leave a vehicle parked in the same spot along a Paris street for more than 24 hours; this also applies to Hauts-de-Seine, Seine-St. Denis, and Val de Marne.

Pay-and-display machines *(horodateurs)* are common throughout France. Larger cities have *Blue Zones* where parking discs or tickets must be displayed on vehicle dashboards. Discs should be displayed on the inside of the windshield, with the clock hands set to show time of arrival and planned time of departure. The limit in *Blue Zones* is 1.5 hours from 9:00 A.M. to 7:00 P.M., except from 11:30 A.M. to 2:30 P.M., with no tickets required on Sundays or public holidays. The discs or tickets may be obtained from tourist offices, certain shops, and police stations. The police charge for the discs, but the tourist offices don't. There are also *Gray Zones* where motorists must plug a meter between 9:00 A.M. and 7:00 P.M. In Paris and some other large cities, illegally parked vehicles may be wheel-clamped or towed.

Camping

Signs reading *Camping a la Ferme* and *Camping rural* indicate modestly sized and spartan campgrounds often located on a farm. An International Camping Carnet is required by some private campgrounds and in national parks. Free-camping without the appropriate permission is not legal, and it's often not tolerated in state forests and national parks and along beach fronts on the Mediterranean. In fact, many parking lots near municipal beaches are guarded by a height barrier which blocks motorhomes from entering. If you have a propane bottle from another country, you'll have trouble filling it in France.

Banks

Open on weekdays from 9:30 A.M. to 4:30 A.M., but times vary. Most banks close for about an hour at lunch time.

Shops

Open from 9:00 A.M. to 12:15 P.M. and from 2:00 P.M. to 6:30 A.M. every day but Sunday. Some shops, however, close on Monday instead of Sunday; and food sellers open at 6:00 or 7:00 A.M.

National Holidays

Jan 1; Easter Mon; Labor Day; May 8; Ascension; Whit Monday; July 14; Aug 15; Nov 1; Nov 11; Dec 25.

BBC Radio Hours and Corresponding Frequencies

In the North:

5:00 A.M. to 7:30 A.M.: 648 and 6195 kHz

7:30 A.M. to 4:00 P.M.: 648, 9760 and 12095 kHz

4:00 P.M. to 10:30 P.M.: 648, 9410 and 12095 kHz

In the South

5:00 A.M. to 7:30 A.M.: 6195, 9410, and 15575 kHz

7:30 A.M. to 4:00 P.M.: 9760 and 12095 kHz

4:00 P.M. to 10:30 P.M..: 6195, 9410, and 12095 kHz

Breakdown, Accident or Emergency

Police, tel. 17; Fire, tel. 18; Ambulance—call the number given on the phone box or call the police. Expressways and main highways have roadside emergency telephones every 2 km. If an accident involving personal injury or substantial damage occurs in a town, contact a policeman (agent de police) to make a report. On country roads, contact a gendarme. If the accident involves damage only, contact a huissier from the nearest town. A huissier is a court official who is part assessor and part bailiff. The party requesting the huissier's services must pay the fee for completing a report on the accident. Accidents also should be re-ported to the Bureau Central Français des Sociétés d'Assurances contre les Accidents Automobiles, 36 ave. du Général de Gaulle, 93171 Bagnolet cedex, tel. 1 49 93 65 50. Automobile Club de France, FIA member, 5 rue Auber, 75009 Paris, tel. 44 65 34 70 or 44 51 53 99, office hours from 9:00 A.M. to 6:00 P.M. on weekdays. Automobile Club National (ACN), FIA and AIT member, 9 rue Anatole de la Forge, 75017 Paris, tel. 42 27 82 00, office hours from 8:30 A.M. to 1:00 P.M. and from 1:45 P.M. to 5:45 P.M. (Friday until 4:45) on weekdays.

Germany

Customs

Non-EC citizens may import the following free of duty: 200 cigarettes or 50 cigars or 250 grams of tobacco, 1 liter of spirits consisting of greater than 22 percent alcohol by volume or 2 liters of spirits consisting of less than 22 percent alcohol by volume, 2 liters of still wine, 50 grams of perfume, 0.25 liters of toilet water, and other goods to a value of DM 115. You may import 10 liters of spare fuel free of duty if your vehicle is registered in an EU country.

Concessions for Hostellers

Scandinavian Seaways offers discounts on its ferry service between Hamburg, Germany, and Harwich or New Castle, England, for groups of 10 or more, members being under 26 years of age.

Stena Sealink Line offers a 10 percent discount on its ferry service between Göteborg, Sweden, and Kiel, Germany; but tickets are obtainable only at Terra Nova Travel Sections in Sweden and are valid for Monday through Thursday travel from June through August.

The ferry service between Luxhaven, Germany, and Helgoland (a Danish Island) is discounted for groups of 6 or more, members being under 23 years of age.

Non-toll Mountain Passes

B307/B181's Aachen Pass, Tegernsee to Jenbach, Austria. 941 meters; usually open in winter; maximum grade is 14.3 percent; minimum width is 5.9 meters (19 ft.); especially scenic; not recommended for caravans.

Fuel

Gasoline costs between DM 1.40 and DM 1.70 per liter. In general, major credit cards are accepted. Leaded super gasoline has an octane rating of 98. Unleaded gasoline is called *bleifrei normal* or *bleifrei super*. Regular unleaded gasoline has an octane rating of 91; the octane rating of super is 95 or 98. Diesel goes by its English name. LPG is called *autogas*.

Road Signs

Alle Richtungen	All directions
Ausfahrt	Exit
Autobahn kreuz	Expressway junction
Baustofflagerung	Roadwork equipment
Einbahnstraße	One-way street
Fahrbahnwechsel	Change lanes
Freiefahrt	Road is clear
Frostschäden	Frost damage
Glatteisgefahr	Icy road
Landschafts Schutzgebiet	No parking
Parkplatz	Parking ramp
Polizei	Police station
Radweg kreutz	Bicycle-track crossing
Rollsplitt	Loose Material
Seitenstreifen nicht befahrbar	Do not use shoulder
Stadtzcentrum	Town center
Stadmitte	Town center
STAU	Slow traffic; drive with care
Straßenschäden	Road damage
Umleitung	Detour
Zentrum	Town center

The word *bahnhof,* whether alone or incorporated in another word, indicates a train station. International *autobahns* are signified by green rectangles bearing an *E;* while the letter *A* is used to signify intranational *autobahns*. National roads are marked by black numbers on a yellow background. If two numbers are given where you would expect to see a speed limit, these numbers represent the speed *range*. A *U* on a blue sign is sometimes used to indicate a detour.

Danger: Sudden fog patches

Tram or bus stop

Driving

The minimum age of a driver is 17 years. Children must be at least 12 years of age to sit in the front seat (unless the seat is equipped with a child restraint). Children under 12 years of age and seated in the rear of the vehicle must be in a child seat if such a seat is fitted; the fine for violating this is 40 DM. The use of seat belts is compulsory for front- and rear-seat passengers. Helmets are compulsory for motorcyclists and their passengers. The legal blood alcohol limit is 80 mg. Speed limits are as follows: 50 kph (30 mph) in built-up areas, 100 kph (62 mph) or 130 kph (81 mph) outside built-up areas, a *recommended* 130 kph (81 mph) on the *autobahn*, and 80 kph (50 mph) for cars with caravans or trailers traveling outside built-up areas or on expressways. When the visibility is below 50 meters, speeds on all roads are limited to 50 kph (31 mph).

Some rules of the road are still different between the former East and West Germany. The former GDR territories (Saxony, Saxony-Anhalt, Brandenburg, Thuringia and Mecklenburg) enforce the following speed limits: 80 kph (50 mph) outside built-up areas, and 100 kph (62 mph) on expressways—except the A24, where the limit is 120 kph (75 mph) or 130 kph (80 mph). The sequence of traffic lights is green + amber (simultaneously), amber, red, red + amber (simultaneously).

Left-turning vehicles must always yield. Trams do not have priority: you can drive on their tracks and basically treat them like cars—they'll stop if they have to. Buses have priority when leaving stops. Pedestrians always have priority when crossing the white-banded crosswalks.

In built-up areas horns should only be used in cases of immediate and extreme danger. Outside built-up areas you can use the horn to indicate that you intend to pass. At night you must flash your headlights to warn of your intention to pass.

Trams can be passed along either side on one-way streets; but on two-way streets they should be passed pon the right only. Outside built-up areas, you cannot pass a school bus which has stopped and has its red lights flashing.

Police are empowered to collect fines of up to 75 DM on the spot, but violators *are* allowed to pay during the following week. Foreigners, however, are often asked to place a deposit; their vehicle may be impounded if they refuse.

Parking

Parking is prohibited within less than 5 meters of a pedestrian crossing, within less than 10 meters in front of a traffic light, and within less than 15 meters of a bus or tram stop. Parking discs may be required in some areas. Parking, except along one-way streets, is allowed only on the right. A sign showing an eagle in a green triangle indicates a wild-life reserve and signifies that parking is limited to designated lots.

You can spend the night in a vehicle parked on the street, but only one night per parking spot.

Camping

The former West Germany's campgrounds are top notch, sporting all the amentities—including excellent restaurants; those in the former East are catching up. Free-camping is allowed for one night at highway rest areas, but it's illegal elsewhere unless you have appropriate permission.

Banks

Generally open weekdays from 8:30 or 9:00 A.M. to 3:00 or 4:00 P.M.(5:00 or 6:00 P.M. on Thursday); some banks close from 12:30 P.M. to 1:30 P.M.

Shops

Open on weekdays from 8:00 A.M. to noon and from 1:00 or 1:30 P.M. to 6:00 or 6:30 P.M. Large stores stay open during lunch hours. Open until 2:00 P.M. on Saturday.

National Holidays

Jan 1; Good Fri; Easter Mon; Labor Day; Ascension; Whit Mon; June 17; Oct 3; Dec 25, 26. Some areas observe Epiphany, Corpus Christi, Assumption, All Saints and Repentance Days.

BBC Radio Hours and Corresponding Frequencies

In the Northeast:

5:00 A.M. to 7:30 A.M.: 6195, 9410 and 15575 kHz

7:30 A.M. to 4:00 P.M.: 9410, 12095 and 15070 kHz

4:00 P.M. to 10:30 P.M.: 6195, 9410 and 12095 kHz

In the Northwest:

5:00 A.M. to 7:30 A.M.: 648, 9410 and 15575 kHz

7:30 A.M. to 4:00 P.M.: 648, 9750 and 12095 kHz

4:00 P.M. to 10:30 P.M.: 6195, 9410 and 12095 kHz

In the South:

5:00 A.M. to 7:30 A.M.: 6195, 9410 and 15575 kHz

7:30 A.M. to 4:00 P.M.: 12095 and 15070 kHz

4:00 P.M. to 10:30 P.M.: 6195, 9410 and 12095 kHz

Breakdown, Accident or Emergency

Police, tel. 110; Fire, tel. 112; Ambulance, tel. 110 in the West, 115 in the former East German states. Roadside emergency telephones are placed along the *autobahns*. Allgemeiner Deutscher Automobil-Club (ADAC), *FIA* and *AIT* member, Am Westpark 8, 81373 Munich, tel. 089 76760, office hours from 8:00 A.M. to 5:00 A.M. on weekdays (8:00 A.M. to noon in other main towns) and until noon on Saturday; grants free assistance to tourists. The ADAC

also offers a 24-hour information service, tel. 089 22222. Automobil-Club von Deutschland (AVD), *FIA* member, Lyonerstraße 16, 60528 Frankfurt am Main, tel. 069 66060, office hours from 8:00 A.M. to 5:00 P.M. on weekdays. Both clubs run emergency patrol services on major roads.

Gibraltar

Customs

Beware of civilians illegally selling bogus tickets for the border crossing. Trailer and motor caravans are not allowed. However, if you do not intend to use yours for camping, Customs may allow it in. You may import 20 liters of spare fuel in a sealed steel container, but you must declare it and pay duty on it.

Fuel

Leaded super gasoline has an octane rating of 98; the octane rating of super is 95. Credit cards are not accepted.

Driving

Helmets are compulsory for motorcyclists and their passengers. Goggles are compulsory for motorcyclists riding a machine with a 50 cc or larger engine. Speed limits are as follows: 40 kph (25 mph) in built-up areas, 40 kph (25 mph)

outside built-up areas. Other limits are posted as necessary. The roads of the Upper Rock are very challenging; consider doing the Rock by taxi or a minibus service.

Parking

Parking on the street is allowed on Devil's Tower Road, Line Wall Road, in Queensway, and on Rosia Road. Parking garages are located at Catalan Bay, Casemates Square, Eastern Beach, and Grand Parade (near the lower cable car station). For the most part, the town center is closed to motor vehicles; park outside the city walls. Vehicles parked illegally are subject to wheel-clamping or towing. Go to the Central Police Station in Irish Town if yours is dispatched as such.

Banks

Open on Monday through Thursday from 9:00 A.M. to 3:30 A.M. Some open on Friday until 6:00 A.M.

Shops

Open on weekdays from 9:00 A.M. to 5:00 P.M. Open until 1:00 A.M. on Saturday.

National Holidays

Jan 1; Mar 13; Easter; May Day; Spring Bank Holiday; Queen's Birthday; Late Summer Bank Holiday; Dec 25.

BBC Radio Hours and Corresponding Frequencies

5:00 A.M. to 7:30 A.M.: 6195, 9410 and 15575 kHz

7:30 A.M. to 4:00 P.M.: 12095, 15070 and 17705 kHz

4:00 P.M. to 10:30 P.M.: 6195, 12095 and 15070 kHz

Breakdown, Accident or Emergency

Police, tel. 190; Fire or Ambulance, tel. 199. Britain's Royal Automobile Club agent is AM Capurro and Sons Ltd., 20 Line Wall Road, tel. 74813 or 75149.

Great Britain (England, Northern Ireland, Scotland and Wales)

Customs

You may import free of duty the following goods if they were *not* taxed in the EC: 400 cigarettes or 200 cigarillos or 100 cigars or 500 grams of tobacco, 1 liter of alcoholic beverages consisting of over 22 percent alcohol by volume, 2 liters of alcoholic beverages consisting of under 22 percent alcohol by volume or 2 liters of fortified or sparkling wine, 2 liters of still table wine, 60 cc/ml of perfume, 250 cc/ml of toilet water, and other goods to the value of £36. You may import free of duty the following goods if they *were* taxed in the EC: 800 cigarettes, 400 cigarillos, 200 cigars, 1 kilogram of pipe tobacco, 10 liters of spirits, 90 liters of wine, and 110 liters of beer. Animals brought into the country are subject to a six month quarantine; penalties for breaching this regulation are severe and rigorously enforced. Overall, British customs officials are particularly fastidious—expect a short delay.

Concessions for Hostellers

B&I Line offers discounts on their service between Britain and Ireland.

Color Line offers a 10 percent reduction on sleeperettes available on their ferry service between Newcastle, England, and Bergen, Norway, or Stavanger, Norway.

North Sea Ferries offers discounts on its service between Rotterdam, Netherlands, and Hull, England.

Scandinavian Seaways offers discounts on its ferry service between Newcastle, England, and Esbjerg, Denmark, or Göteborg, Sweden. Reductions are offered to groups of 10 or more, members being under 26 years of age, on basic fares for the ferry route between Hamburg, Germany, and Harwich or Newcastle, England.

Stena Sealink Line offers a 20 percent discount on standard fares for foot passengers or cars plus up to five passengers between Europe and England. The service between Hoek van Holland, Netherlands, and Harwich, England, offers discounts as high as 40 percent.

Sealink Stena Line offers a 25 percent discount off normal passenger fare on all its ferry services between points in England, Scotland and Wales and points in Ireland. Does not apply to service between Stranraer, Scotland, and Larne, Northern Ireland, on Friday and Saturday sailings during July and August.

Arnold Clark Car Rental offers a 10 percent discount off basic tariff rates on car and van hire (except economy class); network outlets throughout Scotland.

McCauselands Care Hire, Grosvenor Rd., Belfast, BT1, offers a 10 percent reduction on car and van hire.

A discount is offered on the seven-day Scottish Citylink Bus pass.

Fuel

Very few fuel stations are open 24 hours. Gasoline, called *petrol*, is often advertised in terms of imperial gallons (1.19 US gallons per imperial gallon). Pumps, however, measure in liters. Unleaded gasoline costs about £2.05 per imperial gallon. Leaded gasoline is identified by four stars (****) and has an octane rating of 97. Premium unleaded gasoline has an octane rating of 95; the octane rating of super is 98.

Road Signs

Expressways are called *motorways* and are signified by the letter *M*. Highways designated by the letter *A* have multilane sections and are sometimes divided, and *B* highways are single-lane and not divided. A white *R* on a green background indicates a ring road. The black letters *HR* on a yellow background indicate a holiday route.

Driving

Given London's excellent public transport and congested traffic, I recommend that you do not use a motor vehicle there. Rush hours in London occur from 8:30 to 10:00 A.M. and from 5:30 to 7:00 P.M. Avoid the ring road or "orbital" that circles London; traffic will probably be snarled on this overburdened thoroughfare at all times except late evenings and Sunday mornings. If you wanna know how to get from here to there in London, get a *Mini London AZ Street Atlas and Index;* it's used religiously—even by the residents. The *Atlas* illustrates and indexes every street, alleyway, tube line and tube stop in London. You can pick up an *Atlas* in one of the countless shops and bookstores in London.

Driving is on the left-hand side of the road. Seat belts must be worn by all vehicle occupants. Speed limits vary often and greatly; they are generally 30 mph (48 kph) where street lighting is in place in towns and cities, 40 mph (64 kph) in suburban areas, 60 mph (97 kph) on non-divided highways, and 70 mph (113 kph) on motorways and divided highways which provide multiple lanes in your direction—the fast lane being that nearest the median or middle.

Flashing amber traffic lights warn that you must give priority to pedestrians on the crossing. Pedestrians on a striped crosswalk always have legal right-of-way. At intersections a dashed or double-dashed line across your path, or a triangle or a series of triangles pointed toward you on the roadway, indicate that you should give priority to the traffic on the other road. If a triangle or series of triangles points away from you, you have priority. Always give right of way to sheep and cattle.

Parking

Pay-and-display machines are common. A single yellow line painted on the curb means parking in that spot is restricted during daylight hours. A red line or double yellow lines mean more complicated rules apply; look for signs on nearby lamp posts to get the specifics. Of course, you may not park on striped crosswalks; moreover, you cannot park in the zone that precedes a crosswalk, a zone marked by zigzag lines or by rows of studs. In London, wheel clamps are used on illegally parked vehicles: £38 release charge—plus £40 on the Red Route, £30 elsewhere in London, or £20 outside London proper.

Camping

Apart from the small ones run by the major camping clubs, campgrounds don't require an International Camping Carnet. During high season many campgrounds fill up early in the day: show up or reserve early. Most grounds are not replete with the amenities that characterize their continental counterparts. Certain Calor Gas depots can fill German-style propane bottles, but it's very wise to carry adapters. Free-camping without the appropriate permission is illegal; but it's tolerated, as it is in nearly every European country, if practiced discreetly.

Banks

Generally open on weekdays from 9:30 A.M. to 4:30 P.M., perhaps later on Thursdays. Some banks are open on Saturday mornings.

Shops

Open from 9:00 A.M. to 5:30 P.M. every day but Sunday.

National Holidays

England, Wales, and N. Ireland: Jan 1; Mar 17*; Apr 14, 17; May 8, 29; July 12*; Aug 28; Dec 25, 26. *N. Ireland only.

Scotland: Jan 1; Apr 14; May 8, 29; Aug 7; Dec 25, 26.

Breakdown, Accident or Emergency

Police and Ambulance, tel. 999. Royal Automobile Club (RAC), *FIA* member, tel. 0181 686 0088, FAX 0181 681 8710. Automobile Association (AA), tel. 01256 20123, FAX 01256 493389.

Greece

Customs

You may import the following free of duty: one carton of cigarettes or cigars, or 0.25 pounds of smoking tobacco; 1 liter of alcohol or 2 liters of wine; and gifts to a value of 10,000 dr. There is no duty on articles intended for personal use. Foreign bank notes in excess of $1000 must be declared. There are no restrictions on traveler's checks. You may import an unlimited amount of Greek currency and export up to 40,000 dr plus $1400 in foreign currencies. Importation of spare fuel is prohibited. The maximum period for temporary importation of a foreign-registered vehicle is 6 months. Details about your vehicle will be entered in your passport upon entry.

Tolls

Vehicles are classified as follows: (1) car or van with up to 10 seats, (2) caravan, (3) car with caravan, (4) motorcycle.

Vehicle Category

Route	1	2	3	4
Athens to Corinth	400 dr	600	800	200
Corinth to Patras	500	800	1000	200
Corinth to Tripoli	700	1000	1200	400
Athens to Lamia	900	1450	1800	550
Lamia to Larissa	400	600	800	200
Larissa to Katerini	400	600	800	200
Katerini to Evzoni	400	800	800	200

Fuel

Many stations close at 7:00 P.M. Some stations accept credit cards. Gasoline costs between 1.85 dr. and 2.05 dr. per liter. Lead-free is widely available. Regular unleaded gasoline has an octane rating of 91 or 92; the octane rating of super is 96 or 98. Unleaded gasoline is called *amoliwdi wensina*. Unleaded super gasoline has an octane rating of 95.

Road Signs

The word *stathmos* indicates a train station.

Driving

Greece suffers Europe's worst accident rate in terms of the number of collisions per vehicle. Red traffic lights are consistently ignored, and other driving habits are marginally reasonable.

The minimum age of a driver is 18 years. Children must be at least 10 years of age to sit in the front seat. The use of seat belts is compulsory for front-seat passengers. Helmets are compulsory for motorcyclists and their passengers. The legal blood alcohol limit is 50 mg. Speed limits are as follows: 50 kph (30 mph) in built-up areas, 80 kph (50 mph) outside built-up areas, and 100 kph (62 mph) on expressways.

Many roads are three lanes wide: the middle lane is used for passing in both directions. If there is little room to pass on the road, fast drivers expect slow drivers to pull onto the shoulder in order to let them by.

Multitone horns are illegal. Use of a vehicle's horn in towns is allowed only in cases of immediate and extreme danger.

Passing is illegal when approaching a train crossing that isn't equipped with a barrier.

Fines should be paid to the public treasury, not to a police officer.

Parking

Do not park within 3 meters of a fire hydrant, within 5 meters of an intersection, or within 15 meters of a public transportation stop. If you park in a *No Parking* zone in Athens or certain other areas, the police will remove your license plates. A vehicle parked at night in a public place must have its rear red lights turned on. Native drivers in Athens are allowed to park only in metered spaces, but special parking lots are maintained for visitors. Greek-registered vehicles cannot enter the center zone of Athens, but vehicles belonging to visitors who are staying for less than forty days are exempted.

Camping

Greece is a great place to camp, but the campgrounds are not as fancy as those in Northern Europe. Free-camping is illegal without the appropriate permission.

Banks

Open on weekdays from 8:00 A.M. to 2:00 P.M.

Shops

Open from 8:00 A.M. to 2:30 P.M. on Monday, Wednesday and Saturday. Open from 8:00 A.M. to 1:30 P.M. and from 5:30 P.M. to 8:00 P.M. every other day but Sunday.

National Holidays

Jan 1; Epiphany; Shrove Mon; Mar 25; Good Fri; Easter Mon; Labor Day; Whit Mon; Aug 15; Oct 28; Dec 25, 26.

BBC Radio Hours and Corresponding Frequencies

5:00 A.M. to 7:30 A.M.: 9410, 12095 and 15070 kHz
7:30 A.M. to 4:00 P.M.: 9660, 15070 and 17640 kHz
4:00 P.M. to 10:30 P.M.: 9410, 12095 and 15070 kHz

Breakdown, Accident or Emergency

Police, tel. 100 (Athens, Corfu, Patras, Piraeus, Thessaloniki) or 109 (Athens' suburbs); Fire, tel. 199; Ambulance, in Athens tel. 166 (see the phone directory in other towns). The Automobile and Touring Club of Greece (ELPA), *FIA* and *AIT* member, 2-4 Messogion St., 115 27 Athens, tel. 779 1615, office hours from 8:30 A.M. to 7:30 P.M. on weekdays and from 8:30 A.M. to 1:30 P.M. on Saturdays. ELPA provides 24-hour road-side assistance (OVELPA) free of charge to tourists within town limits; tel. 104. Outside town limits, ELPA provides the service for a charge. This service extends to the islands of Crete and Corfu. Another motoring club is the Hellenic Touring Club, *AIT* member, 12 Politechniou St., Athens 104 33, tel. 52 40 854 or 52 48 600, office hours on weekdays from 8:00 A.M. to 3:00 P.M. and from 5:30 P.M. to 9:00 P.M. and on Saturday from 8:00 A.M. to 3:00 P.M.

Hungary

Customs

You may import the following free of duty: 250 grams of tobacco, 2 liters of wine, 1 liter of spirits, and 250 grams of perfume. Items intended for personal use may be imported duty free as well. A 30 percent customs charge is enforced on gifts valued in Hungary at more than 10,000 Ft. Keep all receipts from items purchased from Intertourist, Képcsarnok Vállalat, or Konsumtourist. You need a special permit to export works of art valued at more than 1000 Ft. It's illegal to import or export spare fuel. Visitors must possess the equivalent of at least 5000 Ft in cash, a requirement that's waved, however, for those with a credit card, a letter of invitation, or accommodation vouchers issued by a travel agency.

Fuel

Gasoline or *benzin* costs about 104 Ft per liter. Áfor and Intertag Shell stations at busy locations are open 24 hours. Otherwise, stations are open from 6:00 A.M. to 8:00 P.M. Some stations accept credit cards. Privately owned stations under the aegis of familiar international companies compete with the old state-run stations, but the government regulates the price of fuel.

Since the price of fuel is the same everywhere in Hungary, you might as well patronize the private stations, where you can count on finding rest rooms, an air pump and window-cleaning equipment. The availability of unleaded gasoline is indicated by a blue-bordered white sign bearing figures of two pumps—green for unleaded and black for leaded. Some stations accept major credit cards. Regular leaded gasoline has an octane rating of 86; the octane rating of super is 92. Unleaded gasoline is called *olommentes uzemanyag/benzin*. Unleaded regular gasoline has an octane rating of 92, super has one a rating of 95.

Road Signs

The word *pu* indicates a train station. The word *korut* means *boulevard*, *ter* means *square*, and *utca* means *street*. A sign reading *"Miskolc"* indicates a detour. First class national highways are numbered from 1 to 8; second class roads are numbered from 10 to 89. Minor roads have two numbers, the first being the number of the road and the second reflecting how far relative to other roads the road is from the capital—the higher the number the further away.

Detour for vehicles over 15 metric tons

Lane reserved for buses from 7 A.M. to 7 P.M.

Driving

The minimum age of a driver is 18 years. Unless they're in a child-restraint seat, children must be at least 12 years of age and over 1.5 meters tall to sit up front. The use of seat belts is compulsory for front-seat passengers. Helmets are compulsory for motorcyclists and their passengers riding machines which have 50 cc or larger engines and which can reach speeds of over 50 kph (30 mph). The legal blood alcohol limit is 80 mg. Speed limits are as follows: 50 kph (31 mph) in built-up areas, 80 kph (50 mph) outside built-up areas, 100 kph (62 mph) on divided highways, and 120 kph (74 mph) on expressways. Cars with a trailer or caravan are limited as follows: 50 kph (31 mph) in built-up areas, 70 kph (44 mph) outside built-up areas or on divided highways, 80 kph (50 mph) on expressways.

Trams and buses always have priority. Pedestrians have priority at marked pedestrian crossings and at intersections, but they don't have priority between tram loading islands and the far sidewalks. Bicycle lanes are indicated by a continuous yellow stripe.

Outside built-up areas headlights must be used night and day; motorcycles must use them everywhere. Use of horns is not allowed in built-up areas between 10:00 P.M. and 6:00 A.M.; rather, headlights should be used to give warning. In Budapest and other towns and villages along main roads, horns are always prohibited except in cases of immediate and extreme danger.

Passing should occur on the left. But where tram rails run in the center of the road, trams or other vehicles turning left must be passed on the right. Buses leaving stops have priority after the driver has signalled her intention to pull away.

Fines of up to 5000 Ft may be paid on the spot to police, or you can pay them within 14 days via the mail; credit cards are not accepted.

Parking

The center of Budapest is closed to traffic. Vehicles whose axle weight is less than 1 metric ton (1000 kg) are allowed to park on the sidewalk where parking is not prohibited (a situation indicated by a continuous white line on the pavement) and if a 1-meter wide lane is left for pedestrians. On two-way roads, vehicles must be parked on the right and in the direction of traffic. One one-ways, you can park on either side.

Camping

Camping is quite popular in Hungary. Most grounds stay open from May 1 to September 30 and are crowded during high season. Free-camping is illegal without the appropriate permission.

Banks

Open on weekdays from 8:00 A.M. to 1:00 P.M.

Shops

Open on weekdays from 10:00 A.M. to 6:00 P.M., until 3:00 P.M. on Saturday. Food sellers open at 6:00 or 7:00 A.M. On Thursday some shops stay open until 8:00 P.M. Smaller shops close for lunch.

National Holidays

Jan 1; Apr 4; Easter Mon; Labor Day; Aug 20; Nov 7; Dec 25, 26.

BBC Radio Hours and Corresponding Frequencies

5:00 A.M. to 7:30 A.M.: 9410, 12095 and 15575 kHz

7:30 A.M. to 4:00 P.M.: 12095 and 15070 kHz

4:00 P.M. to 10:30 P.M.: 9410, 12095 and 15070 kHz

Breakdown, Accidents or Emergency

Police, tel. 07; Fire, tel. 05; Ambulance, tel. 04; add another "0" prefix when calling emergency services from outside Budapest. Report accidents to the police and to the Hungarian State Insurance Company within 24 hours. The police give you a document which you must show at the border upon leaving the country; if you don't have this statement, you may face a long delay. The Hungarian Automobile Club operates the "Yellow Angels" breakdown service 24 hours a day, tel. 1 2528 000. Emergency telephones are in place along the major highways. The motoring club is Magyar Autóklub (MAK), FIA and AIT member, Rómer Flóris utca 4/a, Budapest II, tel. 1 2122 938, office hours on weekdays from 7:30 A.M. to 4:00 P.M. and on Friday until 3:00 P.M. For MAK 24-hour breakdown service in Budapest, tel. 1 691 831. Emergency telephones are located every 2 km along expresways.

Republic of Ireland

Customs

You may import free of duty the following goods if they were *not* taxed in the EC: 200 cigarettes or 100 cigarillos or 50 cigars or 250 grams of tobacco, 2 liters of wine, 1 liter of alcoholic beverage consisting of over 22 percent alcohol by volume or 2 liters of alcoholic beverage consisting of under 22 percent alcohol by volume, 50 grams of perfume, 0.25 liters of toilet water, and other goods to a value of IR£34 per person (IR£17 for persons under 15 years of age)—up to 12 liters of beer is included in this last allowance. You may import free of duty the following goods if they *were* taxed in the EC: 800 cigarettes, 10 liters of spirits, 45 liters of wine, and 55 liters of beer. Domestic cats and dogs from outside the United Kingdom, or other types of animals from outside Northern Ireland, cannot be imported. Irish Customs will issue a permit of temporary importation to drivers of caravans and to drivers of cars towing trailers and caravans. A vehicle that is temporarily imported cannot be driven by an Irish citizen.

Concessions for Hostellers

B&I Line offers discounts on their services between Britain and Ireland.

Irish Ferries offers discounts on their services between LeHarve, France, and Rosslare, Ireland, and between Cherbourg, France, and Rosslare, Ireland

Stena Sealink Line offers 25 percent discounts on their services between Britian and Ireland. The discount does not apply to service between Stranraer, Scotland, and Larne, Northern Ireland, on Friday and Saturday sailings during July and August.

Aran Ferries TEO offers a 10 percent discount on round trip to the Aran Islands.

Island Ferry Service offers a 14 percent discount on return journey from Baltimore to Cape Clear and a 25 percent discount on single fares for those over 18 years of age from Burtonport to Aranmore.

Michael Nee Car and MiniBus Hire, Canal Stage, Ballinafad, Co. Galway, offers a 10 percent discount on car and bike hire.

National Bus Company (CIE) offers discounts.

Rail/Bus Rambler Tours make discounted packages available to hostellers. Also, special rates for hostellers wishing to visit the Aran Islands from Indreabheán Youth Hostel.

Rent-a-Bike Centers at Lower Gardiner St., Dublin and Rosslare Harbor, Co. Wexford, offer a 10 percent reduction on bicycle hire.

Available from Killarney Youth Hostel: discounts on local tours and half price on Bus Éireann services from Killarney.

Tolls

There's a thirty-minute car ferry across the River Shannon between Tarbert in Co. Kerry to Killimer in Co. Clare. The ferry leaves Killimer every hour on the hour and Tarbert every hour on the half-hour. The cost per car is IR£7 one way; foot passengers pay IR£1.50. Contact Shannon Ferry Ltd., tel. 065 53124. There's a ten-minute car ferry operating continuously which takes one hour off the driving time between Ballyhack, Co. Wexford, and Passage East, Co. Waterford. First sailing occurs at 7:20 A.M. on weekdays, 9:30 A.M. on Sunday, with last sailing at 10:00 P.M. (summer) or 8:00 P.M. (winter). The cost per car, including passengers, is IR£3.50 one way; foot passengers pay 80p; car loads pay IR£5.50 for return passage; foot passengers pay IR£1, tel. 051 82480.

Fuel

Gasoline costs about IR£0.50/liter. Stations are usually open from 7:30 A.M. to 10:00 P.M., but some stay open 24 hours. Credit cards are accepted. Leaded super gasoline has an octane rating of 98; the octane rating of unleaded super is 95.

Road Signs

Primary highways are marked by an *N* (for *National)* and a number between one and twenty-five. Secondary highways are marked by an *N* and a number above fifty. County roads are marked with an *R* (for *Regional)*. All *T (Trunk)* and *L (Link)* routes are being renumbered as *N* or *R* roads; you'll encounter both old and new signs. What's more, road signs are often in both Irish (Gaelic) and English; but in the northwest, most are solely in Irish. The "yield" sign is a red triangle with its point down and bearing the words "Yield Right of Way" or *"Geill sli"*. Distances are marked in kilometers on the new green signposts and in miles on the old white signposts. Speed limits tend to be listed in miles per hour. Be sure you have the correct papers if you wanna drive between Ireland and Northern

Ireland. Don't drive on roads near the border which are marked "Unapproved Road".

Driving

Driving is on the left. The minimum age of a driver is 17 years. Children must be at least 12 years of age to sit in the front seat (unless the seat is equipped with a child restraint). The use of seat belts is compulsory for front-seat passengers. Helmets are compulsory for motorcyclists and their passengers. The legal blood alcohol limit is 100 mg. Generally, speed limits are as follows: 48 kph (30 mph) in built-up areas, 96 kph (60 mph) outside built-up areas, and 112 kph (70 mph) on expressways. These limits also apply to vehicle combinations.

Horns cannot be used between 11:30 P.M. and 7:00 A.M. It's illegal to use fog lights except in fog or falling snow.

Parking

Except where there are yellow lines on the road and except within a bus stop area, any restrictions you encounter are lifted after 6:00 P.M. Penalties for dangerous parking are stiff. Parking meters are checked from 8:00 A.M. to 6:30 P.M. from Monday through Saturday; maximum parking time is 2 hours. Fines may be collected on the spot for parking violations. Tip lot attendants about 20p when you exit. Cork and Limerick employ the parking disc system in their central areas. A disc allows for 1 to 3 hours of parking.

Banks

Open on weekdays from 10:00 A.M. to 12:30 P.M. and from 1:30 P.M. to 3:00 P.M.

Shops

Open from 9:00 A.M. to 5:30 P.M. every day but Sunday.

National Holidays

Jan 1; Mar 17; Easter; first Mon in June and Aug; last Mon in Oct; Dec 25.

BBC Radio Hours and Corresponding Frequencies

5:00 A.M. to 7:30 A.M.: 648, 9410 and 15575 kHz

7:30 A.M. to 4:00 P.M.: 648, 9750 and 12095 kHz

4:00 P.M. to 10:30 P.M.: 6195, 9410 and 12095 kHz

Breakdown, Accident or Emergency

Police, Fire, and Ambulance, tel. 999. Royal Irish Automoble Club, Dawson St. 34, Dublin, C.2, tel. 01 77 51 41.

Italy

Customs

You may import free of duty the following goods if they were *not* taxed in the EC: 300 cigarettes or 150 cigarillos or 75 cigars, 1.5 liters of spirits, 5 liters of still wine, 75 milliliters of perfume. You may import free of duty the following goods if they *were* taxed in the EC: 400 cigarettes and cigars or 500 grams of tobacco, 1 liter of spirits, and 2 liters of still wine. Two still cameras and one video camera may be imported free of duty. A maximum of 2 million lire in bank notes may be imported or exported. It's illegal to import or carry spare fuel.

Tolls

Tickets are obtained upon entry to the expressway system and paid upon exiting. Tolls (except in Sicily) can be paid with cash or a *Viacard*. Motorists can purchase a 50,000 or 90,000 lire *Viacard* from toll booths, fuel stations, some banks, tourist offices, and tobacconists. *Viacards* are accepted on all routes except the A18 and A20. At automatic barriers, the card should be inserted into a slot on the controlling machine. Credit cards are not accepted as payment for the *Viacard*. Vehicles are classified as follows.

(1) Car whose height as measured vertically from the front axle is less than 1.3 meter, or a motorcycle.

(2) Three-wheeled vehicle or a vehicle whose height as measured vertically from the front axle is greater than 1.3 meters. Tolls for these vehicles are virtually the same amount as tolls for category-1 vehicles.

(3) Vehicle or combination of vehicles with 3 axles. Tolls for these vehicles are, on average, 29 percent greater than tolls for category-1 vehicles.

(4) Vehicle or combination of vehicles with 4 axles. Tolls for these vehicles are, on average, 2 times greater than tolls for category-1 vehicles.

(5) Vehicle or combination of vehicles with 5 axles. Tolls for these vehicles are, on average, 2.42 times greater than tolls for category-1 vehicles.

Route	Toll for a Category-1 Vehicle
A1 Milano to Bologna	16,000 lire
A1 Milano to Roma	44,000
A1 Milano to Napoli	60,500
A1 & A21 Torino to Piacenza	16,000
A3 Napoli to Salerno	1200
A4 Torino to Milano (Ghisolfa)	9500
A4 Milano to Venezia (Mestre)	21,000
A4 & A21 Piacenza to Brescia	6000
A4 & A23 Palmanova to Udine	2100
A5 Torino to Aosta	12,500
A5 Ibrea to Santhià	2500
A6 Torino to Savona	13,000
A7 Milano to Genova	12,000
A8 Milano to Varese/ Sesto Calende	3200
A9 Milano to Como/ Brogeda, Switz.	4100
A10 Genova to Savona Vado	4000
A10 Savona Vado to France	19,000
A11 Firenze to Pisa	6000
A12 Genova to Rosignano	24,500
A12 Rome to Citavecchia	5000
A13 Bologna to Padova	9000
A14 Bologna to Taranto	56,500
A14 & A25 Bologna to Pescara	25,500
A15 Parma to La Spezia	12,500
A16 Napoli to Canosa	20,500
A18 Messina to Catania	4900
A19 & A20 Cefalu to Buonfornello	1300
A20 Messina to Furiano	9500
A21 Torino to Piacenza	16,000
A22 Brénnero to Modena	28,000
A23 Udine to Tarvisio	8000
A24 Roma to L'Aquila to Teramo	11,500
A24 & A14 Brénnero to Verona	21,000
A25 Roma to Pescara	13,500
A26 Genova to Arona	14,000
A26 Voltri to Tortona	6000
A27 Venezia (Mestre) to Vittoria Veneto	5500
A30 Caserta to Nola to Salerno	4500
A31 Vicenza to Piovene Rocchette	2500

The following tunnels connect Italy to Austria, France or Switzerland and require a toll.

SS26D/A40-N205's (E25's) Mont Blanc Tunnel between Entrèves and Chamonix, France: 90–175FF for a car (depending on wheel base), 175FF for a car towing a trailer or caravan, and 90FF for a motorcycle. Special rates for those making the round trip within 72 hours.

SS35/N6's (E70's) Frèjus Tunnel between Bardonecchia and Modane, France, is open all year: 90–175FF for a car (depending on wheel base); 175FF for a car towing a trailer or caravan; 90FF for a motorcycle. Minimum speed of 60 kph, maximum of 80 kph.

SS27/A21's (E27 or E21's) Grand St. Bernard Tunnel runs between Aosta and Bourg St. Pierre, Switzerland, and is open all year: 27 SwF for a car, 27 SwF for a car towing a trailer or caravan, 56.5 SwF for a caravan, and 27 SwF for a motorcycle. Customs is on the Swiss side, where there's a fuel station, money exchange bureau, and restaurant.

SS33-SS337/A9-A19's (E62's) Simplon rail tunnel service that runs from Domodossola to Brig, Switzerland, operates all year.

Tolls are charged on the following mountain passes.

A22/A13's Brenner Pass to the Tyrol: AS 130 for car, van or caravan having up to 9 seats; AS 170 for a car towing a trailer or caravan; AS 100 for a motorcycle.

SS44B/B186's Timmelsjoch Pass from Merano to Ötz, Austria: car single, AS 80; car return, AS 120; motorcycle single, AS 50; motorcycle return, AS 70. 2509 meters; closed from early October to late June; maximum grade is 14.3 percent, minimum width is 3.72 meters (12 ft.); very difficult; open only to private cars not towing trailers or caravans.

Non-toll Mountain Passes

Non-toll mountain passes tend to be much more difficult to negotiate than the passes which charge a toll. If you're driving a vehicle, such as a caravan, that's not allowed on or recommended for some of the following passes or if you wanna travel quickly across or through the mountains, a mountain pass or tunnel which charges a toll tends to be close by.

SS12/B182's Brenner Pass, Bolzano to Innsbruck, Austria. 1375 meters; usually open in winter; tire chains are sometimes necessary in winter; maximum grade is 14.3 percent; minimum width is 6.2 meters (20 ft.); especially scenic; busiest transalpine pass; closed to vehicles towing anything but a luggage trailer; not recommended for caravans.

SS20/N204's Col de Tende Pass, Borgo San Dalmazzo to La Giandola, France. 1321 meters; usually open, but closed from 9:00 A.M. to 6:00 P.M.; maximum gradient 9 percent; minimum width is 5.58 meters (18 ft.); no caravans allowed in the winter.

SS21/D900's Larche/Argentera Pass, Cuneo to Barcelonnette, France. 1994 meters; closed occasionally from December through March; maximum grade is 8.3 percent; minimum width is 3.1 meters (10 ft.); OK for caravans.

SS23's Sestriere Pass, Cesana Torinese to Turin. 2032 meters; usually open; maximum grade is 10 percent; minimum width is 5 meters (16 ft.); especially scenic; OK for caravans.

SS24/N94's Montgenevre Pass, Turin to Briançon, France. 1850 meters; usually open; maximum grade is 9 percent; minimum width is 5 meters (16 ft.); tire chains required in winter; especially scenic; OK for caravans.

SS25/N6's Mt. Cenis Pass, Turin to Chambéry, France. 2083 meters; closed from early November to mid May; maximum grade is 12.5 percent; minimum width is 5 meters (16 ft.); OK for caravans.

SS26/N90's Petit St. Bernard Pass, Aosta to Bourg-St.-Maurice, France. 2188 meters; closed from mid October to mid June; maximum grade is 8.3 percent; minimum width is 5 meters (16 ft.); no vehicles over 15 metric tons (15,000 kg); not recommended for caravans.

SS27/A21's Great St. Bernard Pass, Aosta to Martigny, Switzerland. 2473 meters; closed from October through June; maximum grade is 10 percent; minimum width is 5 meters (16 ft.); chains may be necessary on approach; closed to vehicles towing another vehicle; not recommended for caravans.

SS36's Splügen Pass, Chiavenna to Splügen, Switzerland. 2113 meters; closed from early November through June; maximum grade is 13.3 percent; minimum width is 3.1 meters (10 ft.); maximum vehicle height is 2.84 meters (9 feet 2 inches); maximum vehicle width is 2.32 meters (7.5 ft.); especially scenic; not recommended for caravans.

SS38's Stelvio Pass, Bormio to Spondigna. 2756 meters; closed from October through late June; maximum grade is 12.5 percent; minimum width is 4 meters (13 ft.); especially scenic; no vehicles allowed that are over 9.3 meters (30 ft.); not recommended for caravans.

SS38's Umbrail Pass, Bormio to Santa Maria, Switzerland. 2500 meters; closed from early November through early June; maximum grade is 9 percent; minimum width is 4.34 meters (14 ft.); no trailer or vehicles over 2.32 meters (7.5 ft.) wide; not recommended for caravans.

SS39's Aprica Pass, Edolo to Tresenda. 1176 meters; usually open; maximum grade is 9 percent; minimum width is 4 meters (13 ft.); especially scenic; tire chains may be necessary; OK for caravans.

SS40/B315's Resia Pass, Malles to Landeck, Austria. 1504 meters; usually open; maximum grade is 10 percent; minimum width is 6.2 meters (20 ft.); especially scenic; OK for caravans.

SS42's Mendola Pass, Bolzano to Fondo. 1363 meters; usually open; maximum grade is 12.5 percent; minimum width is 5 meters (16 ft.); especially scenic; OK for caravans.

SS42's Tonale Pass, Edolo to Bolzano. 1882 meters; usually open; maximum grade is 12.5 percent; minimum width is 5 meters (16 ft.); OK for caravans.

SS44's Monte Giovo Pass, Merano to Vipiteno. 2094 meters; closed from November through May; maximum grade is 12.5 percent; minimum width is 4 meters (13 ft.); caravans not allowed.

SS46's Fugazze Pass, Roberto to Vicenza. 1160 meters; usually open; maximum grade is 14.2 percent; minimum width is 3.1 meters (10 ft.); not recommended for caravans.

SS48's Falzarego Pass, Ora to Cortina. 2117 meters; closed occasionally from December through April; maximum grade is 8.3 percent; minimum width is 5 meters (16 ft.); recommended for powerful cars only.

SS48's Pordoi Pass, Arabba to Canazei. 2239 meters; closed occasionally from December through April; maximum grade is 10 percent; minimum width is 5 meters (16 ft.); especially scenic; not recommended for caravans.

SS48's Tre Croci Pass, Cortina to Auronzo. 1809 meters; closed occasionally from December through March; maximum grade is 11 percent; minimum width is 5 meters (16 ft.); especially scenic; OK for caravans.

SS50's Rolle Pass, Predazzo to Primiero. 1971 meters; closed occasionally from December through March; maximum grade is 9 percent; minimum width is 5 meters (16 ft.); especially scenic; OK for caravans.

SS52's Mauria Pass, Pieve di Cadore to Piani. 1297 meters; usually open; maximum grade is 7 percent; minimum width is 5 meters (16 ft.); OK for caravans.

SS52B/B110's Plöcken Pass, Tolmezzo to Kötschach-Mauthen, Austria. 1363 meters; occasionally closed from December through April; maximum grade is 14.3 percent; minimum width is 4.8 meters (16 ft.) at border, expect delays resulting from heavy traffic on summer weekends; marginally negotiable by caravans.

SS239's Campiglio Pass, Tione di Trento to Dimaro. 1682 meters; closed occasionally from December through March; maximum grade is 11.8 percent; especially scenic; OK for caravans.

SS241's Costalunga Pass, Cortina to Bolzano. 1752 meters; closed occasionally from December through April; maximum grade is 14.3 percent; minimum width is 5 meters (16 ft.); especailly scenic; no caravans allowed.

SS242's Sella Pass, Ortisei to Canazei. 2240 meters; closed occasionally from late November to early June; maximum grade is 11 percent; minimum width is 5 meters (16 ft.); especially scenic; not recommended for caravans.

SS243's Gardena Pass, Cortina to Auronzo. 2121 meters; closed occasionally from December through June; maximum grade is 12.5 percent; minimum width is 5 meters (16 ft.); especially scenic; not recommended for caravans.

SS244's Campologno Pass, Cortina to Auronzo. 1875 meters; closed occasionally from December through March; maximum grade is 12.5 percent; minimum width is 5 meters (16 ft.); especially scenic; OK for caravans.

SS300's Gavia Pass, Bormio to Ponte di Legno. 2620 meters; closed from October through July; maximum grade is 18 percent; minimum width is 4.34 meters (14 ft.); especially scenic; not recommended for caravans.

Fuel

Fuel stations along expressways are open 24 hours. Along other roads, fuel stations are open from 7:00 A.M. to 12:30 P.M. and from 3:30 P.M. to 7:30 P.M. from May through September; from October through April the stations close at 7:00 P.M. Credit cards are accepted. Only 25 percent of non-expressway fuel stations are open on Sunday and public holidays; those that are open on Sunday close on Monday. If a fuel station is closed, it displays its hours and the location of the next station. Some stations, however, have pumps that accept bills automatically. Gasoline costs about 1500 lire per liter. Fuel prices are regulated by the government, so don't waste time shopping around. Regular leaded gasoline has an octane rating of 85 or 88; the octane rating of super is 98 or 100. Unleaded gasoline is called *benzina sensa piombo*, *super bleifri*, or *super senza*. Unleaded super gasoline has an octane rating of 95. Diesel is called *gasolio*. LPG is called *GPL (gas liquido)*. It's illegal to carry spare fuel.

Road Signs

Centro Paese	Town center
Entrata	Entrance
Incrocio	Crossroads
Lavori in corso	Roadworks ahead
Parcheggio	Parking ramp
Passaggio a livello	Train crossing
Rallentare	Slow
Senso Vietato	No entry
Sosta Autorizzata	Parking allowed during times shown
Sosta Vietata	No parking
Stazione Di Polizia	Police station
Svolta	Bend
Tutte le Direzion	All directions
Uscita	Exit

Vietato Ingresso Veicoli	No entry for vehicles
Vietato Transito Autocarri	Closed to heavy vehicles

Autostrade (toll expressways), *superstrade* (non-toll express highways), *strade stratali* (main roads), *strade provinciali* (secondary roads) and *strade comunali* (local roads) combine to offer efficient and interesting options for driving. The word *stazione* indicates a train station.

Resticted parking

Stop when meeting public transport bus on mountain road

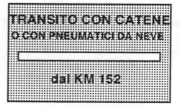

Use snow tires from km 152

Lane reserved for slow vehicles

Traffic in parallel lanes

Driving

The minimum age of a driver is 18 years. Children 4–12 years of age must use a special restraint. The use of seat belts is compulsory both for front- and rear-seat passengers. Helmets are compulsory for motorcyclists and their passengers. The legal blood alcohol limit is 80 mg. Speed limits are as follows: 50 kph (30 mph) in built-up areas, 90 kph (55 mph) on secondary roads outside built-up areas, 110 kph (68 mph) on main roads outside built-up areas, and 130 kph (81 mph) on expressways. On expressways, cars with engines smaller than 1090 cc and motorcycles with engines smaller than 150 cc are limited to 110 kph (68 mph). Cars towing a caravan or trailer, and caravans over 12 tons, are limited to 70 kph (44 mph) outside built-up areas and to 80 kph (50 mph) on expressways. Caravans between 3.5 and 12 tons are limited to 80 kph (50 mph) outside built-up areas, and to 100 kph (62 mph) on expressways. Expressway speeds are reduced to 110 kph (68 mph) during the following: Saturday and Sunday, the Thursday before Easter through the Wednesday after, midweek national holidays, December 20 through January 7, and from the Saturday before the second Sunday in July through the first Sunday in September. All vehicles—including trailers— whose maximum legal speed is less than 30 kph must have a sticker indicating their maximum legal speed affixed to their rear. These stickers are sold at fuel stations. Violation of this requirement may result in fines of between 30,000 and 120,000 lire.

Headlights are required from half an hour after sunset to half an hour before sunrise. Headlights should also be used under bridges and in tunnels. Only use foglights in conditions of poor visibility. Use of the horn is prohibited in built-up areas except in cases of immediate and extreme danger; at night flash your horns instead. Outside built-up areas, however, you must use the horn to signal your intention to pass.

The middle lane of three-lane roads is for passing. Passing on the right is permitted when the driver ahead has signaled a left turn and has moved to the center of the road or when multiple lanes are traveling in your direction.

Anything, such as a bicycle, hanging off the end of a vehicle must be tagged with a reflective red and white striped sign 50 cm square. The signs are sold at most automotive shops in Italy. You may be fined 100,000 lire if you fail to satisfy this requirement.

Police are empowered to revoke your license and to collect fines on the spot. To thwart car theives, police are increasingly subjecting foreign-registered vehicles to spot checks. To pass such a check, operators must present vehicle and personal identification documents— including written permission from the owner if it's a borrowed vehicle. Vehicles which don't pass may be confiscated.

Parking

Generally, parking is on the right side of the road. Parking in a *Blue Zone* or *Zona Disco* is for limited time periods. Parking discs for these zones may be obtained at fuel stations, tourist offices, and motor club offices. When parked in these zones from 9:00 A.M. to 2:30 P.M. and from 4:00 P.M. to 8:00 P.M. on Monday through Saturday (except holidays) your vehicle must display a parking disc. Maximum parking time during these periods is one hour. Some cities also have *Green Zones* or *Zona Verde* where parking is prohibited from 8:00 A.M. to 9:30 A.M. and from 2:30 P.M. to 4:00 P.M. on weekdays.

In Florence, all vehicles are banned from the city center from 7:30 A.M. to 6:30 P.M. on weekdays; visitors may enter the center in their vehicle during these times to load or unload but must then move on to park outside the center.

In Rome a sign reading *"zona tutelato"* indicates that parking is prohibited from 7:30 A.M. to 6:30 P.M. on weekdays; punishment for violating this ordinance may include a prison sentence.

In Venice, parking is very difficult to find. Park instead at one of the mainland car parks; you can take a bus or ferry from there to the city. The parking facility at Mestre, however, is a well-known haunt of thieves. In the Tronchetto garage, park on the left side, not on the right. These mainland facilities are linked to the island by ferry and bus services.

Naples (along with Seville, Spain) is Europe's most infamous lair of thieves. Furthermore, driving in Naples is notoriously difficult. Instead of taking your vehicle into Naples, stay on the Ischia or Sorrento Peninsula. For quick transport to the city, take the catamaran or *aliscafi.*

Camping

In high season it's best to arrive early in the day to get a spot in a popular campground. Free-camping is illegal without the appropriate permission, but it's quite tolerated regardless. Signs reading "Camper Service" or *"Euro-Relais"* indicate water and dumping facilities for motorhomes.

Banks

Open on weekdays from 8:30 A.M. to 1:30 P.M. and from 2:45 P.M. to 3:45 P.M.

Shops

Open on weekdays from 8:30 A.M. to 1:00 P.M. and from 3:30 or 4:00 P.M. to 7:30 or 8:00 P.M. Open until noon on Saturday.

National Holidays

Jan 1, Easter Mon; Apr 25; Labor Day; Aug 15; Nov 1; Dec 8, 25, 26.

BBC Radio Hours and Corresponding Frequencies

In the North:

5:00 A.M. to 7:30 A.M.: 6195, 9410 and 15575 kHz

7:30 A.M. to 4:00 P.M.: 12095 and 15070 kHz

4:00 P.M. to 10:30 P.M.: 6195, 9410 and 12095 kHz

In the South:

5:00 A.M. to 7:30 A.M.: 9410, 12095 and 15575 kHz

7:30 A.M. to 4:00 P.M.: 12095, 15070 and 17640 kHz

4:00 P.M. to 10:30 P.M.: 9410, 12095 and 15070 kHz

Breakdown, Accident or Emergency

Police, Fire, and Ambulance, tel. 113. The Automobile Club d'Italia (ACI), *FIA* and *AIT* member, Via Marsala 8, 00185 Rome, tel. 06 49921, office hours from 8:00 A.M. to 2:00 P.M. on Monday through Saturday, operates a breakdown service on all roads, tel. 116. This service offers free tows to visitors driving in Italy with foreign license plates or with a car rented at the Rome or Milan airports. Renters must show plane tickets and the rental contract to get the service free of charge. Another club is the Touring Club Italiano (TCI), *AIT* member, Corso Italia 10, 20122 Milan, tel. 02 85261, office hours from 9:00 A.M. to 6:00 P.M. on weekdays and from 8:30 A.M. to 12:30 P.M. on Saturday; tel. 8526263 for information on their breakdown service.

Luxembourg

Customs

Equivalent to Belgian customs allowances.

Fuel

Generally, major credit cards are accepted. Leaded super gasoline has an octane rating of 98. Unleaded gasoline is called *essence sans plomb.* Regular unleaded gasoline has an octane rating of 91; the octane rating of super is 95. It's illegal to carry spare fuel.

Road Signs

The word *gare* indicates a train station.

Driving

The minimum age of a driver is 18 years. Children under 12 years of age, or less than 1.5 meters tall, and seated in the front seat must be in a safety seat. The use of seat belts is compulsory for the driver and for passengers. The legal blood alcohol limit is 80 mg. Speed limits are as follows: 50 kph (30 mph) in built-up areas, 90 kph (56 mph) outside built-up areas, and 120 kph (74 mph) on expressways. Limits for cars towing a trailer are as follows: 75 kph (46 mph) outside built-up areas, and 90 kph (56 mph) on expressways.

Generally, traffic on the right has priority. Common knowledge of this rule supplants *Stop* and *Yield* signs in many cities.

Motorcycles must be operated with the headlights on—night and day. Do not use the horn in built-up areas or at night, except in the case of immediate and extreme danger. Use the horn outside built-up areas during daylight hours to warn of your intention to pass or to warn of your approach on mountain roads. Also use the horn in weather conditions that significantly restrict visibility. Flash your lights to indicate your intention to pass.

Passing is allowed on the left only.

Police are empowered to collect fines—usually equaling 500 LF per offense, but occasionally as high as 3000 LF—on the spot.

Parking

Blue Zone parking zones exist in Dudelange, Esch-sur-Alzette, Luxembourg City, and Wiltz.

Parking discs for these zones can be obtained from the ACL motoring club, police stations, shops, and tourist offices. Luxembourg city has parking meters and machines that dispense parking tickets. Wheel clamps are placed on illegally parked vehicles.

Camping

Free-camping without appropriate permission is illegal.

Banks

Generally open on weekdays from 8:30 A.M. to noon and from 1:30 P.M. to 4:30 P.M.

Shops

Open from 9:00 A.M. to noon and from 2:00 P.M. to 6:00 P.M. every day but Sunday.

National Holidays

Jan 1; Easter Mon; May Day; Ascension; Whit Mon; June 23; Aug 15; All Saints; All Souls; Dec 25, 26.

BBC Radio Hours and Corresponding Frequencies

5:00 A.M. to 7:30 A.M.: 648, 9410 and 15575 kHz

7:30 A.M. to 4:00 P.M.: 648, 9750 and 12095 kHz

4:00 P.M. to 10:30 P.M.: 6195, 9410 and 12095 kHz

Breakdown, Accident or Emergency

Police, Fire, and Ambulance, tel. 012. Automobile Club du Grand Duché de Luxembourg (ACL), *FIA* and *AIT*, 13 route de Longwy, Helfenterbruck, Bertrange, tel. 450045, office hours from 8:30 A.M. to noon and from 1:30 P.M. to 6:00 P.M. on weekdays.

Netherlands

Customs

You may import free of duty the following goods if they were *not* taxed in the EC: 200 cigarettes or 50 cigars or 100 cigarillos or 250 grams of tobacco, 2 liters of wine or 1 liter of alcohol consisting of more than 22 percent alcohol by volume, 50 grams of perfume or 25 centiliters of toilet water, and other goods to the value of Fl. 125. Limits are very lax on goods if they *were* taxed in the EC. For example, you may import free of duty the following such goods: 800 cigarettes, 10 liters of liquor consisting of over 22 percent alcohol by volume or 90 liters of wine or 110 liters of beer. Tobacco and alcohol allowances are for those at least 17 years of age. All personal items are considered free of duty, assuming you plan to take them with you when you leave. There is no limit on the import and export of Dutch currency. You can import 10 liters of spare fuel free of duty.

Concessions for Hostellers

North Sea Ferries offers discounts on its service between Rotterdam, Netherlands, and Hull, England.

Stena Sealink Line ferry services between Hoek van Holland, Netherlands, and Harwich, England, offers discounts of up to 40 percent.

Tolls

Between Breskens and Vlissingen and between Perkpolder and Kruiningen a car ferry runs across the Westerschelde estuary. Journey times are 20 minutes and 15 minutes, respectively, and journeys are frequent.

Waalbridge (Prins Willem Alexander Bridge): car (up to 800 kg), 2.90 Fl.; car (over 800 kg), 3.5 Fl.

Kiltunnel (Dordecht to Hoeske): 3.50 Fl. for cars and motorcycles.

Fuel

Gasoline or *benzine* costs around Fl. 1.73 per liter. Major credit cards are accepted. Leaded super gasoline has an octane rating of 98. Unleaded gasoline is called *loodvrije benzine*. Regular unleaded gasoline has an octane rating of 91; the octane rating of super is 95. Diesel is called *dieselolie*. LPG goes by its English name.

Road Signs

Doorgaand Verkeer	All directions
Doorgaand verkeer gestremd	No throughway
Langzaam rijden	Slow
Opspattend Grind	Loose surface
Parkeerplaats	Parking ramp
Politiebureau	Police station
Pas op: filevorming	Attention: single or double lane traffic ahead
Rechtsaf toegeslaan	Right turn allowed
Stadscentrum	Town center
Tegenliggers	Traffic from the opposite direction
Wegomlegging	Detour
Werk in uitvoering	Work in progress

International expressways are denoted by an *E*. Intranational expressways are signified by an *A*. Other highways are marked by an *N*. A blue sign bearing an illustration of a white house can mean children at play, pedestrians have priority, bicycles on the right have priority, or park only where you see a sign marked *P*. The word *station* indicates a train station. A traffic pillar with green on top and yellow running down its long axis indicates that motor vehicles may pass on either side but other traffic must go to the right only.

End of built-up area

Crossing for cyclists and moped riders

Compulsory route for vehicles with dangerous goods

B road (width and axle limits)

Driving

The minimum age of a driver is 18 years. To sit in the front seat, children must be at least 3 years of age and in a safety seat; younger children must sit in a safety seat in the rear. The use of seat belts is compulsory for front-seat passengers. Helmets are compulsory for motorcyclists and their passengers. The legal blood alcohol limit is 50 mg. Speed limits are as follows: 50 kph (30 mph) in built-up areas, 80 kph (50 mph) outside built-up areas, and 100 kph (62 mph) or 120 kph (74 mph) on expressways. The minimum speed limit on expressways is 70 kph (44 mph). Cars towing a trailer or caravan must observe an 80 kph (50 mph) limit outside built-up areas.

Priority roads are denoted by a white-bordered, orange, diamond-shaped sign or, of course, by the international priority sign. Trams have priority where roads of equal importance intersect. Bicyclists proceeding straight through an intersection always have priority. Cycle lanes exist on each side of most main roads. Cycle lanes denoted by broken lines may be used by motor vehicles if this does not interfere with cyclists. Pedestrians on crosswalks always have priority.

Use your horn whenever you present a risk to traffic. At night flash your headlights instead.

It's illegal to cross a continuous white line at any time, even when turning. Trams should be passed on the right unless it's safer to pass on the left. Signs which state that overtaking is prohibited do not apply to motorcycles.

In some areas, police are empowered to collect fines on the spot.

Parking

Vehicles parked publicly overnight need to be somehow illuminated unless they're in a parking ramp or in a built-up area and within 30 meters of a street light. Do not park near a bus stop where the road or curb or pavement is painted black-and-white or yellow. *Blue Zones* exist in most towns and are indicated by the standard No Parking sign bearing the words *"Parkeer Zone"*. (A series of slashes across the sign indicates the end of the zone.) Parking discs for these zones can be obtained from police stations, ANWB motoring club offices, and tobacconists. Wheel clamps are placed on illegally parked vehicles.

Camping

Campgrounds are generally of high quality and are rated from one to five with both stars and flags, the stars signifying the cleanliness of the campground and the flags representing the spectrum of facilities. Dump stations are rare. An International Camping Carnet is not required. There are many small grounds, usually located on farms, limited to ten sites. Free-camping without appropriate permission is illegal and is not well tolerated.

Banks

Open on weekdays from 9:00 A.M. to 4:00 P.M.

Shops

Open from 8:30 or 9:00 A.M. to 5:00 or 5:30 A.M. every day but Sunday. Some close for Monday morning. Some stay open until 9:00 P.M. on Thursday and Friday.

National Holidays

Jan 1; Good Fri; Easter Mon; April 30; May 5; Ascension; Whit Mon; Dec 25, 26.

BBC Radio Hours and Corresponding Frequencies

5:00 A.M. to 7:30 A.M.: 648, 9410 and 15575 kHz

7:30 A.M. to 4:00 P.M.: 648, 9750 and 12095 kHz

4:00 P.M. to 10:30 P.M.: 6195, 9410 and 12095 kHz

Breakdown, Accident or Emergency

Police, Fire, and Ambulance, tel. 0611. The most helpful motoring club is Koninklijke Nederlandsche Toeristenbond (ANWB), *AIT* member, Wassenaarsweg 220, the Hague, tel. 070 314 7147, office hours from 8:00 A.M. to 5:30 P.M. on weekdays. Uniformed ANWB mechanics patrol the highways 24 hours a day in their trademark yellow cars. The ANWB also maintains phone boxes along major roads. You may be required to buy temporary membership in the ANWB to take advantage of these services. Another motoring club is Koninklijke Nederlandsche Automobil Club (KNAC), *FIA* member, Binckhorstlaan 115, Den Haag 2516 BA, tel. 070 383 1612, office hours from 9:00 A.M. to 5:00 P.M. on weekdays.

Norway

Customs

Non-EC citizens over 16 years of age may import the following free of duty: 400 cigarettes or 500 grams of tobacco goods, souvenirs, and gifts to a value of NOK 3500. Persons over 20 years of age may import the following free of duty: 1 liter of wine, 1 liter of liquor or 2 liters of wine or beer. You can import 15 liters of spare fuel free of duty.

Concessions for Hostellers

Color Line offers a 10 percent discount on fares for persons under 26 years of age on its ferry services between Kristiansand, Norway, and Hirtshals,

Denmark, and between Oslo, Norway, and Hirtshals, Denmark.

Fjord Line/Askøy-Bergen Rutlag Coastal Express Service boat service offers a 25 percent discount on fares between Bergen, Norway, and Stavanger, Norway.

Flagg-Renten Coastal Express Service offers a 25 percent discount on fares between Bergen, Norway, and Stavanger, Norway.

Larvik Line offers a 10 percent discount off fares between Larvik, Norway, and Fredrikshavn, Denmark.

Stena Line offers a 10 percent discount off fares on the services below (tickets are obtainable only at Terra Nova Travel Sections and valid for Monday through Thursday travel from June through August).

> Oslo, Norway— —Fredrikshavn, Denmark.
> Moss, Norway— —Fredrikshavn, Denmark.
> Göteborg, Sweden— —Fredrikshavn, Denmark.

Tolls

For a brochure describing in great detail the myriad internal ferry services of Norway, contact the Norwegian Tourist Board.

There's an NOK 11 toll on vehicles up to 3.5 metric tons (3500 kg) entering the center of Oslo, and there's an NOK 10 toll on the E6 west of Oslo, near Drammen. Vehicles entering the center of Bergen must pay an NOK 5 toll on

weekdays but not on weekends or public holidays. There's a similar 10K toll charged on vehicles entering Trondheim's city center.

Road Closings

Several important roads are kept open all year. Road 11 from Oslo to Stavanger to Bergen, across Haukelifjell mountain, is one such road. So is the E6 from Oslo to Trondheim, across Dovrefjell mountain. Some roads are closed for short periods because of snow, and others are closed by decree for the whole winter. The following roads are closed for some period during the year; the road number is given, followed by the road's county or the two cities it connects, and finally the tentative dates during which weather may force the road to be closed.

E89, Skarsvåg to Nordkapp, late October to late April.

Road 13/5, Gaularfjell, late December to mid May.

Road 7, Hardangervidda, normally open all year.

Road 13, Vikafjell, normally open all year.

Road 27, Venabygdefjellet, early January to late March.

Road 45, Hunnendalsveien, normally open all year.

Road 51, Valdresflya, late November to late April.

Road 55, Sognefjellsvegen, early December to mid May.

Road 58, from Highway 15 to Geiranger, November through May.

Road 63, Geiranger, mid November to late May.

Road 63, Trollstigveien, late October to late May.

Road 220, Venabygdfjellet, late February to mid March.

Road 252, from Tyin to Eidsburgarden, late October to early June.

Road 258, Gml. Strynefjellsvei, late September to early June.

Road 520, Hellandsbygd to Røldal, early December to mid June.

Road 882, Storvik to Bardines, normally open all year.

Road 886, from Vintervollen to Gr. Jacobselv, not closed.

Fuel

Gasoline costs about NOK 7.50 per liter. Diesel costs half this much. Fuel stations are closed from 7:00 P.M. to 5:00 A.M. on weekdays. During weekends stations are open only in highly populated areas. Major credit cards are accepted. Leaded super gasoline has an octane rating of 98. Unleaded gasoline is called *blyfritt kraftstoff* or *blyfri* and has an octane rating of 95.

Roads Signs

Arbeide pa Vegen	Roadwork ahead
Bakketopp	Hill top
Enveiskjøring	One-way traffic
Ferist	Cattle grid
Gammel Veg	Old road
Grøfterens	Ditching work
Ikke Møte	No passing, single line traffic
Kjør Sakte	Drive slowly
Løs Grus	Loose surface
Møteplass	Passing bay
Omkjøring	Diversion
Rasteplass	Rest stop
Sentrum	City center
Svake Kanter	Soft shoulder
Veg under Anlegg	Road under construction
Veiarbeide	Roadworks

The Norwegian word *stasjon* indicates a train station.

Parking prohibited (upper panel)
Parking allowed (lower panel)

Sightseeing

2-hour parking from 8 A.M. to 6 P.M. (4 P.M. on Saturday)

2-hour parking from 8 A.M. to 5 P.M.

Road merges (black lane has priority)

Driving

Snow tires are compulsory in the winter. The minimum age of a driver is 17 years, but you must be 18 to rent or borrow a Norwegian-registered vehicle. The use of seat belts is compulsory for front- and rear-seat passengers. Helmets are compulsory for motorcyclists and their passengers. The legal blood alcohol limit is 50 mg. Speed limits are as follows: 50 kph (30 mph) in built-up areas, 80 kph (50 mph) or 90 kph (56 mph) outside built-up areas, and 80 kph (50 mph) or 90 kph (56 mph) on expressways. Cars towing a caravan or trailer are limited outside built-up areas to 80 kph (50 mph) if the towed vehicle has brakes, and to 60 kph (37 mph) if the towed vehicle does not have brakes.

Trams always have priority. In mountainous areas, vehicles traveling downhill have priority; vehicles going up the hill must reverse into a passing bay if there's not enough room for two vehicles to pass.

Headlights must be on at all times while driving. Excessive use of horns is illegal.

Trams in Oslo should be passed on the right, but they may be passed on the left if there's no room on the right or if traveling on a one-way street.

Police are empowered to collect fines on the spot.

Parking

Parking on main roads or on bends is not allowed. A sign that reads *"All stans forbudt"* means *No stopping allowed*. Parking meters are differentiated as follows: Yellow = one-hour, Gray = two-hour, Brown = three-hour. Parking overnight on the roadside is forbidden. Parking regulations are strictly enforced.

Camping

Many campgrounds require an International Camping Carnet. Open fires are not allowed. Often only 2 Amps of power come through the electrical hookups. PRO-GAS plants in Bergen, Kristiansand, Oslo, Stavanger, and Trondheim can fill built-in propane tanks. As described earlier free-camping is generally practiced; just stay at least 150 meters from the nearest residence for no more than two nights, and ask permission if it seems the thing to do.

Banks

Open on weekdays from 8:30 A.M. to 1:30 A.M. and from 2:45 P.M. to 3:45 P.M.

Shops

Open on weekdays from 9:00 A.M. to 5:00 P.M. Open until 1:00 or 2:00 P.M. on Saturday.

National Holidays

Jan 1; Maunday Thur; Good Fri; Easter Mon; Labor Day; May 17; Whit Mon; Ascension; Dec 24 (part), 25, 26.

BBC Radio Hours and Corresponding Frequencies

In the North:

5:00 A.M. to 7:30 A.M.: 9410 and 12095 kHz

7:30 A.M. to 4:00 P.M.: 12095 and 15070 kHz

4:00 P.M. to 10:30 P.M.: 9410, 12095 and 15070 kHz

In the South:

5:00 A.M. to 7:30 A.M.: 6195 and 9410 kHz

7:30 A.M. to 4:00 P.M.: 9410 and 12095 kHz

4:00 P.M. to 10:30 P.M.: 6195, 9410 and 12095 kHz

Breakdown, Accident or Emergency

In Oslo: Police, tel. 002; Ambulance, tel. 003. Elsewhere: Police, tel. 112; Fire, tel. 110; Ambulance, tel. 113. The Norges Automobil-

Forbund (NAF), *AIT* member, Storgt. 2, 0155 Oslo, tel. 22 34 15 00, office hours from 8:30 A.M. to 4:00 P.M. on weekdays and from 8:30 A.M. to 1:00 P.M. on Saturday. The NAF maintains emergency telephones along mountain roads and operates a 24-hour service that patrols main roads, tel. 22 34 16 00. In the Oslo area you can also contact the Falken Redningskorps A/s for assistance, tel. 22 23 25 85. Another motoring club is Kongelig Norsk Automobilklub (KNA), *FIA* member, Drammenasveien 20-C, 0255 Oslo, tel. 22 56 10 09, office hours from 8:30 A.M. to 4:00 P.M. on weekdays (3:00 P.M. in summer). If you must use a telephone directory, look under *redningstjeneste*. During the summer, road patrols monitor most mountain passes and some main roads.

Poland

Customs

Visitors over 17 years of age may import the following free of duty: items for personal use, 2 cameras and up to 24 rolls of film, 250 cigarettes or 50 cigars or 250 grams of tobacco, 5 liters of beer, 2 liters of wine, 1 liter of spirits, and goods to the value of $100. The import or export of Polish legal tender without an appropriate permit is forbidden. There are no limits set on the import of foreign legal tender into Poland. Foreign tourists are requested to declare in writing all currencies which they bring into Poland. Vehicles permanently registered abroad are subject to temporary customs clearance, i.e., for the duration of the traveler's stay in Poland. Should such a vehicle not be taken out of the country, the owner is obliged to pay customs duty and turnover tax. You may import 10 liters of spare fuel free of duty.

The following are designated border crossings.

German: Gubin, Kolbaskowo, Krajnik, Dolny, Lubieszyn, Olszyna, Sieniawka, Slubice, Swiecko, Zgorzelec.

Czech: Boboszow, Chalupki, Cieszyn, Jakuszyce, Kudowa-Slone, Lubawka, Pietrowice, Zawidow.

Slovak: Chyzne, Lysa, Polana, Barwinek, Piwniczna.

Ukrainian: Dorohusk, Hrebenne, Medyka.

Byelorussian: Terespol, Kukuryki.

Lithuanian: Ogrodniki.

The Polish Motoring Association (PZM) maintains offices at all border crossings. These offices provide such services as currency exchange, insurance sales, sales of maps and tourist guides, and information about traveling conditions in Poland.

Road Signs

Expressways are designated by the letter *E*.

Fuel

Gasoline costs zl 12,266 per liter. Fuel stations are usually open 8:00 A.M. to 7:00 P.M. Some stations in large towns stay open 24 hours. Regular leaded gasoline has an octane rating of 86; the octane rating of super is 94 or 98. Unleaded gasoline is called *benzyna bezolowiu*. Regular unleaded gasoline has an octane rating of 82.5; the octane rating of super is 91.

Driving

The minimum age of a driver is 18 years. Children under 10 years of age must be in a safety seat to sit in the front. The use of seat belts is compulsory for front-seat passengers. Helmets are compulsory for motorcyclists and their passengers. The legal blood alcohol limit is 20 mg. Speed limits are as follows: 60 kph (37 mph) in built-up areas, 90 kph (56 mph) outside built-up areas, 110 kph (68 mph) on expressways, and 70 kph (44 mph) for cars with a caravan or trailer traveling outside built-up areas or on expressways. The minimum speed limit on expressways is 40 kph (24 mph). Apart from built-up areas there are residential zones—marked by entry/exit signs—where the speed limit is 20 kph (12 mph).

There are large numbers of horse-drawn wagons carrying agricultural products on the public roads during harvest periods. Unlit horse-drawn wagons are a particular hazard.

Motorcycles outside built-up areas must be operated with headlights on—night and day. Between November 1 and March 1, *all* vehicles must use headlights both night and day.

Use of horns is illegal in built-up areas. Use your vehicle's headlights to warn of your intention to pass. However, when passing in poor visibility you must use your vehicle's horn to give warning.

Trams may be passed on the right; but when a tram stops and there is no island to accept disembarking passengers, drivers must yield to the passengers who cross to the sidewalk.

Police are empowered to collect fines of between zl 25,000 and 500,000 on the spot; they must issue a receipt.

Parking

If parked in darkness on an unlighted street, a vehicle's parking lights must be on. Vehicles weighing less than 2.5 metric tons (2500 kg) can park with one set of wheels on the sidewalk as long as a path remains for pedestrians. Do not park within 5 meters of a pedestrian crossing.

Camping

Most campgrounds are open from mid June to mid September, with the onsite stores open only during July and August. Don't count on finding a washing machine. Though illegal, free-camping without the appropriate permission is quite tolerated.

Banks

Open on weekdays from 8:00 or 9:00 A.M. to 3:00 or 6:00 P.M.

Shops

Open from 9:00 or 11:00 A.M. to 7:00 P.M. every day but Sunday. Food sellers open at 5:00 A.M. Department stores open at 11:00 A.M.

National Holidays

Jan 1; Easter Mon; Labor Day; May 3; Corpus Christi; July 22; Aug 15; Nov 1, 11; Dec 25, 26.

BBC Radio Hours and Corresponding Frequencies

5:00 A.M. to 7:30 A.M.: 6195, 9410 and 15575 kHz

7:30 A.M. to 4:00 P.M.: 9410, 12095 and 15070 kHz

4:00 P.M. to 10:30 P.M.: 6195, 9410 and 12095 kHz

Breakdown, Accident or Emergency

Police, tel. 997; Fire, tel. 998; Ambulance, tel. 999. Polski Zwiazek Motorowy (PZM), *FIA* and *AIT* member, 85 Solec St., 00950 Warsaw, tel. 22 499 361 or 22 499 212 or 22 498 449, office hours from 8:00 A.M. to 4:00 P.M. on weekdays. The PZM operates an assistance service, tel. 981. The service and one hour of mechanical work is free of charge to AAA, AA, CAA and NAC members if the service occurs within 25 km of towns in which the PZM maintains an office. Details of this service can be obtained from PZM offices in towns and at the frontier. POLTOS runs a similar service, tel. 954. Usually these services operate from 7:00 A.M. to 10:00 P.M., but some close at 3:00 P.M. Another motoring club is Auto Assistance, 19 Sandomierska St., 00-950 Warsaw, tel. 22 290 374. Letters of credit issued by the *FIA* or *AIT* may suffice to pay for assistance services nationwide. The holders of such documents should contact the *AUTOTOUR* Motoring Tourism Bureau of Auto Assistance. Accidents must be reported to the police and the Polish Insurance Association. It's illegal to leave the scene of an accident or to not administer first aid to accident victims.

Portugal

Customs

Non-EC citizens over 17 years of age may import the following free of duty: 200 cigarettes or 250 grams of tobacco, 1 liter of liquor consisting of greater than 22 percent alcohol by volume or 2 liters of liquor consisting of less than 22 percent alcohol by volume, 2 liters of wine, 100 milliliters of perfume, and items intended for personal use. There is no limit on the amount of currency that may be imported. But no more than 100,000 Esc or the equivalent of 500,000 Esc in foreign currency may be exported without proof that at least this much was imported. If bringing in a caravan, you must provide—on plain paper or on a form that's available at the border—an inventory of its items.

Tolls

Vehicles are tolled based on the following classifications.

(1)   Vehicle with an axle height, as measured vertically from the front axle, of less than 1.1 meters (with or without a trailer); motor cycle.

(2)   Vehicle with 2 axles and an axle height, as measured vertically from the front axle, of more than 1.1 meters

(3)   Vehicle with 3 axles or an axle height, as measured vertically from the front axle, of greater than 1.1 meters.

	Toll for each Vehicle Category		
Route	1	2	3
A1 Lisbon to Santarém	620 Esc	1080	1390
A1 Santarém to Fatima	470	810	1050
A1 Fatima to Coimbra	710	1250	1610
A1 Coimbra to Aveiro	350	600	780
A1 Aveiro to Porto	550	930	1200
A2 Almada to Setúbal	230	390	490
A3 Porto to Cruz	460	800	1030
A4 Porto to Penafiel	340	610	800
A5 Lisbon to Cascais	200	200	410
A8 Loures to Malveira	110	190	240

A toll is levied on southbound vehicles crossing the 25 de Abril Bridge which links Lisbon with the south bank of the Tagus River at the end of the Vila Franca de Xira expressway.

A car ferry makes ten 30-minute crossings per day of the Sado Estuary between Setúbal and Troia. Other ferries run across the Tagus (Tejo) Estuary between Lisbon and Cacilhas, Barreito, Montijo, and Porto Brandão.

Road Closings

In the winter, roads 231, 232, 338, and 339 through the Serra da Estrela may be closed due to snow.

Fuel

Gasoline costs about 130 Esc per liter. Fuel stations are usually open from 7:00 A.M. to 10:00 P.M. or midnight; otherwise they're open 24 hours. Major credit cards are accepted but entail a surcharge of 100 Esc. Regular leaded gasoline has an octane rating of 85; the octane rating of super is 98. Unleaded gasoline is called *gasolina sin plomo*. Unleaded super gasoline has an octane rating of 95. Diesel is called *gasóleo*. LPG is called *gáz líquido*. It's illegal to carry spare fuel.

Road Signs

The word *estação* indicates a train station. Roads are classified as expressways (AE), principal roads (IP), national roads (EN), municipal roads (EM), and lesser municipal roads (CM). See the "Spain" section for depictions of certain road signs.

Driving

The minimum age of a driver is 17 years. Children must be at least 12 years of age or in a safety seat to sit in the front seat. The use of seat belts is compulsory for front-seat passengers traveling outside built-up areas. Helmets are compulsory for motorcyclists. The legal blood alcohol limit is 50 mg. Speed limits are as follows: 60 kph (37 mph) in built-up areas, 90 kph (56 mph) outside built-up areas, and 120 kph (74 mph) on expressways. Unless otherwise indicated, the minimum speed on expressways is 40 kph (24 mph). Visitors who have held their license for less than a year must obtain from the ACP motoring club and display on their vehicle a yellow disc with the number *90* on it; the *90* indicates that the driver is limited to 90 kph (56 mph). Cars towing a trailer or caravan are limited to 50 kph (31 mph) in built-up areas, 70 kph (43 mph) outside built-up areas, and 90 kph (56 mph) on expressways. When driving across the 25 de Abril Bridge in Lisbon you must travel 30–50 kph (18–31 mph).

Roads are often three lanes wide; the middle lane is used for passing in both directions. At night in rural areas watch out for animal-drawn, unlit carts.

Only use the horn in cases of immediate and extreme danger.

When a tram stops and there is no island to accept disembarking passengers, drivers must yield to passengers crossing to the sidewalk.

Police are empowered to collect fines on the spot.

Parking

You must park in the same direction as moving traffic, except where parking is allowed on one side of the road only. Some towns have *Blue Zones;* obtain a parking disc at police or ACP motoring club offices. Illegally parked vehicles are subject to immobilization.

Camping

Most campgrounds are open year round. Those run by the Portuguese Camping Federation require an International Camping Carnet. Propane gas bottles can be filled in Faro, Lisbon, and Porto. Free-camping without appropriate permission is illegal, but it's tolerated most everywhere but a few of the more popular beach areas.

Banks

Open on weekdays from 8:30 A.M. to 3:00 P.M.

Shops

Open on weekdays from 9:00 A.M. to 1:00 P.M. and from 3:00 P.M. to 7:00 P.M. Open until 1:00 P.M. on Saturday. Shopping centers are open daily from 10:00 A.M. to midnight.

National Holidays

Jan 1; Shrove Tues; Good Fri; Apr 25; Labor Day; Corpus Chrisit; June 10, 13 (Lisbon), 24 (Porto); Aug 15; Oct 5; Nov 1; Dec 1, 8, 24, 25, 26.

BBC Radio Hours and Corresponding Frequencies

5:00 A.M. to 7:30 A.M.: 6195, 9410 and 15575 kHz

7:30 A.M. to 4:00 P.M.: 12095, 15070 and 17705 kHz

4:00 P.M. to 10:30 P.M.: 6195, 12095 and 15070 kHz

Breakdown, Accident or Emergency

Police, Fire, and Ambulance, tel. 115. Orange emergency telephones are along main roads. The national motoring club is Automóvel Club de Portugal (ACP), *FIA* and *AIT* member, Rua Rosa Araújo 24-26, 1200 Lisbon, tel. 01 56 3981, office hours from 9:00 A.M. to 1:00 P.M. and from 2:00 P.M. to 4:45 P.M. on weekdays. South of Coimbra the ACP breakdown service can be contacted at tel. 01 942 50 95, FAX 01 941 94 99 (8:00 A.M. to 11:30 P.M. everyday); to the north of Coimbra call 02 31 67 32 or 01 830 1127, FAX 02 31 66 98 (8:00 A.M. to 11:30 P.M. weekdays, 9:00 A.M. to 8:00 P.M. on the weekend). First aid can be called at these numbers 24 hours a day. Other Portuguese drivers readily assist stranded motorists. Use your best judgment if another driver comes to your aid; consider asking them to phone for help.

Romania

Customs

You may import the following free of duty: 1 small movie camera, 2 rolls of movie film, 2 cameras, 20 rolls of photographic film, 1 radio/tape recorder, 1 typewriter, 1 pair of binoculars, camping and sports equipment, 200 cigarettes, 2 liters of liquor, 4 liters of wine or beer, and 5 liters of fuel in a spare can. Gifts are allowed free of duty. You may, however, be charged duty for some electronic goods. Declare expensive items upon arrival. You may export gifts and souvenirs, but their value must not exceed 50 percent of the currency you legally exchanged; so keep all your receipts. You are also allowed to export up to 5 paintings from the Plastic Artist's Union. You need a license to export antiques. You may import up to 5 liters of spare fuel free of duty. You may export up to 10 liters. A tax is levied on all exported fuel.

Tolls

From Giurgiu to Ruse, Bulgaria, and from Giurgeni to Vadu Oii, tolls are charged for crossing the Danube River.

Fuel

There are about 30 PECO stations which sell unleaded fuel. Generally, fuel stations are located along main roads exiting towns. The Automobil Clubul Roman and tourist offices provide a *Tourist and Motor Car Map* that locates each fuel station. Prices are substantially lower than those in Western European countries, but shortages may cause delays. Regular leaded gasoline has an octane rating of 88 or 90; the octane rating of super is 96 or 98. Unleaded gasoline is called *benzina fara plumb*. Unleaded super gasoline has an octane rating of 98. Diesel is called *motorina*.

Road Signs

The word *gara* indicates a train station.

Driving

The minimum age of a driver is 18 years. Children must be at least 12 years of age to sit in the front seat. Helmets are compulsory for motorcyclists and their passengers. The legal blood alcohol limit is 0 mg. Speed limits are as follows: 60 kph (37 mph) in built-up areas, and 70 kph (44 mph) or 80 kph (50 mph) or 90 kph (56 mph) outside built-up areas and on expressways. These latter speed limits apply respectively to vehicles with an engine that is smaller than 1100 cc, vehicles with an engine between 1100 cc and 1800 cc, and vehicles with an engine larger than 1800 cc. Motorcycles are limited to 40 kph (25 mph) in built-up areas, 60 kph (37 mph) elsewhere.

Attention: priority on roundabouts must be given to vehicles entering on the right.

It's illegal to use a horn in towns from 10:00 P.M. to 6:00 A.M.; use headlights instead. In Bucharest and many other towns, use of horns is illegal at all times; signs reading *"claxonarea interzisa"* alert drivers to this prohibition.

Trams are the only vehicles which may be passed on the right.

Police can levy fines on the spot. Random vehicle checks are common.

Parking

Parking must be done on the right side of the road and in the direction of traffic.

Banks

Open on weekdays from 9:00 A.M. to 12:30 or 1:00 P.M. Licensed exchanged bureaus, *schimb*, stay open in the afternoons and on Saturday morning.

Shops

Open from 8:00 A.M. to noon and from 4:00 P.M. to 8:00 P.M. every day but Sunday. Some open until noon on Sunday.

National Holidays

Jan 1, 2; May 1, 2, 9; Aug 23, 24; Dec 24, 25, 30.

BBC Radio Hours and Corresponding Frequencies

5:00 A.M. to 7:30 A.M.: 9410, 12095 and 15070 kHz

7:30 A.M. to 4:00 P.M.: 9660, 15070 and 17640 kHz

4:00 P.M. to 10:30 P.M.: 9410, 12095 and 15070 kHz

Breakdown, Accident or Emergency

Police, tel. 955; Fire, tel. 981, Ambulance, tel. 961. The national motoring club is the Automobil Clubul Român (ACR), *FIA* and *AIT* member, Strada Tache Ionescu 27, 70154 Bucharest 22, tel. 1 615 5510 or 1 659 3910, office hours from 8:00 A.M. to 4:30 P.M. on weekdays and from 8:00 A.M. to 1:30 P.M. on Saturday. The ACR provides roadside assistance—along, in case of accident, with medical and legal assistance at fixed rates. Contact the ACR at tel. 927 in Bucharest and at tel. 12345 elsewhere. Another motoring service is operated by the National Tourist Office *"Carpati-Bucaresti"*, 7 Bulvardue Magheru, Bucharest 1, tel. 145160, office hours from 8:00 A.M. to 4:30 P.M. on weekdays, 8:00 A.M. to 1:30 P.M. on Saturday. In case of an accident, the state insurance administration *CAROM* will assist you as well. All accidents must be reported to the police, who will issue a report to ease export of a damaged vehicle. Carry spare parts: they're scarce. In fact, theft of parts from vehicles undergoing repair is common.

Slovak Republic

Customs

You may import the following free of duty: 250 cigarettes or the equivalent in tobacco, 2 liters of wine, 1 liter of spirits, 0.5 liters of eau de cologne, and gifts to the value of 1000 Sk. Declare valuable items. As when exiting the Czech Republic, crystal not purchased with hard currency may be subject to a tax of 100 percent of its retail price. Only antiques bought at government-specified shops may be exported. Keep all receipts. You can import 20 liters of spare fuel free of duty. A map showing the locations of fuel stations which sell unleaded gasoline is available at the border.

Fuel

Gasoline costs about 22.50 Sk per liter. Fuel stations are located on main roads exiting towns and are open 24 hours. It's difficult to find a station in Brataslava; fuel up on the way in or out. Credit cards are accepted in main towns and in popular tourist areas. Leaded regular gasoline has an octane rating of 90; the octane rating of super is 96. Lead-free gasoline is known as *natural* and is only available at select stations; its octane rating is 95. Diesel is designated by a sign that reads *"TT Diesel."*

Road Signs

The following signs are unique to the Czech and Slovak Republics.

CHODTE VLAVO	Pedestrians walk on the left
DIALKOVA PREMAVKA	Bypass
H NEMOCNICA	Hospital
JEDNOSMERNY PREMAVKA	One-way traffic
OBCHADZKA	Diversion
PRUJEZD ZAKAZANY	Closed to vehicles

The Czech word *nádrazí* indicates a train station.

Driving

The minimum age of a driver is 18 years. Children must be at least 12 years of age and over 1.5 meters tall to sit in the front seat. The use of seat belts is compulsory for front- and rear-seat passengers. Helmets are compulsory for motorcyclists and their passengers. Goggles are compulsory for motorcyclists riding a machine having a 50 cc or larger engine. The legal blood alcohol limit is 0 mg. Speed limits are as follows: 50 kph (30 mph) in built-up areas, 90 kph (56 mph) outside built-up areas, 110 kph (68 mph) on expressways, 80 kph (50 mph) for a car with a caravan or trailer traveling outside built-up areas or on expressways, and 90 kph (56 mph) for motorcycles outside built-up areas.

A tram signalling a right turn and set to cross the line of a vehicle on its right has priority.

Headlights must be used when weather slightly impairs visibility. Motorcycles must be operated with headlights on—night and day. Horns can be used only to warn of danger or to signal that you're about to pass. The use of horns is always prohibited in Brataslava.

Trams should be passed on the right; if there is no room on the right, trams can be passed on the left—except in Brataslava. When near a tram stop do not pass.

Police are empowered to collect fines of up to 2000 SK on the spot.

Parking

Parking is allowed only on the right side of the road, unless the road is one way, then parking is on the left. Parking along a tram line is prohib-

ited unless a 3.5-meter wide lane is left between the vehicle and the tram lane.

Banks

Open on weekdays from 8:00 A.M. to 3:00 P.M.

Shops

Open on weekdays from 9:00 A.M. to 6:00 P.M. Some close from noon to 2:00 P.M. Some open until noon on Saturday.

National Holidays

Jan 1; Easter Mon; May Day; May 9; Dec 25, 26.

BBC Radio Hours and Corresponding Frequencies

5:00 A.M. to 7:30 A.M.: 6195, 9410 and 15575 kHz

7:30 A.M. to 4:00 P.M.: 9410, 12095 and 15070 kHz

4:00 P.M. to 10:30 P.M.: 6195, 9410 and 12095 kHz

Breakdown, Accident or Emergency

Police, tel. 158; Fire, tel. 150,; Ambulance, tel. 155. Any accident resulting in injury or in damage in excess of 1000 SK must be immediately reported to police. If your vehicle is registered in Slovakia, the accident must also be reported to the State Insurance Company. In Brataslava, contact the 24-hour road service by phoning 07 363711. The *Auto Atlas CSFR*, sold

in Slovakia, lists the telephone numbers of roadside assistance services nationwide. The national motoring club is Ustredni Automotoklub SR, Wolkrova ul. c. 4, 851 01 Brataslava, tel. 07 850910, office hours from 7:45 A.M. to 4:45 P.M. on weekdays.

Slovenia

Customs

It's illegal to import spare fuel.

Tolls

Charged on the A1/E63 from Ljubljana to Kranj, the A10/E70 from Ljubljana to Razdrto, and the A10/E57 from Maribor to Celje.

Fuel

Fuel stations at border entry points and along expressways are open 24 hours; others are open from 7:00 A.M. to 8:00 P.M. Monday–Saturday. Credit cards are not accepted. Leaded super gasoline has an octane rating of 98. Lead-free gasoline has an octane rating of 91 or 95.

Driving

The minimum age of drivers is 18 years. Children must be at least 12 years of age to sit in the front seat. The use of seat belts is compulsory for front- and rear-seat passengers. The legal blood alcohol limit is 50 mg. Speed limits are as follows: 60 kph (37 mph) in built-up areas, 80 kph (50 mph) outside built-up areas, 120 kph (75 mph) on expressways, 80 kph (50 mph) for a car with a caravan or trailer traveling outside built-up areas or on expressways, and 90 kph (56 mph) for motorcycles outside built-up areas.

Motorcyclists must use headlights night and day. Spare bulbs should be carried.

Police are empowered to collect fines on the spot.

Banks

Open on weekdays from 8:00 A.M. to 6:00 P.M., noon on Saturday.

Shops

Open on weekdays from 7:30 A.M. to 7:00 P.M., and on Saturday till 1:00 P.M.

National Holidays

Jan 1, 2; Feb 8; Easter Monday; April 27; May 1, 2; June 25; Aug 15; Oct 31; Nov 1; Dec 25, 26.

BBC Radio Hours and Corresponding Frequencies

5:00 A.M. to 7:30 A.M.: 9410, 12095 and 15575 kHz

7:30 A.M. to 4:00 P.M.: 12095 and 15070 kHz

4:00 P.M. to 10:30 P.M.: 9410, 12095 and 15070 kHz

Breakdown, Accident or Emergency

Police, tel. 92; Fire, tel. 93; Ambulance, tel. 94. Police must be called to an accident scene. To ease export of your vehicle, they'll issue a report detailing any damage done to it.

Spain

Customs

Visitors may enter with unlimited foreign and Spanish currency. You can't leave with more than 100,000 ptas and foreign currency to a value of 500,000 ptas, unless you can prove that you declared to customs any excess when you entered the country. You may import 10 liters of spare fuel free of duty.

Tolls

Private cars (with or without caravans) and motorcycles pay tolls as follows.

Route	Toll
A1 & A68 Burgos to Mirands de Ebro	1085 ptas
A2 from A7 juntion to Zaragoza	2140
A4 Sevilla to Cadiz	1275
A6 Madrid to Adanero	1025
A7 La Jonquera to Barcelona	1530
A7 Barcelona to Salou	1015
A7 Salou to Valencia	3220
A7 Valencia to Alicante	2130
A8 Bilbao to Irun	1780
A9 La Coruña to Santiago de Compostela	550
A9 Pontevedra to Vigo	395
A15 Pamplona to Tudela	1245
A18 Barcelona to Manresa	670
A19 Barcelona to Mataró	255
A66 Oveido to Leon	1225
A68 Bilbao to Zaragoza	4650

A16's Tunnel de Graf between Castelldefels & Sitges charges a toll of 445 ptas for cars (with or without trailers or caravans) and motorcycles.

C138/D929's Bielsa Tunnel runs through the Pyrénées between Aragnouet and Bielsa, France; usually open all year, but closes from 10:00 P.M. to 6:00 A.M. from November through April.

C1411's Cadi Tunnel between Bellver de Cerdanya and Bagá. The tunnel runs west of the Tosas Pass: 935 ptas for cars (with or without trailers or caravans) and motorcycles.

Compania Transmediterranea SA operates year-round ferry services to the Balearic and Canary Islands:Barcelona—Palma (Mallorca); Valencia—Palma; Barcelona—Mahón (Menorca); Valencia—Mahón ; Barcelona—Ibiza; Valencia—Ibiza; Palma—Mahón—Ibiza; Cádiz—Las Palmas (Grand Canaria); Cádiz—Santa Cruz (Tenerife); Fuerteventrua—Lanzarote—Gomera—Hierro—La Palma.

Non-toll Mountain Passes & Tunnels

Non-toll mountain passes and tunnels tend to be much more difficult to negotiate than those which charge a toll. If you're driving a vehicle (such as a caravan) that's not allowed on or recommended for some of the following passes, or if you wanna travel quickly across or through the mountains, note that a mountain pass or tunnel which charges a toll tends to be close by.

NIII's Contreras Pass, Tarancon to Requena. 890 meters; maximum grade is 7 percent; minimum width is 6.82 meters (22 ft.); OK for caravans.

NVI's Guadarrama Pass, Madrid to La Coruña. 1510 meters; closed occasionally; maximum grade is 12.5 percent; minimum width is 8 meters (26 ft.); OK for caravans.

N111's Lizarraga Pass, Logroño to Donostia/San Sebastián. 1030 meters; maximum grade is 7 percent; minimum width is 5.42 meters (17.5 ft.); OK for caravans.

N152's Tosas Pass, Barcelona to Puigcerdà. 1800 meters; usually open; maximum grade is 10 percent; minimum width is 5 meters (16 ft.); marginally negotiable by caravans.

N230's Viella Tunnel runs 6 km from Viella and Vilaller; approaches to this tunnel are very narrow.

N240's Azpiroz Pass, Pamplona to Donostia/San Sebastián. 615 meters; usually open; maximum grade is 10 percent; minimum width is 5.9 meters (19 ft.); OK for caravans.

N240's Barazar Pass, Gasteiz/Vitoria to Bilbao. 605 meters; maximum grade is 9 percent; minimum width is 6.5 meters (21 ft.); OK for caravans.

N330/N134's Somport Pass, Huesca to Pau, France. 1632 meters; usually open; maximum grade is 10 percent; minimum width is 3.72 meters (12 ft.); OK for caravans.

N400's Cabrejas Pass, Tarancon to Cuenca. 1167 meters; usually open; maximum grade is 14.3 percent; minimum width is 5 meters (16 ft.); OK for caravans.

N525's Canda Pass, Zamora to Orense. 1260 meters; sometimes closed; maximum grade is 12.5 percent; minimum width is 7.1 meters (23 ft.); OK for caravans.

N601's Navacerrada Pass, Madrid to Segovia. 1860 meters; usually open; maximum grade is 9 percent; minimum width is 6 meters (19.5 ft.); not recommended for caravans.

N623's Carrales Pass, Burgos to Santander. 1020 meters; maximum grade is 6 percent; minimum width is 6.82 meters (22 ft.); not recommended for caravans.

C135/D933's Ibaneta Pass, Pamplona to St.-Jean-Pied-de-Port, France. 1058 meters; usually open; maximum grade is 10 percent; minimum width is 4 meters (13 ft.); especially scenic; OK for caravans.

C136/D934's Pourtalet Pass, Huesca to Pau, France. 1791 meters; closed from late October to early June; maximum grade is 10 percent; minimum width is 3.4 meters (11 ft.); not recommended for caravans.

C138/D929's Bielsa Tunnel runs through the Pyrénées between Bielsa and Aragnouet, France; open 8:00 A.M. to 10:00 P.M. from Easter Sunday to mid November.

C142's Bonaigua Pass, Esterri d'Aneu to Viella. 2072 meters; closed from late October to early June; maximum grade is 8.3 percent; minimum width is 4.34 meters (14 ft.); not recommended for caravans.

Fuel

Gasoline costs about 97 ptas per liter. Prices are government regulated, so don't waste time shopping around. Some fuel stations accept credit cards. Regular leaded gasoline has an octane rating of 92; the octane rating of super is 97. Unleaded gasoline is called *gasolina sin plomo*. Unleaded super gasoline has an octane rating of 95. Diesel is called *gas-oil*. LPG is called *gases licuados del petróleo*.

Road Signs

Aparcamiento	Parking ramp
Ceda el Paso	Give Way
Centro	Town center
Comisaria	Police station

Cuidado	Drive with care
Desvío	Detour
Dirreción Única	One-way street
Obras	Roadworks
Peligro	Danger
Todas Direcciones	All directions

Roads marked *A* for *autopista* are toll roads. Roads marked *N* are known as *autovias* and are the main, non-toll highways; these are often virtually as fast as—and more scenic than—the autopistas. A sign showing a stylized picture of a camera indicates an especially good view. The word *estación* indicates a train station.

End of parking prohibition

Take care

Tourist office

Compulsory lane for motorcycles

No entry

Driving

The minimum age of a driver is 18 years. Children under 12 years of age must be seated in an approved child seat to sit in the front of a vehicle. Seat belts are compulsory for front- and rear-seat passengers. Helmets are compulsory for motorcyclists and their passengers riding motorcycles which have an engine larger than 125 cc. The legal blood alcohol limit is 80 mg. Speed limits are as follows: 50 kph (30 mph) in built-up areas, 90 kph (56 mph) or 100 kph (62 mph) outside built-up areas, and 120 kph (74 mph) on expressways. In residential areas the maximum speed is 20 kph (12 mph). Cars towing a trailer are limited to 80 kph (50 mph) on divided highways, 70 kph (44 mph) on other roads.

Immediately outside many towns are sensors which detect your speed as you approach the town. If you're going over the speed limit, a traffic light at the edge of the town is automatically turned to red so that you must come to a stop before entering the town. Two red lights mean *No entry*. Jaywalking is illegal and its prohibition is strictly enforced. Generally, traffic on the right has priority. Normally where a minor road intersects a major road there's a sign reading "Stop" or "*Ceda el Paso*" (give way); if such a sign is not in place, the traffic on the major road still has priority.

Motorcycles must be operated with headlights on—day and night. All vehicles must have headlights on in tunnels. In built-up areas horns may be used only in cases of immediate and extreme danger. Elsewhere don't use the horn unnecessarily, but don't hesitate to use it in warning.

When in daylight and outside a built-up area, you must use the horn to indicate your intention to pass; at night, flash the headlights instead. It's illegal not to use your vehicle's directional to indicate your intention to pass. And if a vehicle comes up behind you signaling that it wants to pass and if you see that the road ahead is clear, you must signal with your vehicle's right blinker to acknowledge the situation. Trams which are stopped and accepting or letting off passengers may not be passed.

Police are empowered to collect fines of up to 50,000 ptas on the spot. Foreigners must pay on the spot unless they can present a Spanish bail bond or an address of a Spanish friend or company who will guarantee payment of the fine. If the fine cannot be paid or guaranteed, the vehicle will be impounded and the driver detained until the fine is paid. There's usually a discount of 20 percent for immediate settlement. The police will issue a *Boletin de Denuncia* which specifies the offense and the amount of the fine. Check carefully that the fine amount noted on the document matches the amount you paid. Follow the English instructions on the back of the document if you wanna dispute the charge; you have 10 days to file a written dispute, and you can write your argument in English.

Parking

In some cities a blue line on the street indicates resident-only parking; in other cities, check for signs. Don't leave anything of value in a parked vehicle. Parking garages are a safer alternative to the street, but you might wanna check prices before you enter with your vehicle. On one-way streets, parking is allowed on even dates along the side with even addresses and on odd dates along the side with odd addresses; in both cases, park in the direction of traffic flow. Do not park within 5 meters of intersections or entrances to public buildings. *Blue Zones* or *Zona Azul* are indicated by signs. Parking in these zones is allowed for 1–2 hours from 8:00 A.M. to 9:00 P.M. Parking discs can be obtained from hotels, travel agents, or the town hall. Some large towns have *Zona ORAs* in the center of the town; parking in such a zone is allowed in conjunction with display of a ticket which must be bought at a tobacconist; tickets are valid for 30, 60, or 90 minutes. Illegally parked vehicles may be towed.

Camping

Campgrounds are rated on a 1 to 3 scale based on their spectrum of facilities, not on their quality. An International Camping Carnet isn't required at most. Amperage offered through electrical hookups tends to be low, sometimes as lows as 2 Amps. Free-camping without appropriate permission is illegal but quite tolerated.

Banks

Open Monday through Saturday from 9:00 A.M. to 2:00 P.M. from October through June. Closed on Saturday during the summer.

Shops

Open on weekdays from 9:00 or 10:00 A.M. to 1:00 P.M. and from 4:00 P.M. to 7:00 P.M. Open and close one hour later on summer afternoons. Open until noon on Saturday.

National Holidays

Jan 1; Epiphany; Mar 19; Maunday Thur; Good Fri; Labor Day; Ascension; Corpus Christi; July 25; Aug 15; Oct 12; Nov 1; Dec 6, 8, 25. Many local variations.

BBC Radio Hours and Corresponding Frequencies

5:00 A.M. to 7:30 P.M.: 6195, 9410 and 15575 kHz

7:30 A.M. to 4:00 P.M.: 12095, 15070 and 17705 kHz

4:00 P.M. to 10:30 P.M.: 6195, 12095 and 15070 kHz

Breakdown, Accident or Emergency

In Madrid, Barcelona and other large towns: Police, tel. 091; Fire, tel. 080; Ambulance, tel. 092. Elsewhere refer to the telephone directory. The Traffic Control Department maintains a network of emergency phones along main roads and provides roadside assistance; call the operator and ask for *auxilio en carretera*. The national motoring club is Real Automóvil Club de España (RACE), *FIA* and *AIT* member, José Abascal 10, 28003 Madrid, tel. 447 3200, office hours from 9:00 A.M. to 2:00 P.M. on weekdays.

Sweden

Customs

You may import the following free of duty: 400 cigarettes or 200 cigarillos or 500 grams of tobacco; 1 liter of spirits and 1 liter of wine, or 2 liters of wine and 2 liters of beer; a reasonable amount of perfume; and other goods to a value of SEK 600. There is no limit on the amount of currency that may be imported or exported. Spare fuel imported in a separate container(s) is subject to duty and VAT.

Concessions for Hostellers

Stena Line offers a 10 percent discount on fares between Göteborg, Sweden, and Kiel, Germany, and between Göteborg, Sweden, and Fredrikshavn, Denmark. Discounted tickets, however, are obtainable only at Terra Nova Travel Sections and are valid for Monday through Thursday travel from June through August.

At the following travel bureaus you can obtain tickets such as BIGE, Inter Rail and Nordtourist, as well as various regular tickets for domestic and international air, train, boat, ferry and bus transportation. You can also rent a car, book charter bus tours, buy insurance, and obtain maps and travel literature.

> STF Travel Bureau, Box 25, Drottninggatan 33, 10120 Stockholm, tel. 08 7903200.

> STF Travel Bureau, Poshuset, Drottninterget 6, Box 305, 40124 Göteborg, tel. 031 150930.

> STF Travel Bureau, Skeppsbron 1, 21120 Malmö, tel. 0040 341260.

Fuel

Gasoline costs about SEK 7.80 per liter. Some *pumps* actually accept SEK 50 or SEK 100 bills; These pumps are called *sedel automat;* old-fashioned self-serve pumps are called *tanka själv*. Generally, fuel stations are open from 7:00 A.M. to 7:00 P.M., but in cities and along main roads they syay open until 8:00 or 10:00 P.M., or for 24 hours. You'll have to exit the expressway to find fuel stations; but on the expressway, signs abound pointing to them. In general, credit cards are accepted. Leaded super gasoline has an octane rating of 96 (normal) or 98 (premium). Unleaded gasoline is called *blyfri 95* (or *98);* and it has an octane rating of 95 (or 98). Diesel goes by its English name. LPG is called *autogas*. Propane is called *gasol*. Gasoline and diesel are both dispensed from green pumps. You may carry 30 liters of spare fuel.

Road Signs

International expressways are designated by white characters on a green background. Intranational roads are denoted by white characters on a blue background. The word *station* indicates a train station.

Passing place (on narow roads)

Driving

The minimum age of a driver is 18 years. Children 7 years of age and under need to be seated in a special child restraint or in a device which allows them to use the fitted seat belts. Seat belts are compulsory for front- and rear-seat passengers. Helmets are compulsory for motorcyclists and their passengers. The legal blood alcohol limit is 20 mg. Speed limits are as follows: 50 kph (30 mph) in built-up areas, 70 kph (44 mph) or 90 kph (56 mph) outside built-up areas, and 110 kph (68 mph) on expressways (though this is reduced to 90 kph near major towns). Cars towing a trailer are limited to 80 kph (50 mph).

Trams have priority. When a tram stops and there is no island to accept disembarking passengers, drivers must yield to passengers crossing to the sidewalk. Pedestrians have priority on a crosswalk, but they're required to cross streets via crosswalks only.

You must use headlights at all times when operating a vehicle. Use of the horn is illegal in built-up areas except in cases of immediate and extreme danger. Outside built-up areas, you're encouraged to signal with the horn or headlights if you intend to pass another vehicle. If a vehicle behind you signals that it wants to pass, you must acknowledge it with your vehicle's right blinker if from your vantage point the road ahead is clear.

If you're driving relatively slowly, other drivers will expect you to move over onto the shoulder of the road to let them pass; the road shoulders in Sweden are extra wide to accommodate this practice. On steep hills this shoulder takes on the status of a full-fledged lane. Do not, however, use the shoulder as if it were another lane. Some narrow roads forego using a solid white line to indicate a zone where passing is dangerous; instead these roads are divided by elongated white lines at short intervals. These lines mean that visibility is impaired in one or both directions and that any passing should be undertaken with special care. Trams must be passed on the right. If there isn't an island at a tram stop, give way to boarding and alighting passengers. Trams operate in Göteborg, Malmo, and Norrköping.

Police are not empowered to collect fines on the spot. Fines range from 300 to 1200 Kr, but if two or more offences are already on record and the new fine or fines brings the total over 2500 Kr the offender must go to court.

Parking

Maps showing parking regulations and zones in major cities may be obtained from police or local offices of the national motoring clubs. Parking meters are usually checked between 8:00 A.M. and 6:00 P.M. Park on the right-hand side of the road. If parking on the street overnight, check the signs to be sure you're not parking on a street that's slated to be cleaned that night. A yellow sign with a red line across its bottom means parking is somehow restricted in the vicinity. Sweden imposes incredibly high fines for parking violations.

Camping

Most campgrounds are open from June 1 to September 1; though some stay open year round. They're rated with from one to three stars based on their spectrum of facilities. Parties without an International Camping Carnet will likely have to buy a Swedish Camping Card. Many campgrounds offer reduced fees to campers who check in after 9:00 P.M. and leave before 9:00 A.M. the next day. Motorhomes must have a closed drainage system; if yours doesn't, you can rent an approved tank at the campground. Foreign propane tanks can be filled at AGA Gas AB and Primus stations. As mentioned earlier *Allmansaratten* (everyman's right) lets anyone free-camp on unfenced land less than 100 meters from the nearest dwelling; this doesn't apply to motorhomes, though, and you should ask permission from the owner—and note that, as with other fines Swedish, the penalties for littering are severe.

Banks

Open on weekdays from 9:30 A.M. to 3:00 P.M., but some stay open until 5:30 P.M.

Shops

Open on weekdays from 9:30 A.M. to 6:00 P.M. Open until 1:00 or 4:00 P.M. on Saturday. Some larger stores stay open from 7:00 A.M. to 10:00 or 11:00 P.M. every day but Sunday.

National Holidays

Jan 1; Epiphany; Good Fri; Easter Mon; Labor Day; Ascension; Whit Sun; Whit Mon; Sat btw June 20 and 26; Sat btw Oct 31 and Nov 6; Dec 25, 26.

BBC Radio Hours and Corresponding Frequencies

5:00 A.M. to 7:30 A.M.: 9410 and 12095 kHz

7:30 A.M. to 4:00 P.M.: 12095 and 15070 kHz

4:00 P.M. to 10:30 P.M.: 9410, 12095 and 15070 kHz

Breakdown, Accident or Emergency

Police, Fire, and Ambulance, tel. 115. Larmtjänst, a roadside service run by a confed-eration of Swedish insurance companies, can be contacted 24 hours a day by calling 020 91 00 40 (toll-free) for towing, 020 22 00 00 for other reasons. There are two national motoring clubs: Motormännens Riksförbund (M), *AIT* member, Sturegatan 32, Stockholm, tel. 08 7 82 38 00, office hours from 8:30 A.M. to 5:00 P.M. weekdays; and Kungl Automobil K l u b b e n (KAK), *FIA* member, Gyllenstiernsgatan 4, S-11526, Stockholm, tel. 0890 0055, office hours from 9:00 A.M. to 4:00 P.M. Monday through Thursday and from 9:00 A.M. to 1:00 P.M. on Friday.

Switzerland

Customs

Persons 17 years of age or older may import the following free of duty: 400 cigarettes or 100 cigars or 500 grams of tobacco or half of these amounts if entering from a European country, 2 liters of alcoholic beverage consisting of under 15 percent alcohol by volume, and 1 liter of alcoholic beverage consisting of over 15 percent alcohol by volume. There are no limits on the amount of currency you can import or export. You can import 25 liters of spare fuel free of duty. Caravans and trailers less than 2.3 meters wide and 8 meters long can be imported without hassle. Those between 2.3 and 2.5 meters wide may enter if towed by a four-wheel drive vehicle or a vehicle weighing more than 3.5 tons. The total length of the combo must not exceed 18 meters.

Tolls

Note that cars rented in Switzerland come with a visible disk or *vignette* which allows the vehicle to travel Switzerland's express highways until the end of the year. If you don't have this disk but still wanna use these expressways, you can purchase it at a border station or from a Swiss National Tourist Office for 30 SwF (about $22). By using the expressways instead of other roads, you'll save a lot of fuel; the *vignette* will probably pay for itself in terms of these fuel savings alone. Road numbers on green signs indicate toll expressways (unlike France, where blue signs indicate toll expressways or *autoroutes* and green signs indicate non-toll expressways).

Because the following two tunnels are part of the expressway system, a *vignette* is required of drivers who use them.

N2's (E35's) St. Gotthard Tunnel runs 16.3 km under the Gotthard Pass from Göschenen to Airolo.

N13's (E43's) San Bernardino tunnel runs 6.6 km parallel to the Pass.

The following tunnels require tolls.

N6-A6/SS33-SS337's Lötschberg rail tunnel from Kandersteg to Goppenstein operates all year: 23 SwF for a car, 33 SwF for a van, 15 SwF for a motorcycle; 15 minute travel time; Kandersteg departures every 30 minutes starting at 5:05 A.M. and lasting till 11:05 P.M.; Goppenstein departures every 30 minutes starting at 5:35 A.M. and lasting till 11:35 P.M.; schedule varies on Saturday from roughly July 2 to August 6 and from September 24 to October 1.

A9-A19/SS33-SS337's (E62's) Simplon rail tunnel allows car-carrying trains to run year round from Brig to Domodossola, Italy.

A13-A27's Albula rail tunnel service runs between Thusis, Tiefencastel, and Samedan at least five times a day each way: 85 SwF for a car, 140 SwF for a car towing a trailer or caravan, 10.50 SwF per passenger.

A19's Furka rail tunnel from Oberwald to Realp: 28 SwF for a car.

A19's Oberlap rail tunnel from Andermatt to Disentis: 68 SwF per car; operates only in winter; other times the road is open to traffic.

A21/SS27's (E27 or E21's) Grand St. Bernard Tunnel runs 6 km between Bourg St. Pierre and Aosta, Italy, and is open all year: 27 SwF for a car, 27 SwF for a car towing a trailer or caravan, 56.5 SwF for a caravan, 27 SwF for a motorcycle. Customs is on the Swiss side, where there's a fuel station, money exchange bureau, and restaurant.

A car ferry sails between Horgen and Meilen across Lake Zurich all year, and another sails between Beckenreid and Gersau on Lake Lucerne from April through October. There are also ferry services between Constance and Meersburg, Germany, and between Romanshorn and Frederichshafen, Germany, on Lake Constance.

Non-toll Mountain Passes

Non-toll mountain passes tend to be much more difficult to negotiate than the passes which charge a toll. If you're driving a vehicle, such as a caravan, that's not allowed on or recommended for some of the following passes, or if you wanna travel quickly across or through the mountains, note that a mountain pass or tunnel which charges a toll tends to be close by. The Touring Club Suisse, tel. 022 35 80 00, provides English descriptions of the current conditions of mountain passes. The same information is available in French, German and Italian by phoning 123 or 163.

N2's St. Gotthard Pass, Andermatt to Bellinzona. 2108 meters; closed from mid October to early June; maximum grade is 10 percent; minimum width is 6.2 meters (20 ft.); no vehicles over 2.54 meters (8 feet 2 1/2 inches) wide or 3.64 meters (11 feet 9 inches) tall; Swiss tax is charged; OK for caravans.

N5's Faucille Pass, Geneva to Morez, France. 1322 meters; usually open; maximum grade is 10 percent; minimum width is 5 meters (16 ft.); scenic view of Mont Blanc; difficult; not recommended for caravans.

N8 & N4's Brünig Pass, Meiringen to Lucerne. 1008 meters; usually open; maximum grade is 8.3 percent; minimum width is 6.2 meters (20 ft.); no vehicles over 2.54 meters (8 feet 2 1/2 inches) wide; tire chains are sometimes necessary; OK for caravans.

N9-N19/SS33-SS337's (E62's) Simplon Pass, Brig to Domodossola, Italy. 2006 meters; closed occasionally from November through April; maximum grade is 11 percent; minimum width is 7.1 meters (23 ft.); no vehicles over 2.54 meters (8 feet 2 inches) wide; no trailers over 2 metric tons (2000 kg); OK for caravans.

N13's San Bernardino Pass, Chur to Bellinzona. 2005 meters; closed from October to late June; maximum grade is 10 percent; minimum width is 4 meters (13 ft.); no vehicles over 2.32 meters (7.5 ft.) wide; not recommended for caravans.

A3's Julier Pass, Tiefencastel to Silvaplana. 2284 meters; usually open; maximum grade is 13.3 percent; minimum width is 4 meters (13 ft.); no vehicles over 2.54 meters (8 feet 2 1/2 inches) wide; OK for caravans.

A3's Maloja Pass, Chiavenna to Silvaplana. 1814 meters; usually open; maximum grade is 9 percent; minimum width is 4 meters (13 ft.); no vehicles over 2.54 meters (8 feet 2 1/2 inches) wide; no trailers allowed; OK for caravans.

A6's Grimsel Pass, Gletsch to Innertkirchen. 2165 meters; closed from mid October to late June; maximum grade is 10 percent; minimum width is 5 meters (16 ft.); no vehicles over 2.32 meters (7.5 ft.) wide; no trailers over 2.5 metric tons (2,500 kg); OK for caravans.

A11's Col des Mosses Pass, Aigle to Saanen. 1445 meters; usually open; maximum grade is 8.3 percent; minimum width is 4 meters (13 ft.); especially scenic; no vehicles over 2.32 meters (7.5 ft.) wide; chains necessary in winter; no buses allowed; OK for caravans.

A11's Susten Pass, Innertkirchen to Wassen. 2223 meters; closed from late October to early June; maximum grade is 9 percent; minimum width is 6.2 meters (20 ft.); especially scenic; no vehicles over 2.54 meters (8 feet 2 1/2 inches) wide; OK for caravans.

A17's Klausen Pass, Altdorf to Glarus. 1948 meters; closed from late October to early June; maximum grade is 9 percent; minimum width is 5 meters (16 ft.); no vehicles over 2.32 meters (7.5 ft.) wide; no caravans allowed.

A19's Furka Pass, Andermatt to Brig. 2430 meters; closed from October through June; maximum grade is 10 percent; minimum width is 4 meters (13 ft.); no vehicles over 2.32 meters (7.5 ft.) wide; not recommended for caravans.

A19's Oberlap Pass, Andermatt to Disentis. 2045 meters; closed from early November to late May; maximum grade is 10 percent; minimum width is 5 meters (16 ft.); no vehicles over 2.32 meters (7.5 ft.) wide; marginally negotiable by caravans.

A21/SS27's Great St. Bernard Pass, Martigny to Aosta, Italy. 2473 meters; closed from October through June; maximum grade is 10 percent; minimum width is 5 meters (16 ft.); tire chains may be necessary on approach; closed to vehicles towing another vehicle; not recommended for caravans.

A28's Flüela Pass, Landquart to Susch. 2383 meters; closed occasionally from November through May; closed at night; maximum grade is 12.5 percent; minimum width is 5 meters (16 ft.); no vehicles over 2.32 meters (7.5 ft.) wide; no vehicles over 3.46 meters (11 feet 2 inches) tall; OK for caravans.

A28's Ofen Pass, Zernez to Santa Maria. 2149 meters; usually open; maximum grade is 12.5 percent; minimum width is 3.72 meters (12 ft.); tire chains may be required; no vehicles over 2.32 meters (7.5 ft.) wide; OK for caravans.

A29's Bernina Pass, Celerina to Tirano. 2329 meters; closed occasionally from late December through March; closed at night; maximum grade is 12.5 percent; minimum width is 5 meters (16 ft.); no vehicles over 2.32 meters (7.5 ft.) wide; especially scenic; not recommended for caravans.

A189's Juan Pass, Bulle to Spiez. 1509 meters; usually open; maximum grade is 10 percent; minimum width is 4 meters (13 ft.); no vehicles over 2.32 meters (7.5 ft.) wide; especially scenic; not recommended for caravans.

A203-A9-A21/N506's Forclaz Pass, Martigny to Chamonix, France. 1527 meters; usually open; maximum grade is 8.3 percent; minimum width is 5 meters (16 ft.); no vehicles over 2.54 meters (8 feet 2 1/2 inches) wide; no trailers over 5 metric tons; especially scenic; marginally negotiable by caravans.

A461's Lukmanier Pass, Disentis to Biasca. 1916 meters; closed from early November to late May; maximum grade is 9 percent; minimum width is 5 meters (16 ft.); caravans are not allowed.

A203-A9-A21/N506's Col de Montes Pass, Martigny to Chamonix, France. 1460 meters; closed occasionally from December through early April; maximum grade is 12.5 percent; minimum width is 3.1 meters (10 ft.); OK for small caravans.

SS36's Splügen Pass, Splügen to Chiavenna, Italy. 2113 meters; closed from early November through June; maximum grade is 13.3 percent; minimum width is 3.1 meters (10 ft.); maximum vehicle height is 2.84 meters (9 feet 2 inches); maximum vehicle width is 2.32 meters (7.5 ft.); especially scenic; not recommended for caravans.

SS38's Umbrail Pass, Santa Maria to Bormio, Italy. 2500 meters; closed from early November through early June; maximum grade is 9 percent; minimum width is 4.34 meters (14 ft.); no vehicles over 2.32 meters (7.5 ft.) wide; no trailers allowed; not recommended for caravans.

Unclassified road's Albula Pass from Tiefencastel to La Punt (via Bergün). 2315 meters; closed from early November to early June; maximum grade is 10 percent; minimum width is 3.72 meters (12 ft.); no vehicles over 2.32 meters (7.5 ft.) wide; no trucks or trailers; not recommended for caravans.

Unclassified road's Col du Pillon Pass from Aigle to Saanen (via Gstaad). 1546 meters; closed occasionally from January through February; maximum grade is 9 percent; minimum width is 4 meters (13 ft.); no vehicles over 2.32 meters (7.5 ft.) wide; tire chains may be necessary; OK for caravans.

Unclassified road's Nufenen Pass from Brig to Airolo, Italy (via Bedretto). 2478 meters; closed from mid October to mid June; maximum grade is 10 percent; minimum width is 4 meters (13 ft.); no vehicles over 2.32 meters (7.5 ft.) wide; marginally negotiable by caravans weighing less than 1.5 metric tons (1500 kg).

Fuel

Lead-free gasoline costs 0.98 SwF per liter. Fuel stations along expressways are usually open from 6:00 A.M. to 10:00 P.M. or midnight. Those along Basel North, Pratteln North/South, and Coldrério North/South (N2), however, stay open 24 hours. Along other roads, fuel stations are open from 6:00 or 7:00 or 8:00 A.M. to 6:00 or 8:00 P.M. Outside of open hours fuel is commonly available from automatic pumps that accept 10 and 20 SwF notes or credit cards. And some stations which do not always stay open 24 hours do stay open 24 hours during the summer. Many stations do *not* accept major charge cards like Visa, MasterCard or American Express. Unleaded gasoline has an octane rating of 98. Unleaded gasoline is called *bleifrei, essence sans plomb,* or *benzina sensa piomba,* depending on whether you're in a German-, French-, or Italian-speaking part of Switzerland, respectively. Likewise, diesel is called *diesel, diesel,* or *gasolio;* and LPG is called *autogas, Gaz de pétrole liquéfié (GPL),* or *gas liquido (GPL).* Unleaded super gasoline has an octane rating of 95.

Road Signs

A sign depicting a tire with chains on it or a sign reading *"chaines à neige" obligatoires* means that snow chains are necessary to navigate the road ahead. Snow chains for your tires can be rented from fuel sations marked *"Service de Châines à Neige"* or *"Schneekettendienst".* The word indicating a train station will be either *gare, bahnhof* or *stazione* depending on whether you are in a French-, German- or Italian-speaking portion of Switzerland, respectively.

Flashing red light (level crossing)

Alternatively flashing red lights (level crossing)

Semi-expressway

Postal vehicles have priority

Driving

You can recieve helpful information in French, German and Italian by calling the following numbers: general, tel. 111; snow conditions and tourist infor, tel. 120; weather, tel. 162; road conditions, tel. 163; avalanche bulletin, tel. 187. Many roads are closed to caravans and trailers.

It's often impossible to "make good time" in this mountainous country if you don't use the expressways; roads rarely approximate a straight line between destinations. Check your Switzerland road map carefully when planning your schedule. But besides realizing the limits that these roads impose, you should realize the potential they offer—you'll be enveloped by natural beauty on every turn. Plan to drive for driving's sake, and try to minimally constrain yourself with time-related issues. Ask yourself this question: Why do I wanna drive quickly through Switzerland?

The minimum age of a driver is 18 years. If in the front seat, children under 7 years of age must be seated in an approved child seat. Seat belts are compulsory for front-seat passengers. Helmets are compulsory for motorcyclists and their passengers. The legal blood alcohol limit is 80 mg. Speed limits are as follows: 50 kph (30 mph) in built-up areas, 80 kph (50 mph) outside built-up areas, and 100 kph (62 mph) or 120 kph (74 mph) on expressways. Cars/trailer combos which weigh less than 1000 kg are limited to 80 kph (50 mph) outside built-up areas; if the combo weighs over 1000 kg, it's limited to 60 kph (37 mph) outside built-up areas and to 80 kph (50 mph) on expressways.

The mountain resort towns of Braunwald, Murren, Wengen and Zermatt cannot be reached directly by private motor vehicle. Park at the railway or sky tram station and complete the journey via public transport.

Trams always have priority. Buses have priority when leaving a bus stop. Blue posts are used to indicate an upcoming intersection with a priority road. Traffic going up a mountain has priority, except where signs displaying a yellow posthorn on a blue background signal that postal buses have priority. A red slash going through such a sign indicates the end of the postal priority zone. Some of these mountain postal roads are one way; such cases are indicated by a white rectangle placed below the blue rectangle/yellow horn sign. Some mountain roads require one-way traffic during certain hours only; these hours will be posted at either end of such roads.

Use headlights in tunnels. Motorcycles must be operated with headlights on—night and day. Use the horn in cases of immediate and extreme danger only; flash your headlights instead.

When passing, do not cross a double white line. When completing a passing maneuver, you must signal with your vehicle's right blinker before you re-enter the right lane. Moving trams must be passed on the right if there's enough room; otherwise they may be passed on the left. A stationary tram should be passed on the left, unless it's stopped at a passenger island, in which case it may be passed on the right. Motorcyclists are not allowed to pass long columns of vehicles or to weave in and out of traffic.

Police are empowered to collect fines on the spot.

Parking

Do not park where you see a sign that reads "Stationierungsverbot" or "Interdiction de Stationner". Parking on the sidewalk is illegal except where signs indicate otherwise. Many towns have Blue Zones that restrict parking during the period 8:00 A.M. to 7:00 P.M. on weekdays. Obtain discs free of charge from ACS or TCS motoring club offices. In Basel, Berne, and Geneva you can get discs at fuel stations, restaurants, kiosks, police stations, and garages. In Laussann a Red Zone system is also in effect; discs good for both zones (one side for each zone) can be obtained from the TCS offices or the tourist information offices. Wheel clamps are in use.

Parking disc is compulsory

Camping

Most campgrounds stay open from mid April to mid October, but some are open year round. Most are of high quality and offer a wide range of amenities. Swiss campgrounds use a unique three-prong plug which can be rented from most campgrounds. Overnight parking at rest stops is OK. Otherwise free-camping without the appropriate permission is illegal, and it's not tolerated in the canton of Tessin and near a few other resort areas.

Banks

Open on weekdays from 8:30 A.M. to 4:30 or 5:00 A.M.

Shops

Open on weekdays from 8:00 A.M. to 12:15 P.M. and from 1:30 P.M. to 6:30 P.M. Open from 9:00 A.M. to 4:00 P.M. on Saturday. Department stores stay open during lunch hours.

National Holidays

Jan 1; Good Fri; Easter Mon; Ascension; Whit Mon; Dec 25.

BBC Radio Hours and Corresponding Frequencies

5:00 A.M. to 7:30 A.M.: 6195, 9410 and 15575 kHz

7:30 A.M. to 4:00 P.M.: 12095 and 15070 kHz

4:00 P.M. to 10:30 P.M.: 6195, 9410 and 12095 kHz

Breakdown, Accident or Emergency

Police, tel. 117; Fire, tel. 118; Ambulance, tel. 144 or 177. The breakdown service *Touring Secours* can be reached by dialing 140. Anglo-phone, tel. 157 5014, is a 24-hour hotline that provides data ranging from weather reports to English-speaking doctor referals; it's available in Switzerland only and costs 1.4 SwF per minute. Touring Club Suisse (TCS), *AIT* member, 9 Rue Pierre Fatio, 1211 Genèva 3, tel. 022 737 12 12 (022 735 8000 for road and touring info), FAX 022 786 0992, varying office hours from Monday through Saturday, offers 24-hour

roadside service. Automobile Club de Suisse (ACS), *FIA* member, 39 Wasserwerkgaße, 3000 Berne 13, tel. 031 311 77 22, FAX 031 311 03 10, office hours weekdays from 8:00 A.M. to noon and from 2:00 P.M. to 5:30 P.M.

Turkey

Customs

You may import the following free of duty: 400 cigarettes, 50 cigars, 200 grams of tobacco, 1.5 kilograms of instant coffee, 500 grams of tea, and 2.5 liters of alcohol. An additional 600 cigarettes, 100 cigars, or 500 grams of tobacco is allowed if these goods were bought at Turkish duty-free shops. Register in your passport all valuables. Your vehicle will be noted on your passport as imported goods; it must be exported within a certain amount of time. If your vehicle belongs to another private party, you must present a letter of authorization from the owner and certified by a lawyer. Keep all receipts to prove that items you obtained in Turkey were bought with legally exchanged currency. You must have authorization to export antiques. If an item you plan to export could possibly be an antique, go to great lengths to determine its actual antique status. Punishment for improperly exporting antiques can be severe. Don't even think of messing around with illicit drugs in Turkey. You may import 25 liters of spare fuel free of duty.

Tolls

Tolls are charged between Edirne and Istanbul, Istanbul and Izmut, Tsarsus and Pozanti, and Ankara and Gerede. In the direction Europe to Asia, tolls are charged on the Bosphorus and Faith Sultan Mehment bridges: 50,000 TRL for cars and vans, 20,000 TRL for motorcycles

Fuel

Many fuel stations along main highways are open 24 hours; others are open from 6:00 A.M. to 10:00 P.M. Fuel stations are not as numerous as in other countries, so fill up your vehicle's tank whenever you can. Credit cards are generally not accepted. Regular uleaded gasoline has an octane rating of 91; the octane rating of super is 96. Unleaded gasoline is called *kursunsuz benzin*. Unleaded super gasoline has an octane rating of 95. Diesel alos goes by the name *mersin*.

Road Signs

Dikkat	Attention
Dur	Stop
Gümrük	Customs
Hastahane	Hospital
Nufus	Population
Rakin	Altitude
Tamirat	Roadworks
Yabancilara Yasaktir	Photography forbidden
Yasak Bolge	Photography forbidden
Yavas	Slow

Historical sites are designated by yellow signposts.

Driving

Turkey—with its surprisingly good roads and maddeningly slow trains—is best seen by motor vehicle. Generally, driving habits conform those of other Southern European countries. Signposts, however, are much less frequent. Turkey also has a relatively high accident rate. Watch out at night for livestock and for unlit farm vehicles.

Foreign drivers who are under 18 years of age may drive foreign-registered vehicles in Turkey if they have a valid license from their home country. Seat belts are compulsory for front- and rear-seat passengers. Helmets are compulsory for motorcyclists. The legal blood alcohol limit is 50 mg. Speed limits are as follows: 50 kph (30 mph) in built-up areas, 90 kph (56 mph) outside built-up areas, and 90 kph (56 mph) on expressways. Cars towing a trailer or caravan are limited to 40 kph (25 mph) in built-up areas, and 70 kph (44 mph) outside built-up areas.

Headlights must be used in built-up areas after sunset. Use of the horn is illegal except in cases of immediate and extreme danger.

Police are empowered to collect fines on the spot.

Parking

A sign reading *"Park Yapilmaz"* means *No parking*. Do not park within 25 meters of danger signs.

Camping

Camprounds can be sparsely scattered and vary greatly in terms of quality. Free-camping *is* legal. Many motorhomers choose to spend the night in the safety of a militia or police station parking lot. Propane bottles can be filled at the AYGAS station at Ambarli, on the road to Edirne 10 km west of Istanbul.

Banks

Open on weekdays from 8:30 A.M. to noon and from 1:30 P.M. to 5:00 P.M.

Shops

Open on weekdays from 9:00 A.M. to 1:00 P.M. and from 2:30 P.M. to 7:00 P.M. Open from 9:00 A.M. to 1:00 P.M. and from 1:30 P.M. to 8:00 P.M. on Saturday.

National Holidays

Jan 1; Apr 23; May 19; Seker Bayrami and Kurban Bayrami are moveable religious festivals; Aug 30; Oct 28 (part), 29. When a holiday falls on a Fri, the following Sat is also observed as a holiday.

BBC Radio Hours and Corresponding Frequencies

5:00 A.M. to 7:30 A.M.: 6180, 12095 and 15070 kHz

7:30 A.M. to 4:00 P.M.: 9660, 15070 and 17640 kHz

4:00 P.M. to 10:30 P.M.: 6180, 12095 and 15070 kHz

Breakdown, Accident or Emergency

Police, tel. 155; Fire, tel. 110; Ambulance, tel. 112. Tourist Police: in Ankara, tel. 434 1756; Istanbul, tel. 527 4503; Izmir, tel. 218 652. Ask at your hotel and/or at a tourist information office about how to contact one of the roadside services. The Türkiye Turing Ve Otomobil Kurumu (TTOK), *FIA* and *AIT* member, Halaskargazi Cad. 364 Sisli, 80222 Instanbul, tel. 212 231 4631, office hours from 8:30 A.M. to noon and from 12:30 P.M. to 5:00 P.M. on weekdays, offers a repair service. All accidents must be reported to the police so the police can prepare a report for the Turkish Insurance Bureau. If your vehicle must be repaired, prices are generally not too high; just give a little tip to the mechanic doing the work, and take all vehicle documents with you if you leave the shop.

14. ferries & the chunnel

I begin this chapter with a general description of European ferry services, a description that culminates, nevertheless, in a close look at the new Channel Tunnel. I then map the ferry services that connect the central continent with its most significant marginal constituents—the British Isles, Scandinavia, and the Eastern Mediterranean—numbering the routes to facilitate cross-referencing with the lists of operators' reservation numbers that I include after each map, and tacking on after each list detailed fare schedules of representative routes. Dozens of less significant ferry services, left unmapped herein, operate between European destinations; I describe many in the previous chapter, and any map you buy should show these if they terminate or originate within its domain.

General

A recent revolution in ferry quality has made modern and generously appointed ships the norm. The overnight and one- or two- or three-day routes are becoming more like *Love Boat* cruises than anything else. Many ferries now include plush seats, televisions, cinemas, pools, saunas, silver-service restaurants, bars, live entertainment, casinos, children's playrooms, duty-free shops, and exchange bureaus. The food served aboard ferries is expensive, however; consider bringing your own sandwiches and drinks. Also expensive is the merchandise in the duty-free shops—except for the tobacco and alcohol, that is. In good weather, you can stroll or sunbathe on the decks, throw bread to the playful gulls, and snap dramatic photos.

Cabins come in economy, standard, and luxury classes of varying capacity: single-berth, double-berth, triple-berth, and quad-berth. You *can* pay for a single berth in a multiple-berth room, but the ferry company retains the right to assign roommates. For some people the comfortable chairs or pullman's coaches may suffice as makeshift beds on overnight routes. Some budget travelers who embark on their first overnight sailing of the Mediterranean opt to sleep on the ferry's deck to save some cash. *Bad idea.* Summer nights on the open Mediterranean are surprisingly—and painfully—cold.

Many sources preach that you should book your ferry passage in advance if you plan to transport a vehicle across a principal ferry route during the high season. This is true, but the proper definition of "advance" may surprise you. Remember the fecundity of the unexpected that a motor vehicle allows to blossom? Most bookings entail high cancellation penalties, so booking ferry passage too far in advance stunts this important factor. Wait until you arrive overseas and settle into your trip before you make any "advance" booking for ferry passage—if you book at all. Besides, passage booked through domestic brokers is more expensive than passage booked directly with a ferry company. Many offer a simplified price structure, constant throughout the year, for tickets purchased outside Europe. Even during high season you may be able to pull up at the port unannounced, stop into the office, and succeed in securing a spot on the next ferry. However, don't expect this method to work as well as, say, flying standby: the high cancellation fees associated with ferry bookings oblige people to fulfill their reservations. But the ferries always have enough room for foot passengers; I recommend that foot passengers do not make a booking.

In at least two cases, however, you should definitely book ahead. First, if vehicle-passenger fares are cheaper than foot-passenger fares, you need to book ahead and declare then the passengers who'll be making the crossing with you. If you don't do this, the ferry company will require your passengers to pay foot-passenger fares—which are more expensive. This policy discourages drivers from offering passage to hitchhikers or other foot passengers in exchange for cash. Second, if you plan to secure a cabin on an overnight ferry, definitely reserve the cabin and your passage in advance. When reserving space for your vehicle, you must describe the type of vehicle, its license number, its length, and its height—including any roof luggage or equipment.

Fares or "tariffs" charged by a particular ferry company for a particular sailing might depend on the time of day, the day of the week, the time of the year, the age and organizational affiliation of the passenger, and the size and type of vehicle being transported.

Overnight sailings long enough to allow for a good night's sleep tend to be more expensive than long daytime sailings; whereas short daytime sailings tend to be more expensive than short nighttime sailings. Holiday and weekend (usually defined as Friday afternoon to Sunday) sailings tend to be more expensive than normal weekday sailings. And peak summer sailings are, of course, more expensive than shoulder and low season sailings (except for those sailings around, say, Christmas).

Fares also depend on whether a passenger is in a vehicle or on foot, and on whether he's a child, youth, student, senior citizen, handicapped person, HI member, holder of a rail pass, auto club member, soldier, or diplomat.

Finally, the fares for vehicle transport depend on the size (length, height, width) and/or type of vehicle or combination of vehicles.

The fares I list in the representative schedules are per person (except where otherwise indicated); and they model non-weekend, budget-oriented, single (one-way) passage.

Most ferry companies calculate return (two-way) fares using the single fares applicable *at the time of the passenger's departure* instead of those applicable at the time of their return, simply doubling these fares or taking roughly 10 to 20 percent off the sum. Some companies, however, compute return fares as the average of the outward and inward single fares or offer them at single—or even lower—rates providing you return on a specific scheduled but unpopular sailing or on the same day.

Several groups of ferry companies have joined up to offer "Landbridge" tickets that cover passage from, say, Ireland to Britain to France to Ireland; or from, say, Britain to the Netherlands and from Denmark to Sweden, both legs being return. It's usually cheaper to buy such a ticket than to buy separate tickets to achieve the same end.

After widdling down the selection of ferry services, contact the remaining few. Begin each inquiry by explaining to the ferry representative your planned date or dates of ferry travel. Ask about the sailing schedule for that day or days. Ask if the different departures during the day charge different fares. Ferries tend to service relatively short routes many times a day. On the other hand, ferries may service relatively long routes only once or twice a week. The frequency of ferry service also varies with the season: more ferries ply the waters in summer than in winter, and some may halt service altogether in the off season. If you definitely need a two-way ticket, be sure to ask for *return* fares. If not, ask how the company calculates return fares. If

you're arranging passage for a large group, ask about special group rates. Describe the height and length of your vehicle and, if it's a large van or minibus, the number of seats it has. Ask if any special offers applying to your type of vehicle will be in effect around your planned dates of travel. If you're under 26 years of age, ask if the company offers youth discounts. If you'll be traveling with children, note the age range for which children's fares are valid. If you're a student, determine if the company offers student fares; if they do, ask what documents (ISIC, for example) they require as evidence of your student status. If you consider yourself a senior citizen, determine if the company offers reduced fares for seniors and if the *company* considers you a senior. (You may need to be a member of a certain senior citizen organization.) Handicapped persons, ask if you're entitled to a discount. Hostellers, ask if discounts apply to card-carrying HI members. Railpass holders, ask if you qualify for a discount or free passage. Members of auto clubs, determine if reductions apply to you and your family. Soldiers and diplomats, ask if reductions apply to you and your family. In all cases, ask if the discounts apply to both persons *and* vehicles.

Reductions are not cumulative, so opt for the one that gives you the greatest discount. Be sure to determine what cancellation charges apply. If pertinent, ask whether the company allows stop-overs. If stopovers are possible, note how far in advance you must declare your intention to stopover and what embarkation/disembarkation fees apply. Finally, ask how early you must report for check-in; plan to arrive at the port at least one hour before a scheduled departure. Signs depicting car-bearing boats radiate for miles around a ferry port, so it's easy to find the dock. And note that it's usually illegal to carry containers of spare fuel on ferries. Quite a few ferries do, however, allow you to carry tanks of propane.

If you plan to cross the English Channel, you should consider using the new Channel Tunnel instead of a ferry. The much pooh-poohed delays in the Tunnel's opening pale when one considers that the Romans mused over the idea, that Napolean approved a Channel Tunnel project (designed for stagecoaches and to be ventilated by "chimneys" rising above the water's surface) in 1802, and that the British made an abortive stab at it in 1880. Begun again in earnest in 1987, the

"Chunnel" runs 50 kilometers (31 miles) from Folkestone, England, to Calais, France, 37 of those kilometers through chalk marl, the roof just 25–45 meters below the seabed. (But it's only the second longest rail tunnel in the world; the longest runs under Japan's Strait of Tsugaru.) The project took some $15 billion, 15,000 workers, and seven years to complete.

Not just one tunnel, the Chunnel consists of two large parallel train tunnels serviceable through a third parallel tunnel between them. That's right, *train* tunnels: you can't drive your vehicle straight through. Instead, after paying at a toll booth and passing through frontier controls, you'll be directed to drive onto a long train called *Le Shuttle.* There are four *Le Shuttle,* one departing every fifteen minutes during peak times, every hour during the night; each can carry up to 180 cars and is confined to the Chunnel and its approaches. Thus the Channel Tunnel allows up to 720 vehicles per hour to come off England's M22 motorway, drive onto a *Le Shuttle,* ride piggy-back under the ocean, roll off the train, and roll onto France's A16 or A26 *autoroute,* or vice versa. Of course connections to lesser roads are accessible as well. Unless passengers wanna stretch or use the toilets, there's no reason for them to get out of their vehicles: the chambers are brightly lit, sound-proofed and air-conditioned but extremely spartan, and while enroute Customs officials walk from vehicle to vehicle, checking passports. Motorcyclists, however, travel in a special compartment, separated from their cycles. The whole process, including the embarking and disembarking, takes an average of only one hour—compared to three if you employ a conventional ferry to achieve the same end.

Fares are charged per vehicle, no matter the number of passengers, with four sets according to the time of year. A standard round trip for a car ranges from $340 in November or December to $480 on a Friday or Saturday in July or August. There are no advance reservations; though tickets can be pre-paid through travel agents.

For people without a vehicle to transport, 394-meter-long "Eurostar" trains run through the Chunnel twice daily (once on Sunday, no service on Saturday) at 300 kph (186 mph) non stop between London's brand-new landmark Waterloo Station and the Midi Station in Brussels (with occasional stops in Lille, France) or the Gare du Nord in Paris—the London-to-Paris trip taking just three hours instead of the grueling six associated with ferry passage, and the standard class approximating a typical airliner's business class, complete with reading lamps and footrests. Starting soon, daily service will also run beyond London, from Paris and Brussels direct to Edinburgh, York, Manchester, and Birmingham, for example. Night sleepers will depart from Amsterdam, Dortmund, Frankfurt and Paris, direct to destinations such as the Welsh capital Cradiff, Bristol, and Glasgow.

It's said that travel through the Chunnel—protected by antiterrorism security measures similar to those at international airports—is at least 20 times safer than conventional rail travel, which in turn is much safer than ferry or car travel.

If you're curious about the construction of the Chunnel, you should check out the Eurotunnel Exhibition Center at Cheriton, near Folkestone. Besides a large operating model of the link, there's an observation tower giving a bird's-eye view of the Folkestone terminal. A simulator makes it possible to "drive" a tunnel construction train. You can take in an audiovisual show. And you can inspect a fullsize mock-up of a *Le Shuttle.*

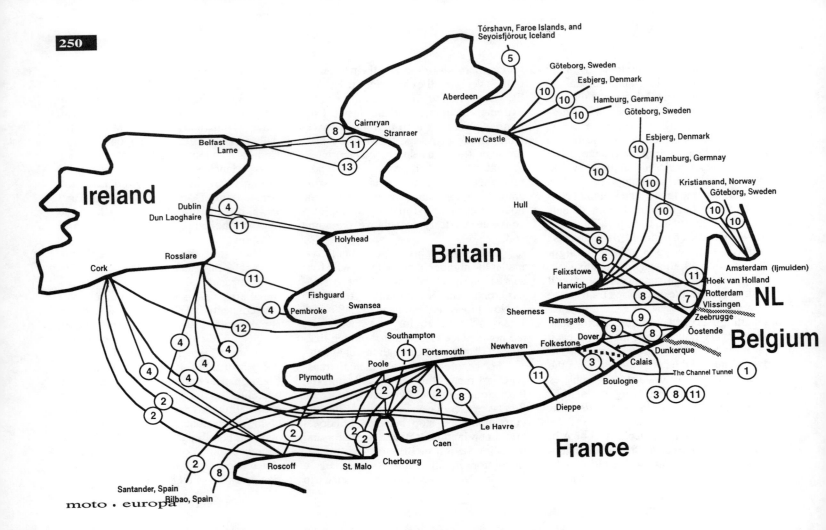

Tórshavn, Faroe Islands, and
Seyoisfjörour, Iceland
⑤

Göteborg, Sweden
⑩
Esbjerg, Denmark
⑩
Hamburg, Germany
⑩
Göteborg, Sweden
⑩
Esbjerg, Denmark
⑩
Hamburg, Germnay
⑩
Kristiansand, Norway
Göteborg, Sweden
⑩
⑩

Aberdeen

New Castle
⑩
⑩
⑩

Cairnryan
⑧ ⑪ Stranraer
⑬

Belfast
Larne

Ireland

Dublin ④
Dun Laoghaire ⑪

Rosslare
Holyhead

Cork

Britain

Hull
⑥
⑥

Amsterdam (Ijmuiden)

Felixstowe
Harwich ⑪ Hoek van Holland
⑧ ⑦ Rotterdam
NL
Vlissingen
Sheerness ⑨ Zeebrugge
Ramsgate ⑨
⑨ ⑧ Öostende Belgium
Dover
Folkestone
⑪ Southampton
⑪ Portsmouth Newhaven ③ Calais
Poole ⑪ Dunkerque
② ⑧ ② ⑧ Boulogne The Channel Tunnel ①
Plymouth Dieppe ③ ⑧ ⑪

② ② Le Havre
② ② ②
St. Malo Caen
⑧ Cherbourg
② Roscoff France
⑧

Santander, Spain
Bilbao, Spain

moto · europa

Fishguard
Pembroke ④
Swansea ⑫
④ ④
④ ④
④ ④
② ②

Principal Ferry Companies Serving the British Isles

1. The Channel Tunnel

For information, call 21 00 69 01 or FAX 21 35 89 89 in France. Call *Le Shuttle* in Britain at 01303 271100. Or call BritRail Travel in the US at 800 677 8585 or 212 575 2667, or Rail Europe at 800 387 6782.

2. Brittany Ferries

Tel. 01752 221 321 in Plymouth, England; tel. 01705 827 701 in Portsmouth. Tel. 31 96 88 80 in Caen, France; tel. 33 43 43 68 in Cherbourg; tel. 99 40 64 41, FAX 99 82 55 01 in Saint-Malo; tel. 98 29 28 28 or 98 29 28 29 in Roscoff. Tel. 021 277801, FAX 021 277801 in Cork, Ireland. Tel. 22 00 00 in Santander, Spain.

3. Hoverspeed

Tel. 01304 240241 in England; tel. 01303 221281 in Folkestone; tel. 01304 240101 in Dover. Tel. 21 30 27 26 in Boulogne, France; tel. 21 46 14 14 in Calais.

4. Irish Ferries

Tel. 800 243 8687 or 212 972 5600 in the United States. Tel. 01 661 0511, FAX 01 661 0743 in Dublin; tel. 021 504 333 or FAX 021 504 651 in Cork, Ireland; tel. 053 33158 or FAX 053 33544 in Rosslare. Tel. 0151 2273131 in England. Tel. 01407 760222 in Holyhead, Wales; tel. 01646 68416 in Pembroke. Tel. 01 42 66 90 90 in Paris; tel. 33 44 28 96 in Cherbourg, France; tel. 35 53 28 83 in Le Havre.

5. Strandfaraskip Landsins

Tel. 14550 or 16450, FAX 16000 in the Faroe Islands (Denmark).

6. North Sea Ferries

Tel. 201 768 5505 in the United States. Tel. 01482 377177 for reservations, FAX 01482 706438 in Britain. Tel. 305 491 7909 in the Netherlands.

7. Olau Lines

Tel. 01795 666666, FAX 01795 666919 in Britain. Tel. 01184 88000 in the Netherlands.

8. P&O European Ferries

Tel. 201 768 1187 in the United States. Tel. 0181 575 8555 in London; tel. 01304 212121 in Dover, England; tel. 01394 604040 in Felixstowe; tel. 01705 827677 in Portsmouth. Tel. 01581 200276 in Cairnryan, Scotland; tel. 01574 274321 in Larne. Tel. 1 800 409 049 in Dublin, Ireland. Tel. 1 44 51 00 51 in Paris; tel. 21 46 04 40 in Calais, France; tel. 35 19 78 50 in Le Havre; tel. 33 88 65 70 in Cherbourg. Tel. 050 542 222 in Zeebrugge, Belgium; tel. 059 559 995 or 059 707 601 in Öostende. Tel. 02503 21888 in Hoofdorp, Netherlands. Tel. 0211 38 70 60 in Düsseldorf, Germany. Tel. 0660 8412 in Austria. Tel. 94 423 4477 in Bilbao, Spain. Tel. 01 822 038889 in Switzerland.

9. Sally Line

Tel. 0181 858 1127 or 01843 595522, FAX 01843 589329 in Britain. To contact the motoring information and help hotline, tel. 01843 580 900 on weekdays from 9:00 A.M. to 6:00 P.M. Tel. 28 21 43 44 in Dunkerque, France. Tel. 59 55 99 54 in Öostende, Belgium.

10. Scandinavian Seaways

Tel. the DFDS Travel Center in the United States at 800 533 3755 or 305 491 7909. Tel. 01255 240240, FAX 01255 244382 in Harwich, England; tel. 0191 293 6262, FAX 0191 293 6222 in New Castle. Tel. 75 12 48 00 in Esbjerg, Denmark. Tel. 040 389 0371 in Hamburg, Germany. Tel. 031 65 06 00 in Göteborg, Sweden.

11. Stena Sealink Line

Tel. Britrail at 800 677 8585 in the United States. Tel. 0171 233 5832 or 01233 647047 in Britain; tel. 01233 647022 in Dover; tel. 01273 612999 in Newhaven; tel. 01255 242000 in Harwich; tel. 01703 235506 in Southampton. Tel. 01348 872881 in Fishguard, Wales; tel. 01407 762304 in Holyhead. Tel. 01574 273616 in Larne, Scotland; tel. 01776 703531 in Stranraer. Tel. 01 2808844 in Dublin; for 24-hour recorded information about timetables and fares tel. 01 2807046 for Dun Laoghaire/Holyhead, and 01 2807096 for Rosslare/Fishguard. Tel. 01 2807777 in Dun Laoghaire, Ireland; tel. 053 33115 in Rosslare. Tel. 21 46 80 80 in Calias, France; tel. 33 20 43 38 in Cherbourg; tel. 35 06 39 00 in Dieppe. Tel. 1747 89333 in Hoek van Holland, Netherlands; tel. 020 622 9105 or 020 624 4041 in Amsterdam. You can also reserve by calling the following: Belgium/Luxembourg, 02 513 3818; Denmark, 98 42 43 66; France, 1 47 42 86 87 or 20 06 29 44; Germany, 021 19 05 51 50 or 04 31 90 92 00; Italy, 2 65 35 63; Netherlands, 20 62 55 33 56; Spain, 91 542 4376; Sweden, 31 75 30 30 or 08 14 14 75.

moto · europa

12. Swansea Cork Ferries

Tel. 01792 456116 or FAX 01792 644356 in Swansea, Wales. Tel. 021 271 166, FAX 021 275 061 in Cork, Ireland.

13. Seacat

Tel. 01345 523523.

Hoverspeed:

Dover, England—Calais, France; 35 minutes by Hovercraft, 55 minutes by Seacat catamaran (Folkestone—Boulogne). The Seacat fares are significantly lower than those below, which are for the Hovercraft.

	low	med	high
Vehicle + driver	£109	142	166
Vehicle + up to 2 passengers	124	162	181
Vehicle + up to 5 passengers	130	169	188
Extra passengers	10	10	10
Extra charge for each meter over 5.5 meters	15	18	20
Motorcycle & driver + passenger	59	69	75
Bicycle	5	5	5
Adult on foot	25	25	25
Child (aged 4–15) on foot	15	15	15

Stena Sealink Line:

Dover, England—Calais, France; 1.5 hours. High and medium season mixed: roughly April 1 to December 31. Low season: roughly January 4 to March 31. Discount of 20 percent on normal passenger fare for HI members; tickets available at port ticket office only, not from travel agents. Cheaper "Nightrider" fares offered.

	low	med	high
Car (less than 6 m long and 2.2 m high + driver	£60	100	130
Car + 2 passengers	70	110	140
Car + up to 9 passengers	80	120	150
Vehicle or vehicle combo over 6 m long or 2.2 m high	110	150	200
Motorcycle + up to 3 passengers	46	50	60
Adult on foot	25	25	25
Child (aged 4–13), senior (over 60), or student with ISIC	14	14	14

Irish Ferries:

Pembroke, Wales—Rosslare, Ireland; Holyhead, Wales—Dublin, Ireland; crossing time: 4.25 hours from Pembroke, 4 hours from Holyhead. Sails twice daily. High season: roughly July 14 to September 3. Medium Season: roughly April 20 to April 23 and from June 1 to June 4. Low season: roughly June 5 to July 13 and from September 4 to October 12. Irish travel tax of $7.50 applies to all sailings from Ireland; this tax is not included in the fares below.

	v. low*	low*	med.*	high*
Vehicle** + up to 5 adults	£84	119	149	159
Motorcycle or bicycle	free	free	free	free
Adult	19	21	25	25
Senior or student	17	18	22	22
Child (aged 5–15)	9.50	10.50	12.50	12.50

*Fares for the early sailings from Rosslare (8:30 A.M.) and Pembroke (2:15 P.M.) are £10–25 cheaper than those listed above—except for the early sailing from Pembroke during very low season, which is £10 more. And fares for the late sailings from Rosslare (20:30 P.M.) and Pembroke (2:55 A.M.) during medium season are £5 more

**Vehicles in excess of 1.82 meters high or 6.5 meters long must be declared at time of booking or a supplement may apply.

Stena Sealink Line Sea Lynx Catamaran or HHS:

Holyhead, Wales—Dun Laoghaire, Ireland; 110 minutes for the Sea Lynx, 99 minutes for the HHS. High Season: roughly July 14 to September 3. Medium season: roughly May 28 to high season, and from high season to roughly September 30. Stena Line offers a reduction of 25 percent off normal passenger fare for HI members; tickets available at port ticket offices only, not from travel agents. Irish travel tax of $7.50 applies to all sailings from Ireland; this tax is not included in the fares below.

	low	med	high
Car + driver	£86	106	146

ferries & the chunnel

Vehicle + 2 adults	96	106	156
Vehicle + up to 9 adults	106	126	166
Vehicles over 6 m long or 2.2 m high	182	222	282
Motorcycle + up to 3 adults	40	48	54
Adult on foot	22	22	22
Student* or Senior** or Child (aged 4–13) on foot	12	12	12

*student fares are only valid on presentation of a current <u>usit</u> card.
**over 60 years old.

Student/senior* on foot or in vehicle	16	17	21	21
Child** on foot or in vehicle	10	10	13	13
Adult cabin*** supplement	16	16	16	16
Child cabin*** supplement	16	16	16	16

^up to 5 meters in length; add £15 for each additional meter. Vehicles with a
height exceeding 2 meters must be declared at time of booking or a supplement
will apply.
*aged over 60 years.
**5–16 years of age.

***cabins are rented whole, not by berth.

Swansea Cork Ferries:

Swansea, Wales—Cork, Ireland; 10 hours. High season: roughly July
19 to August 21. Medium season: roughly August 23 to September 4,
April 11 to 14, May 25 to 29, and December 17 to 30. Low season: roughly
May 30 to July 17, and roughly September 6 to October 9. Irish travel tax
of $7.50 applies to all sailings from Ireland; this tax is not included in the
fares below.

	v. low	*low*	*med.*	*high*
Vehicle^ + up to 5 adults	£95	115	149	165
Van or caravan supplement	10	10	10	10
Motorcycle	41	46	51	55
Bicycle	7	7	7	7
Adult on foot or in vehicle	20	20	26	27

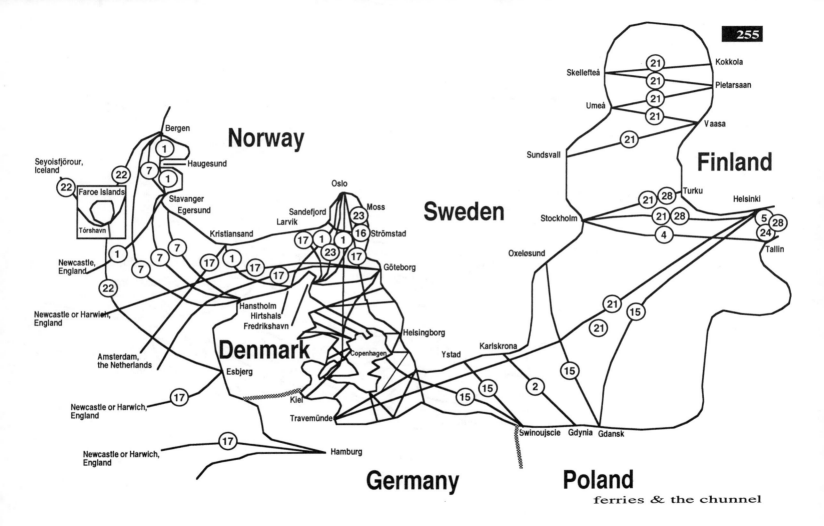

ferries & the chunnel

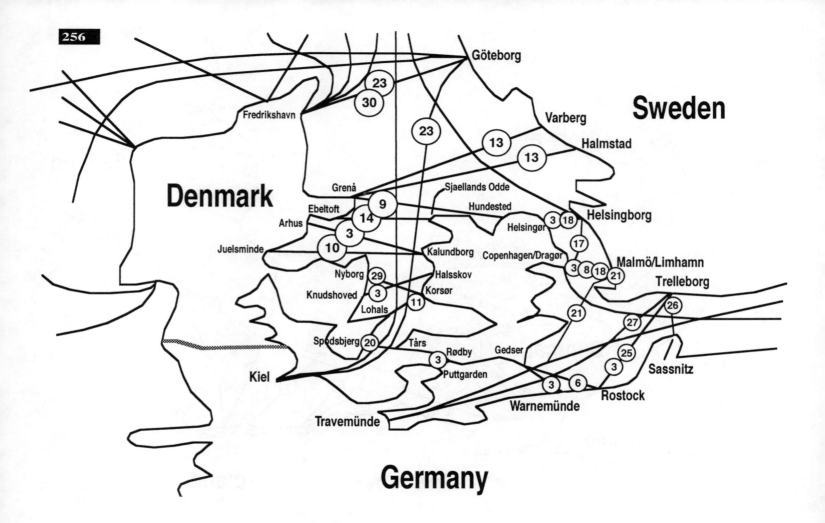

Principal Ferry Companies Serving Scandinavia

1. Color Line

In the United States contact the Bergen Line at 800 323 7436 or 212 986 2711, FAX 212 983 1275, or call 800 666 2374 for brochure orders. In England contact the Color Line at 091 296 1313, FAX 091 296 1540. Tel. 99 56 1977, FAX 98 94 56 92 in Hirtshals, Denmark. Tel. 55 54 86 00, FAX 55 54 86 01 in Bergen, Norway; tel. 38 07 88 88, FAX 38 07 88 13 in Kristiansand; tel. 22 94 44 70, FAX 22 83 07 76 in Oslo.

2. Corona Line

Tel. 58 213524, FAX 58 216667 in Poland. Tel. 45 54 66 00, FAX 45 54 66 73 in Sweden.

3. DSB

Tel. 86 18 17 88 in Århus, Denmark; tel. 33 15 15 15 in Copenhagen; tel. 32 53 15 85 in Dragør; tel. 53 87 91 45 in Gedser; tel. 53 57 15 77 in Halsskov; tel. 59 56 08 81 in Kalundborg; tel. 49 26 26 83 in Helsingør; tel. 65 31 40 54 in Knudshoved; tel. 54 60 51 66 in Rødby. Tel. 04319 81133 in Kiel, Germany; tel. 04371 865111 in Puttgarden; tel. 03815 195151 for Rostock and Warnemünde. Tel. 42 18 61 00 in Helsingborg, Sweden; tel. 40 36 20 41 in Limhamn.

4. Estline

Tel. 800 688 3876 or 212 691 2099, FAX 212 366 4747 in the United States. Tel. 0142 441434, FAX 0142 247704 in Tallin, Estonia. Tel. 08 66 70 001, FAX 08 20 62 48 in Sweden.

5. Estonian New Line

Tel. 0 680 2499, FAX 0 680 2475 in Finland.

6. Europa-Linien

Tel. 53 87 00 55, FAX 53 87 96 33 in Denmark. Tel. 366 31030, FAX 366 21789 in Germany.

7. Fjord Line

Tel. 800 545 2204, FAX 201 835 3030 in United States. Tel. 97 96 14 01, FAX 97 96 27 43 in Hanstholm, Denmark. Tel. 55 14 11 00 or 55 32 37 70, FAX 55 32 38 15 in Bergen, Norway; tel. 51 49 33 88, FAX 47 55 31 20 77 in Egersund. For the Askøy-Bergen Rutlag service between Bergen and Stavanger, tel. 55 32 74 91, FAX 55 32 38 15 in Bergen.

8. Flyvebådene

Tel. 33 12 80 88, FAX 33 93 33 10 in Copenhagen, Denmark. Tel. 40 10 39 30, FAX 40 12 04 84 in Sweden.

9. Grenaa-Hundested

Tel. 86 32 16 00 in Grenå, Denmark; tel. 42 33 82 33 in Hundested.

10. Kattegatbroen

Tel. 75 69 48 00 in Juelsminde, Denmark; tel. 53 51 51 33 in Kalundborg; FAX 75 69 44 65 in Denmark.

11. Langelandsfærgen

Tel. 62 55 21 24, FAX 62 55 19 45 in Denmark.

12. Larvik Line

Tel. the DFDS Travel Center in the United States at 800 533 3755 or 305 491 7909. Tel. 98 41 14 00, FAX 98 43 25 74 in Denmark. Tel. 22 52 45 00, FAX 22 43 41 56 in Norway. Contact Scandinavian Seaways in Britain at tel. 01255 240240.

13. Lion Ferry

Tel. 86 32 03 00, FAX 86 32 75 25 in Grenå, Denmark. Tel. 31 85 80 00 in Sweden; tel. 34 01 80 30, FAX 34 08 51 25 in Varberg; tel. 35 13 51 70, FAX 35 13 08 75 in Halmstad.

14. Mols Linien

Tel. 89 52 52 52 in Ebeltoft, Denmark; tel. 59 32 32 32 in Sj. Odde.

15. Polferries (known in Poland as Polish Baltic Navigation or PZB)

Tel. 800 688 3876 or 212 691 2099, FAX 212 366 4747 in the United States and Canada. Tel. 0171 251 3398, FAX 0171 250 3625 in England. Tel. 33 11 46 45, FAX 33 11 95 78 in Denmark. Tel. 0 680901, FAX 0 6809633 in Finland. Tel. 0936 5174, FAX 0936 4818 in Swinoujscie, Poland; tel.

058 431887, FAX 058 430975 in Gdansk. Tel. 41 11 60 10, FAX 41 11 69 22 in Ystad, Sweden.

16. Scandi Line

Tel. 33 46 08 00, FAX 33 46 25 08 in Norway.

17. Scandinavian Seaways

Tel. the DFDS Travel Center in the United States at 800 533 3755 or 305 491 7909. Tel. 01255 240240, FAX 01255 244382 in Harwich, England; tel. 0191 293 6262, FAX 0191 293 6222 in New Castle. Tel. 75 12 48 00 in Esbjerg, Denmark. Tel. 31 65 06 00 Göteborg, Sweden. Tel. 04038 90371 in Hamburg, Germany.

18. Scandlines

Tel. 32 53 15 85, FAX 49 26 11 24 in Copenhagen, Denmark; tel. 49 26 26 83 in Helsingør. Tel. 42 18 61 00, Helsingborg, Sweden; tel. 40 36 20 41 in Limhamn.

19. Scarlett Line

Tel. 39 27 37 00, FAX 39 27 12 72 in Denmark. Tel. 41 82 80 65, FAX 41 82 63 63 in Sweden.

20. SFDS

Tel. 62 50 10 22 in Spodsbjerg, Denmark; tel. 53 93 13 23 in Tårs.

21. Silja Line

Tel. 800 533 3755 or 305 491 7909 in the United States. Tel. 800 461 8651 or 416 222 0740, FAX 416 222 5004 in Canada. Tel. Scandinavian Seaways in Britain at 0255 240 240. Tel. 90 180 4555, FAX 90 180 4353 in Helsinki, Finland; tel. 92 165 2255, FAX 92 165 26375 in Turku. Tel. 04502 4077 in Germany. Tel. 08 22 21 40, FAX 86 67 14 60 in Stockholm, Sweden; tel 09 04 09 80 in Umeå; tel. 60 12 93 10 in Sundsvall; tel. 91 01 41 60 in Skellefteå.

22. Smyril Line

Tel. 800 688 3876 or 212 691 2099, FAX 212 366 4747 in the United States. Tel. 75 12 48 00, FAX 75 18 11 01 in Denmark.

23. Stena Line

Tel. 800 688 3876 or 212 691 2099, FAX 212 366 4747 in the United States. Tel. 96 20 02 00, FAX 96 20 02 80 in Fredrikshavn, Denmark. Tel. 431 9090, FAX 431 909200 in Kiel, Germany; tel. 4502 4037 in Travemünde. Tel. 22 41 22 10, FAX 22 41 44 40 in Oslo, Norway; tel. 69 25 75 00 in Moss. Tel. 31 85 80 00, FAX 31 85 85 86 in Göteborg, Sweden.

24. Tallink

Tel. 800 688 3876 or 212 691 2099 in the United States. Tel. 0 2282 1211 or 0 2282 1228, FAX 0 635 311 in Finland

25. TR-Line

Tel. 800 688 3876 or 212 691 2099 in the United States. Tel. 0381 670790, FAX 0381 6707980 in Rostock, Germany. Tel. 0410 56200, FAX 0410 56 170 in Trelleborg, Sweden.

26. TS-Line (Hansa Ferry)

Tel. 41 01 03 90 or 40 20 20 00, FAX 41 01 33 86 or 40 12 02 19 in Sweden.

27. TT-Line

Tel. 800 688 3876 or 212 691 2099 in the United States. Tel. 04502 8010, FAX 04502 5983 in Travemünde, Germany. Tel. 0410 56200, FAX 0410 56169 in Trelleborg, Sweden.

28. Viking Line

Tel. 800 688 3876 or 212 691 2099 in the United States. Tel. 800 387 1876 or 416 364 2738 in Canada. Tel. 02 273 381 in Australia. Tel. 0171 839 2927 or 0345 581 400, FAX 0171 839 5891 in England. Tel. 90 12351, FAX 90 123 5327 in Helsinki, Finland; tel. 921 63311 in Turku. Tel. 86 44 07 65, FAX 86 41 32 72 in Sweden.

29. Vognmandstruten

Tel. 65 31 03 33, FAX 65 31 55 89 in Nyborg, Denmark; tel. 53 57 12 33, FAX 53 57 07 05, in Korsør.

30. SeaCatamaran Danmark

Tel. 98 42 83 00 in Fredrikshavn, Denmark. Tel. 31 77 75 08 00 in Göteborg, Sweden.

Vognmandsruten:

Nyborg, Denmark—Korsør, Denmark; 1 hour, 17–24 sailings per day.

Car or van	$36
Caravan	49

ferries & the chunnel

Motorcycle	7
Bicycle	4
Adult in vehicle or on foot	7
Child (13 years and under)	4

Larvik Line:

Fredrikshavn, Denmark—Larvik, Norway; 6 to 12 hours. A 10 percent discount is offered to HI members. High season: roughly June 17 to August 7.

	low	*high*
Car + driver	$71	104
Car + 2 passengers	102	147
Car + up to 6 passengers	105	154
Van or caravan	105	136
Motorcycle	23	31
Adult on foot	33	48
Child on foot	17	24
Adult cabin supplement	17	23
Child cabin supplement	11	14

DSB:

Copenhagen, Denmark—Malmö, Sweden; 1 hour.

Car or van + up to 5 passengers	$43
Caravan + up to 5 passengers	65
Motorcycle + up to 2 passengers	15
Bicycle	3
Adult on foot	3
Child (aged 7–15)	2

Flyvebædene:

Copenhagen, Denmark—Malmö, Sweden; 0.75 hours. NO MOTOR VEHICLES. Discount of 15 percent for groups of 10 or more.

Adult	$12
Child (aged 2–12)	5
Youth (aged 13–17) or Senior	9
Bicycle	4

DSB:
Helsingør, Denmark—Helsingborg, Sweden; 0.40 hours.

Car or van + up to 5 passengers	$39
Caravan + up to 5 passengers	59
Adult on foot	3
Child (aged 7–11) or senior	2

Stena Line:
Fredrikshavn, Denmark—Göteborg, Sweden; 4.5 hours. High season: roughly June 17 to August 14. A discount of 10 percent is offered to HI members, but tickets are obtainable only at Terra Nova Travel Sections and valid for Monday through Thursday travel from June through August.

	low	high
Car or van + up to 5 passengers	$67	88
Caravan + up to 5 passengers	105	141
Motorcycle + 2 passengers	29	47
Adult on foot	15	23
Child (aged 6–15) on foot	8	12
Student or senior on foot	8	14

Tallink:
Tallinn, Estonia—Helsinki, Finland; 4 hours. Also operate a hydrofoil service that does not carry vehicles and takes only 1.5 hours. Passenger fares below apply to hydrofoil too.

Car	$36
Van or caravan	63
Motorcycle	9
Adult	22
2 children (aged 6–11) per adult	free

DSB:
Puttgarden, Germany—Rødby, Denmark; 1 hour, 28–40 sailings/day.

Car or van + up to 5 passengers	$50
Caravan + up to 5 passengers	63
Motorcycle + up to 2 passengers	27
Bicycle	3
Adult on foot	6
Child (aged 4–11) on foot	3

DSB:
Warnemünde, Germany—Gedser, Denmark; 2 hours, 4–7 sailings/day.

Car or van + up to 5 passengers	$40

Caravan + up to 5 passengers	59
Motorcycle + up to 2 passengers	27
Bicycle	3
Adult on foot	6
Child (aged 4–11) on foot	3

TR-Line:

Rostock, Germany—Trelleborg, Sweden; 5–8 hours. Day and night sailings. High Season: roughly June 10 to August 28. Discounts of roughly 10 percent for groups of 10 or more.

	day/night low	high
Car + driver, or motorcycle + up to 2 passengers, or up to 2 bicyclists	$32/63	39/79
Car + up to 5 passengers, or motorcycle + up to 3 passengers, or up to 5 bicyclists	50/79	74/103
Van or caravan + up to 5 passengers	100/153	137/166
Adult on foot	21/42	21/42
Child (aged 6–14) on foot	11/21	11/21
Senior or student on foot	16/32	16/32
Adult cabin supplement	13/21	13/21
Child (aged 6–14) cabin supplement	9/16	9/16

TS-Line (Hansa Ferry):

Rostock or Sassnitz, Germany—Trelleborg, Sweden; 6 or 4 hours, respectively. High season: roughly June 1 to August 31.

	low	high
Car or van + up to 5 passengers	$62	65
Caravan + up to 5 passengers	80	93
Motorcycle + up to 2 passengers	27	27
Bicycle + passenger	8	8
Adult on foot	6	6
Child (aged 4–11) or senior	3	3
Adult cabin supplement	11	12
Child (aged 4–11) cabin supplement	9	10

Polferries:

Gdansk, Poland—Oxelösund, Sweden; 19 hours overnight. Seniors deduct $10 off cabin charge. Children under 6 years of age can travel free of charge without their own berth. Discounts available to students, families, and groups. Also offered are vehicle + passengers packages offered that should reduce the average fare.

Car	$120
Van or caravan	185
Motorcycle	37
Adult in 2-berth cabin	87
Adult in 4-berth cabin	74
Child (under 16) in cabin	55

Polferries:

Swinoujscie, Poland—Ystad, Sweden; 7 hours at day, 9 hours overnight. High season: roughly June 12 to August 13. Seniors deduct $9 off cabin charge. Children under 6 years of age can travel free of charge without their own berth. Discounts available to students, families, and groups. Also offered are vehicle + passengers packages that should reduce the average fare.

	low	high
Car	$75	85
Van or caravan	111	130
Motorcycle	19	19

Adult	46	46
Child (aged 6–12)	30	30
Adult in 2-berth cabin	72	72
Adult in 4-berth cabin	63	107
Child (aged 6–12) in cabin	47	91

Viking Line:

Stockholm, Sweden—Helsinki, Finland; 15 hours overnight. High season: roughly June 17 to August 14. Fares include buffet breakfast. Children under 12 travel free. Reductions of 25 percent offered to railpass holders, etc. A combination ticket with TR-Line is offered as well.

	low	high
Car or van	$27	32
Caravan	98	109
Adult on foot	18	32
Family member, student, senior	12	21
Cabin	49	49

Viking Line:

Stockholm, Sweden—Turku, Finland; 10 hours at day, 12 hours at night. High season: roughly June 17 to August 14. Fares include buffet breakfast. Children under 12 travel free. Discounts of 25 percent offered to senior citizens, rail pass holders, etc. A combination ticket with TR-Line is offered as well.

	day/night	
	low	*high*
Car or van	$20	32
Caravan	78	109
Motorcycle	10	16
Adult	14	32
Group member or child or senior	8	21
Cabin	25	25

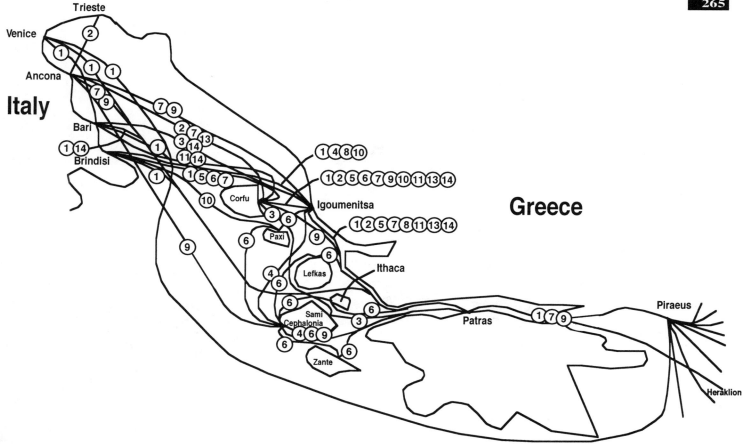

ferries & the chunnel

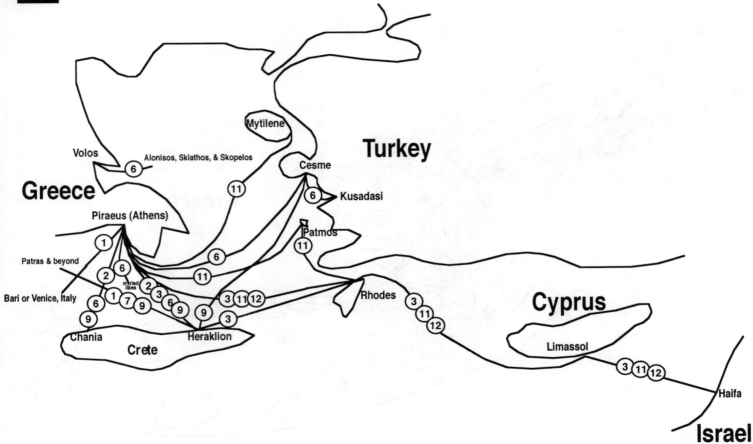

Greece

Turkey

Cyprus

Israel

Mytilene

Volos

Alonisos, Skiathos, & Skopelos

⑥

⑪

Cesme

⑥ Kusadasi

Piraeus (Athens)

①

Patras & beyond

⑥

②

Bari or Venice, Italy

⑥ ① ⑦ ⑨

⑨

② ③

⑥ ⑨

myriad isles

⑥

⑪

Patmos

⑪

③ ⑪ ⑫

⑨

③

⑨

③

Rhodes

③

⑪

⑫

Limassol

③ ⑪ ⑫

Haifa

Chania

Heraklion

Crete

moto · europa

Ferry Companies Serving the Eastern Mediterranean

Many of the ferry services I describe in this section stop running for substantial periods during the year. Furthermore, although daily services abound, the long duration of many of the sailings in the Eastern Mediterranean—especially the non-stop sailings—means that some services make only one or two sailings per week. Thus it's very important that you call ahead.

1. Adriatica

Contact Extra Value travel, Inc., tel. 813 394 3384 in the United States. Tel. 0661 38089, FAX 0661 35416 in Corfu, Greece; tel. 081 227 003, FAX 081 223 749 in Heraklion; tel. 0665 26715, FAX 0665 22101 in Igoumenitsa; tel. 061 422 138, FAX 061 653 510 in Patras; tel. 01 429 1396, FAX 01 429 1299 in Piraeus. Tel. 080 330 360, FAX 080 330 628 in Bari, Italy; tel. 0831 523 825, FAX 0831 568 332 in Brindisi; tel. 041 781 867, FAX 041 781 894 in Venice.

2. Anek Lines

Contact Viamare Travel Limited in London, tel. 071 431 4560, FAX 071 431 5456.

3. Arkadia Line

Tel. 800 367 1789 or 310 544 3551, FAX 310 541 0166 in the United States. Contact Viamare Travel Limited in London, tel. 071 431 4560, FAX 071 431 5456. Tel. 080 521 7699 or FAX 080 521 8229 in Bari, Italy.

Tel. 01 61 23 402–7 or 01 61 23 461–6 or FAX 01 61 26 206 in Athens, Greece; tel. 0665 22797 in Igoumenitsa; tel. 081 242 226 in Heraklion; tel. 0241 24 955 on Rhodes. Tel. 05 362223 in Limassol, Cyprus. Tel. 04 671743 or FAX 04 670530 in Haifa, Israel.

4. European Seaways

Tel. 800 367 1789 or 310 544 3551, FAX 310 541 0166 in the United States. Tel. 0831 527667 or 0831 527668, FAX 0831 564070 in Brindisi, Italy. Tel. 0661 44455 in Corfu, Greece; tel. 0665 22409 in Igoumenitsa; tel. 0674 22456 in Cephalonia; tel. 061 270948, FAX 061 226110 in Patras.

5. Fraglines

Contact Time & Tide, tel. 800 472 8999 or 212 861 2500, FAX 212 517 9867 in the United States. Contact Viamare Travel Limited in London, tel. 071 431 4560, FAX 071 431 5456. Tel. 822 1285 in Greece.

6. Hellenic Mediterranean Line

Contact all Leisure Travel in San Francisco, tel. 415 989 7434, FAX 415 986 4037. Tel. 071 499 0076, FAX 071 495 2617 in London. Tel. 831 528531, FAX 831 526872 in Brindisi, Italy. Tel. 6742 2150 in Cephalonia, Greece; tel. 6652 5682, FAX 6652 4960 in Igoumenitsa; tel. 6743 3120, FAX 6743 3130 in Ithaca; tel. 6142 9520, FAX 6142 1352 in Patras; tel. 6623 2201, FAX 6623 2036 in Paxi; tel. 1422 5341, FAX 1422 5317 in Piraeus.

7. Marlines

Contact Viamare Travel Limited in London, tel. 071 431 4560, FAX 071 431 5456. Tel. 071 50062, FAX 071 54268 in Ancona, Italy. Tel. 411 0777 in Greece.

8. Mediterranean Lines

Contact Viamare Travel Limited in London, tel. 071 431 4560, FAX 071 431 5456. Tel. 061 274451 in Patras, Greece.

9. Minoan Lines

Tel. 800 367 1789 or 310 544 3551, FAX 310 541 0166 in the United States. Tel. 071 201 708, FAX 071 201 933 in Ancona, Italy. Tel. 0665 22952, FAX 0665 22101 in Igoumenitsa, Greece; tel. 0661 25000, FAX 0661 46555 in Corfu; tel. 0674 23021, FAX 0674 22635 in Cephalonia; tel. 061 421500, FAX 061 420800 in Patras; tel. 01 4113819, FAX 01 4118631 in Piraeus; tel. 081 229646, FAX 081 226479 in Heraklion; tel. 0821 45911, FAX 0821 45654 in Chania. Tel. 0232 7127230, FAX 0232 7128987 in Cesme, Turkey.

10. Misano Lines

Tel. 831 562043, FAX 831 562081 in Brindisi, Italy; tel. 06 4440527, FAX 06 4940777 in Rome.

11. Poseidon Lines

Tel. 800 367 1789 or 310 544 3551, FAX 310 541 0166 in the United States. Contact Viamare Travel Limited in London, tel. 071 431 4560, FAX 071 431 5456. Tel. 080 521 0022 or FAX 080 521 1204 in Bari, Italy. Tel. 01 42 92 046 or 01 42 92 041, FAX 01 42 92 041 in Piraeus, Greece.

12. Stability Lines

Contact Viamare Travel Limited in London, tel. 071 431 4560, FAX 071 431 5456. Tel. 4132 392 in Greece.

13. Strintzis Lines

Tel. 800 367 1789 or 310 544 3551, FAX 310 541 0166 in the United States. Contact Viamare Travel Limited in London, tel. 071 431 4560, FAX 071 431 5456. Tel. 4132 392 in Greece.

14. Ventouris Ferries

Contact Viamare Travel Limited in London, tel. 071 431 4560, FAX 071 431 5456. Tel. 482 8901 in Greece.

Hellenic Mediterranean Lines:
Brindisi, Italy—Corfu, Greece—Igoumenitsa, Greece—Paxi, Greece—Cephalonia, Greece—Patras, Greece; 8 hours to Corfu, 10 hours to Igoumenitsa, 18 hours to Patras. Day and night sailings. High season: Italy to Greece from roughly July 22 to August 14, Greece to Italy from roughly August 13 to September 3. Reduction of 20 percent on passenger and vehicle fares for return portion of round trip ticket. Reduction of 10 percent on passenger and vehicle fares for auto club members.

	low	high
Car	$46	79
Van or caravan	82	179
Motorcycle	33	36

Adult in seat	60	87
Child (aged 2–12) in seat	30	44
Adult in cabin	122	207
Child (aged 2–12) in cabin	61	104

Service continues from Cephalonia to Ithaca, Zante, or Lefkas.

(low/high)

	Ithaca	Zante	Lefkas
Car	$60/93	76/108	79/111
Van or caravan	120/217	105/202	144/241
Motorcycle	40/43	39/42	40/43
Adult in seat	63/90	65/92	65/92
Child (aged 2–12) in seat	32/45	33/46	33/46
Adult in cabin	122/207	122/207	122/207
Child (aged 2–12) in cabin	61/104	61/104	61/104

Misano:

Brindisi, Italy—Igoumenitsa, Greece—Corfu, Greece; 4 hours.
Brindisi, Italy—Paxi, Greece; 6 hours. HYDROFOIL; DOES NOT
TAKE VEHICLES. High season: Italy to Greece from roughly July 22 to
August 15, Greece to Italy from roughly August 13 to September 4.

Reduction of 10 percent off fare on return portion of round-trip ticket.
Group rates available.

	Corfu		Paxi	
	low	high	low	high
Adult	$57	84	75	105
Child (aged 2–12)	29	42	38	53
Youth (under 26)	42	60	60	81

Adriatica:

Venice, Italy—Patras, Greece; 43 hours. High season: Italy to Greece
from roughly July 1 to August 15.

	low	high
Car up to 4 meters long	$96	100
Car over 4 meters long	141	151
Van or caravan up to 6 meters long	176	196
Van or caravan over 6 meters long	206	256
Motorcycle	46	46
Adult cabin supplement	276	296
Child (aged 2–12) cabin supplement	118	126

Adriatica:

Piraeus, Greece—Bari, Italy; 23 hours. High season: Greece to Italy from roughly July 10 to September 19.

	low	*high*
Car up to 4 meters long	$80	90
Car over 4 meters long	110	120
Van or caravan up to 6 meters long	145	160
Van or caravan over 6 meters long	165	185
Motorcycle	35	35
Adult cabin supplement	225	250
Child (aged 2–12) cabin supplement	95	103

Adriatica:

Piraeus, Greece—Venice, Italy; 48 hours. High season: Greece to Italy from roughly July 10 September 19.

	low	*high*
Car up to 4 meters long	$110	120
Car over 4 meters long	160	175
Van or caravan up to 6 meters long	205	230
Van or caravan over 6 meters long	240	260
Motorcycle	50	55

Adult cabin supplement	320	355
Child (aged 2–12) cabin supplement	135	145

Hellenic Mediterranean Lines:

Piraeus, Greece—Heraklion on Crete; 12 hours. **Piraeus, Greece—Chania on Crete;** 12 hours. One child under 2 years of age travels free of charge. Additional children under 2 years of age in the same family pay half fare each. Children over 2 and under 12 years of age pay half fare each. Discount of 10 percent for departures from January 1 to May 31 and from October 16 to December 31.

Car	$76
Van	161
Caravan	218
Motorcycle	16
Adult in cabin	68

Hellenic Mediterranean Lines:

Piraeus, Greece—Cesme, Turkey—Kusadasi, Turkey; 15 hours to Ceseme, 16 hours to Kusadasi. One child under 2 years of age travels free of charge. Additional children under 2 years of age in the same family pay half fare each. Children over 2 and under 12 years of age pay half fare each. Discount of 10 percent for departures from January 1 to May 31 and from October 16 to December 31.

	Cesme	*Kusadasi*
Car	$196	$228

Van	325	359
Caravan	456	502
Motorcycle	39	47
Adult on deck	90	85

part 3

· · · · · · · · · · · ·

appendices

a. questions renters should ask

On the Phone With Your Auto-Insurance Agent, Credit or Charge Card Company, or Other Potential Auto-Insurance Provider

Name of person you're speaking with?

Are you covered for renting and driving a vehicle abroad?

What countries does the insurance cover you in?

Does it cover drivers besides yourself? If so, is there a charge for additional drivers?

What is the deductible?

Does the insurance cover damage from collision, fire, natural disaster, vandalism or attempted theft?

Does it cover theft?

Does it cover at-fault drivers?

What types of vehicles is it limited to?

Does it cover fines for traffic violations?

Is baggage insurance included?

Is there a consecutive-day limit?

Does it cover "loss of use" charges?

Does it cover damages poor roads may cause to, say, the underbelly of a vehicle?

If investigating credit or charge card insurance, ask if the coverage is primary or secondary. Can the rental company bill your account directly? If so, will the status of such a billing require you to pay the charge immediately to avoid incurring a finance charge? Will it eat into your credit line? Are credit holds which the rental company may want to put on a card in line with your policies?

On the Phone With the Rental Company Agent

Person's name you're speaking with?

What are the age criteria?

For how long must you have had your license?

If you don't have a credit card, ask how you can go about paying for the rental and for any deposit.

Tell the rep where you want to take delivery.

Do you need an IDP?

Is the company a consolidator? If so, which local independent supplier will provide your vehicle? Will the policies quoted by the consolidator be exactly the same as those of the supplier? If so, tell the rep that you want this promise in writing.

Establish the class and type of vehicle you want the price quotes based on. If you're a gambler or just want a small car, ask for economy class.

Establish the time period you want the price quotes based on—the longer the cheaper.

Note the company's definition of a *week*.

Ask that the rates be quoted in dollars and that they include tax. If you've determined that you don't need to buy a CDW or LDW or TP, ask that the cost of these not be included either.

Ask if you can stipulate that you neither have to buy TP nor place a deposit on the vehicle. Ask that this stipulation be put in writing and that it state that any foreign agent will honor the agreement.

If you must buy TP or place a deposit, ask how much the TP costs and the amount and means of the deposit.

Is unlimited mileage included?

Is there a surcharge for additional drivers?

Are alteration or cancellation fees associated with a reservation?

In what countries does the basic included insurance and the registration allow you to drive the vehicle?

Is the insurance Green Card insurance?

If you plan to transport the vehicle on ferries, make sure the included insurance and the registration allows this.

Is the basic included insurance liability-only?

What is the amount of the liability coverage?

Does it cover multiple drivers?

Does it cover at-fault drivers?

Are bail bonds included for Spain and Greece?

Does the included insurance cover damage done to the vehicle as a result of bad roads (especially in Greece)?

If the basic included insurance covers more than liability, does it cover damage from collision, fire, natural disaster, vandalism or attempted theft. Does it cover theft? What's the deductible?

If you need to buy the CDW or LDW, ask the above questions about it. How much does the waiver cost? If theft protection is extra, how much does it cost?

Is baggage insurance offered? What does it cover? How much does it cost?

Is personal accident insurance (PAI) offered? What does it cover? How much does it cost?

How will you be served in the event of an accident or breakdown? Is this service guaranteed to be timely?

Are any special services (such as translation services) or materials (such as maps) offered?

Is there a surcharge for taking delivery of or returning your vehicle at the airport(s) you plan to use?

If your itinerary demands that you return the vehicle at another location, what is the return charge for this location? Is there a cheaper alternative?

Ask what the daily charge will be if you decide to extend your tour. Ask how much notice you must give of such an extension.

Is there a refund for early return? Or will an early return result in your having to pay a daily rate instead of, say, a weekly rate.

What are the business hours during which you can take delivery of and return the vehicle?

What safety accouterments are included? If the items included don't satisfy the requirements of all the countries in which you'll be driving the vehicle, negotiate for inclusion of all the necessary items.

If inquiring about a motorhome, what is included in the price? Bedding? Kitchen utensils? Cleaning? etc.

If you plan to take a British vehicle to the continent, or vice versa, ask if headlight conversion kits are available free of charge.

If you need a luggage rack, a bicycle rack, a ski rack, tire chains, etc., ask if these items are available free of charge.

Ask if a parking disc or "blue card" is included.

If renting outside Switzerland but planning to drive there, ask if a Swiss toll sticker or *vignette* can be included.

Ask that the rental company deliver the vehicle with a full tank and that they agree not to charge you for fuel unless you return the vehicle with less than a full tank. At least feign disinterest if the representative claims this is not possible.

Ask about programs associated with airlines or ferries or the Chunnel.

Ask about special rates or terms associated with your employer or with national organizations you belong to.

If the representative will not disclose the rates associated with special programs or groups, just call back later.

Can you get a written price guarantee in the foreign currency, along with a written guarantee—which should include a clause stating that any foreign agent or local independent supplier will honor the guarantee—of your other agreements?

If you decide to rent from this particular company, get a confirmation number. Ask that this number be placed on your written guarantee.

Taking Delivery of the Vehicle

If an agent compels you to buy insurance or place a deposit contrary to your contract, don't worry; you'll have recourse to settle things with the company after you return home.

Ask for a free upgrade.

Press for a discount if you're given a smaller vehicle than the one you reserved.

Refuse to pay more if forced to rent a vehicle that's more expensive than the one you reserved.

If necessary, put the names of additional drivers on the contract.

Think twice before buying the personal accident insurance that will probably be offered.

Do you have a Green Card for driving across borders?

Do you have bail bonds for Spain and Greece?

Does your vehicle have a nationality sticker?

Does it have a Swiss toll sticker or *vignette?*

Do you have a parking disc or "blue card"?

Do you have the appropriate numbers and addresses in case of accident or breakdown?

Do you have a list of return charges at various locations?

Do you know the business hours in which you can return the vehicle?

Are the required accouterments in the vehicle?

Where is the jack and how does it work?

Where is the lug wrench?

Where is the spare? How do you get it out?

Are the tires in good condition? Do the headlights and tail lights work? Do the windshield wipers work? How about the wiper fluid? Do the seat adjustments and seat belts work?

Make sure any potentially dangerous mechanical flaws are fixed and that any others are noted on the contact. If these fixes can't be made in time, demand a different vehicle.

Is there any cosmetic damage to the vehicle? If yes, make sure the damage is recorded on the contract.

How much fuel is in the tank? Make sure the fuel level is recorded on the contract.

Do you have a European Accident Statement form in the glove compartment or driver's-side door?

Solicit any more instructions you may need to operate the vehicle.

Returning the Vehicle

If returning a motorhome, make sure its sanitary system is empty and clean.

Confirm with the agent that no damage was done to the vehicle. Have this fact written on the contract.

Furthermore, be sure the counter agent removes any hold or block the company placed on your credit or charge card.

If there was damage, have it noted accurately and precisely on the contract; and take pictures of the vehicle.

Check the amount of fuel in the vehicle and have this fuel level noted on the contract.

Keep copies of all documents associated with the rental.

b. u.s. military bases in europe

Germany

Bitburg Base, APO AE 09132–5000, Germany, tel. 6561 61 1110. Located 15 miles north of Trier, Germany. 3400 military personnel; 1125 civilians.

Ramstein Air Base, APO AE 09094–5000, Germany, tel. 6371 47 113. Located adjacent to Ramstein, 10 miles west of Kaiserslautern. The base's 8330 military personnel and 3612 civilians comprise the largest concentration of US citizens outside the United States.

Rhein-Main Air Base, APO AE 09097–5000, Germany, tel. 69 699 1110. Located 5 miles south of Frankfurt, Germany. 3546 military personnel; 1051 civilians.

Sembach Air Base, APO AE 09130–5000, tel. 6302 67 113. Located 9 miles northeast of Kaiserslautern, Germany. 2617 military personnel; 600 civilians.

Spangdahlem Air Base, APO AE 09126–5000, Germany, tel. 6565 61 1110. Located 8 miles east of Bitburg, Germany; 20 miles northeast of Trier, Germany. 4600 military personnel; 600 civilians.

Great Britain

Lakenheath Royal Air Force Base, APO AE 09464-5000, United Kingdom, tel. 638 523000. Located 70 miles northeast of London, England; 25 miles from Cambridge. 4480 military personnel; 2025 civilians.

Mildenhall Royal Air Force Base, APO AE 09459-5000, United Kingdom, tel. 638 511110. Located 30 miles northeast of Cambridge, England. 3492 military personnel; 193 civilians.

Italy

Aviano Air Base, APO AE 09601, Italy, tel. 434 667111. Located adjacent to Aviano, 50 miles north of Venice, Italy. 2592 military personnel; 730 civilians.

Turkey

Incirlik Air Base, APO AE 09824, Turkey, tel. 71 221774 through 71 221780. Located 10 miles east of Adana, Turkey. 2094 military personnel; 2055 civilians.

c. evaluating a vehicle before buying it

When a vehicle catches your eye, evaluate it as I describe below. If the owner can easily help you complete this evaluation, he or she is probably a responsible owner with a good mechanical understanding of the vehicle; in other words, he or she probably took good care of it.

When the engine is cold, open the **radiator** cap and inspect the coolant; it shouldn't be rusty colored. Also, greenish-white stains on the radiator cap suggest pinholes and the prospect of growing leakage.

Look for dark stains or puddles underneath the vehicle: they indicate leaks from the cooling system, transmission, or engine. Other bad signs include excessive residue of lubricants on the engine, transmission, hoses or other under-the-hood components.

Rust, if it eats through the vehicle, can let deadly exhaust fumes inside. And if left unchecked, rust can compromise the structural integrity of the body and suspension. Lift one of the front floor carpets to check the condition of the sheet metal underneath. Inspect other vulnerable areas such as wheel wells and rocker panels, the door edges, and the trunk floor. If you place a small magnet against these areas, you can tell if plastic putty patches cover rust or accident damage.

Fresh **welds** in the underbody, ripply **body work,** a part whose **color** or fit doesn't seem quite right, new **paint** on a late-model vehicle, or fresh undercoating on an old vehicle testify that it's has been in an accident.

A vehicle with 31,000 kilometers or less should have its original **tires;** new tires may indicate an odometer that's been tampered with.

Uneven tread wear indicates an accident or poor wheel alignment. Uneven tread on the front tires may signal serious suspension damage.

Grab the top of each tire and shake it; if you feel play or hear a clunking sound, suspect loose or worn wheel bearings or suspension joints. Look behind the front wheels of front-wheel-drive vehicles to check the covers on the **universal joints:** torn or missing covers are expensive to replace.

Check the **shock absorbers** by pushing down hard at each corner of the vehicle and then letting go. If the vehicle needs more than one rebound to level off, the shock absorbers may be worn.

Step back about ten feet (three meters) and check if one side is lower than the other. Do the same looking perpendicular to the long axis of the vehicle, noting if the front or rear sags. A lopsided vehicle may need new **springs.**

A saggy **driver's seat** suggests heavy use. On a low-kilometer vehicle the **pedals** shouldn't be brand new or worn flat. Musty **odors** in the vehicle suggest a water leak that may be hard to find and costly to fix.

You shouldn't have to push the brake pedal any further than three inches above the floor to stop the vehicle. Speed up to 60 kph on a flat stretch of road; apply the **brakes** firmly, without locking the wheels; repeat: the vehicle should stop quickly and in a straight line. With the engine idling, press firmly on the brake pedal for thirty seconds. The pedal should feel firm and steady; if it sinks to the floor or feels spongy, the hydraulic brake system may be leaking.

A **clutch** that doesn't engage smoothly could signal trouble. The pedal shouldn't have more than two inches (four and a half centimeters) of play. You can test the clutch by turning on the vehicle, setting the parking brake, and slowly letting out the clutch as if to drive away; if the vehicle stalls without the clutch slipping, it's a good sign.

Test the **transmission** by going through all the gears. At the point that you would shift up to the next gear, *don't* shift up. Instead, take your foot off the accelerator; if the transmission pops out of any gear upon deceleration, it's faulty. Do this in reverse gear too. If the clutch doesn't engage until the pedal is all the way up or if the pedal doesn't have an inch or so of free play at the top, you could face an expensive clutch job.

An **automatic transmission** shouldn't slam into gear or slip as you drive. With the engine warmed up, let it idle in *Park*. Inspect the dipstick for the transmission fluid; the fluid should be reddish, with a faint odor of chestnuts. A dark brown color, a rancid smell, or metal particles on the dipstick signal trouble.

With the **engine** warm, accelerate to about 60 kph, take your foot off the accelerator for a few seconds, and then accelerate fast. A friend should be with you, watching out the rear window. Black exhaust may mean only that the fuel system needs adjusting, but blue exhaust means that the vehicle is an oil-burner—the engine will probably have to be rebuilt or replaced. Persistent billowy white exhaust means coolant is getting into the engine's combustion chambers, probably through a blown gasket or a crack in the cylinder head or engine block. (But white vapory exhaust upon start-up on a damp, frosty morning is nothing to worry about.)

The vehicle should hold the road nicely. **Steering** should be smooth and precise, without much free play or vibration. Have your friend stand behind you in the road, watching as you drive straight ahead (if possible through a puddle so you can just look at the wet tire tracks to see if the front and rear wheels travel precisely in line); if the vehicle sidles along like a crab, an accident has probably bent the body or frame; give up on such a vehicle. If the vehicle's steering just pulls to one side, however, a wheel alignment may be all that's needed.

Here are some other important things to determine when you test a vehicle.

Do the windshield wipers work? How do you fill them?

Do the demisters work? Do they pump exhaust into the car?

How far does the hand brake come up?

Do all the windows operate correctly?

Do the indicators work?

Do the brake lights work?

Look at the spare wheel. Check its tread and air pressure.

Examine the wheel nut spanner. Does it fit and work?

Try the jack. Does it really work?

Are the jacking points in good condition?

Does the vehicle have a fuel cap?

How do you replace the fan belt? (Tightening the fan belt is easy.)

Are the heater hoses fitted firmly?

How do you check the battery's water level?

Is the engine seal in good condition?

Does the sink pump work? How do you refill it?

appendix c

Does the sink plug fit?

Is a tool kit included? If so, is it in good condition?

Where are the spare fuses?

Does the horn work?

With campers, check if there's a built-in, two-burner stove with a detachable propane tank. Besides being convenient and odorless, propane refills are obtainable all over Europe at stores, service stations and campgrounds. An electric refrigerator would be another plus in a camper.

d. preventive maintenance

Simple preventive maintenance and inspection prior to your journey can save many headaches.

Oil Change

Get an oil change every 3000 miles or every three months, whichever comes first. Change after the first 1000 miles, however, if you're driving a new car.

Lube Job

Get a lub job every 5000 miles or less.

Battery

Never smoke while working near a battery: the battery could be giving off explosive gas. When disconnecting or reconnecting the live battery terminal, be very careful not to allow the spanner to contact any of the vehicle's metalwork. Such a connection could give you a bad burn; or even worse, the resulting spark could cause the battery to explode. To be on the safe side, always remove the battery's earth cable—the one connected to the bodywork, chassis, or engine—first.

Most problems with a battery are related to the two electrical connections of the battery terminals. When corrosion occurs the resulting green or white powder fungus growing on the terminal can prevent power from getting to the starter motor. Even if the connections appear clean on the exterior, it's advisable to remove the terminal connector and clean the contact surfaces with a wire brush or emery paper. To prevent recurrence of corrosion, apply a smear of petroleum jelly to the connections before re-making them and again afterwards, covering all outermost surfaces of the connector and battery terminal.

Another common cause of a failing starter motor, apart from the obvious dead battery, is a battery earth connection that is not making proper contact with the body or chassis of the vehicle. If this is the problem, remove the connector and clean it.

Check both battery cables and any earth straps for breakage or fraying (this usually occurs at the terminal ends); replace them if necessary. Finally, check the level of the battery electrolyte, the fluid inside the battery. This fluid should reach slightly above the battery plates. If the battery plates are exposed, use distilled water to fill the battery to the proper level. Some batteries, however, are sealed for life; it's impossible to fill these batteries as such.

Ignition System

Before attempting to carry out any checks or adjustments on any part of the ignition system, you must ensure that the ignition is switched off.

Contact Points

Remove the distributor cap to expose the contact points. These are the most common cause of breakdown in the ignition system. If the faces of the contact points appear badly pitted or burned, they should be replaced or cleaned.

In cars that don't employ an electronic ignition system, the contact point *gap* is critical; this gap can close up after a period of time. Contact point gaps vary from one model to another, so consult your vehicle handbook. To check and adjust the contact point gap, you must rotate the engine until one of the lobes on the distributor cam has pushed the moving arm of the contact points to its fullest open position. Using a feeler gauge, make any adjustment to the gap by slackening the contact breaker retaining screw or screws and moving the positions of the contact points relative to the distributor base plate. Adjust the contact point gap until the feeler gauge will barely fit between the contact points. Finally, lock the adjusting screw and re-check the gap: sometimes the setting can change when the retaining screw is tightened.

Distributor Cap

The distributor cap is another potential problem area. Carry out the following simple checks.

- Check if the H. T. leads are secure in the cap.

- Make sure the inside and outside of the distributor cap are free of any oil residue, dirt, and moisture.

- Look for hairline cracks or tracking caused by the H. T. current on the inside and outside of the rotor arm and distributor cap.

- While the distributor cap is removed, check the entire connector. This should protrude far enough to contact the rotor arm when the cap is replaced. If the carbon brush is badly worn, a replacement cap will be needed.

H. T. Leads

The H. T. leads are the thick cables coming out of the distributor cap. Any breakdown either in the conductive center, the insulation, or at the connections will cause faulty operation of the ignition system. Wipe the outer insulation material clean and examine for cracking or deterioration. Check the connectors at both ends for security and cleanliness.

Remember that the H. T. leads to the spark plugs must be fitted in the correct positions; if the leads become mixed up, the car will not start. It's a good idea to number the leads to facilitate correct re-installation. Alternatively, you could remove only one H. T. lead at a time. Modern vehicles are fitted with carbon-core leads which can break down internally. Only an auto electrician can properly test such leads.

Coil Connections

The coil is the source of power for the ignition system, make sure the connections for the two low-tension wires on either side of the main H. T. lead are secure and clean. Also, check the main H. T. lead; it should be secure. Examine the plastic top of the coil for any hairline cracks or tracking caused by the H. T. current short-circuiting; replace it if necessary. Finally, ensure the coil top is clean of grease, dirt and moisture.

Fuel System

A breakdown in the fuel system is difficult to anticipate. However, you can carry out some simple tests to minimize the risk.

- Examine any rubber fuel pipes for cracking, softening, and leakage; and make sure they're secure at the connections.

- Most vehicle fuel systems incorporate a fuel filter or dirt trap to prevent any debris from being transmitted through the fuel lines to the carburetor. Carry out periodic checks of these fillters as called for by the vehicle handbook.

- Check for any evidence of fuel leakage around the carburetor gasket joints, jet assemblies, and feed pipes. Such a leak may require the services of a specialist.

- The efficiency of the engine greatly depends upon the correct mixture setting for the carburetor. Only a properly equipped workshop can check and reset modern carburetors.

Cooling System

The efficiency of the engine cooling system is vital to the vehicle's ability to handle the various climates and terrain inherent in a continental tour. Check the radiator to ensure it's free from external blockage or restrictions. Remove any debris such as leaves, paper, or accumulated dirt.

Inspect all the rubber coolant hoses for cracking or bulges (particularly adjacent to the securing clips). Check the tightness of hose clips; avoid over-tightening, however, as this will cut into the hose material. When filling up the cooling system, do so with anti-freeze solution: anti-freeze contains a corrosion inhibitor to minimize corrosion build-up. Check the fan belt for fraying, general deterioration, or excessive glazing on the V-shape drive surfaces: these may promote slippage. If the belt's length has more than half an inch of free play, some adjustment is necessary.

Safety Tips

If the fan belt has not been replaced during the preceding twelve months, consider replacing it. Keep the old fan belt as a spare. A broken fan belt will be signaled by the generator/ignition warning light and an increased reading on the water temperature gauge. If the belt breaks, stop immediately and replace the it.

Miscellaneous

Don't forget other parts of the vehicle that can break down and cause you considerable inconveniences. Tires, for example, should be checked for condition, tread depth and pressure. It may be necessary to increase tire pressures because of the load or high speeds you'll be carrying. Refer to the vehicle owner's handbook for correct tire pressures.

appendix d

e. conversions

Time

Britain, Iceland, Ireland, Morocco and Portugal are on Greenwich mean time, 5 hours ahead of New York time. Bulgaria, Greece, Finland, Estonia, Latvia, Lithuania, Romania, western Russia, and Turkey are two hours ahead of GMT. Every other place mentioned in this book is one hour ahead of GMT.

Distance

Miles	Kilometers	Kilometers	Miles
1	1.60	1	0.62
2	3.21	2	1.24
3	4.82	3	1.86
4	6.43	4	2.48
5	8.04	5	3.10
6	9.65	6	3.72
7	11.26	7	4.34
8	12.87	8	4.97
9	14.48	9	5.59
10	16.09	10	6.21
15	24.13	15	9.32
20	32.18	20	12.32
25	40.23	25	15.53
30	48.27	30	18.64
35	56.32	35	21.74
40	64.37	40	24.85
45	72.41	45	27.96
50	80.46	50	31.07
100	160.93	100	62.14

1 centimeter = 0.4 inches, 1 meter = 3.28 feet, 1 kilometer = 0.62 miles
1 inch = 2.54 centimeter, 1 foot = 0.31 meter, 1 mile = 1.61 kilometer

Volume

US Gallons	Liters	Liters	US Gallons
1	3.79	1	0.26
2	7.57	5	1.32
3	11.36	10	2.64
4	15.27	20	5.28
5	19.06	25	6.61
6	22.85	30	7.93
7	26.63	40	10.57
8	30.42	50	13.21
10	34.20	75	19.82
15	53.13	100	26.42

Imp. Gallons	Liters	Liters	Imp. Gallons
1	4.54	1	0.22
2	9.09	5	1.10
3	13.63	10	2.20
4	18.18	20	4.40
5	22.73	25	5.50
6	27.27	30	6.60
7	31.82	40	8.80
8	36.36	50	11.00
10	45.46	75	16.50
15	68.19	100	22.00

16 ounces = 2 cups = 1 pint, 2 pints = 1 quart, 4 quarts = 1 gallon
1 US gallon = 0.833 Imperial gallons

Pressure

lbs./in.²	kg/cm²
18	1.27
20	1.41
22	1.55
24	1.69
26	1.83
28	1.97
30	2.11
32	2.25
34	2.39
36	2.53
38	2.67
40	2.81

20	48.06	56.24
21	50.46	59.06
22	52.86	61.87
23	55.27	64.68
24	57.67	67.49
25	60.07	70.30
26	62.47	73.12
27	64.88	75.93
28	67.28	78.74
29	69.68	81.55
30	72.09	84.37

Fuel Efficiency

km/Liter	mi./US Gallon	mi./Imp. Gallon
1	2.40	2.81
2	4.81	5.62
3	7.21	8.44
4	9.61	11.25
5	12.02	14.06
6	14.42	16.87
7	16.82	19.69
8	19.22	22.50
9	21.63	25.31
10	24.03	28.12
11	26.43	30.93
12	28.83	33.75
13	31.24	36.56
14	33.64	39.37
15	36.04	42.18
16	38.44	45.00
17	40.85	47.81
18	43.25	50.62
19	45.65	53.43

Weight

1 gram = 0.035 ounces, 16 ounces = 1 pound, 1 kilogram = 2.2 pounds

1 ounce = 28.35 grams, 1 pound = 0.45 kilograms,

1 metric ton = 0.98 tons

1 short ton = 2000 pounds = 907 kilograms

1 long ton = 2240 pounds = 1016 kilograms

Gradients

1 in 4	25.0%
1 in 5	20.0%
1 in 6	16.4%
1 in 7	14.2%
1 in 8	12.4%
1 in 9	11.1%
1 in 10	10.0%
1 in 11	9.1%
1 in 12	8.4%
1 in 13	7.9%
1 in 14	7.2%
1 in 15	6.6%

appendix e

Temperature

°C	°F	°C	°F	°C	°F
-20	-4.0	0	32.0	21	69.8
-19	-2.2	1	33.8	22	71.6
-18	-0.4	2	35.6	23	73.4
-17	1.4	3	37.4	24	75.2
-16	3.2	4	39.2	25	77.0
-15	5.0	5	41.0	26	78.8
-14	6.8	6	42.8	27	80.6
-13	8.6	7	44.6	28	82.4
-12	10.4	8	46.4	29	84.2
-11	12.2	9	48.2	30	86.0
-10	14.0	10	50.0	31	87.8
-9	15.8	11	51.8	32	89.8
-8	17.6	12	53.6	33	91.4
-7	19.4	13	55.4	34	93.2
-6	21.2	14	57.2	35	95.0
-5	23.0	15	59.0	36	96.8
-4	24.8	16	60.8	37	98.6
-3	26.6	17	62.6	38	100.4
-2	28.4	18	64.4	39	102.2
-1	30.2	19	66.2	40	104.0
		20	68.0		

f. what to do in case of an accident

To accomplish some of the steps that I describe below, see the *Motorists' Phrasebook* chapter for useful phrases in eight European languages. If you have a European Accident Statement form in your glove compartment or driver's-side door, get it out and use it to record the information I mention below. On the EAS it doesn't matter which vehicle you designate as "A" and which you designate as "B". But be sure to have the other driver sign the form. Or if the other driver produces it—and if when completed it's acceptable to you—make sure you sign it and take a carbon a copy. You should mail a copy of your copy to your insurer. Required procedures are more lax in some countires, such as the **United Kingdom** and **Sweden;** see the end of this appendix for the procedures to follow in such countries.

- If you must move the vehicles, first mark with chalk the position of their wheels on the pavement.
- Note the license number of the other vehicle and whether the vehicle is right- or left-hand drive.
- Note the full name, address, and occupation of the other vehicle's driver. Note also the number and other information on their driver's license. If the other driver does not own the vehicle he or she was driving, try to note the above information about the owner too.
- Note the names and addresses of persons injured and the nature of their injuries.
- Try to determine the names, addresses and occupations of witnesses.

- Note the date, time, and exact place of the accident. Make a rough sketch showing the position and speeds of the vehicles both before and at the instant of the collision, indicating also the directions in which the vehicles were traveling. Note any signals that were given by yourself and the other driver immediately before the accident.
- Note the condition of the brakes, lights, and tires of both vehicles.
- Note the weather and road conditions.
- Photograph the damages and vehicle positions from several telling angles.
- It is usually compulsory to contact the police when the accident involves personal injury. If this is the case and you're in a populated area, stick to the spot like glue and wait for a police officer; if it seems no police officer will arrive soon, lock your vehicle and go with the driver of the other vehicle to call a policeman. In some countries, however, especially in the South, it *may* be acceptable to abstain from involving the police in an accident that doesn't cause personal injury. In such a case, the accident may be settled by a small exchange of funds between drivers or by filling out a European Accident Statement form and mailing it to the respective insurance companies. See the appropriate country section of the *Country-by-Country Information* chapter to determine the requirements of the particular country you're in.
- The police officer will make out a report in triplicate. The report will state where the accident occurred, the names of both owners and their insurance companies, and the damage done.

- Note the address of the police to whom the accident was reported and the names and badge numbers of the attending officers.

- Accidents involving a third party must be reported immediately to the appropriate insurance bureau of the host country; see your Green Card for details.

- Record the date and time of any correspondence you have with an insurance company, and note the name of the representative with whom you speak.

- Contact your insurance company; they'll probably tell you to make a copy of your copy of the police report and send it to them.

- Under no circumstances should you sign any document or make any statement—especially an admittance of guilt—without the advice of a lawyer or competent official of the local automobile club.

- If you own the vehicle and you plan to ship it home and if the vehicle is still safe to drive, ask your insurance company if they'll cover repairs done in your home country. If they will, wait until you return home to have the vehicle repaired. The damage to the vehicle will substantially lower its value; thus the duty and taxes you must pay upon importing the vehicle will be lower.

If you're involved in an accident in a country such as the **United Kingdom** or **Sweden** where the required post-accident procedure is more lax, and the accident causes damage or injury to any other person, vehicle, animal not in your vehicle, or to roadside property, you must do the following.

- Give your and the vehicle owner's name and address and the registration number of the vehicle to anyone having reasonable grounds for requiring them.

- If you don't give your name and address at the time of the accident, report the accident to the police within 24 hours. Moreover, you should within seven days present your insurance certificate to the police at any police station in the country where the accident occurred.

g. motorists' phrasebook

English

gasoline
diesel
LPG (Liquefied Petroleum Gas)

Nothing to declare.
Something to declare.
passport
visa
driver's license
vehicle registration
green card
bail bond

Fill it up, please.
Do you have a map?
Which is the best road to . . .?

Can I park here?
Where can I park?

campsite
May we light a fire?
Is the water drinkable?
I am leaving early tomorrow.
Where are the nearest shops?
Where is the chemical toilet disposal area?

How much will it cost?
When will it be ready?
How much do I owe you?

Danish—*Dansk*

benzin
dieselolie
LPG (gas)

Intet at fortolde.
Noget at fortolde.
pas
visum/visere
kørekort
indregistreringstattest
grønt kort
kautionbevis

Vær så venlig at fylde den op.
Har De et kort?
Hvad er den nemmeste vej til . . .?

Kan jag parkere her?
Hvor kan jeg parkere?

campingplads
Må vi tænde bål?
Er vandet drikkeligt?
Jeg tager af sted tidligt i morgen.
Er der de nærmeste butikker?
Er der tømning af kemisk toilet?

Hvor meget vil det koste?
Hvornår vil den være klar?
Hvor meget skylder jeg Dem?

Dutch—*Nederlands*

benzine
dieselolie
LPG

Niets aan te geven.
Let aan to geven.
paspoort
visum
rijbewijs
kentekenbewijs
groene kaart
schriftelijk bewjis van borgsteling

Helemall vol graag.
Hebt U een wagenkaart?
Wat is de beste wag naar . . .?

Kan ik hier parkeren?
Waar kan ik parkeren?

camping
Mogen wij een vuur maken?
Is het water drinkbaar?
Ik vertrek morgen vroeg.
Waar zijn de dichtstbijzijnde?
Waar is plaats voor ledigen van chemisch toilet?

Hœveel gaat dat kosten?
Wanneer is hij klaar?
Hoeveel ben ik U schuldig?

English	Danish—*Dansk*	Dutch—*Nederlands*
Please adjust . . .	De bedes venligst . . .	Wilt U . . . bijstellen
Please change . . .	**Vær vanlig at udskifte . . .**	**Wilt U . . . vernieuwen**
Please check . . .	Vær vanlig at efterse . . .	Wilt U . . . nakijken
Something is wrong with . . .	**Der er noget galt med . . .**	**Er is iets mis met . . .**
air filter	luftfilter	luchtfilter
alternator	**vekselstrómsgenerator**	**wisselstroomdynamo**
anti-freeze	frosrvæske/kølervæske	antivries
brakes	**bremserne**	**remmen**
battery	batteri	accu
carburetor	**karburator**	**carburator**
clutch	kobling	koppeling
crankshaft	**krumtapaksel**	**krukas**
differential	differentialet	differentieel
distributor	**strømfordeler**	**verdeler**
exhaust pipe	udstødningsrør	gedeelte uitlaatpijp
fan belt	**ventilatorrem**	**V-snaar**
front suspension	forhjulsophængning	Voorwielophanging
fuel filter	**filter**	**filter**
fuel pump	benzinpumpe	brandstofpomp
fuel tank	**benzintank**	**brandstoftank**
fuse	sikring	zekering
gasket	**paking**	**pakking**
generator	dynamo	dynamo
glowplug	**startgløderør**	**gloeipatroon**
horn	horn	claxon/toeter
hose	**slange**	**slang**
muffler	lyddæmperen	knalpot
oil	**olien**	**olie**
oil filter	olie filter	oliefilter
oil pump	**oliepump**	**oliepomp**
radiator	køler	radiator
shock absorbers	**støddæmper**	**schokbreker**
snow chains	sne kæder	sneeuwkettingen
spark plug	**tændrør**	**bougie**
starter	starteren	starter
steering	**styretøjet**	**stuurinrichting**
thermostat	termostaten	thermostaat
tires	**dækkene**	**buitenbanden**

English	Danish—*Dansk*	Dutch—*Nederlands*

English

transmission
universal joint
water
water pump
wheel
valves

I am a member of . . . automobile club.
Can your club provide free emergency service?

Can you direct me to the nearest garage?

My car has broken down.
My car has run out of gas.
Can you tow the car to a garage?
Please tow it to a garage.
Can you repair the car?
You will be repaid by your country's automobile club.

My car has been towed.
Where is the auto pound?
Someone has stolen . . .
I have lost . . .
I have had an accident.
There has been an accident.
Will you serve as a witness?

Call the police.
lawyer
ambulance
Did you see the accident?
Please write down . . .
your name and address.
details of your insurance company and policy number.

Danish—*Dansk*

transmission
kardanled
vandet
vandepumpe
hjul
ventilerne

Jeg er medlem af . . . motorklub.
Kan Deres Klub yde gratis vejhjælp?

Kan De vise mig den nærmeste vej til garage?
Min bil er brudt sammen.
Min bil er løbet tør for benzin.
Kan De slæbe bilen til et værksted?
Træk den venligst til et værksted.
Kan De reparere min bil?
De vil få belobet refunderet af Deres egen klub.

Min bil er blevet slæbt væk.
Hvor er politiets parkeringsplads?
Nogen har stjålet . . .
Jeg har mistet . . .
Jeg har været ude for en ulykke.
Der er sket en ulykke.
Vil De vidne?

Tilkad politiet.
sagfører
ambulance
Så De ulykken ske?
Skirv venligst . . .ned
Deres navn og adresse.
enkeltheder om Deres forsikringsselskab og policenummer.

Dutch—*Nederlands*

transmissie
cardankoppeling
water
waterpomp
wiel
kleppen

Ik ben lid van de . . . toeristenclub.
Verstrekt uw club gratis hulp bij pech?

Kunt U mij de weg wijzen naar de dichtsbijzijnde?
Mijn auto heeft motorpech.
Mijn heeft geen benzine meer.
Kunt u de auto naar een slepen?
Wilt u het naar een garage laten slepen.
Kunt u de auto repareren?
Het bedrag zal u worden uitbetaald door de club van uw eigen land.

Mijn auto is weggesleept.
Waar staan de weggesleepte auto's opgeslagen?
Iemand heeft . . .gestolen.
Ik heb . . .verloren.
Ik heb een ongeluk gehad.
Er is een ongeluk gebeurd.
Zoudt u als getuige willen optreden?

Wilt U de politie waarschuwen.
advocaat
ambulance
Hebt u het ongelukzien gebeuren?
Wilt u . . .opschrijven.
uw naam en adres.
uw verzekeringsmaatschappij en polisnummer.

English	French—*Français*	German—*Deutsch*
gasoline	essence	benzin
diesel	**diesel**	**diesel**
LPG (Liquefied Petroleum Gas)	Gaz de pétrole liquéfié (GPL)	autogas
Nothing to declare.	**Rien à déclarer.**	**Nichts zu verzollen.**
Something to declare.	Quelque chose à déclarer.	Etwas zu verzollen.
passport	**passeport**	**paß**
visa	visa	visa
driver's license	**permis de conduire**	**Führerschein**
vehicle registration	carte grise	Kfz-Schein
green card	**carte verte**	**grüne Versicherungskarte**
bail bond	titre de cautionnement	Bürgschaftßchein
Fill it up, please.	**Faites le plein, s'il vous plaît.**	**Bitte füllen Sie den Tank auf.**
Do you have a map?	Avez-vous une carte?	Haben Sie Straßenkarten?
Which is the best road to . . .?	**Quel est le meilleur chemin pour aller à . . .?**	**Was ist der beste Weg nach . . .?**
Can I park here?	Puis-je stationner ici?	Darf ich hier parken?
Where can I park?	**Où puis-je stationer?**	**Wo darf ich parken?**
campsite	terrain de camping	campingplatz
May we light a fire?	**Pouvons-nous faire du feu?**	**Dürfen wir ein Feuer anmachen?**
Is the water drinkable?	L'eau est-elle potable?	Ist das Wasser trinkbar?
I am leaving early tomorrow.	**Je partirai demain matin de bonne heure.**	**Ich fahre morgen früh ab.**
Where are the nearest shops?	Où est les magasins les plus proches?	Wo sind die nächstgelegenen Geschäfte?
Where is the chemical toilet disposal area?	**Où est un lieu d'évacuation pour W.C. chimiques?**	**Wo ist Klärgrube für chemische Toiletten?**
How much will it cost?	Quel sera le coût de la réparation?	Wievel kostet sie?
When will it be ready?	**Quand sera-t-elle prête?**	**Wann wird der Wagen fertig sein?**
How much do I owe you?	Combien vous dois-je?	Wievel habe ich zu bezahlen?
Please adjust . . .	**Veuillez régler . . .**	**Wollen Sie bitte . . .**
Please change . . .	Voulez-vous changer . . .	Bitte wechseln Sie . . .
Please check . . .	**Voulez-vous vérifier . . .**	**Bitte prüfen Sie . . .**
Something is wrong with . . .	Quelque chose ne va pas . . .	Irgend etwas ist nicht in Ordnung mit . . .

English	French — Français	German — Deutsch
air filter	**le filtre à air**	**Luftfilter**
alternator	le alternateur	Drehstromlichtmaschine
anti-freeze	**mettre de l'antigel**	**Frostschutzmittel**
brakes	freins	Bremsen
battery	**batterie**	**Batterie**
carburetor	carburateur	Vergaser
clutch	**embrayage**	**Kupplung**
crankshaft	vilebrequin	Kurbelwelle
differential	**différentiel**	**Differential**
distributor	distributeur	Verteiler
exhaust pipe	**tuyauterie d'échappement**	**Auspuffrohr**
fan belt	courroige du ventilateur	Ventilatorriemen
front suspension	**suspension avant**	**Vorderradaufhängung**
fuel filter	filtre	Filter
fuel pump	**pompe à essence**	**Kraftstoffpumpe**
fuel tank	réservoir de carburant	Kraftstoffbehälter
fuse	**fusible**	**Sicherung**
gasket	joint	Dichtung
generator	**dynamo**	**Lichtmaschine dinamo**
glowplug	bougie de préchauffage	Glühkerze
horn	**avertisseur**	**Hupe**
hose	durite	Schlauch
lights	**éclairage**	**Lampen**
muffler	silencieux	Auspufftopf
oil	**huile**	**Ölstand**
oil filter	filtre d'huile	Ölfilter
oil pump	**pompe à huile**	**Ölpumpe**
radiator	radiateur	Kühler
shock absorbers	**amortisseurs**	**Stossdämpfer**
snow chains	chaînes de neige	Schneeketten
spark plug	**bougie**	**Zündkerze**
starter	démarreur	Starter
steering	**direction**	**Steuerung**
thermostat	thermostat	Thermostat
tires	**pneus**	**Reifen**
transmission	transmission	Kraftübertragung
universal joint	**cardans**	**Kardangelenk**
water	l'eau	Wasser

appendix g

English	French—*Français*	German—*Deutsch*
water pump	**pompe à eau**	**Wasserpumpe**
wheel	roue	Rad
valves	**soupapes**	**Ventile**
I am a member of . . . automobile club.	Je suis membre du . . . club automobile	Ich bin Mitglied des . . . Automobilclub
Can your club provide free emergency service?	**Votre club peut-il me dépanner sans frais?**	**Leistet Ihr Club kostenlose Pannenhilfe?**
Can you direct me to the nearest garage?	Pouvez-vouz m'indiquer le plus proche garage?	Können Sie mir bitte angeben die Garage?
My car has broken down.	**Ma voture est en panne.**	**Mein Wagen hat eine Panne.**
My car has run out of gas.	Ma voiture n' a plus d'essence.	Mein Wagen hat kein Benzin mehr.
Can you tow the car to a garage?	**Pouvez-vous remorquer la voiture à un garage?**	**Würden Sie das Auto zu einer Werkstatt abschleppen?**
Please tow it to a garage.	Veuillez le remorquer jusqu'à un garage.	Bitte schleppen Sie ihn zu einer Garage ab.
Can you repair the car?	**Pouvez-vous réparer la voiture?**	**Würden Sie das Auto reparieren?**
You will be repaid by your country's	Le remboursement sera fait pa le club	Die Rückvergütung erfolgt durch den
automobile club.	**automobile de votre pays.**	**Automobilclub Ihres Landes.**
My car has been towed.	La police e enlevé ma voiture.	Mein Auto ist abgeschleppt worden.
Where is the auto pound?	**Où se trouve la fourriére?**	**Wo ist die Verwahrstelle für Kraftfahrzeuge?**
		Jemand har . . . gestohlen.
Someone has stolen . . .	On m' a volé . . .	
I have lost . . .	**J'ai perdu . . .**	**Ich habe . . . verloren.**
I have had an accident.	Je veins d'avoir un accident.	Ich hatte einen Unfall.
There has been an accident.	**Il y a eu un accident.**	**Es gab einen Unfall.**
Will you serve as a witness?	Voulez-vous aervir de témoin?	Wollen Sie als Zeuge aussagen?
Call the police.	**Appelez la police.**	**Wollen Sie bitte die Polizei rufen.**
lawyer	avocat	**Rechtsanwalt**
ambulance	**ambulance**	**Krankenwagen**
Did you see the accident?	Avez-vous vu l'accident?	Haben Sie den Unfall gesehen?
Please write down . . .	**Veuillez écrire**	**Bitte notieren Sie . . .**
your name and address.	votre nom et votre adresse.	Ihren Namen und Ihre Adresse.
details of your insurance company and policy number.	**le nom et l'addresse de votre assurance et le numéro de votre police.**	**Angaben zu Ihrer Versicherungsgesellschaft und-police.**

English	Italian—*Italiano*	Portuguese—*Português*
gasoline	benzina	bensin
diesel	**gasolio**	**gasóleo**
LPG (Liquefied Petroleum Gas)	GPL (gas liquido)	gáz líquido
Nothing to declare.	**Nulla da dichiarare.**	**Nada a declarar.**
Something to declare.	Qualcosa da dichiarare.	Tenho algo a declarar.
passport	**passaporto**	**pasaporte**
visa	visto	visto
driver's license	**patente di guida**	**carta de condução**
vehicle registration	certificato di immatricolazione	livrete
green card	**carta verde**	**carta verde**
bail bond	cauzione	fiança
Fill it up, please.	**Mi faccia il pieno, per favore.**	**Encha-o por favor**
Do you have a map?	Ha una carte stradale?	Tem un mapa?
Which is the best road to . . .?	**Qual'è la strada migliore per andare a . . .?**	**Qual é a melhor estrada para . . .?**
Can I park here?	Posso fermarmi qui?	Posso estacionar aqui?
Where can I park?	**Dove posso posteggiare?**	**Ondo posso estacionar?**
campsite	campeggio	parque de campismo
May we light a fire?	**Possiamo accendere il fuoco?**	**Posso acender uma foguéira?**
Is the water drinkable?	L'acqua è potabile?	A água é potável?
I am leaving early tomorrow.	**Partiró domattina presto.**	**Parto amahã cedo.**
Where are the nearest shops?	Dove sono i negozi più vicini?	Onde estão as loj mais próxima?
Where is the chemical toilet disposal area?	**Dov'è il pozzetto per vuotare i W.C. chimici?**	**Onde está detritos?**
How much will it cost?	Quanto costerà la riparazione?	Quanto vai custar?
When will it be ready?	**Quando sarà pronta?**	**Quando é que está pronto?**
How much do I owe you?	Quanto le devo?	Quanto Ihe devo?
Please adjust . . .	**Regoli . . .**	**é favor adjustar . . .**
Please change . . .	Mi vuol cambiare . . .	é favor mudar . . .
Please check . . .	**Mi vuol verificare . . .**	**é favor limpar . . .**
Something is wrong with . . .	Qualcosa non va . . .	Passa-se qualquer coisa com . . .
air filter	**filtro aria**	**filtro de ar**
alternator	alternatore	alternador
anti-freeze	**antigelo**	**anti-congelante**

English	Italian—*Italiano*	Portuguese—*Português*
brakes	freni	travões
battery	**batteria**	**bateria**
carburetor	carburatore	carburador
clutch	**frizione**	**embraiagem**
crankshaft	albero motore	cambota
differential	**differenziale**	**diferencial**
distributor	spinterogeno	distribuidor
exhaust pipe	**tubo di scarico**	**tubo de escape**
fan belt	cinghietta ventilatore	correia do ventoinha
front suspension	**sospensione anteriore**	**suspensão da frente**
fuel filter	filtro	filtro
fuel pump	**pompa carburante**	**bomba de alimentção de combustível**
fuel tank	serbatoio carburante	depósito de combustível
fuse	**fusibile**	**fusivel**
gasket	**guarnizione**	**junta**
generator	dínamo	dínamo
glowplug	**candela ad incandescenza**	**vela de incandescência**
horn	tromba	buzina
hose	**manicotto in gomma**	**tubo**
lights	fari	luzes
muffler	**silenziatore**	**silencioso/panela**
oil	olien	óleo
oil filter	**filtro dell'olio**	**filtro de óleo**
oil pump	pompa dell'olio	bomba d'óleo
radiator	**radiatore**	**radiador**
shock absorbers	stabilizzatore	amortecedor
snow chains	**catene da neve**	**correntes para neve**
spark plug	candela	vela de ignição
starter	**messa in moto**	**motor de arranque**
steering	sterzo	direcção
thermostat	**termostato**	**termostato**
tires	gomme	pneus
transmission	**transmissione**	**transmissão**
universal joint	giunto articolato	cruzeta do cardan
water	**vandet**	**água**
water pump	pompa dell'acqua	bomba de água
wheel	**ruota**	**roda**
valves	valvole	válvulas

English

I am a member of . . . automobile club.
Can your club provide free emergency
service?

Can you direct me to the nearest garage?
My car has broken down.
My car has run out of gas.
Can you tow the car to a garage?

Please tow it to a garage.
Can you repair the car?
**You will be repaid by your country's
automobile club.**

My car has been towed.
Where is the auto pound?
Someone has stolen . . .
I have lost . . .
I have had accident.
There has been an accident.
Will you serve as a witness?

Call the police.
lawyer
ambulance
Did you see the accident?
Please write down . . .
your name and address
**details of your insurance company and
number.**

Italian — *Italiano*

Sono socio del . . . automobile club.
Il suo Automobile Club puó assistermi
gratuitamente?

Volete indirizzarmi al più vicino garage?
La mia automobile è guasta.
La mia automobile è rimasta senza benzina.
Potete rimorchiare l'automobile in un
garage?
Per favore lo rimorchi in un garage.
Potete riparare l'automobile?
**Il rimborso sarà effettuato dall'Auto-
mobile Club del suo Paese.**

La mia auto è stata rimorchiata via.
Dov'è il deposito della polizia?
Mi hanno rubato . . .
Ho perso . . .
Ho avuto un incidente.
C'è stato un incidente.
Vuol fare da testimonio?

Chiami la polizia.
avvocato
ambulanza
Ha assistito all'incidente?
Per favore scriva . . .
il suo nome e indirizzo
**i dat della sua assicurazione e il
numero di polizza.**

Portuguese — *Português*

En sou membro de . . . automóvel clube.
O seu club fornece serviço de desempa-
nagem gratuito?

Pode indicar-me a mais próxima garage?
O meu carro avariou.
O meu carro ficou sem gasolina.
Pode rebocar o carro para uma garagem?

Por favor reboque-o para uma garagem.
Pode arranjar o carro?
**Você será reembolsado através do
Automóvel Club de seu país.**

O meu carro foi rebocado.
Onde fica o parque da policia?
Alguém roubou . . .
Eu perdi . . .
Eu tive um acidente.
Houve um acidente.
Pode testemunhar?

Chame a policia.
advogodo
ambulancia
Viu o acidente?
Por favor escreva . . .
o seu nome e morada
**detalhes para a companhia de seguros e
e número de apólica.**

English	Spanish — *Español*	Swedish — *Svenska*
gasoline	bensin	bensin
diesel	**gas-oil**	**diesel**
LPG (Liquefied Petroleum Gas)	gases licuados del petróleo	motorgas
Nothing to declare.	**Nada que declarar.**	**Ingenting att förtulla.**
Something to declare.	algo que declarar.	Någonting att förtulla.
passport	**pasaporte**	**pass**
visa	visado	visum
driver's license	**licencia de conducir**	**körkort**
vehicle registration	matrícula	besiktningsinstrument
green card	**carta verde**	**grönt kort**
bail bond	libertad bajo fianza	borgen
Fill it up, please.	**Lleno, por favor.**	**Full tank, tack.**
Do you have a map?	¿Tiene usted mapas?	Har Ni vägkarta?
Which is the best road to . . .?	**¿Cuál es el mejor camino para ir a . . .?**	**Vilken är den bästa vägen til . . .?**
Can I park here?	¿Puedo aparcar aqui?	Kan jag parkera här?
Where can I park?	**¿Dónde puedo aparcar?**	**Var kan jag parkere?**
campsite	sitio de acampada	campingplats, tältplats
May we light a fire?	**¿Podemos encender un fuego?**	**Får vi göra upp eld?**
Is the water drinkable?	¿Es potable el agua?	Är vattnet drickbart?
I am leaving early tomorrow.	**Me marcharé mañana temprano.**	**Vi far tidgit i morgon bitti.**
Where are the nearest shops?	¿Dónde están la tienda más cercana?	Var finns närmaste affär?
Where is the chemical toilet disposal area?	**¿Dónde está lugar para residuous quimicos?**	**Var finns tömning av kemisk toalett?**
How much will it cost?	¿Cuánto costará?	Hur mycket kostar det?
When will it be ready?	**¿Cuándo estará listo?**	**När blir den färdig?**
How much do I owe you?	¿Cuánto le debo?	Hur mycket blir det?
Please adjust . . .	**Quiere Usted reglar . . .**	**Var vänlig och justera . . .**
Please change . . .	Quiere Usted cambiar . . .	Var vänlig och byt . . ., tack.
Please check . . .	**Quiere Usted Verificar . . .**	**Kontrollera . . .tack.**
Something is wrong with . . .	Algo va mai con/Algo pasa en . . .	Något är fel mel . . .
air filter	**filtro del aire**	**luftrenare**
alternator	alternador	växelströmsgenerator
anti-freeze	**anti-congelante**	**glykol/anti-freeze**
brakes	frenos	bromsarna

English	Spanish — *Español*	Swedish — *Svenska*
battery	batería	batteri
carburetor	**carburador**	**förgasare**
clutch	embrague	koppling
crankshaft	**cigüeñal**	**vevaxel**
differential	diferencial	differentialen
distributor	**distribuidor**	**fördelare**
exhaust pipe	tubo de escape	avgasrör
fan belt	**correa del ventilador**	**fläktrem**
front suspension	suspensión de las ruedas delanteras	framhjulsupphängning
fuel filter	**filtro**	**filter**
fuel pump	bomba de gasolina	bränslepump
fuel tank	**tanque de combustible**	**bränsletank**
fuse	fusible	propp
gasket	**junta**	**packning**
generator	dínamo	generator
glowplug	**bujía incandescente**	**glödstift**
horn	bocina	signalhorn
hose	**tubo flexible**	**slang**
lights	instalación eléctrica	glödlamporna
muffler	**silenciador**	**ljuddämparen**
oil	aceite	olja
oil filter	**filtro de aceite**	**oljerenarhus**
oil pump	bomba de aceite	oljepump
radiator	**radiador**	**kylare**
shock absorbers	amortiguador	stötdämparen
snow chains	**cadenas para la nieve**	**snökedjor**
spark plug	bujía	tändstift
starter	**motor de arranque**	**startmotorn**
steering	dirección	styrningen
thermostat	**termostato**	**termostaten**
tires	cubiertas	däcket
transmission	**transmisión**	**kraftöverföring**
universal joint	junta de cardán	knut
water	**agua**	**vatten**
water pump	bomba de agua	vattenpump
wheel	**rueda**	**hjulen**
valves	válvulas	ventilerna

English

I am a member of . . . automobile club.
Can your club provide free emergency service?

Can you direct me to the nearest garage?

My car has broken down.
My car has run out of gas.
Can you tow the car to a garage?
Please tow it to a garage.
Can you repair the car?
You will be repaid by your country's automobile club.

My car has been towed.
Where is the auto pound?
Someone has stolen . . .
I have lost . . .
I have had accident.
There has been an accident.
Will you serve as a witness?

Call the police.
lawyer
ambulance
Did you see the accident?
Please write down . . .
your name and address
details of your insurance company and policy number.

Spanish — *Español*

Soy un miembro de . . . club de automóvil.
¿Puede su Club facilitar sevicio gratuito de asistencia?

¿Puede usted indicarme el más próximo garage?
Mi coche se ha averiado.
Mi coche se ha quedado sin gasolina.
¿Podría remolcar el coche al garaje?
Por favor remólquele hasta un garaje.
¿Podría reparar el coche?
El reembolso se efectuará por medio del club de automóvil de su pais.

Mi coche ha sido remolcado.
¿Dónde está el depósito de la policía?
Alguien ha robado . . .
He perdido . . .
He tenido un accidente.
Ha habido un accidente.
¿Quiere actuar como testigo?

Llame a la policía.
abogado
ambulancia
¿Vió Vd. el accidente?
Por favor, escriba . . .
su nombre y dirección
datos de su compañía de seguros y número de póliza.

Swedish — *Svenska*

Jag är medlem av . . . motorklubb.
Kan er klubb lämna fri bilbärgning?

Var ligger närmaste garage/verkstaden?

Min bil är sönder.
Min bil har slut på bensin.
Kan ni bogsera min bil till en verkstad?
Var snäll bogsera bilen till verkstad.
Kan ni reparera bilen?
Ni får betalning genom ert lands motorklubb.

Min bil har bogserats bort.
Var är uppställningsplatsen?
Någon har stulit . . .
Jag har förlorat . . .
Jag har haft en olycka.
Det har inträffat en olycka.
Vill ni vittna?

Ring efter polisen.
advokat
ambulans
Såg ni olyckan?
Var snäll skirv ned . . .
ert namn och adress
namn på försäkringsbolag och nummer på försäkringen.

h. country telephone codes

Austria	43	Gibraltar	350	Norway	47
Belgium	32	Great Britain	44	Poland	48
Bulgaria	359	Greece	30	Portugal	351
Cyprus	357	Hungary	36	Romania	40
Czech Republic	42	Iceland	354	Slovak Republic	42
Denmark	45	Ireland	353	Spain	34
Finland	358	Italy	39	Sweden	46
France	33	Luxembourg	352	Switzerland	41
Germany (former East)	37	Netherlands	31	Turkey	90
Germany (former West)	49				

i. motorail

Motorail services allow you and your vehicle to travel long distances by train. See the *Itinerary Suggestions* chapter for a discussion of the nature and the pros and cons of Motorail travel. Motorail is known as *"Traines -autos-couchettes"* in France, *"Autoreisezuge"* in Germany, *"Treni per Auto Accompagnate"* in Italy, and *"Trenes de Autos"* in Spain. In this appendix I give specifics about the French, Italian and Spanish Motorail services; similar services are offered in most countries. Few sources outside Europe know much about Motorail. To get more info or to make reservations, call the French National Railway's *(SCNF's)* English and Spanish Hotline in Paris at 1 45 82 08 41, or call 0171 203 7000 in Britain.

Vehicles are generally loaded two hours before departure of the train, but double check this upon booking. Free parking is usually available one day before departure and one day after arrival. In most stations a free car wash voucher is given to Motorail clients. In some cases the loading and collection of vehicles take place in the same station as that in which passengers board and leave the train. When this is not the case a free bus service is usually provided to transfer passengers between the two stations.

Note that the size of your vehicle may limit your ability to use the trains. To fit on the *SNCF* trains, a vehicle, in combination with any attachments, should be no more than 1.63 meters in height (except on the Lisbon service where 1.6 meters is the limit; and except for cars towing trailers, which must not exceed 1.55 meters), clear the ground by no less than 0.1 meters, have a track no greater than 1.85 meters, and a width no more than 1.95 meters. (Some Motorail trains *will* carry larger vehicles however.) Bicycles must be transported inside your vehicle. For safety reasons bicycles carried on specially designed roof racks will be refused on Motorail and will be forwarded as registered luggage on the next available parcels train (subject to a handling fee and delivery within five days). Trailers are carried on all Motorail services. On the Calais, Paris and Lille routes, rates for trailers are the same as for cars: take the "Car + driver" fare and deduct the "Additional adult" fare.

To find the station look for signs depicting car-carrying flat beds or box cars and/or reading "auto/train". When you check in, leave heavy luggage in your vehicle; just take what you need for the journey. In Italy *you* must drive the vehicle onto and off of the train.

There's usually a whole range of sleeping accommodation to choose from. *Couchettes* are the ideal choice for families, with four-berth compartments in first class and six-berth compartments in second class. Although the sheets and blankets are provided, passengers do not usually undress, as cabins are not segregated according to sex. Washrooms and toilets are located at either end of each carriage. A real bed and washing facilities in each compartment make a *Sleeper* the most comfortable option. They can accommodate up to three people; although children under 12 years of age can share with an adult or another child. Each sleeper carriage has an attendant who will serve snacks and drinks to passengers in their compartments. *T2 Sleepers* come in two types: "upper" in which the two beds are at head height on opposite sides of the compartment, and "lower" where they're one above the other. I advise elderly or less agile passengers to request the latter type for ease of access. Not more than two persons may occupy one couchette berth or bed in a sleeping car, and then only on condition that at least one person is under 12 years of age (under 10 years of age on *international* Motorail services). Children under 4 years of age who occupy a separate couchette berth or bed in a sleeping car (or seat on a daytime service) must be in possession of a valid rail ticket.

Breakfast is included in your fare. By the time you've finished, your vehicle is ready for collection.

In what follows, all prices are in terms of British £s and pertain to a single (one-way) journey on the cheapest departures which occur more or less at least once per week—that is, more or less continually—during the period from July through early September. Thus there's a good chance that cheaper departures than the ones listed may be available to you; but, likewise, if you're not travelling during the above period you may have no choice but a departure more expensive than that listed, as some routes actually offer the cheapest fares of the year during the above, peak period. The cheapest departures usually occur on, say, Monday or Tuesday; the most expensive on Thursday or Friday; with those on Saturday and Sunday tending to be moderately priced. The price jumps are usually only in the "Car + driver" fares and come in increments of £20–25. Trains traveling at least partially in France or Spain consider children to be 4–11 (inclusive) years of age; those traveling in only Italy consider them to be 4–12 (inclusive) years of age. In either case younger children travel free of charge. The first row of a listing below corresponds to first class travel, the second to second class. Where a "—" is used instead of the word *to*, this indicates that fares are the same in both directions. Note that for some routes there is only one departure per week, and many routes are serviced during spring and summer only.

Sleeping Accommodation on Motorail Trains Originating or Terminating in France (compulsory on all overnight services):

First class	Single-bed sleeper	£105 per bed
	Smaller single-bed sleeper	80 per bed
	Two-bed sleeper	47 per bed
	Four-berth couchette	13 per berth
Second class	Two-bed sleeper	47 per bed
	Three-bed sleeper	34 per bed
	Six-berth couchette	10 per berth

Sleeping Accommodation on Spanish Domestic Motorail (compulsory on all overnight services):

First class	Single-bed sleeper	£54 per bed
	Two-bed sleeper	30 per bed
Second class	Six-berth couchette	6 per berth

Sleeping Accommodation on Italian Domestic Motorail (compulsory on all overnight services):

First class	Single-bed sleeper	£77 per bed
	Smaller single-bed sleeper	56 per bed
	Two-bed sleeper	40 per bed
Second class	Two-bed sleeper	40 per bed
	Three-bed sleeper	33 per bed
	Four-berth couchette	12 per berth
	Six-berth couchette	9 per berth

appendix i

Routes and Fares:

	Car + driver	Additional adult	Child	Motorcycle + driver
Calais, France—Avignon, France	£197	82	41	159
	169	54	27	131
Calais, France —Biarritz, France	225	84	42	168
	197	57	28	140
Calais, France—Bordeaux, France	183	70	36	138
	159	46	23	113
Calais, France to Brive, France	165	63	32	127
	144	42	21	104
vice versa	145	63	32	127
	124	42	21	104
Calais, France—Frejus/St. Raphael, Fra.	247	91	46	185
	218	63	32	156
Calais, France—Moutiers, France	*************** a winter route *****************			
Calais, France to Narbonne, France	251	93	47	180
	221	63	32	149
vice versa	231	93	47	180
	201	63	32	149
Calais, France—Nice, France	253	106	53	205
	215	70	36	168
Calais, France—Toulouse, France	217	82	41	162
	189	54	27	126
Calais, France—Bologna, Italy	299	120	60	not allowed
	259	80	40	not allowed
Paris, France—Bologna, Italy	242	92	46	not allowed
	210	61	30	not allowed
Calais, France—Livorno, Italy	320	119	60	not allowed
	284	82	41	not allowed
Calais, France—Milan, Italy	270	98	49	not allowed
	237	65	33	not allowed
Paris, France—Milan, Italy	231	88	44	not allowed
	202	58	29	not allowed
Paris, France—Rimini, Italy	301	108	55	not allowed
	264	70	36	not allowed
Calais, France—Rome, Italy	336	129	65	not allowed
	293	86	43	not allowed

	Car up to 3.80 m	Car up to 4.42 m	Car over 4.42 m	Adult	Child	Motorcycle
Lille/Seclin, France—Avignon, France	£89	105	133	78 52	39 26	53
Paris, France—Avignon, France	95	112	142	61 41	31 20	58
Lille, France—Biarritz, France	136	160	203	81 54	40 27	81
Paris, France—Biarritz, France	101	119	150	65 43	32 22	61
Lille, France—Bordeaux, France	109	129	164	68 45	34 23	66
Paris, France—Bordeaux, France	74	88	110	51 34	25 17	44
Paris, France—Evian, France	85	101	128	57 38	28 19	52
Paris, France—Frejus/St. Raphael, Fra.	131	155	195	79 52	39 26	79
Paris, France—Marseille, France	110	130	165	69 46	35 23	66
Lille, France—Narbonne, France	145	172	216	85 56	42 28	88
Paris, France—Narbonne, France	110	130	165	69 46	35 23	66
Lille, France—Nice, France	174	206	260	98 65	49 33	105
Paris, France—Nice, France	138	165	208	82 55	41 27	83
Paris, France—St. Gervais, France	89	105	133	58 39	29 19	53
Paris, France—Toulon, France	119	141	177	73 49	37 24	71
Paris, France—Toulouse, France	91	107	136	62 41	31 21	56
Bilbao, Spain—Alicante, Spain	32	45	57	46 32	23 16	not allowed
Bilbao, Spain—Cadiz, Spain	45	62	79	52 36	26 18	not allowed
Barcelona, Spain—Malaga, Spain	45	62	79	50 30	25 15	40
Bilbao, Spain—Malaga, Spain	45	62	79	49 34	25 17	not allowed

appendix i

# of people in car	Car* up to 3.80 m				Car* up to 4.42 m				Car* over 4.42 m				Adult ** 1st class	Adult** 2nd clss	Motorcycle
	1/2	3	4	5/6	1/2	3	4	5/6	1/2	3	4	5/6			
Bologna,Italy—Bari, Italy	£71	57	50	44	85	68	59	51	126	102	89	76	34	24	not allowed
Milan,Italy—Bari, Italy	92	74	65	55	111	89	78	67	166	133	116	100	46	27	not allowed
Milan,Italy—Napoli, Italy	88	92	62	53	106	85	74	64	159	127	111	95	44	26	not allowed
Bologna,Italy—Villa San Giovani, Italy	109	87	76	65	131	104	91	78	196	157	137	117	53	31	not allowed
Milan,Italy—Villa San Giovani, Italy	133	107	93	80	160	128	112	96	240	192	168	144	58	34	not allowed

* trailers up to 2.5 meters long are charged at half the lowest category car rate; trailers over 2.5 meters long are charged at the normal car rate, according to length.

** children 4–12 (inclusive) years of age pay half fare

Discounts on Ferry and Chunnel Travel for Motorailers:

The following single (one-way) fares are valid on any crossing between Dover and Calais or Newhaven and Dieppe on Hoverspeed, P&O European Ferries or Stena Sealink. See the *Ferries & the Chunnel* chapter for the normal fares.

Friday and Saturday

	Car + driver	Additional adult	Child (aged 4–13)	Motorcycle + driver	Trailer up to 3 m	Trailer over 3 m
November–April	£36	10	5	20	8	8
May–October	70	15	9	50	20	38

Sunday through Thursday

	Car + driver	Additional adult	Child (aged 4–13)	Motorcycle + driver	Trailer up to 3 m	Trailer over 3 m
November–April	£36	10	5	20	8	8
May–October	62	15	9	48	16	31

The following single fares are valid on the listed Brittany Ferries routes during high season, roughly July 14 to September 3.

Monday through Thursday

	Car + 2 adults	Additional adult	Child (aged 4–13)
Portsmouth—Caen or Poole—Cherbourg	£105	22	10
Plymouth—Roscoff	117	22	13
Portsmouth—St. Malo or Poole—St. Malo	135	27	14

Friday through Saturday

	Car + 2 adults	Additional adult	Child (aged 4–13)
Portsmouth—Caen or Poole—Cherbourg	£140	22	10
Plymouth—Roscoff	149	22	13
Portsmouth—St. Malo or Poole—St. Malo	173	27	14

The following single fares apply to the *Le Shuttle* service through the Chunnel. Fares are charged per vehicle. There are no charges for passengers. Maximum of five passenger per vehicle.

	Friday and Saturday	Sunday through Thursday
December–April	£58	58
May–October	110	106

index

The listings in this index do not reflect the information in the country-by-country portion of the *Country-by-Country Information* chapter, the detailed fare schedules of the *Ferries and the Chunnel* chapter, and the appendices: the nature and organization of that information is such that indexing it would prove worthlessly redundant.